This Is Your First Rock Garden, Isn't It?

An *Other Coast* Collection
by Adrian Raeside

Andrews McMeel
Publishing

Kansas City

The Other Coast® is a registered trademark of Adrian Raeside and is syndicated by Creators Syndicate. For information, write Creators Syndicate, 5777 W. Century Blvd., Suite 700, Los Angeles, California 90045.

 For information, write Andrews McMeel Publishing, an Andrews McMeel Universal company, 4520 Main Street, Kansas City, Missouri 64111.

05 06 07 08 09 BBG 10 9 8 7 6 5 4 3 2 1

ISBN-13: 978-0-7407-5450-0
ISBN-10: 0-7407-5450-5

Library of Congress Control Number: 2005925664

www.andrewsmcmeel.com

Also by Adrian Raeside

The Other Coast: Road Rage in Beverly Hills

Introduction

The Other Coast was born in 1990 as *Toulose*, a color Sunday-only feature in the *Victoria Times Colonist*. The cartoon initially revolved around the life of Toulose, an appallingly bad painter who bears a vague resemblance to the pint-sized hero in the pages that follow. Over the next few years, *Toulose* evolved into *The Other Coast*, the cartoon strip you know today that now appears in more than 150 newspapers worldwide.

Who lives on *The Other Coast?* Talentless television scriptwriters, rabid environmentalists (as long as what they're saving can't be turned into luggage), gluttons, finicky vegans, convicted embezzlers, mind-numbing bands, and assorted paranoid wackos. Along with whales, dogs, and other offbeat inhabitants of the animal kingdom, these characters bring utter absurdness to *The Other Coast* on a daily basis.

What exactly is *The Other Coast?* It's a place where dogs get hooked on nicotine gum, oilmen drill for coffee, and environmentalists do their bit to save the depleted oceans by sharing the shark fin soup.

It's a parody of life . . . sort of.

Adrian Raeside
adrian@raesidecartoon.com

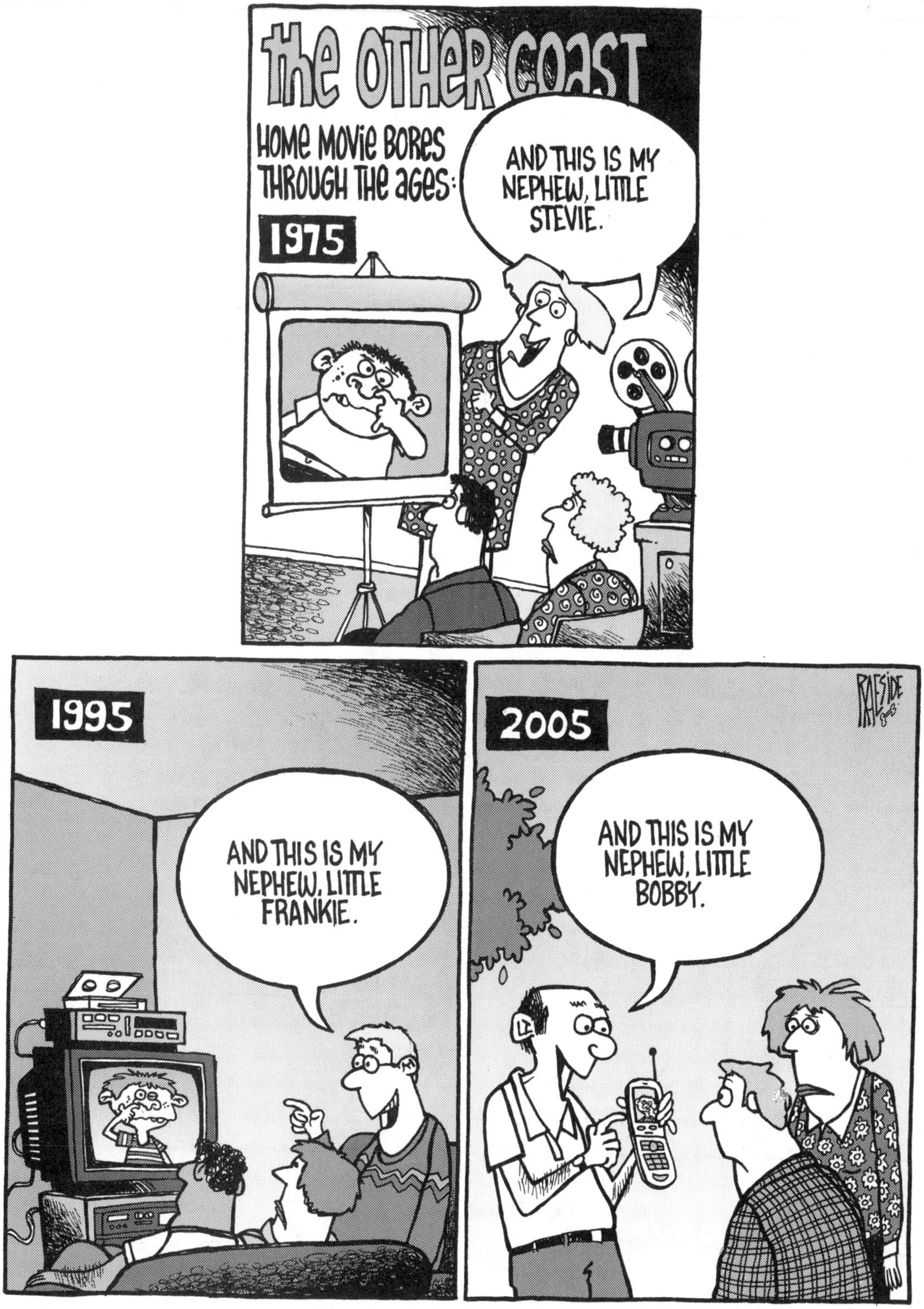
THE OTHER COAST
HOME MOVIE BORES THROUGH THE AGES:
1975
AND THIS IS MY NEPHEW, LITTLE STEVIE.
1995
AND THIS IS MY NEPHEW, LITTLE FRANKIE.
2005
AND THIS IS MY NEPHEW, LITTLE BOBBY.
RAESIDE

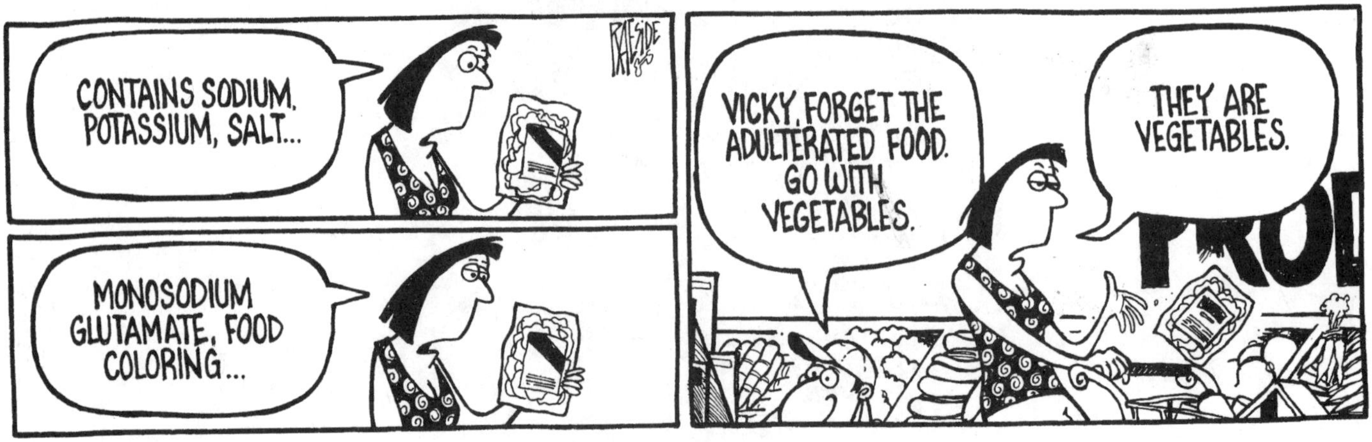
CONTAINS SODIUM, POTASSIUM, SALT...
MONOSODIUM GLUTAMATE, FOOD COLORING...
VICKY, FORGET THE ADULTERATED FOOD. GO WITH VEGETABLES.
THEY ARE VEGETABLES.

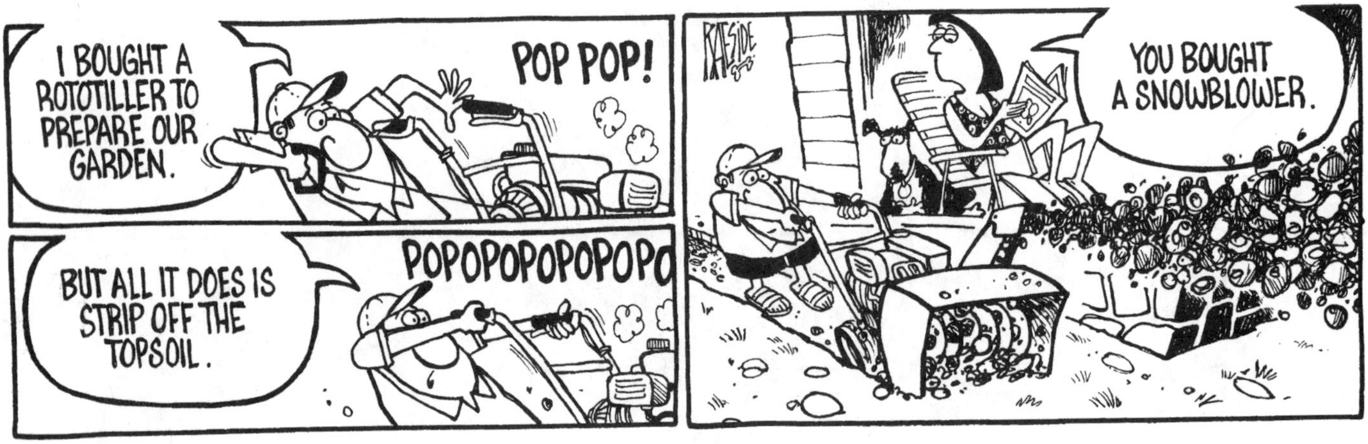
I BOUGHT A ROTOTILLER TO PREPARE OUR GARDEN.
POP POP!
BUT ALL IT DOES IS STRIP OFF THE TOPSOIL.
POPOPOPOPOPOPO
YOU BOUGHT A SNOWBLOWER.

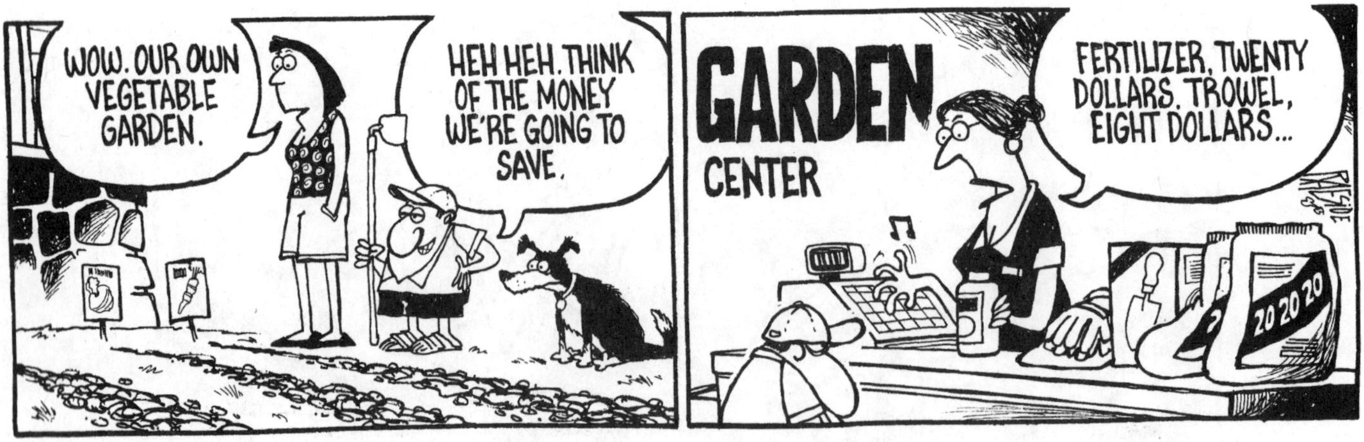
WOW. OUR OWN VEGETABLE GARDEN.
HEH HEH. THINK OF THE MONEY WE'RE GOING TO SAVE.
GARDEN
CENTER
FERTILIZER, TWENTY DOLLARS. TROWEL, EIGHT DOLLARS...
20 20 20

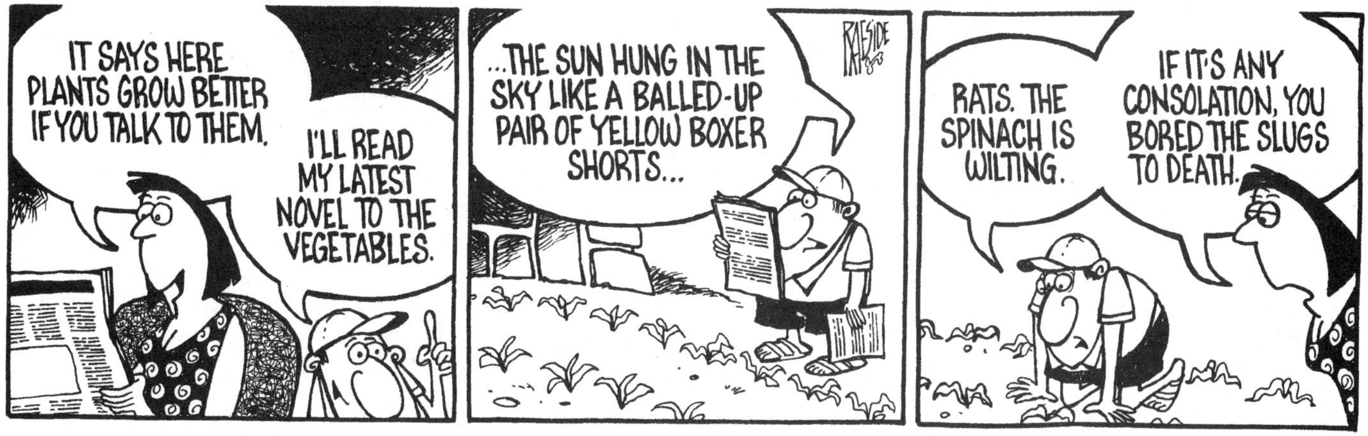
IT SAYS HERE PLANTS GROW BETTER IF YOU TALK TO THEM.
I'LL READ MY LATEST NOVEL TO THE VEGETABLES.
...THE SUN HUNG IN THE SKY LIKE A BALLED-UP PAIR OF YELLOW BOXER SHORTS...
RATS. THE SPINACH IS WILTING.
IF IT'S ANY CONSOLATION, YOU BORED THE SLUGS TO DEATH.

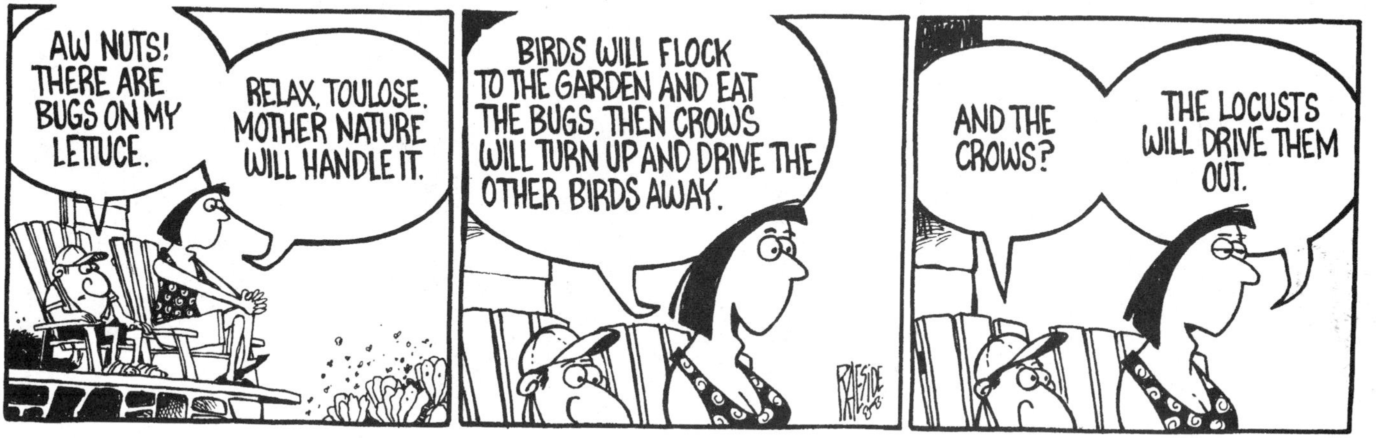
AW NUTS! THERE ARE BUGS ON MY LETTUCE.
RELAX, TOULOSE. MOTHER NATURE WILL HANDLE IT.
BIRDS WILL FLOCK TO THE GARDEN AND EAT THE BUGS. THEN CROWS WILL TURN UP AND DRIVE THE OTHER BIRDS AWAY.
AND THE CROWS?
THE LOCUSTS WILL DRIVE THEM OUT.

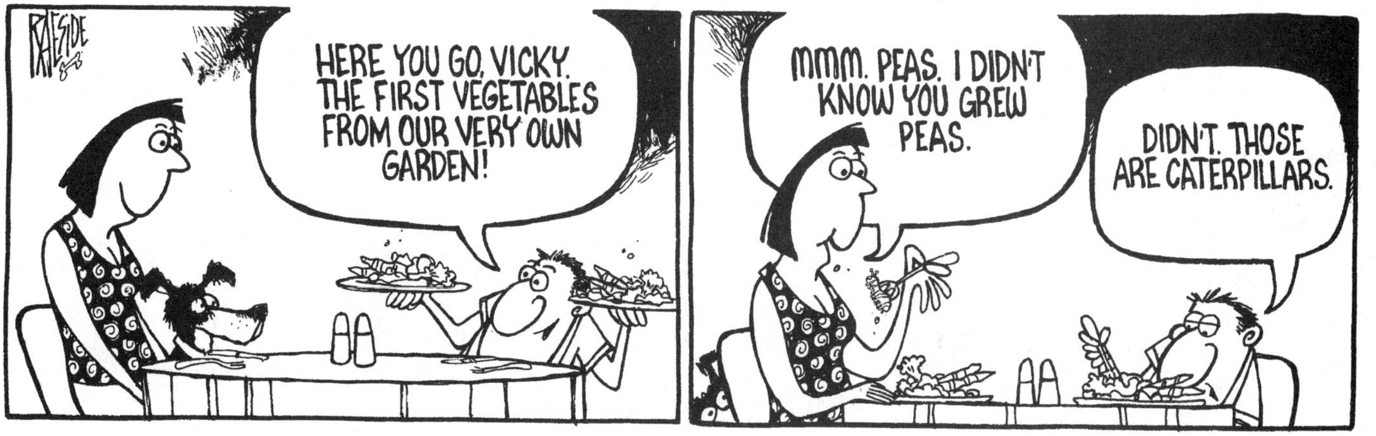
HERE YOU GO, VICKY. THE FIRST VEGETABLES FROM OUR VERY OWN GARDEN!
MMM. PEAS. I DIDN'T KNOW YOU GREW PEAS.
DIDN'T. THOSE ARE CATERPILLARS.

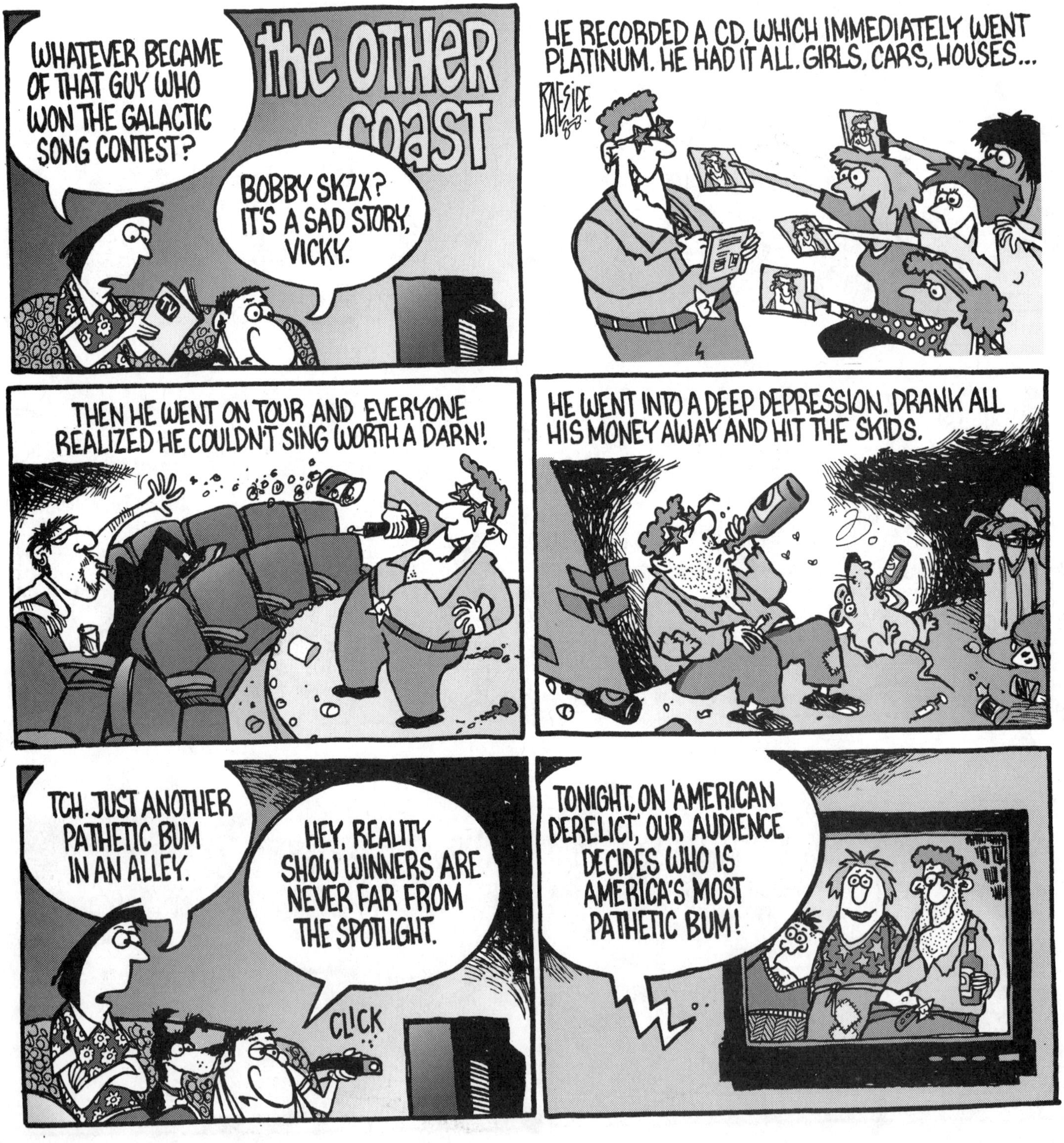
the OTHER COAST
WHATEVER BECAME OF THAT GUY WHO WON THE GALACTIC SONG CONTEST?
BOBBY SKZX? IT'S A SAD STORY, VICKY.
TV
HE RECORDED A CD, WHICH IMMEDIATELY WENT PLATINUM. HE HAD IT ALL. GIRLS, CARS, HOUSES...
THEN HE WENT ON TOUR AND EVERYONE REALIZED HE COULDN'T SING WORTH A DARN!
HE WENT INTO A DEEP DEPRESSION. DRANK ALL HIS MONEY AWAY AND HIT THE SKIDS.
TCH. JUST ANOTHER PATHETIC BUM IN AN ALLEY.
HEY, REALITY SHOW WINNERS ARE NEVER FAR FROM THE SPOTLIGHT.
CLICK
TONIGHT, ON 'AMERICAN DERELICT,' OUR AUDIENCE DECIDES WHO IS AMERICA'S MOST PATHETIC BUM!

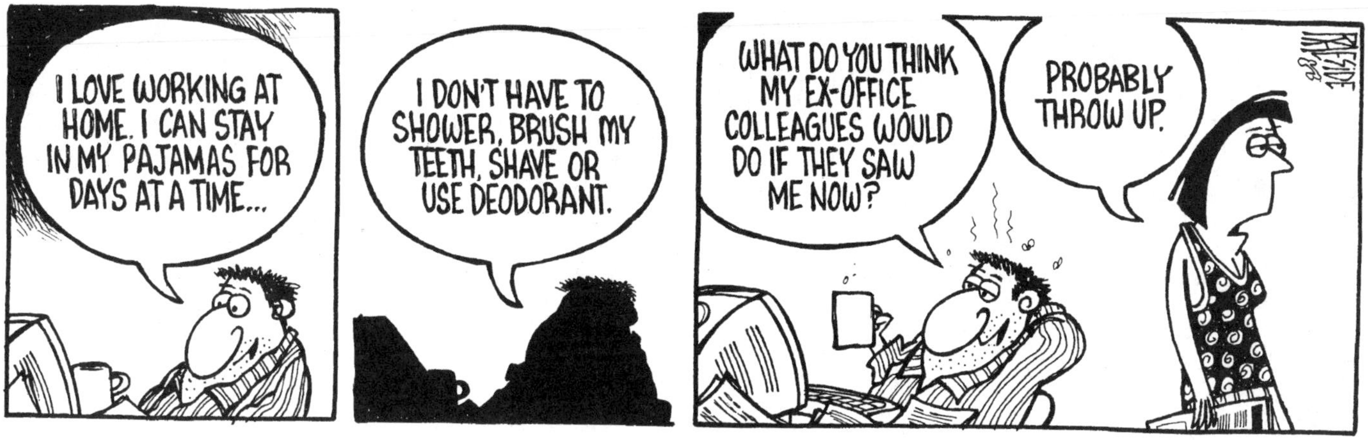
I LOVE WORKING AT HOME. I CAN STAY IN MY PAJAMAS FOR DAYS AT A TIME...
I DON'T HAVE TO SHOWER, BRUSH MY TEETH, SHAVE OR USE DEODORANT.
WHAT DO YOU THINK MY EX-OFFICE COLLEAGUES WOULD DO IF THEY SAW ME NOW?
PROBABLY THROW UP.

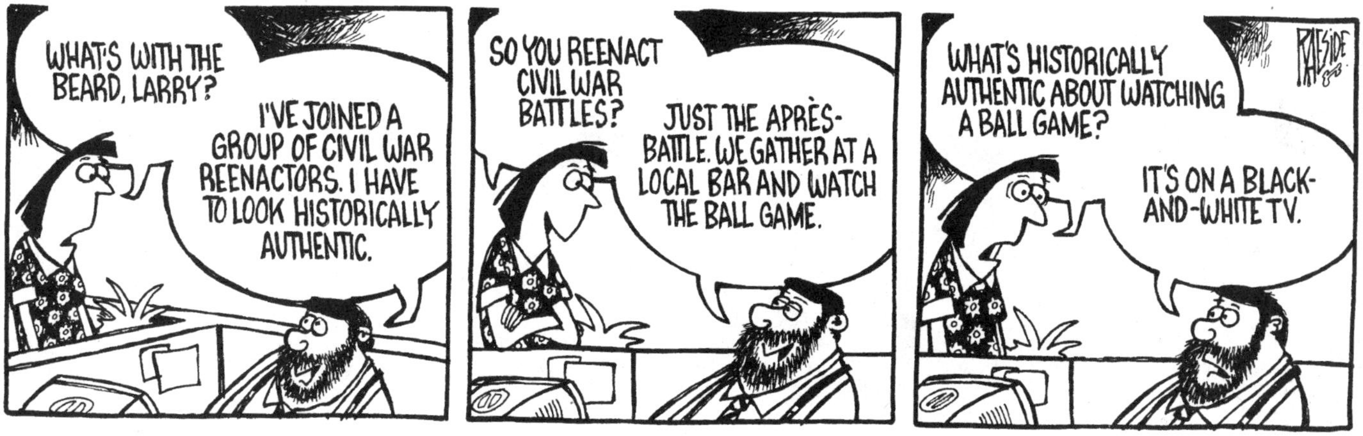
WHAT'S WITH THE BEARD, LARRY?
I'VE JOINED A GROUP OF CIVIL WAR REENACTORS. I HAVE TO LOOK HISTORICALLY AUTHENTIC.
SO YOU REENACT CIVIL WAR BATTLES?
JUST THE APRÈS-BATTLE. WE GATHER AT A LOCAL BAR AND WATCH THE BALL GAME.
WHAT'S HISTORICALLY AUTHENTIC ABOUT WATCHING A BALL GAME?
IT'S ON A BLACK-AND-WHITE TV.

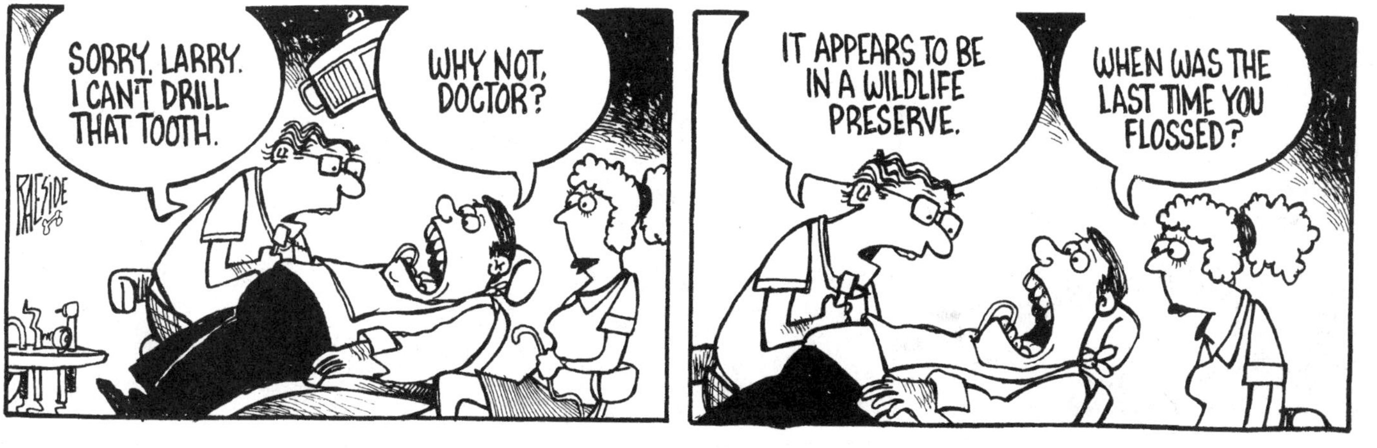
SORRY, LARRY. I CAN'T DRILL THAT TOOTH.
WHY NOT, DOCTOR?
IT APPEARS TO BE IN A WILDLIFE PRESERVE.
WHEN WAS THE LAST TIME YOU FLOSSED?

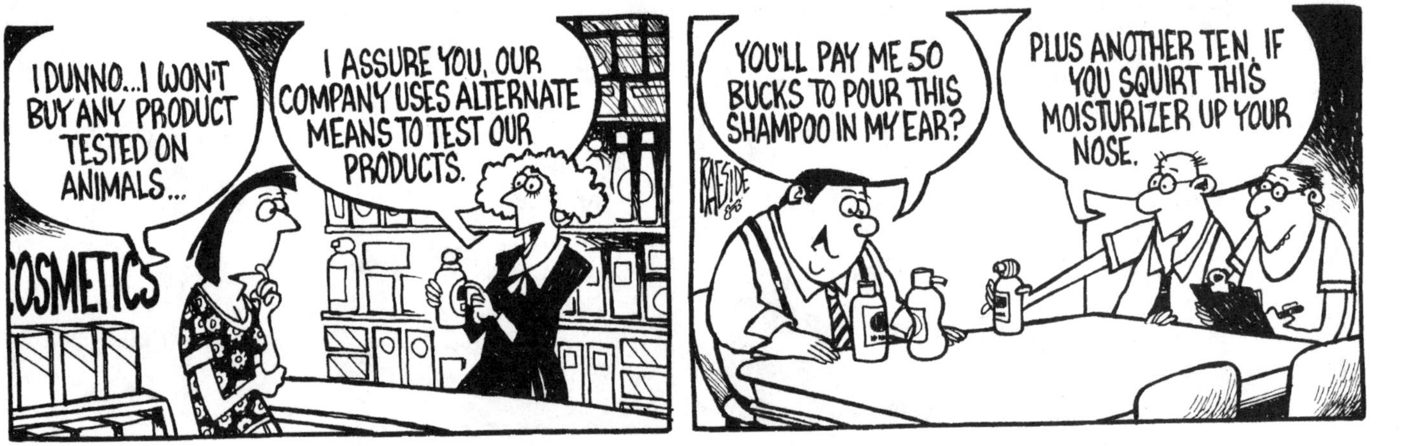
COSMETICS
I DUNNO...I WON'T BUY ANY PRODUCT TESTED ON ANIMALS...
I ASSURE YOU, OUR COMPANY USES ALTERNATE MEANS TO TEST OUR PRODUCTS.
YOU'LL PAY ME 50 BUCKS TO POUR THIS SHAMPOO IN MY EAR?
PLUS ANOTHER TEN, IF YOU SQUIRT THIS MOISTURIZER UP YOUR NOSE.

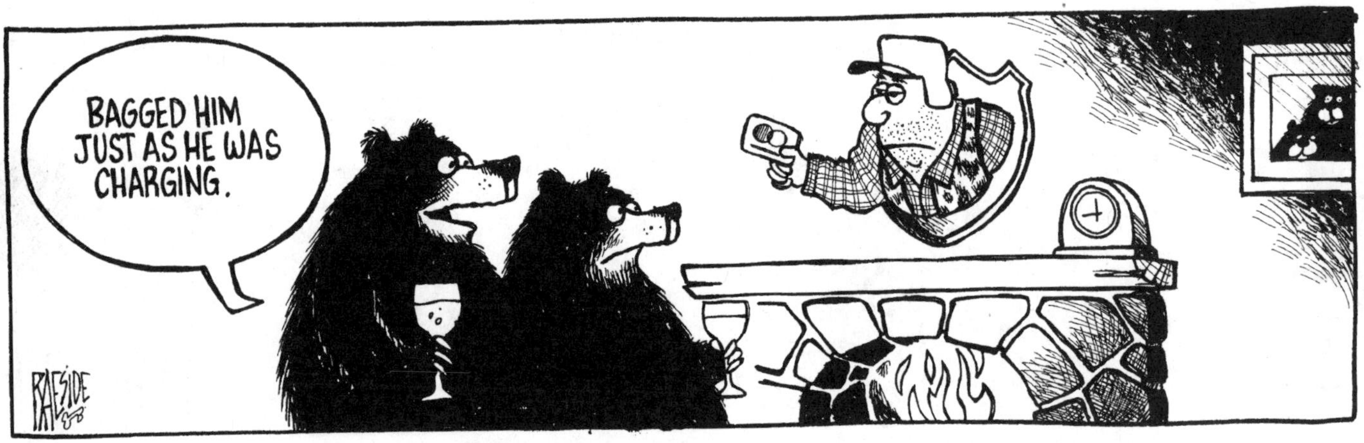
BAGGED HIM JUST AS HE WAS CHARGING.

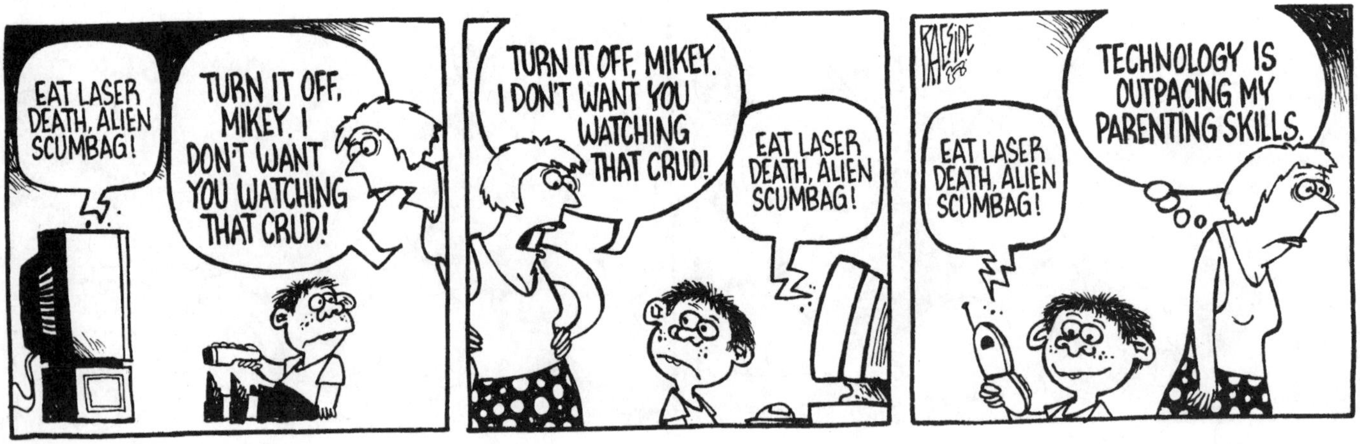
EAT LASER DEATH, ALIEN SCUMBAG!
TURN IT OFF, MIKEY. I DON'T WANT YOU WATCHING THAT CRUD!
TURN IT OFF, MIKEY. I DON'T WANT YOU WATCHING THAT CRUD!
EAT LASER DEATH, ALIEN SCUMBAG!
EAT LASER DEATH, ALIEN SCUMBAG!
TECHNOLOGY IS OUTPACING MY PARENTING SKILLS.

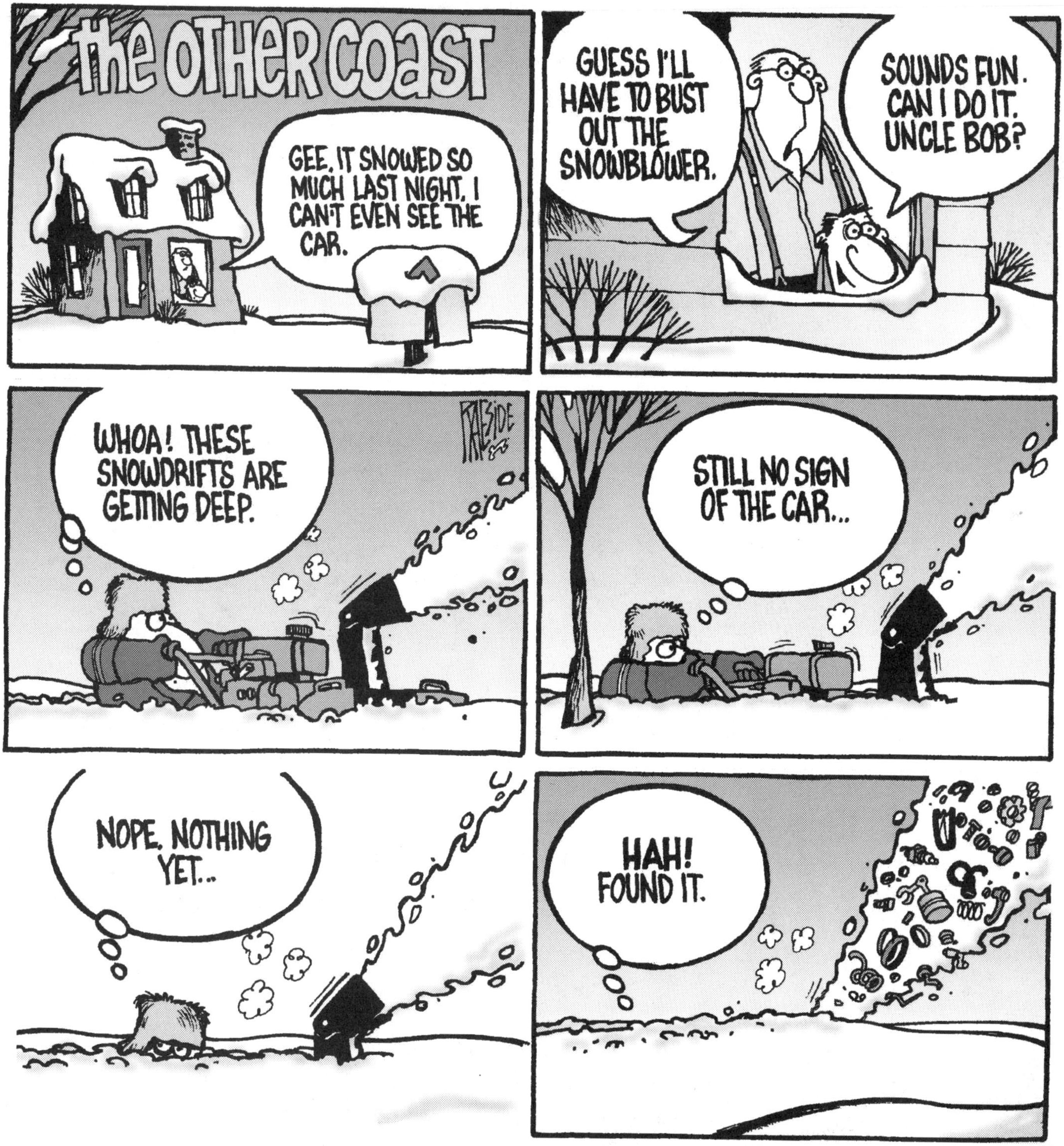

the OTHER COAST
GEE, IT SNOWED SO MUCH LAST NIGHT, I CAN'T EVEN SEE THE CAR.
GUESS I'LL HAVE TO BUST OUT THE SNOWBLOWER.
SOUNDS FUN. CAN I DO IT, UNCLE BOB?
WHOA! THESE SNOWDRIFTS ARE GETTING DEEP.
STILL NO SIGN OF THE CAR...
NOPE, NOTHING YET...
HAH! FOUND IT.

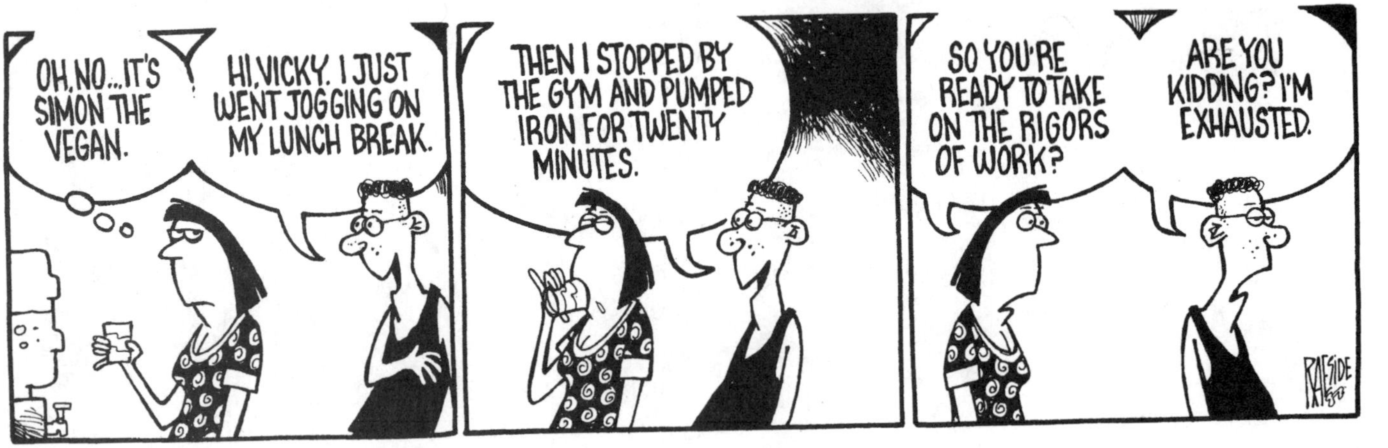
OH, NO... IT'S SIMON THE VEGAN.
HI, VICKY. I JUST WENT JOGGING ON MY LUNCH BREAK.
THEN I STOPPED BY THE GYM AND PUMPED IRON FOR TWENTY MINUTES.
SO YOU'RE READY TO TAKE ON THE RIGORS OF WORK?
ARE YOU KIDDING? I'M EXHAUSTED.

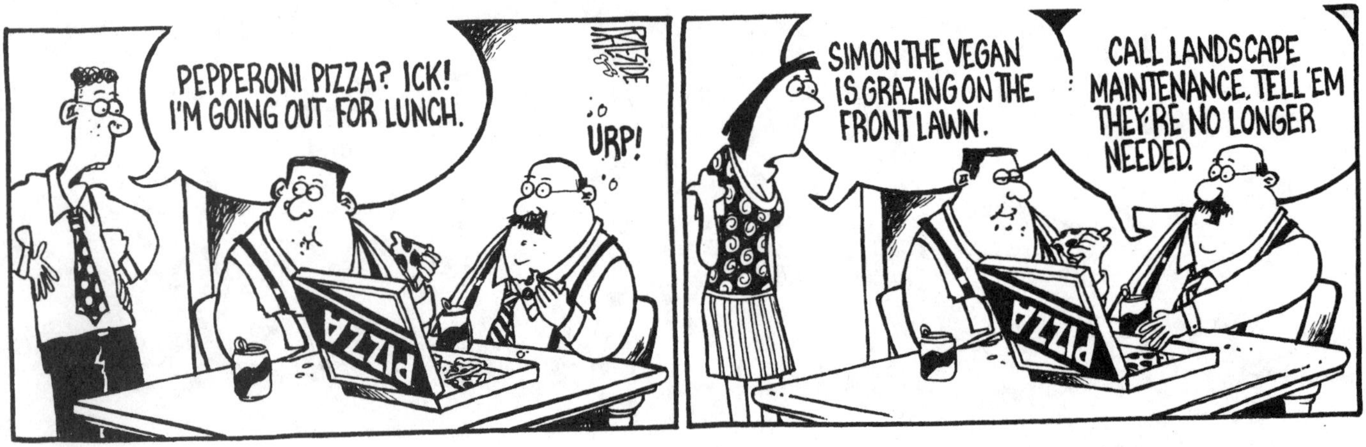
PEPPERONI PIZZA? ICK! I'M GOING OUT FOR LUNCH.
URP!
PIZZA
SIMON THE VEGAN IS GRAZING ON THE FRONT LAWN.
CALL LANDSCAPE MAINTENANCE. TELL 'EM THEY'RE NO LONGER NEEDED.
PIZZA

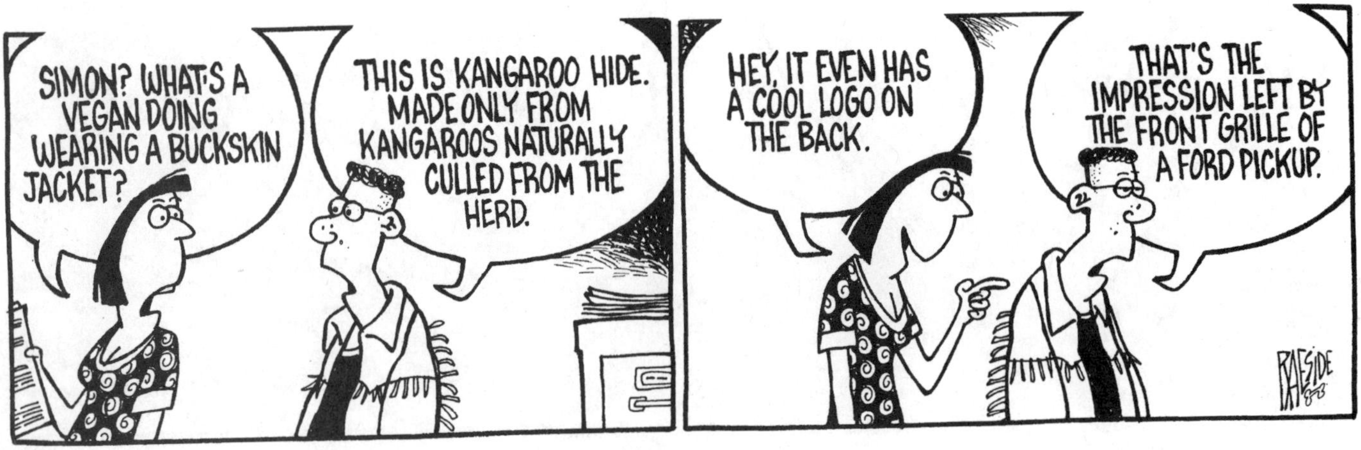
SIMON? WHAT'S A VEGAN DOING WEARING A BUCKSKIN JACKET?
THIS IS KANGAROO HIDE. MADE ONLY FROM KANGAROOS NATURALLY CULLED FROM THE HERD.
HEY, IT EVEN HAS A COOL LOGO ON THE BACK.
THAT'S THE IMPRESSION LEFT BY THE FRONT GRILLE OF A FORD PICKUP.

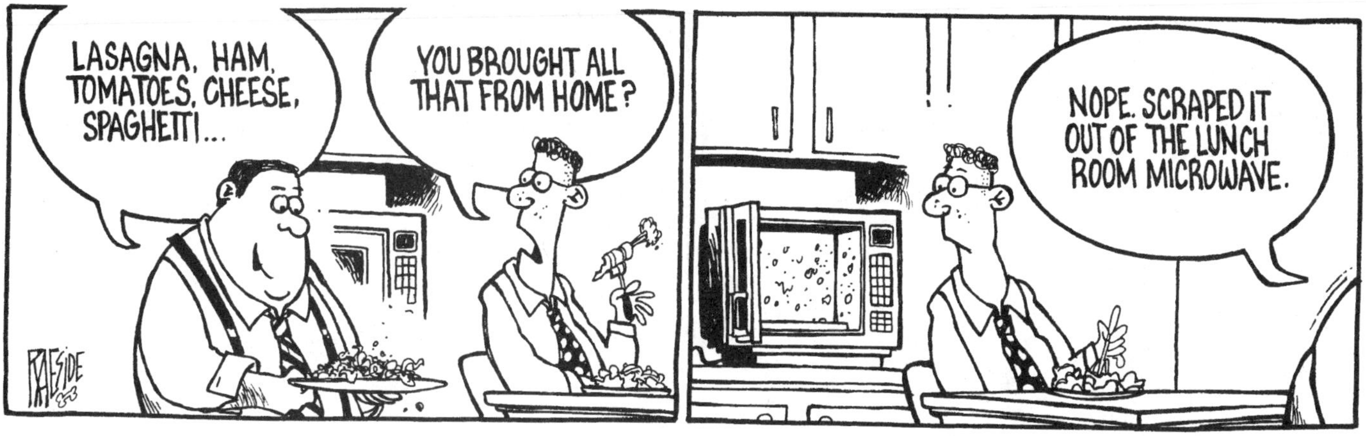
LASAGNA, HAM, TOMATOES, CHEESE, SPAGHETTI...
YOU BROUGHT ALL THAT FROM HOME?
NOPE. SCRAPED IT OUT OF THE LUNCH ROOM MICROWAVE.

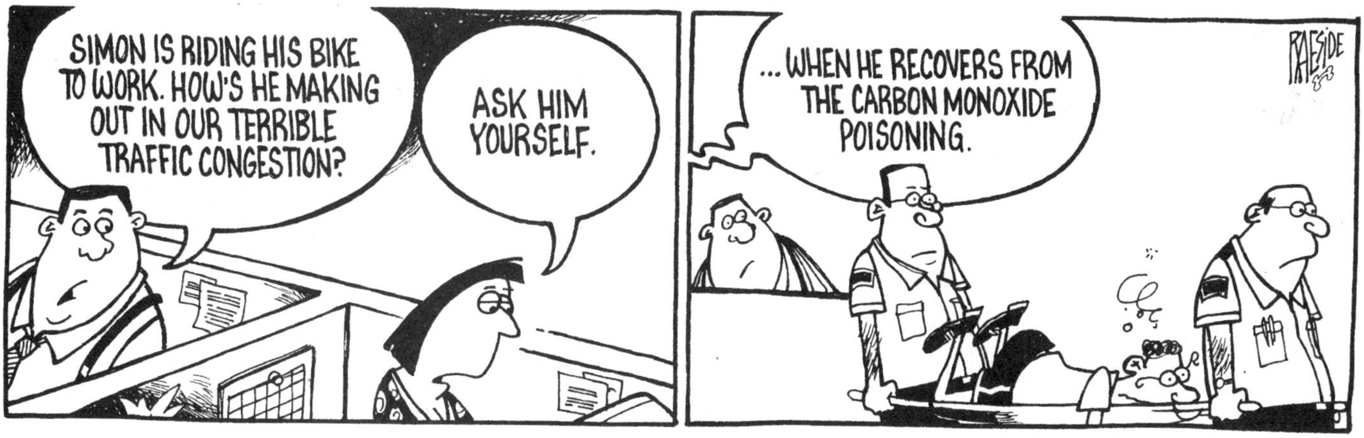
SIMON IS RIDING HIS BIKE TO WORK. HOW'S HE MAKING OUT IN OUR TERRIBLE TRAFFIC CONGESTION?
ASK HIM YOURSELF.
...WHEN HE RECOVERS FROM THE CARBON MONOXIDE POISONING.

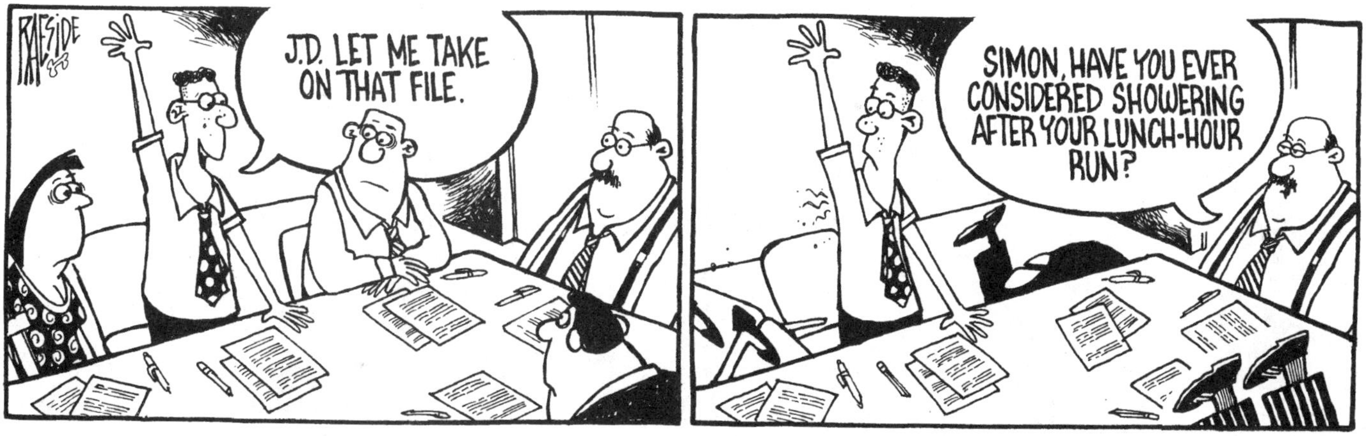
J.D. LET ME TAKE ON THAT FILE.
SIMON, HAVE YOU EVER CONSIDERED SHOWERING AFTER YOUR LUNCH-HOUR RUN?

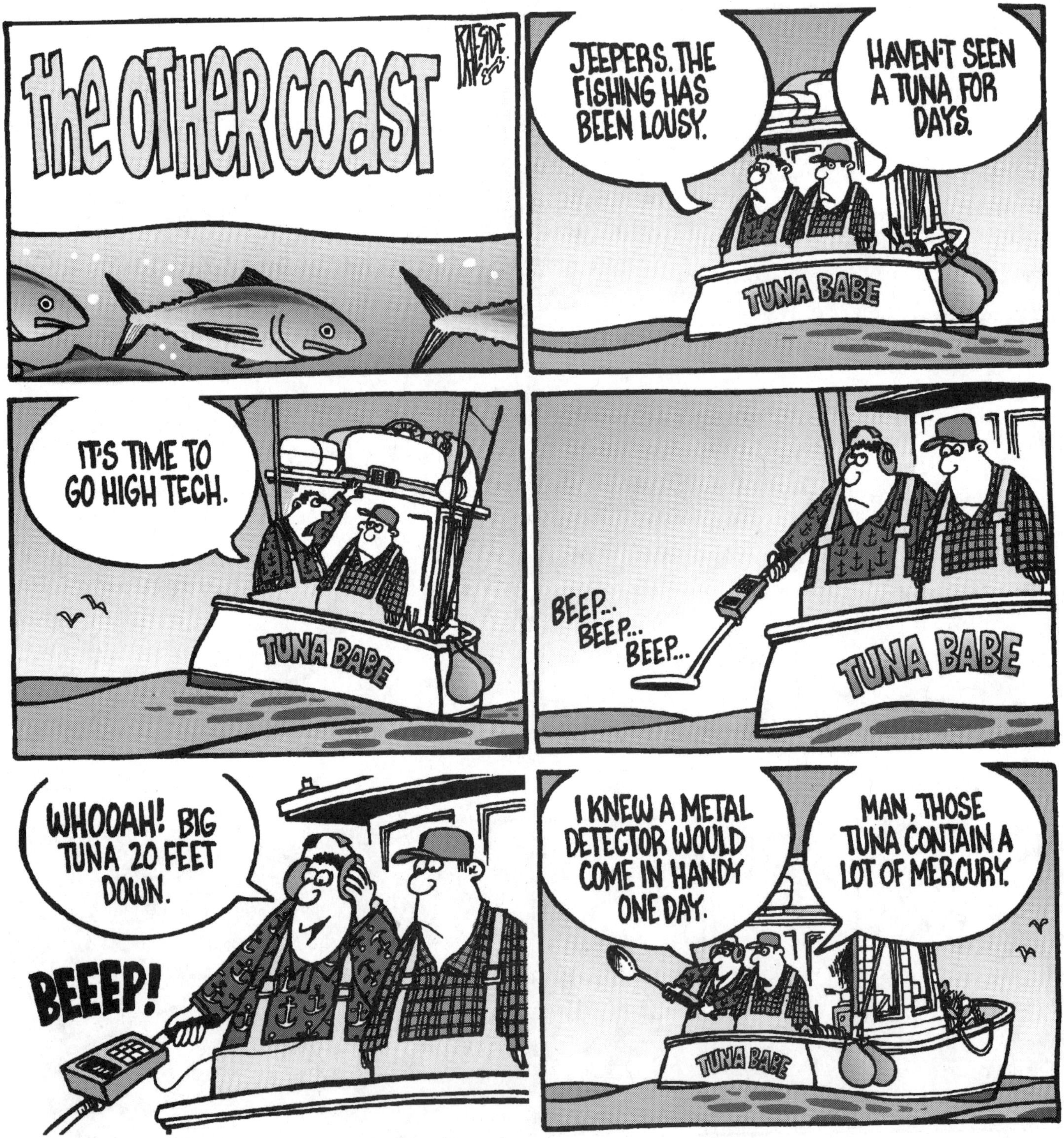
the OTHER COAST
RAESIDE
JEEPERS. THE FISHING HAS BEEN LOUSY.
HAVEN'T SEEN A TUNA FOR DAYS.
TUNA BABE
IT'S TIME TO GO HIGH TECH.
TUNA BABE
BEEP... BEEP... BEEP...
TUNA BABE
WHOOAH! BIG TUNA 20 FEET DOWN.
BEEEP!
I KNEW A METAL DETECTOR WOULD COME IN HANDY ONE DAY.
MAN, THOSE TUNA CONTAIN A LOT OF MERCURY.
TUNA BABE

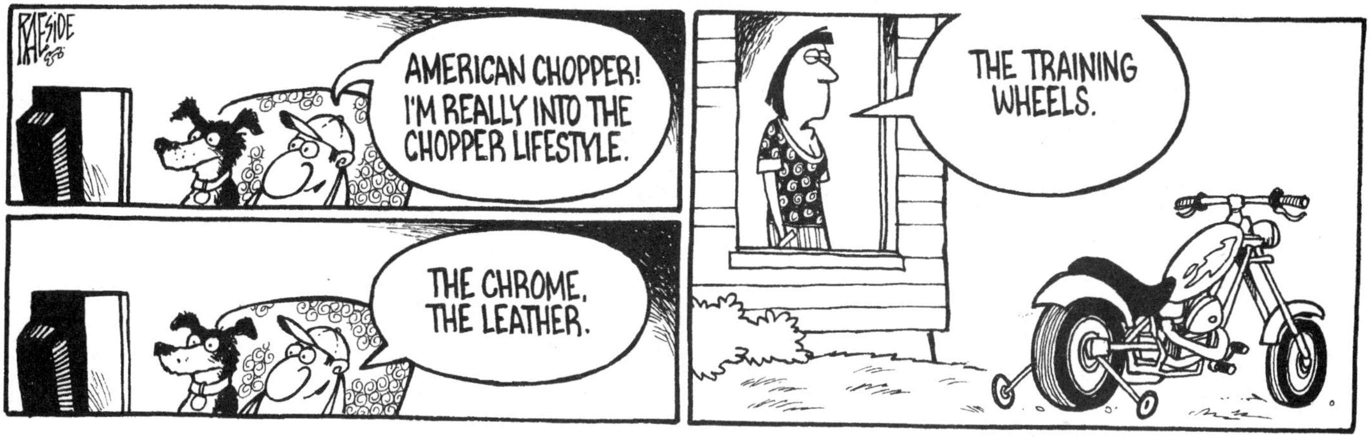
AMERICAN CHOPPER! I'M REALLY INTO THE CHOPPER LIFESTYLE.
THE CHROME, THE LEATHER.
THE TRAINING WHEELS.

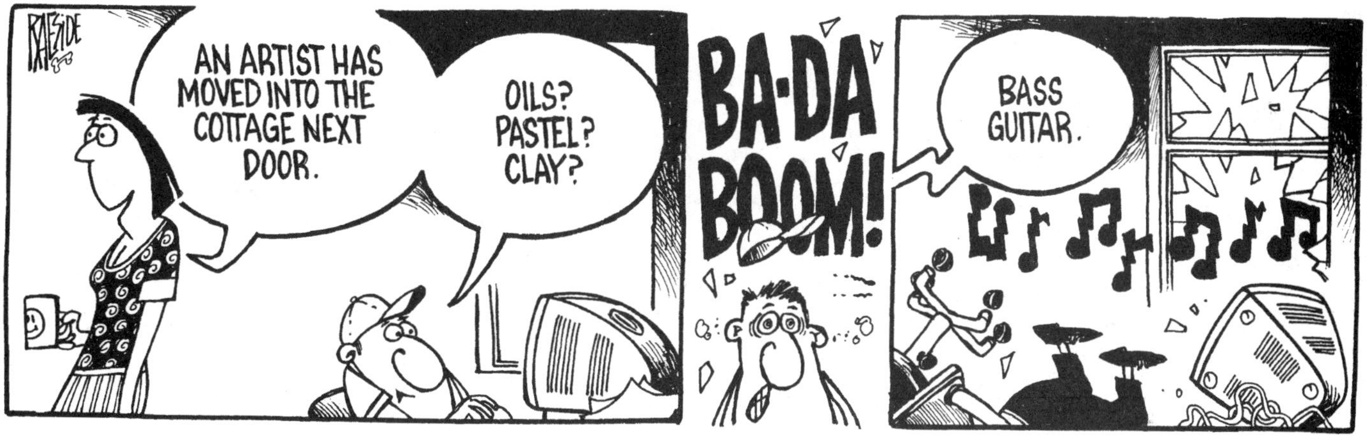
AN ARTIST HAS MOVED INTO THE COTTAGE NEXT DOOR.
OILS? PASTEL? CLAY?
BA-DA BOOM!
BASS GUITAR.

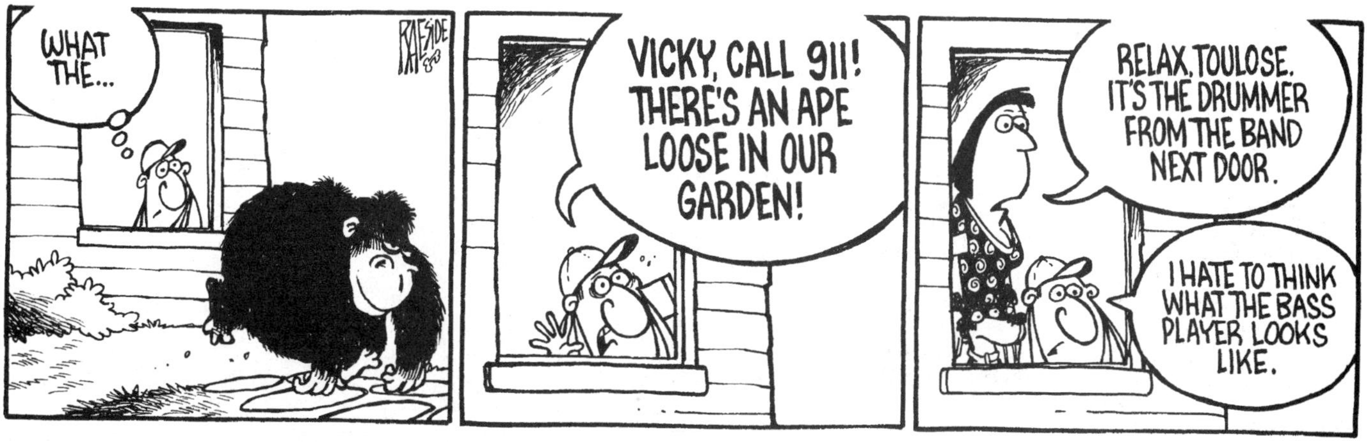
WHAT THE...
VICKY, CALL 911! THERE'S AN APE LOOSE IN OUR GARDEN!
RELAX, TOULOSE. IT'S THE DRUMMER FROM THE BAND NEXT DOOR.
I HATE TO THINK WHAT THE BASS PLAYER LOOKS LIKE.

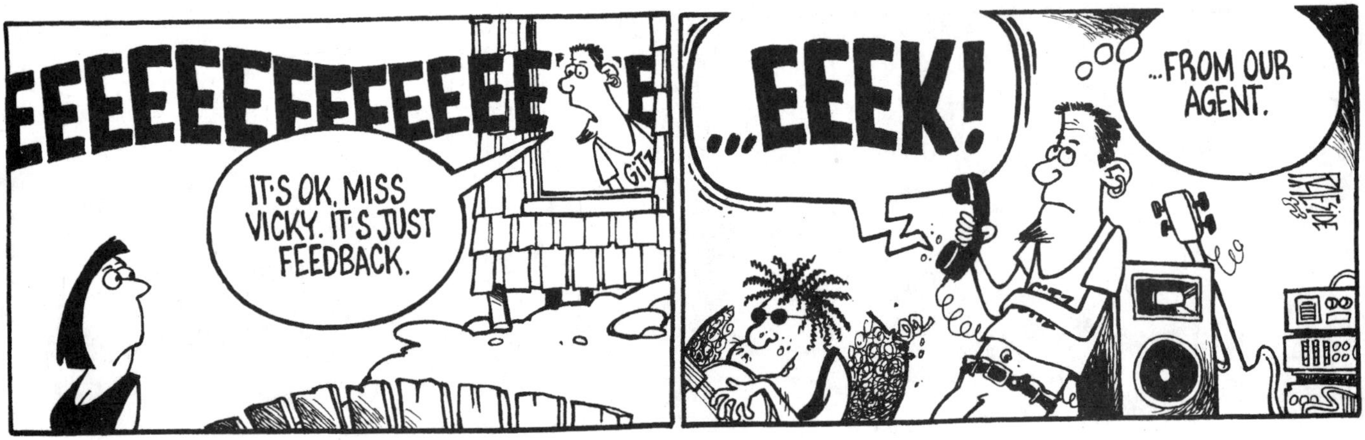
EEEEEEEEEEEEEEE
IT'S OK, MISS VICKY. IT'S JUST FEEDBACK.
...EEEK!
...FROM OUR AGENT.

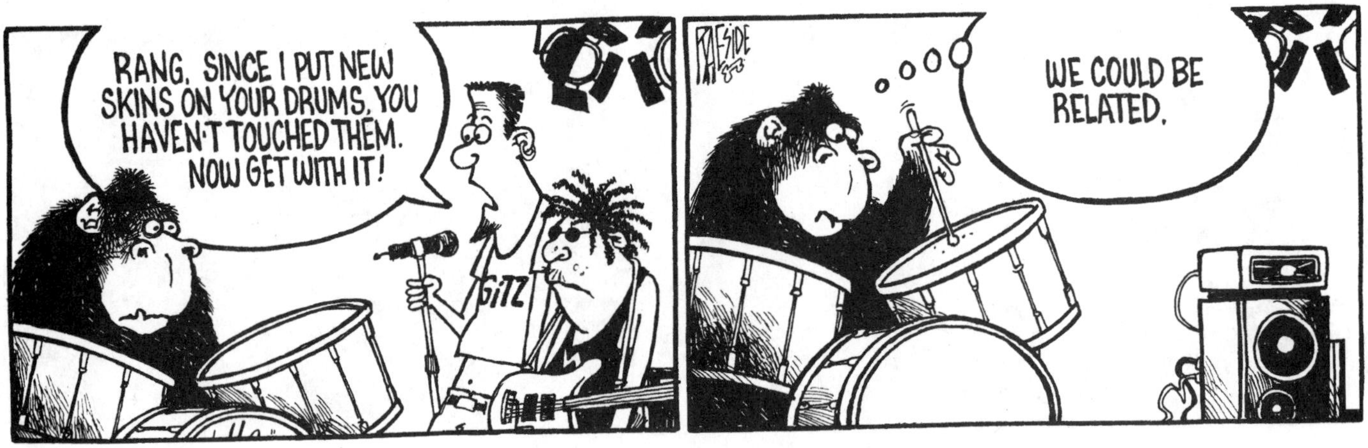
RANG, SINCE I PUT NEW SKINS ON YOUR DRUMS, YOU HAVEN'T TOUCHED THEM. NOW GET WITH IT!
WE COULD BE RELATED.

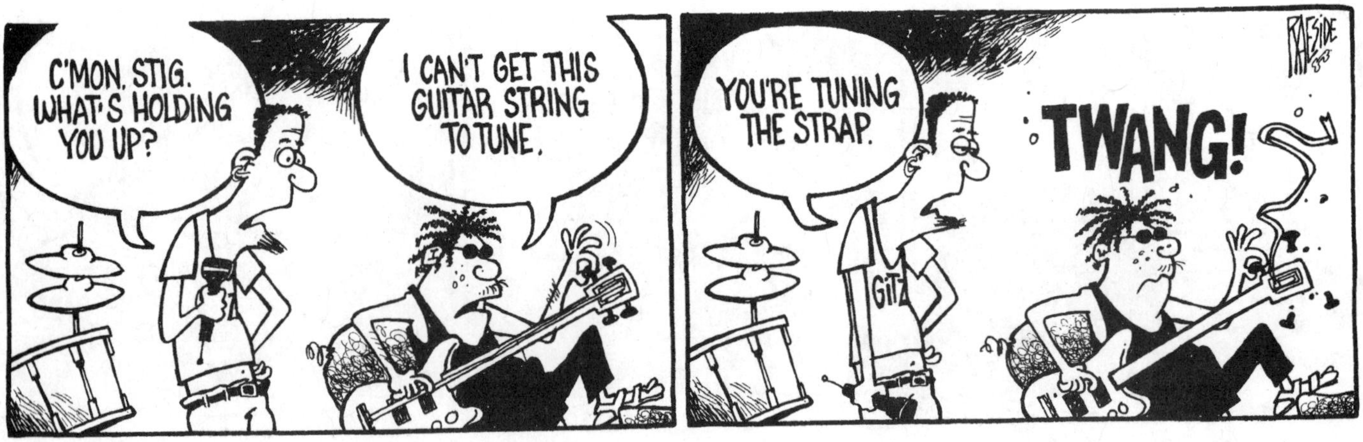
C'MON, STIG. WHAT'S HOLDING YOU UP?
I CAN'T GET THIS GUITAR STRING TO TUNE.
YOU'RE TUNING THE STRAP.
TWANG!

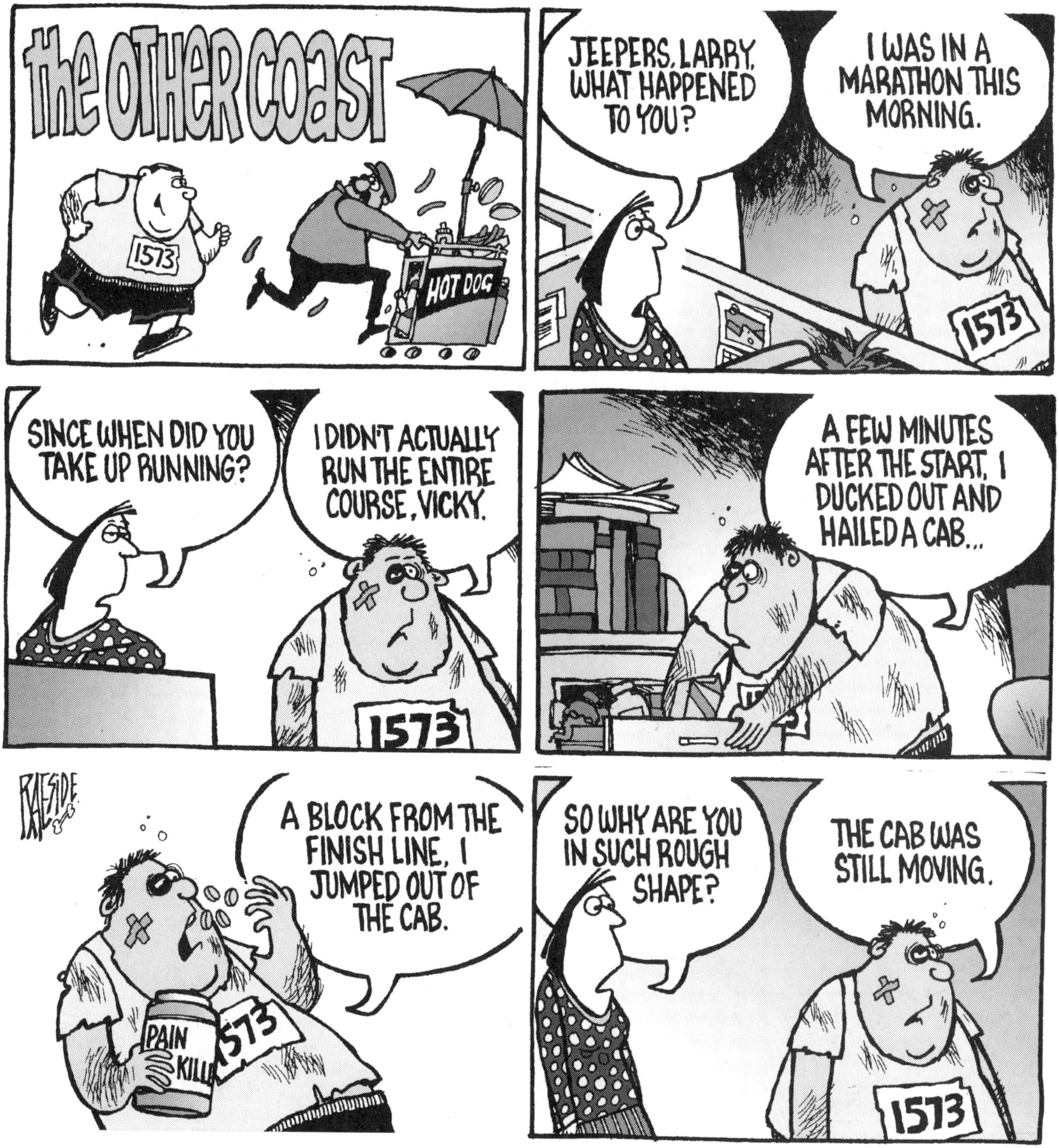
the OTHER COAST
1573
HOT DOG
JEEPERS, LARRY, WHAT HAPPENED TO YOU?
I WAS IN A MARATHON THIS MORNING.
1573
SINCE WHEN DID YOU TAKE UP RUNNING?
I DIDN'T ACTUALLY RUN THE ENTIRE COURSE, VICKY.
1573
A FEW MINUTES AFTER THE START, I DUCKED OUT AND HAILED A CAB...
RAESIDE
A BLOCK FROM THE FINISH LINE, I JUMPED OUT OF THE CAB.
PAIN KILL
1573
SO WHY ARE YOU IN SUCH ROUGH SHAPE?
THE CAB WAS STILL MOVING.
1573

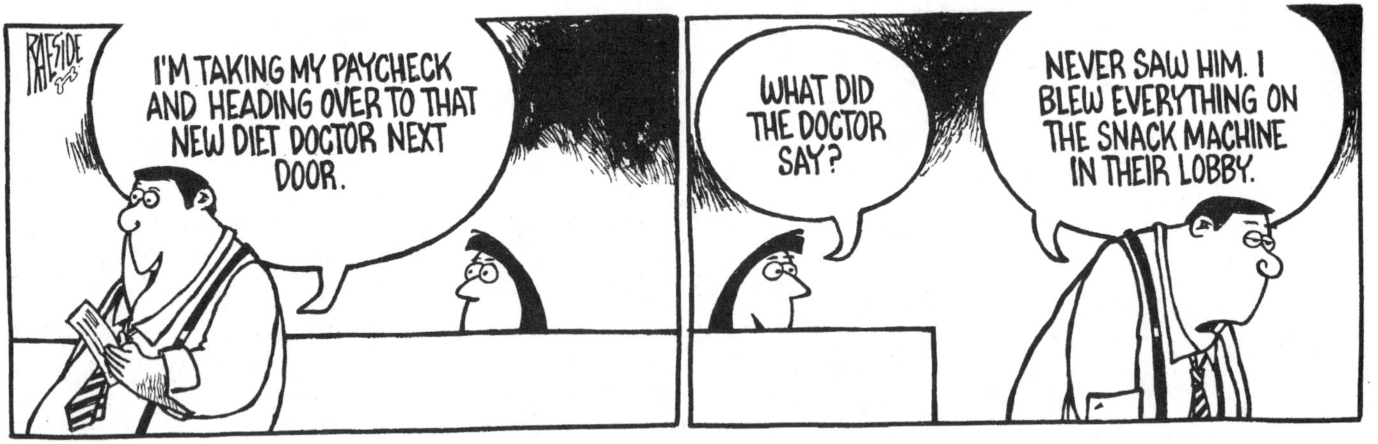
I'M TAKING MY PAYCHECK AND HEADING OVER TO THAT NEW DIET DOCTOR NEXT DOOR.
WHAT DID THE DOCTOR SAY?
NEVER SAW HIM. I BLEW EVERYTHING ON THE SNACK MACHINE IN THEIR LOBBY.

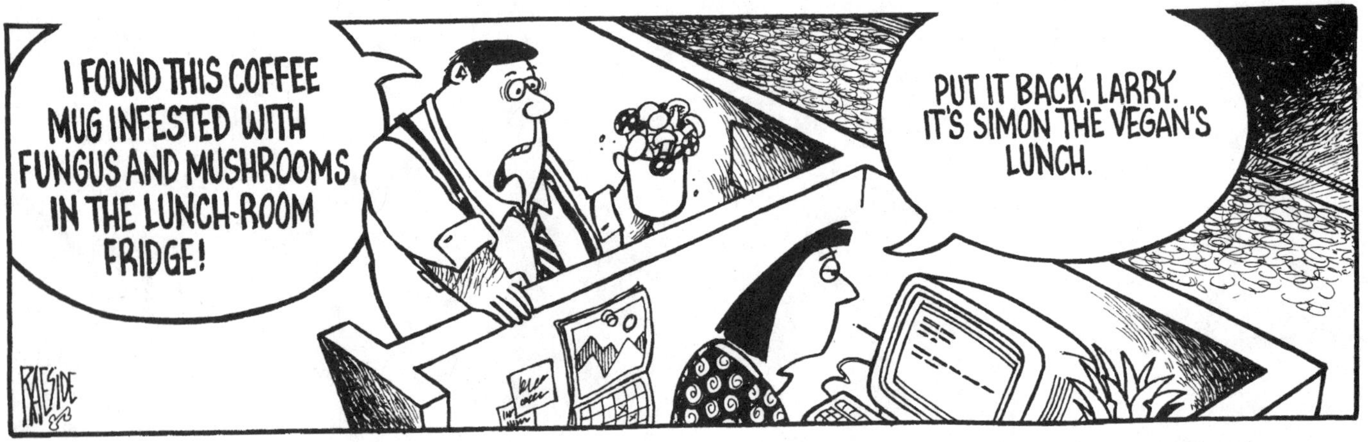
I FOUND THIS COFFEE MUG INFESTED WITH FUNGUS AND MUSHROOMS IN THE LUNCH-ROOM FRIDGE!
PUT IT BACK, LARRY. IT'S SIMON THE VEGAN'S LUNCH.

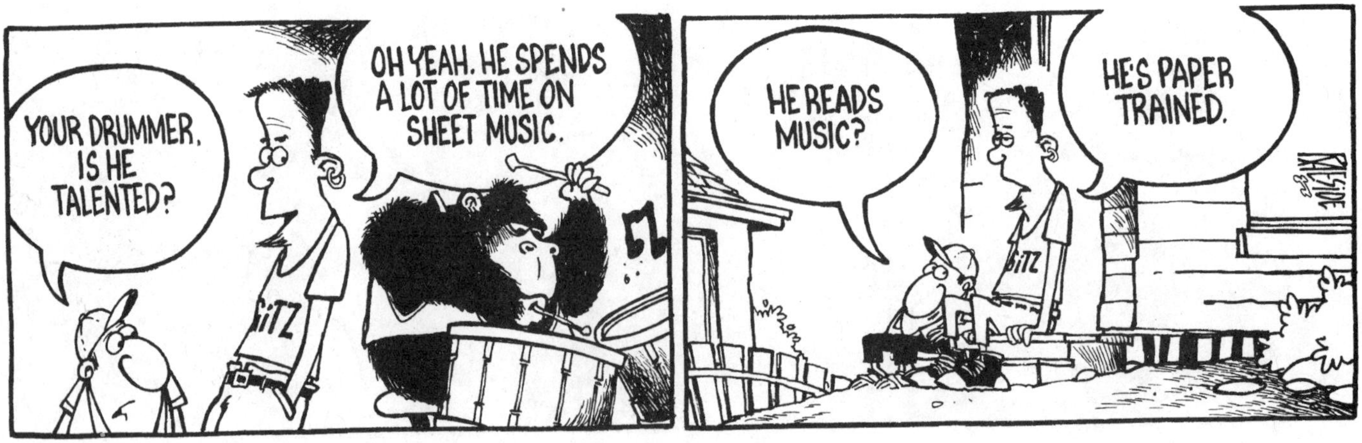
YOUR DRUMMER, IS HE TALENTED?
OH YEAH. HE SPENDS A LOT OF TIME ON SHEET MUSIC.
HE READS MUSIC?
HE'S PAPER TRAINED.

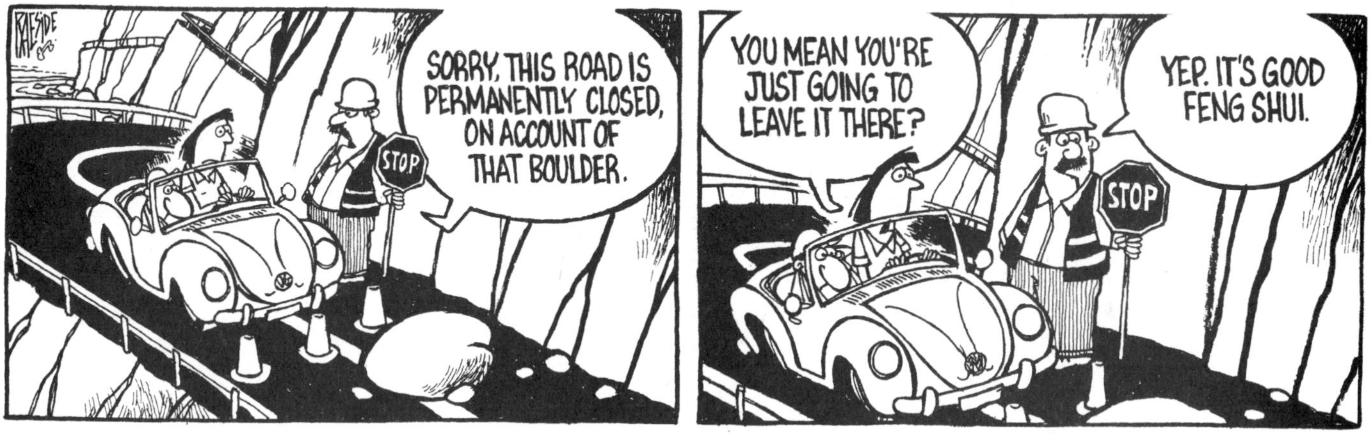
SORRY, THIS ROAD IS PERMANENTLY CLOSED, ON ACCOUNT OF THAT BOULDER.
STOP
YOU MEAN YOU'RE JUST GOING TO LEAVE IT THERE?
YEP. IT'S GOOD FENG SHUI.
STOP

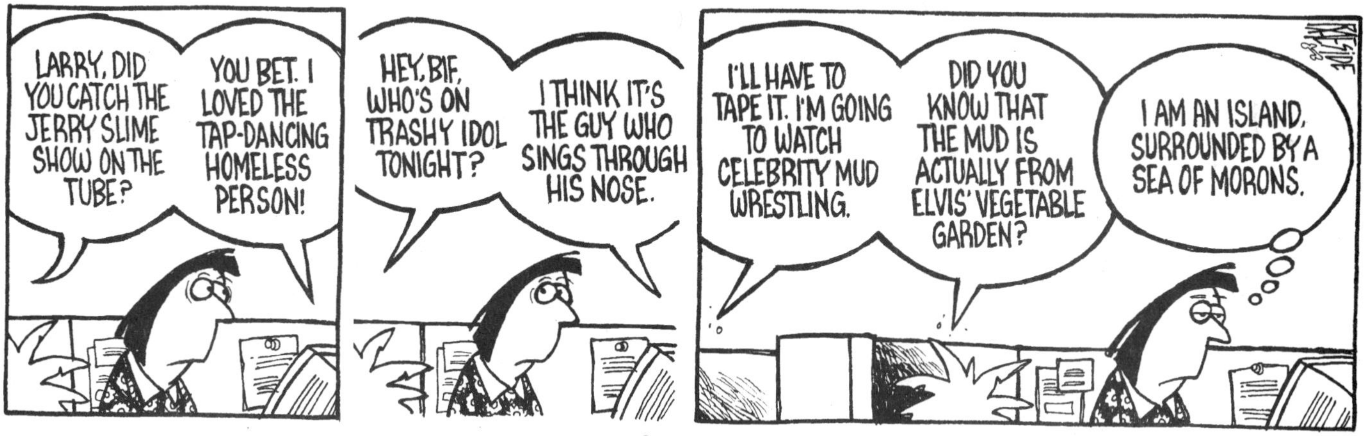
LARRY, DID YOU CATCH THE JERRY SLIME SHOW ON THE TUBE?
YOU BET. I LOVED THE TAP-DANCING HOMELESS PERSON!
HEY, BIF, WHO'S ON TRASHY IDOL TONIGHT?
I THINK IT'S THE GUY WHO SINGS THROUGH HIS NOSE.
I'LL HAVE TO TAPE IT. I'M GOING TO WATCH CELEBRITY MUD WRESTLING.
DID YOU KNOW THAT THE MUD IS ACTUALLY FROM ELVIS' VEGETABLE GARDEN?
I AM AN ISLAND, SURROUNDED BY A SEA OF MORONS.

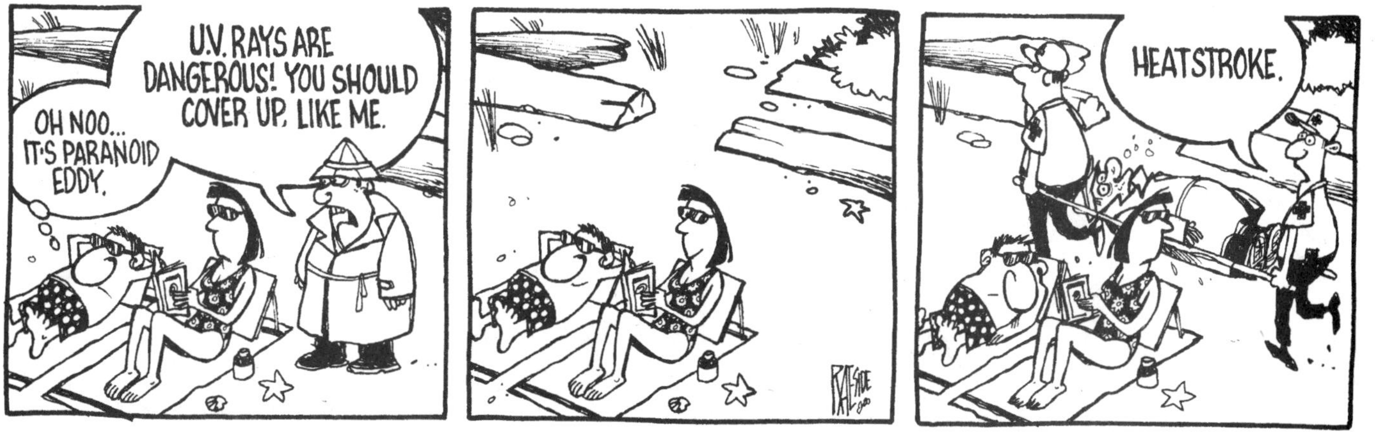
OH NOO... IT'S PARANOID EDDY.
U.V. RAYS ARE DANGEROUS! YOU SHOULD COVER UP, LIKE ME.
HEATSTROKE.

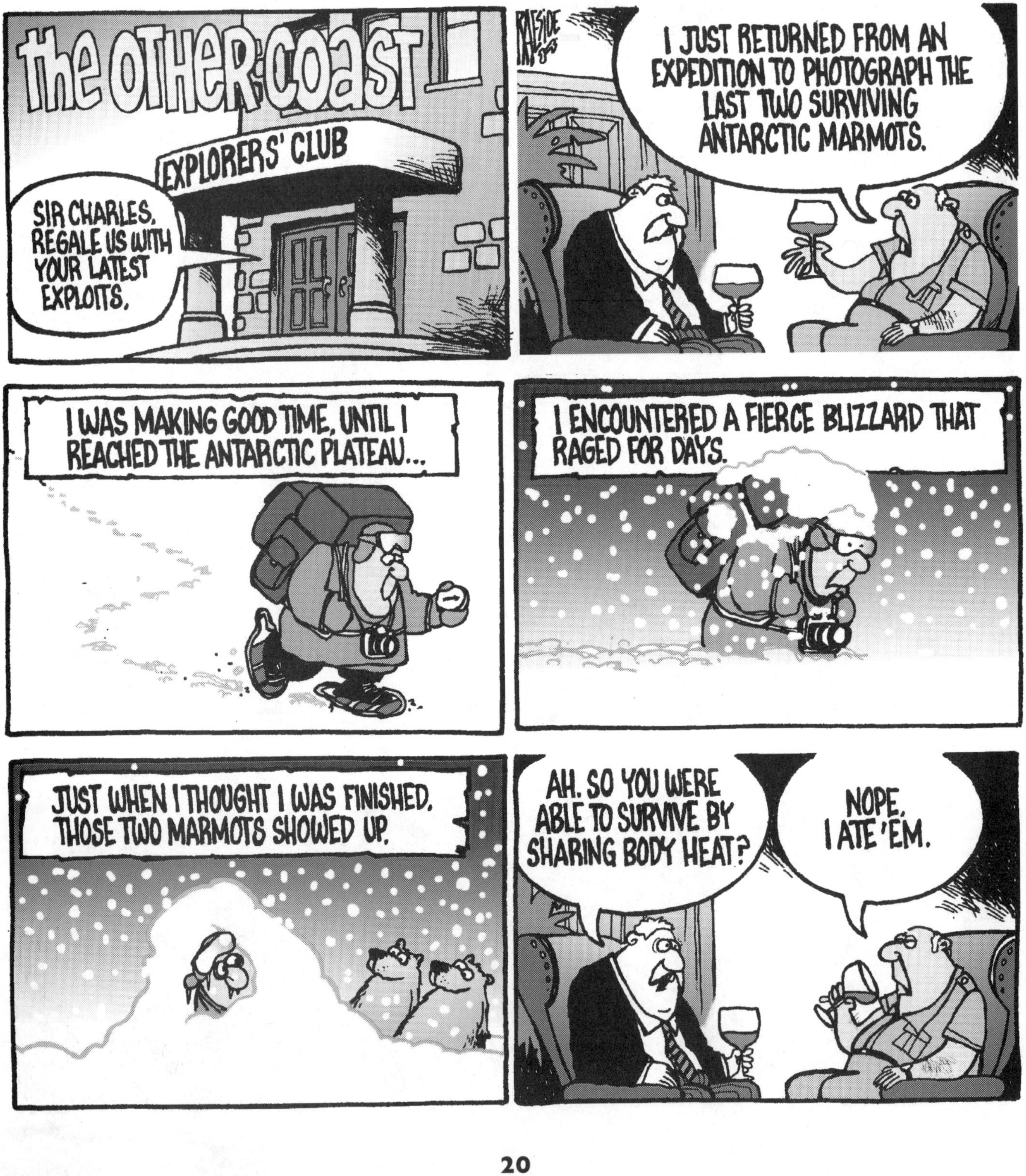
the OTHER COAST
EXPLORERS' CLUB
SIR CHARLES, REGALE US WITH YOUR LATEST EXPLOITS.
I JUST RETURNED FROM AN EXPEDITION TO PHOTOGRAPH THE LAST TWO SURVIVING ANTARCTIC MARMOTS.
I WAS MAKING GOOD TIME, UNTIL I REACHED THE ANTARCTIC PLATEAU...
I ENCOUNTERED A FIERCE BLIZZARD THAT RAGED FOR DAYS.
JUST WHEN I THOUGHT I WAS FINISHED, THOSE TWO MARMOTS SHOWED UP.
AH. SO YOU WERE ABLE TO SURVIVE BY SHARING BODY HEAT?
NOPE, I ATE 'EM.

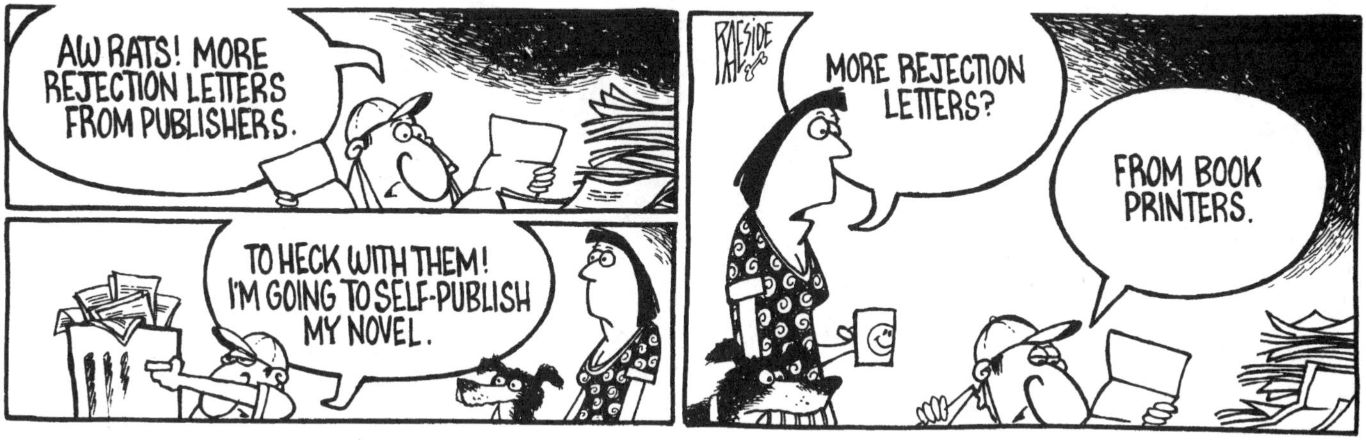
AW RATS! MORE REJECTION LETTERS FROM PUBLISHERS.
TO HECK WITH THEM! I'M GOING TO SELF-PUBLISH MY NOVEL.
MORE REJECTION LETTERS?
FROM BOOK PRINTERS.

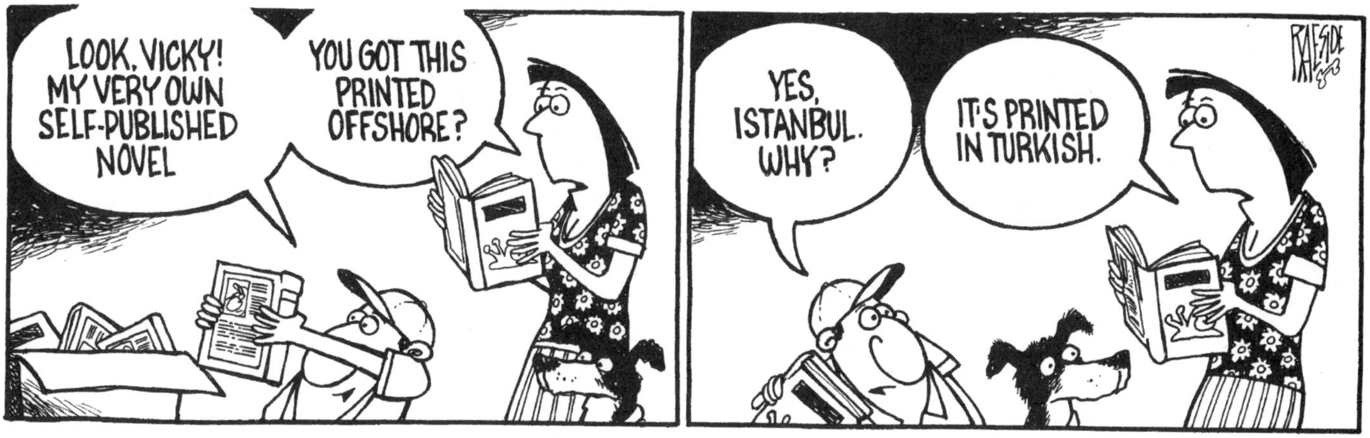
LOOK, VICKY! MY VERY OWN SELF-PUBLISHED NOVEL
YOU GOT THIS PRINTED OFFSHORE?
YES, ISTANBUL. WHY?
IT'S PRINTED IN TURKISH.

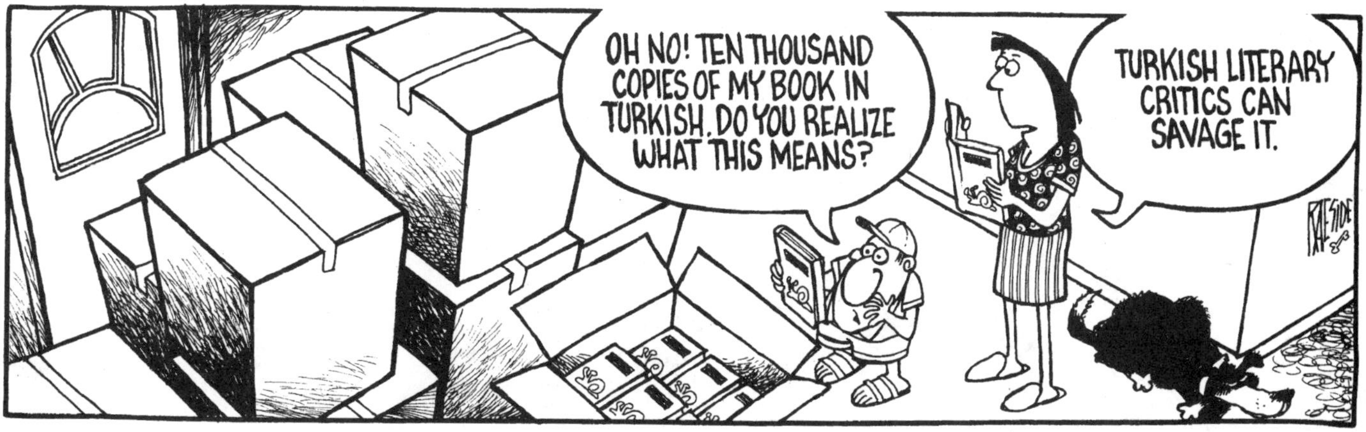
OH NO! TEN THOUSAND COPIES OF MY BOOK IN TURKISH. DO YOU REALIZE WHAT THIS MEANS?
TURKISH LITERARY CRITICS CAN SAVAGE IT.

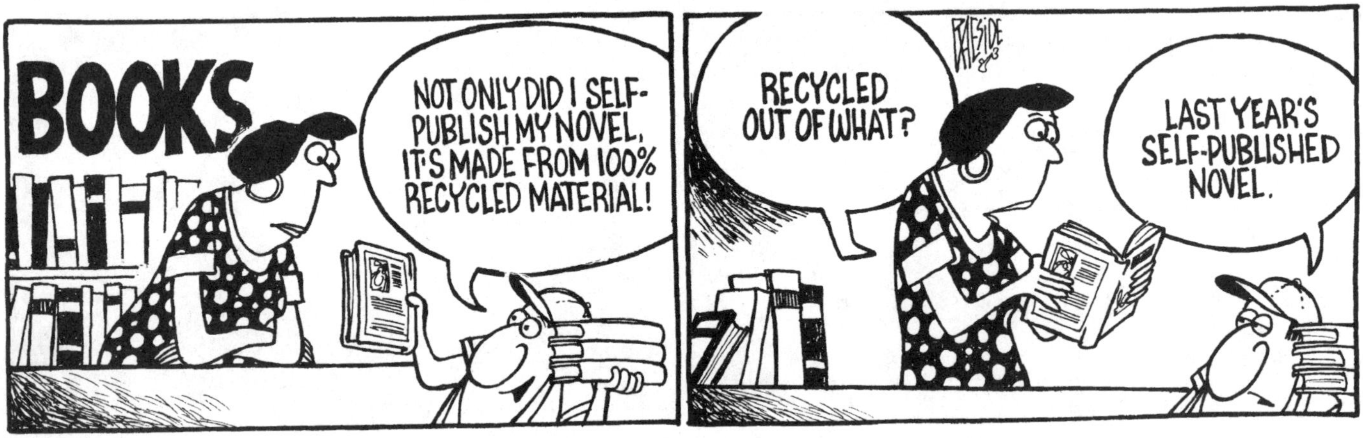
BOOKS
NOT ONLY DID I SELF-PUBLISH MY NOVEL, IT'S MADE FROM 100% RECYCLED MATERIAL!
RECYCLED OUT OF WHAT?
LAST YEAR'S SELF-PUBLISHED NOVEL.
RAESIDE

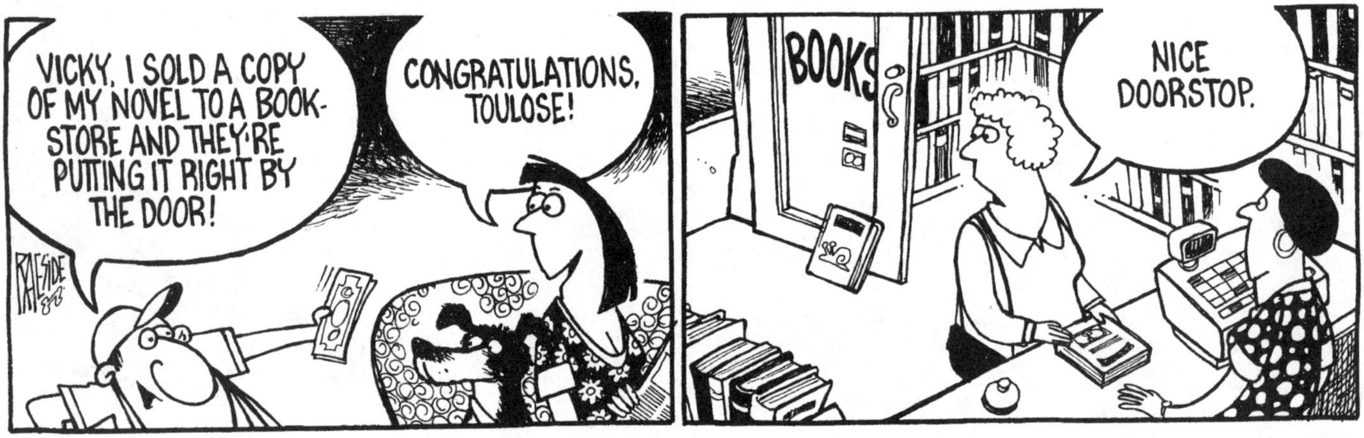
VICKY, I SOLD A COPY OF MY NOVEL TO A BOOK-STORE AND THEY'RE PUTTING IT RIGHT BY THE DOOR!
CONGRATULATIONS, TOULOSE!
RAESIDE
BOOKS
NICE DOORSTOP.

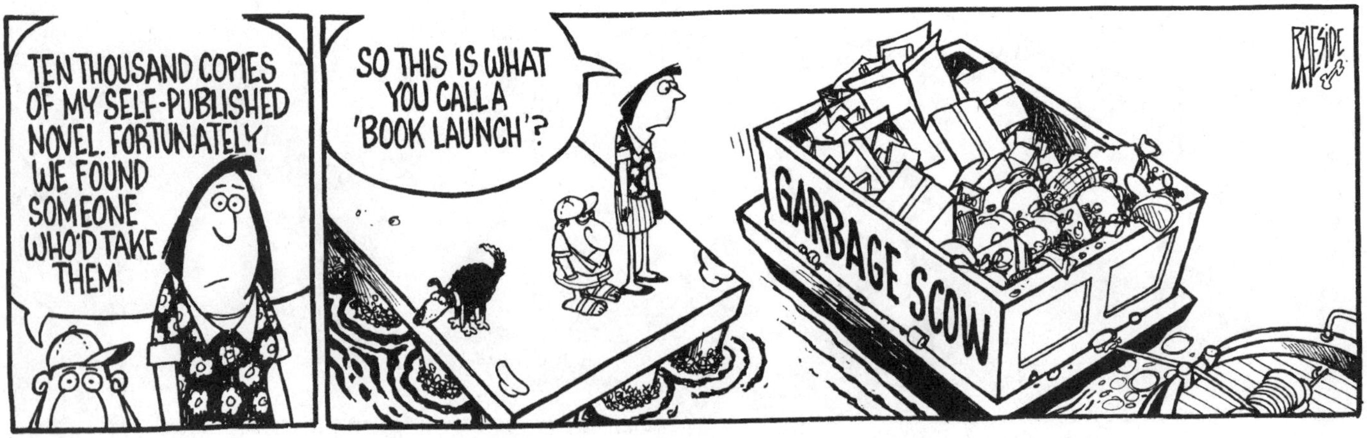
TEN THOUSAND COPIES OF MY SELF-PUBLISHED NOVEL. FORTUNATELY, WE FOUND SOMEONE WHO'D TAKE THEM.
SO THIS IS WHAT YOU CALL A 'BOOK LAUNCH'?
GARBAGE SCOW
RAESIDE

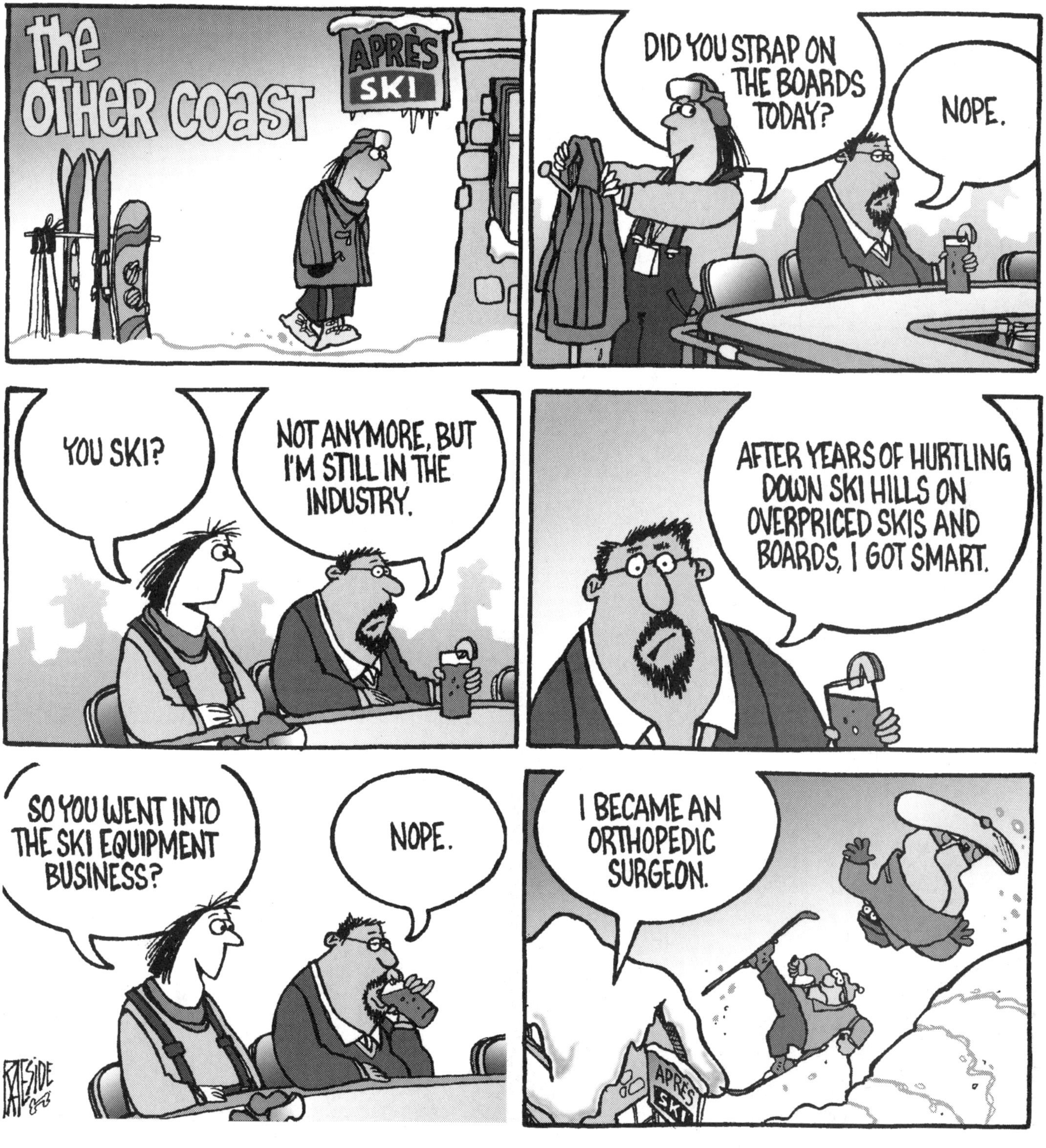
the OTHER COAST
APRÈS SKI
DID YOU STRAP ON THE BOARDS TODAY?
NOPE.
YOU SKI?
NOT ANYMORE, BUT I'M STILL IN THE INDUSTRY.
AFTER YEARS OF HURTLING DOWN SKI HILLS ON OVERPRICED SKIS AND BOARDS, I GOT SMART.
SO YOU WENT INTO THE SKI EQUIPMENT BUSINESS?
NOPE.
I BECAME AN ORTHOPEDIC SURGEON.
APRÈS SKI
RALESIDE

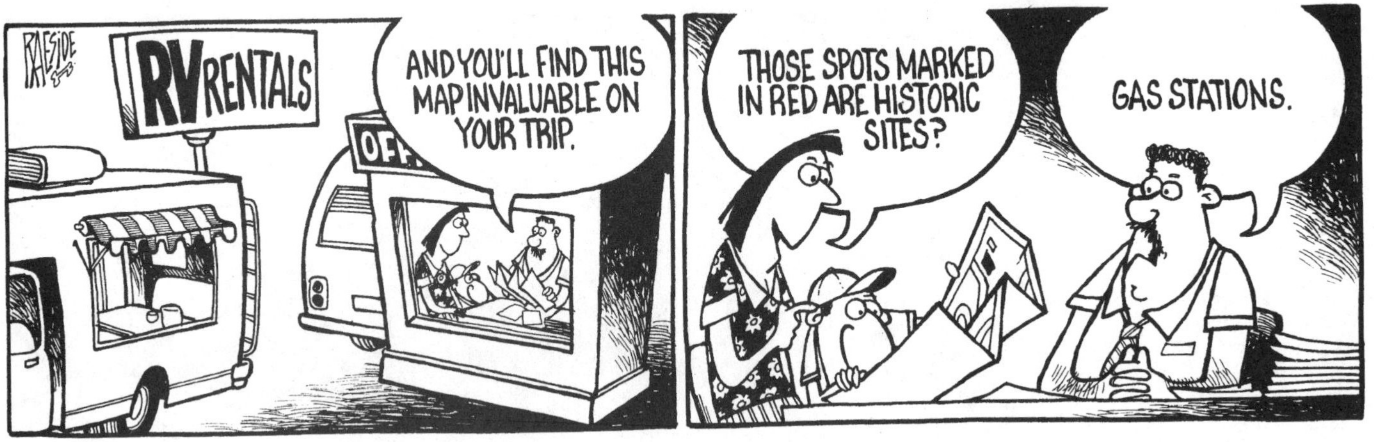
RV RENTALS
AND YOU'LL FIND THIS MAP INVALUABLE ON YOUR TRIP.
THOSE SPOTS MARKED IN RED ARE HISTORIC SITES?
GAS STATIONS.

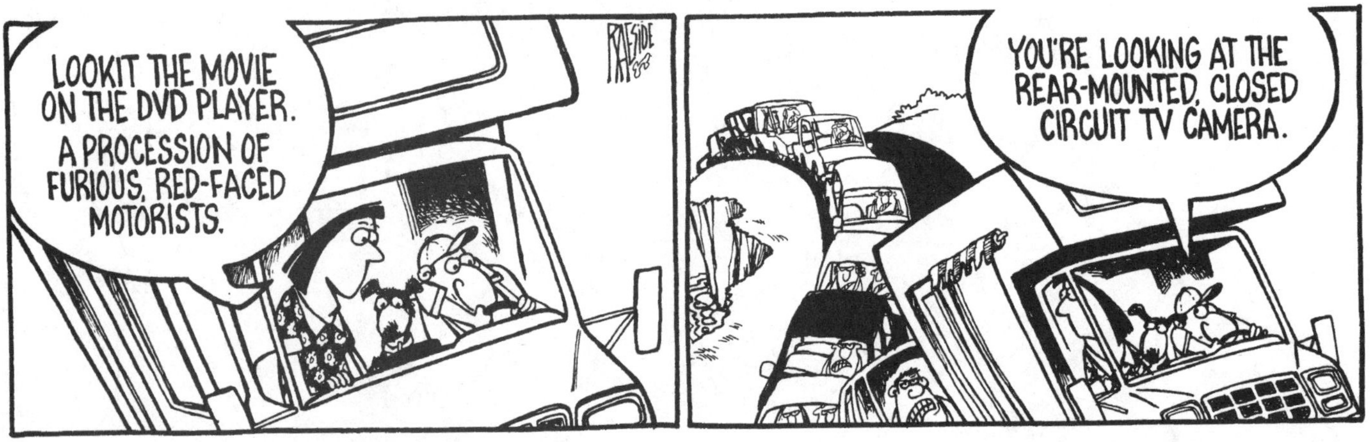
LOOKIT THE MOVIE ON THE DVD PLAYER. A PROCESSION OF FURIOUS, RED-FACED MOTORISTS.
YOU'RE LOOKING AT THE REAR-MOUNTED, CLOSED CIRCUIT TV CAMERA.

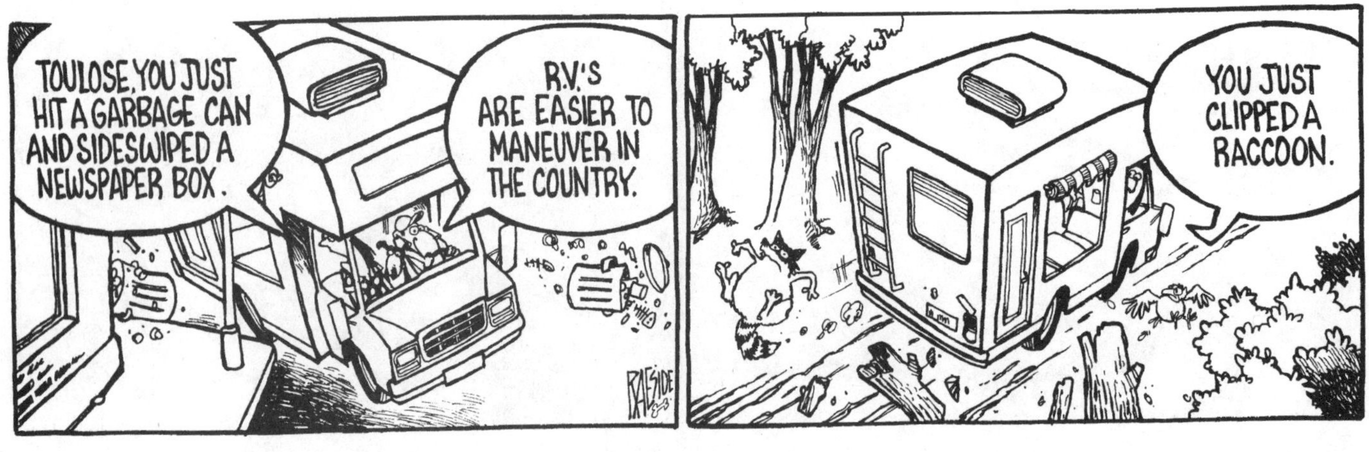
TOULOSE, YOU JUST HIT A GARBAGE CAN AND SIDESWIPED A NEWSPAPER BOX.
R.V.'S ARE EASIER TO MANEUVER IN THE COUNTRY.
YOU JUST CLIPPED A RACCOON.

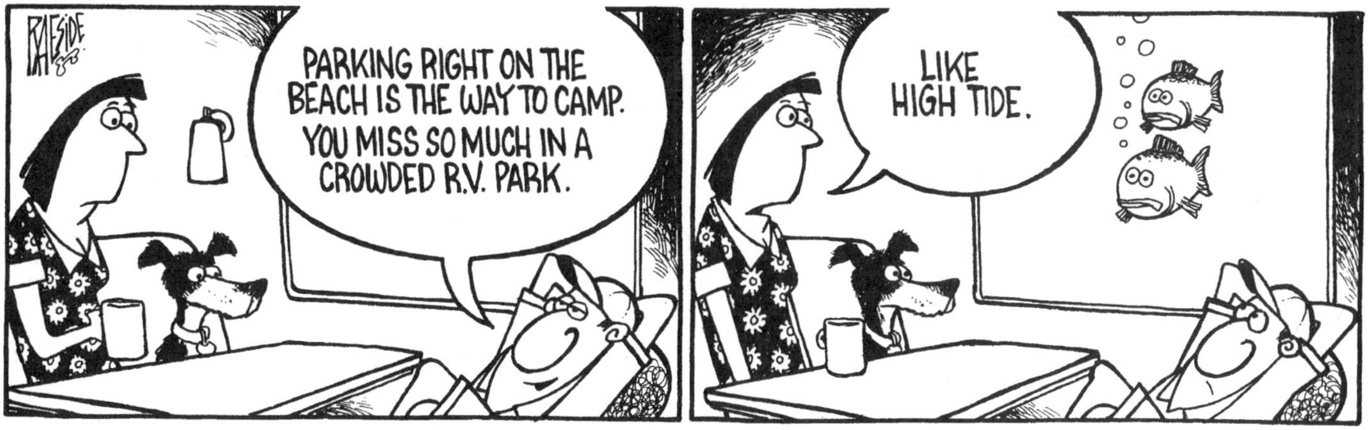
PARKING RIGHT ON THE BEACH IS THE WAY TO CAMP. YOU MISS SO MUCH IN A CROWDED R.V. PARK.
LIKE HIGH TIDE.

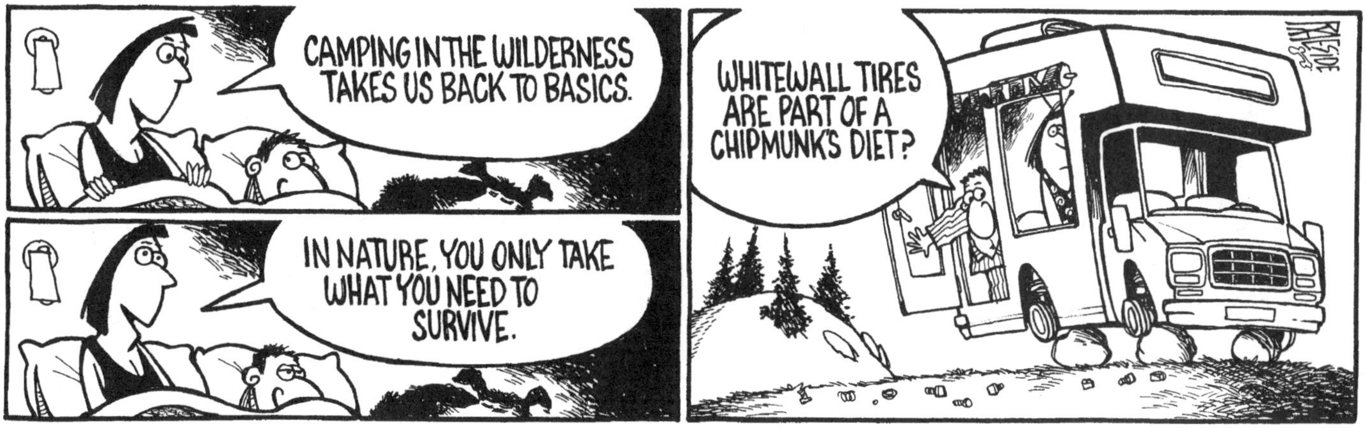
CAMPING IN THE WILDERNESS TAKES US BACK TO BASICS.
IN NATURE, YOU ONLY TAKE WHAT YOU NEED TO SURVIVE.
WHITEWALL TIRES ARE PART OF A CHIPMUNK'S DIET?

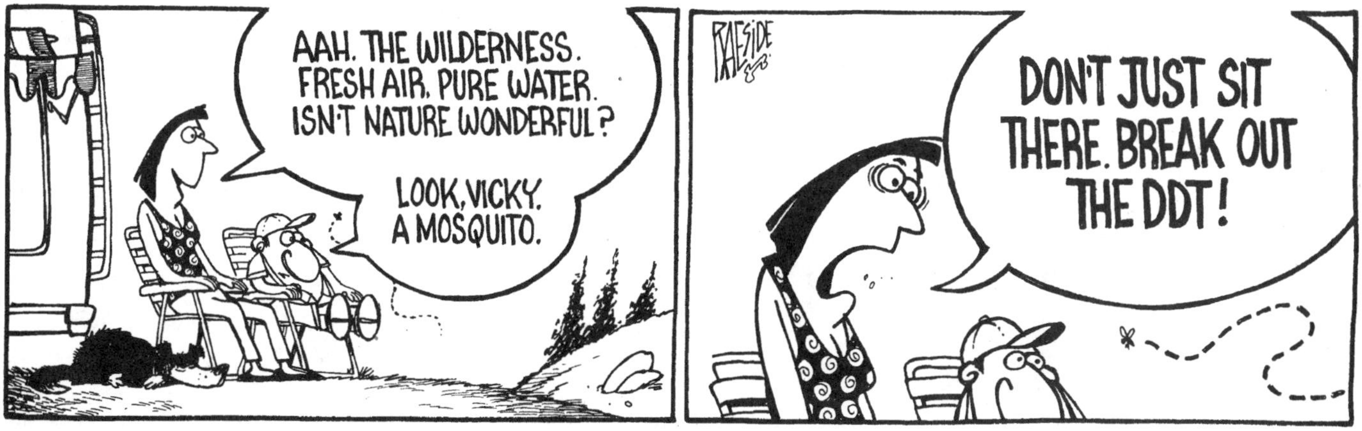
AAH. THE WILDERNESS. FRESH AIR. PURE WATER. ISN'T NATURE WONDERFUL?
LOOK, VICKY. A MOSQUITO.
DON'T JUST SIT THERE. BREAK OUT THE DDT!

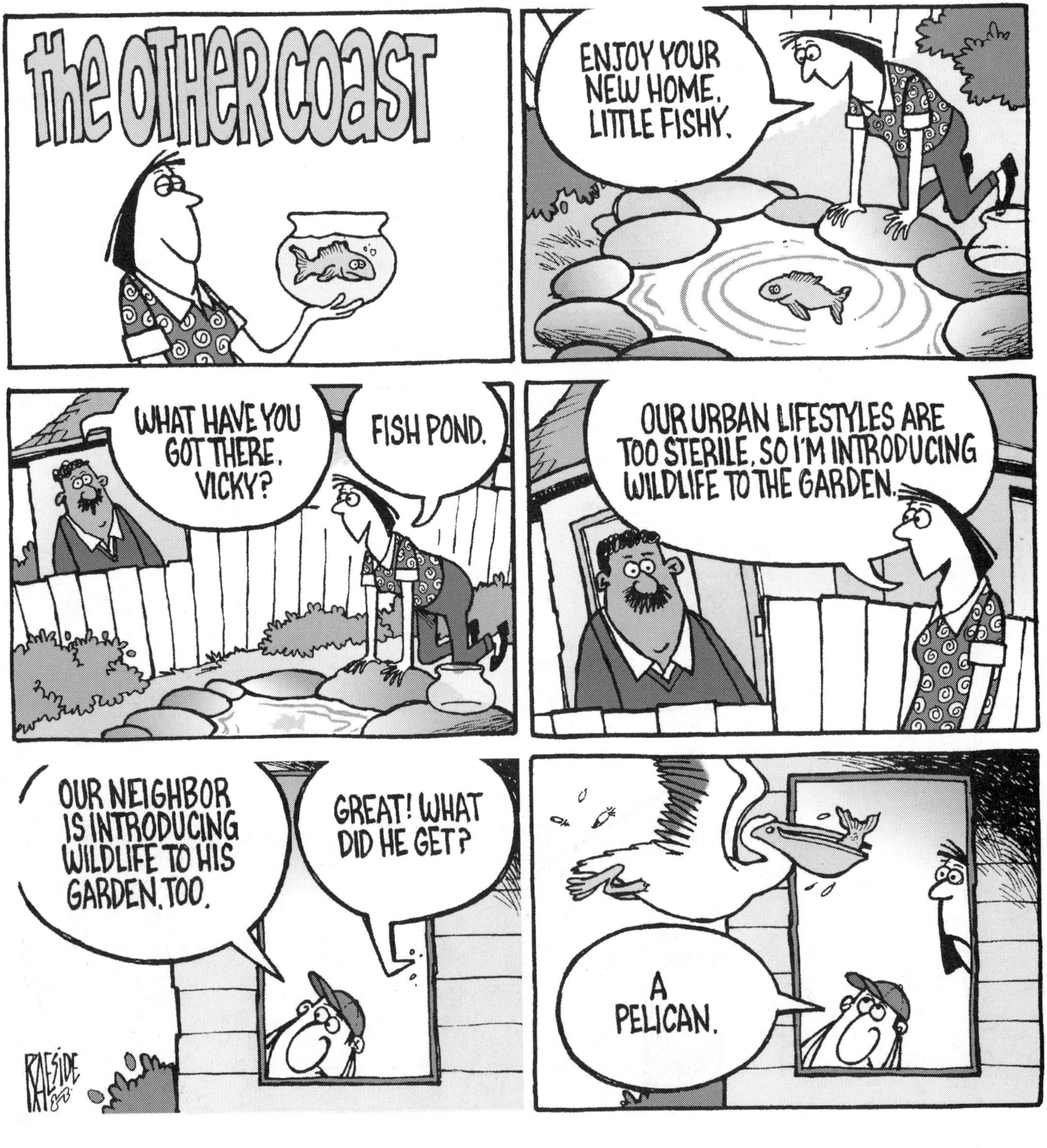
the OTHER COAST
ENJOY YOUR NEW HOME, LITTLE FISHY.
WHAT HAVE YOU GOT THERE, VICKY?
FISH POND.
OUR URBAN LIFESTYLES ARE TOO STERILE, SO I'M INTRODUCING WILDLIFE TO THE GARDEN.
OUR NEIGHBOR IS INTRODUCING WILDLIFE TO HIS GARDEN, TOO.
GREAT! WHAT DID HE GET?
A PELICAN.
RAESIDE

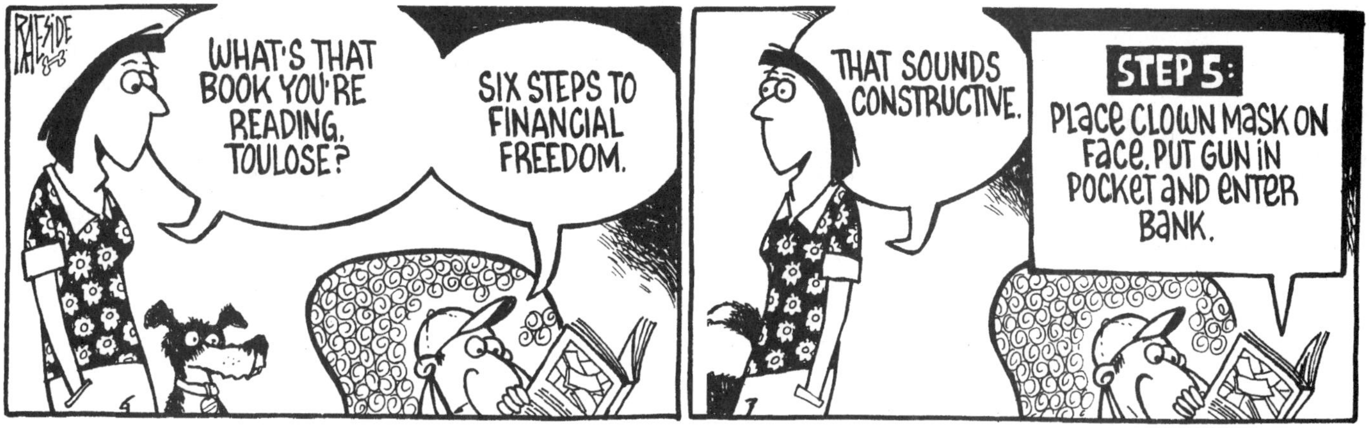
WHAT'S THAT BOOK YOU'RE READING, TOULOSE?
SIX STEPS TO FINANCIAL FREEDOM.
THAT SOUNDS CONSTRUCTIVE.
STEP 5:
PLACE CLOWN MASK ON FACE, PUT GUN IN POCKET AND ENTER BANK.

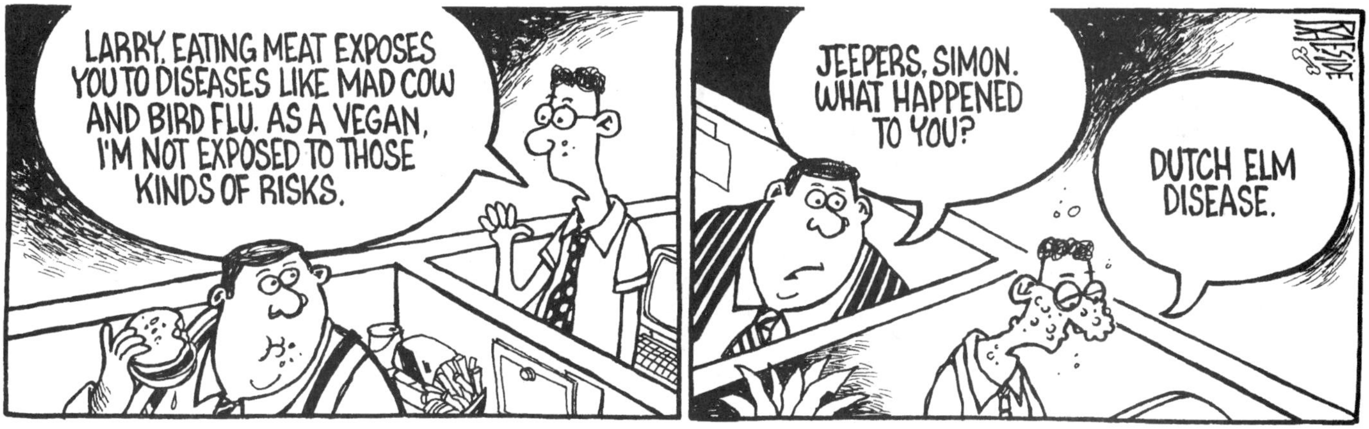
LARRY, EATING MEAT EXPOSES YOU TO DISEASES LIKE MAD COW AND BIRD FLU. AS A VEGAN, I'M NOT EXPOSED TO THOSE KINDS OF RISKS.
JEEPERS, SIMON. WHAT HAPPENED TO YOU?
DUTCH ELM DISEASE.

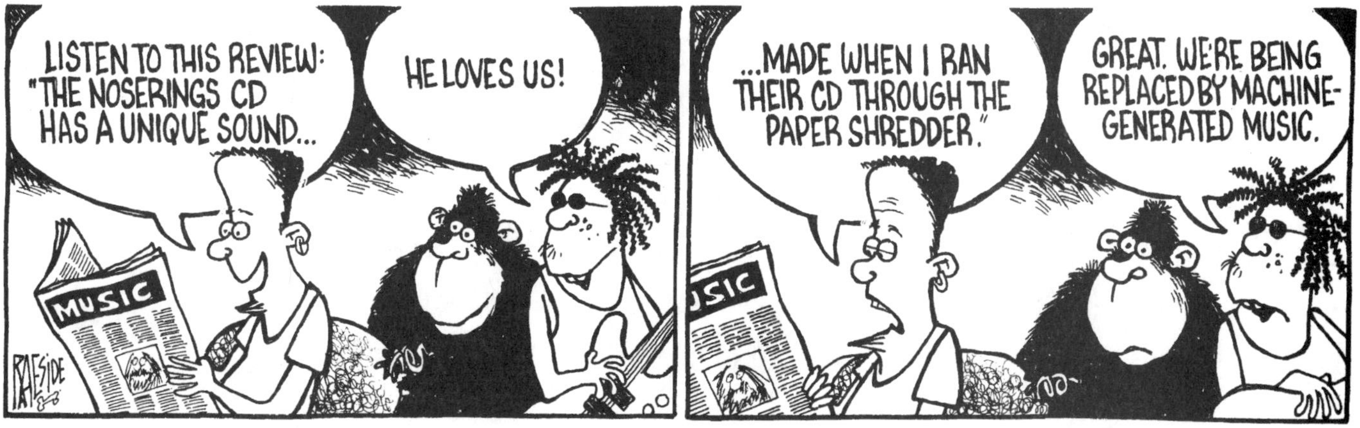
LISTEN TO THIS REVIEW: "THE NOSERINGS CD HAS A UNIQUE SOUND...
HE LOVES US!
MUSIC
...MADE WHEN I RAN THEIR CD THROUGH THE PAPER SHREDDER."
GREAT. WE'RE BEING REPLACED BY MACHINE-GENERATED MUSIC.

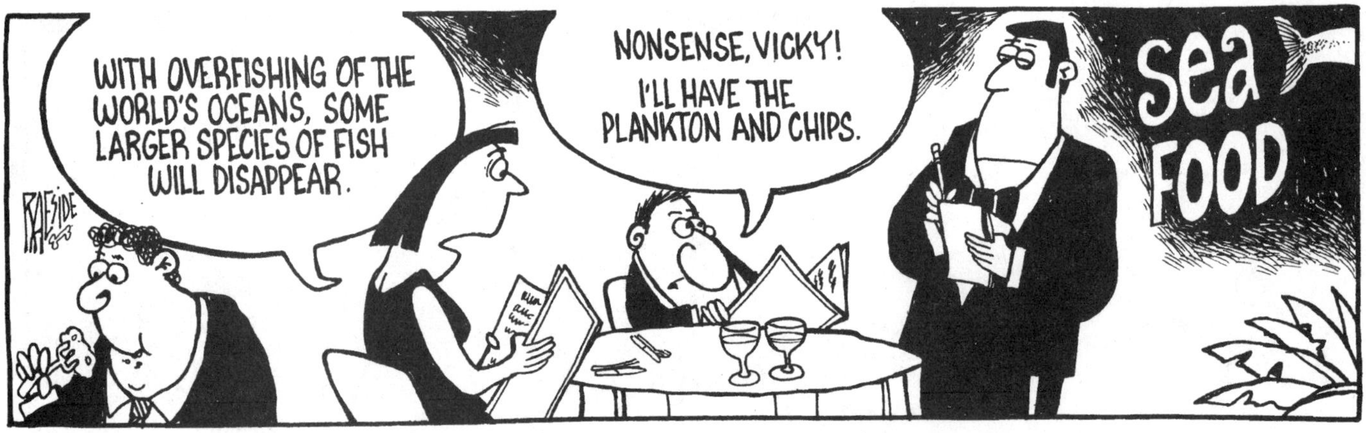
WITH OVERFISHING OF THE WORLD'S OCEANS, SOME LARGER SPECIES OF FISH WILL DISAPPEAR.
NONSENSE, VICKY!
I'LL HAVE THE PLANKTON AND CHIPS.
sea FOOD
RAESIDE

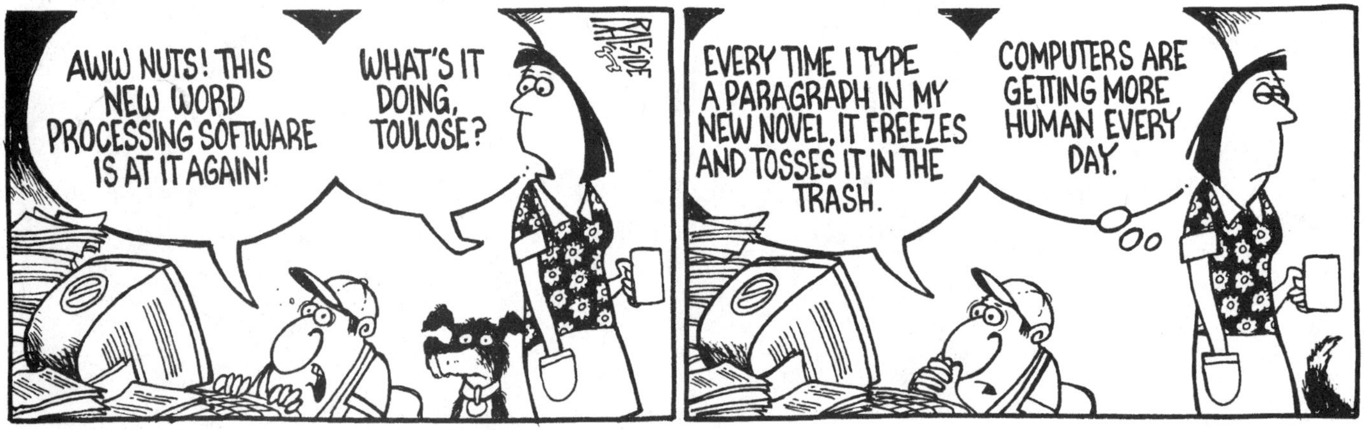
AWW NUTS! THIS NEW WORD PROCESSING SOFTWARE IS AT IT AGAIN!
WHAT'S IT DOING, TOULOSE?
RAESIDE
EVERY TIME I TYPE A PARAGRAPH IN MY NEW NOVEL, IT FREEZES AND TOSSES IT IN THE TRASH.
COMPUTERS ARE GETTING MORE HUMAN EVERY DAY.

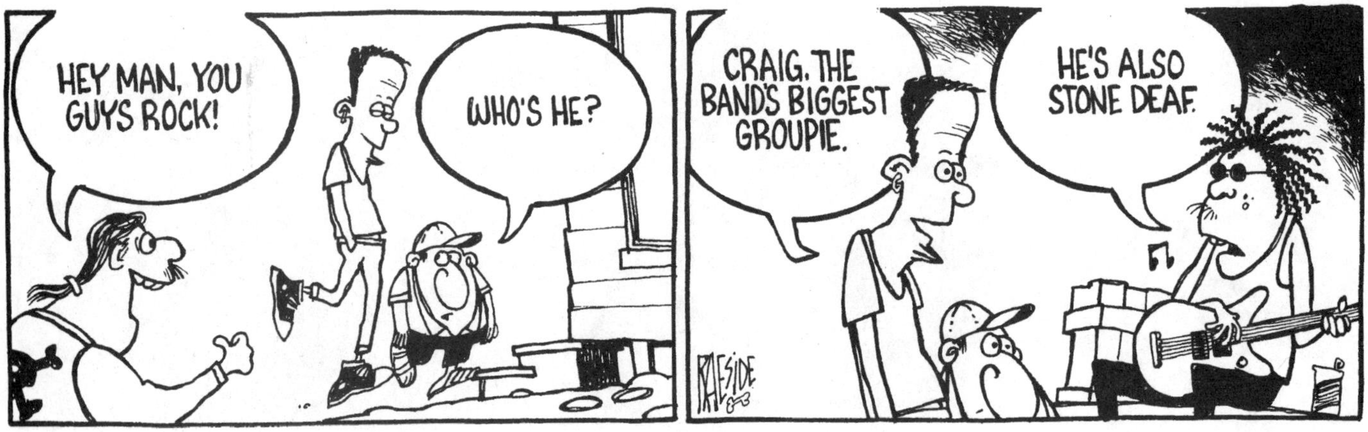
HEY MAN, YOU GUYS ROCK!
WHO'S HE?
CRAIG. THE BAND'S BIGGEST GROUPIE.
HE'S ALSO STONE DEAF.
RAESIDE

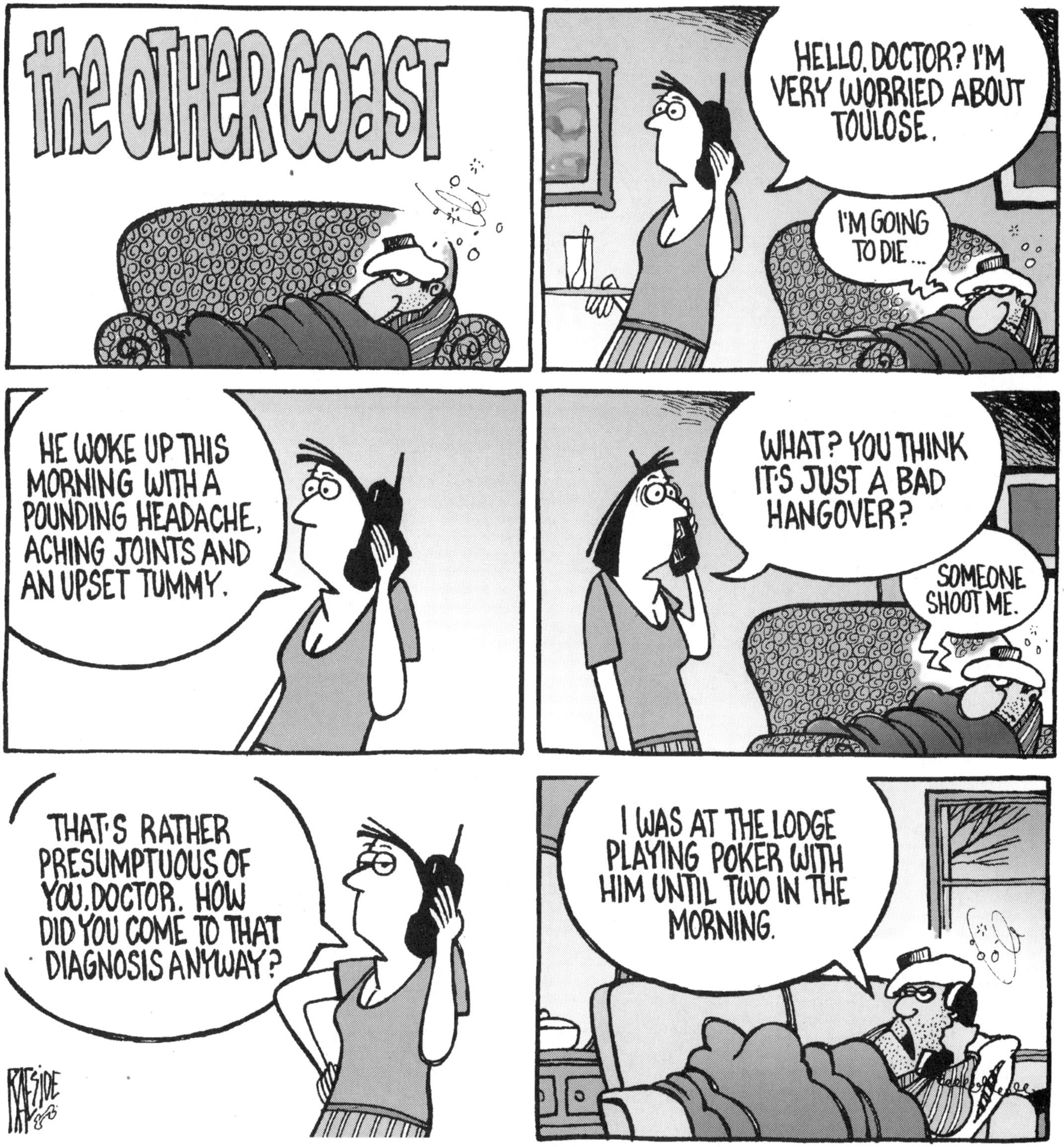
the OTHER COAST
HELLO, DOCTOR? I'M VERY WORRIED ABOUT TOULOSE.
I'M GOING TO DIE...
HE WOKE UP THIS MORNING WITH A POUNDING HEADACHE, ACHING JOINTS AND AN UPSET TUMMY.
WHAT? YOU THINK IT'S JUST A BAD HANGOVER?
SOMEONE SHOOT ME.
THAT'S RATHER PRESUMPTUOUS OF YOU, DOCTOR. HOW DID YOU COME TO THAT DIAGNOSIS ANYWAY?
I WAS AT THE LODGE PLAYING POKER WITH HIM UNTIL TWO IN THE MORNING.
RAESIDE

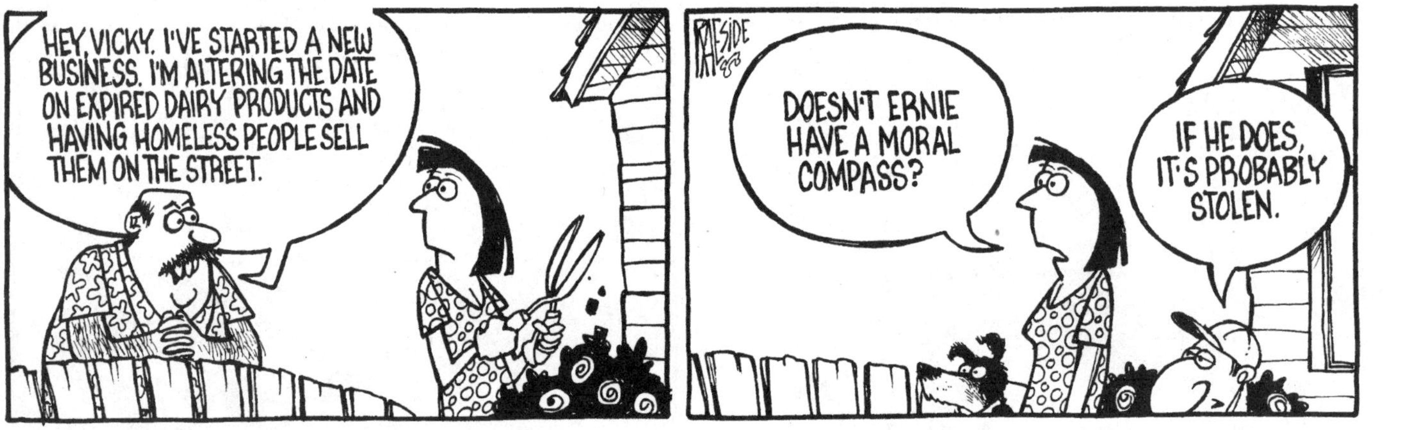
HEY, VICKY. I'VE STARTED A NEW BUSINESS. I'M ALTERING THE DATE ON EXPIRED DAIRY PRODUCTS AND HAVING HOMELESS PEOPLE SELL THEM ON THE STREET.
RAESIDE
DOESN'T ERNIE HAVE A MORAL COMPASS?
IF HE DOES, IT'S PROBABLY STOLEN.

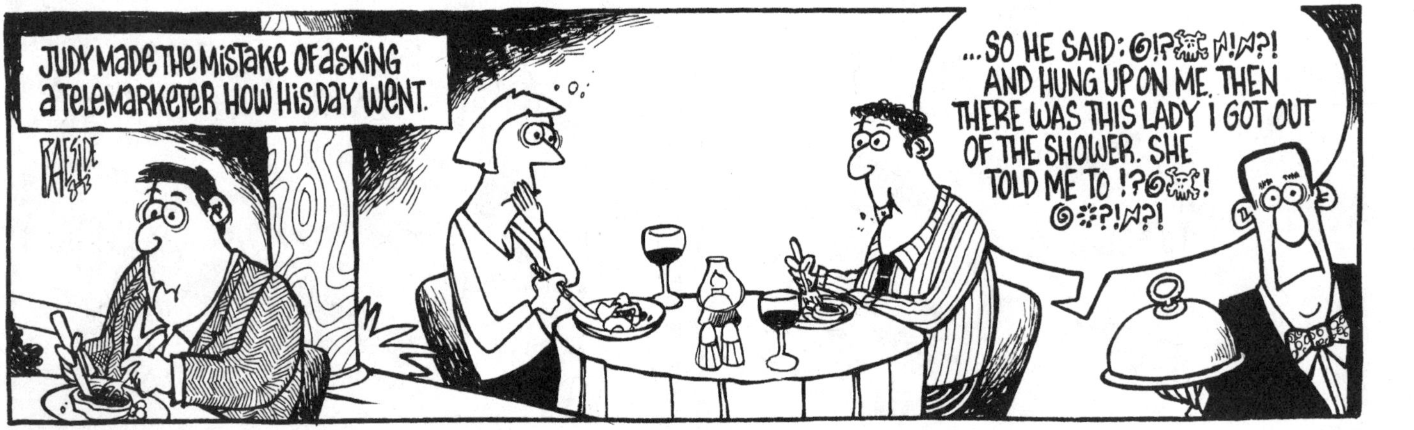
JUDY MADE THE MISTAKE OF ASKING A TELEMARKETER HOW HIS DAY WENT.
RAESIDE
...SO HE SAID:
AND HUNG UP ON ME. THEN THERE WAS THIS LADY I GOT OUT OF THE SHOWER. SHE TOLD ME TO

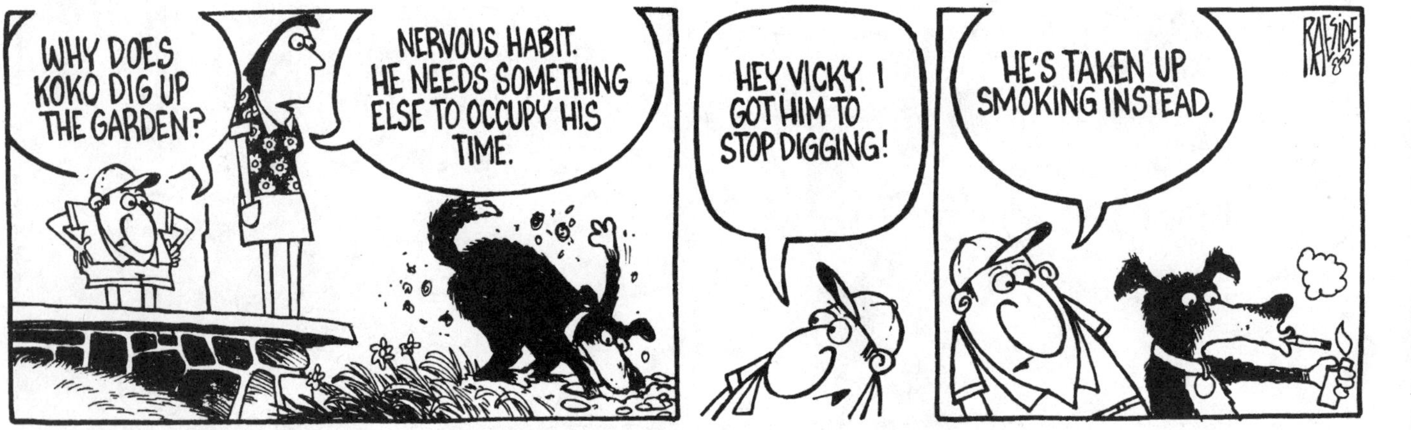
WHY DOES KOKO DIG UP THE GARDEN?
NERVOUS HABIT. HE NEEDS SOMETHING ELSE TO OCCUPY HIS TIME.
HEY, VICKY. I GOT HIM TO STOP DIGGING!
HE'S TAKEN UP SMOKING INSTEAD.
RAESIDE

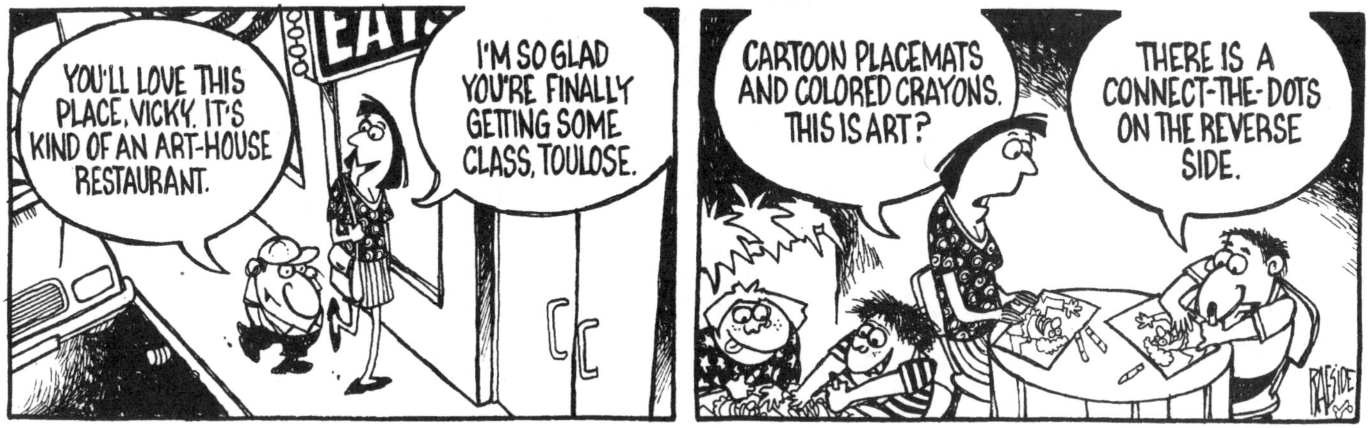
YOU'LL LOVE THIS PLACE, VICKY. IT'S KIND OF AN ART-HOUSE RESTAURANT.
I'M SO GLAD YOU'RE FINALLY GETTING SOME CLASS, TOULOSE.
CARTOON PLACEMATS AND COLORED CRAYONS. THIS IS ART?
THERE IS A CONNECT-THE-DOTS ON THE REVERSE SIDE.
RAESIDE

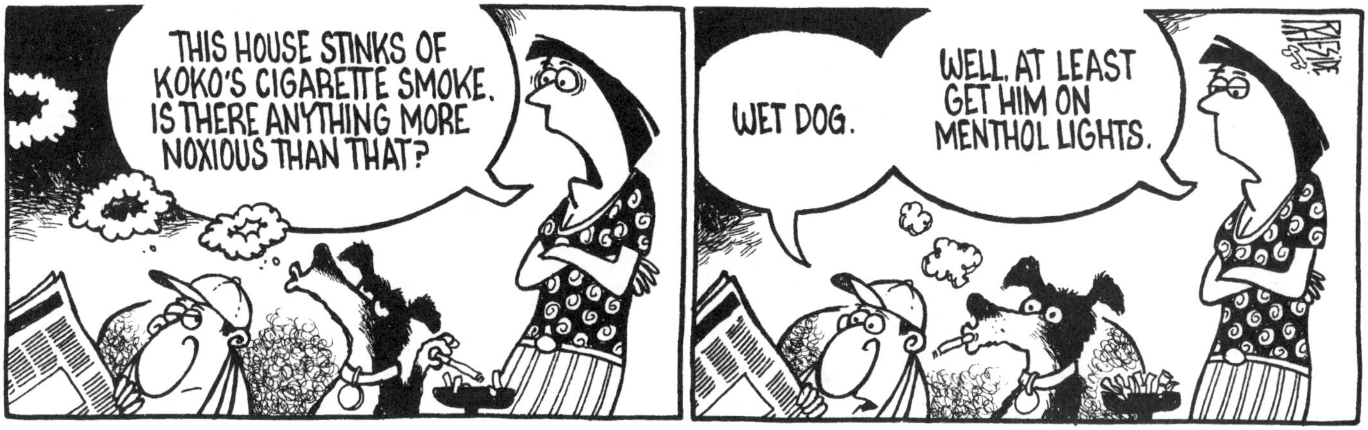
THIS HOUSE STINKS OF KOKO'S CIGARETTE SMOKE. IS THERE ANYTHING MORE NOXIOUS THAN THAT?
WET DOG.
WELL, AT LEAST GET HIM ON MENTHOL LIGHTS.
RAESIDE

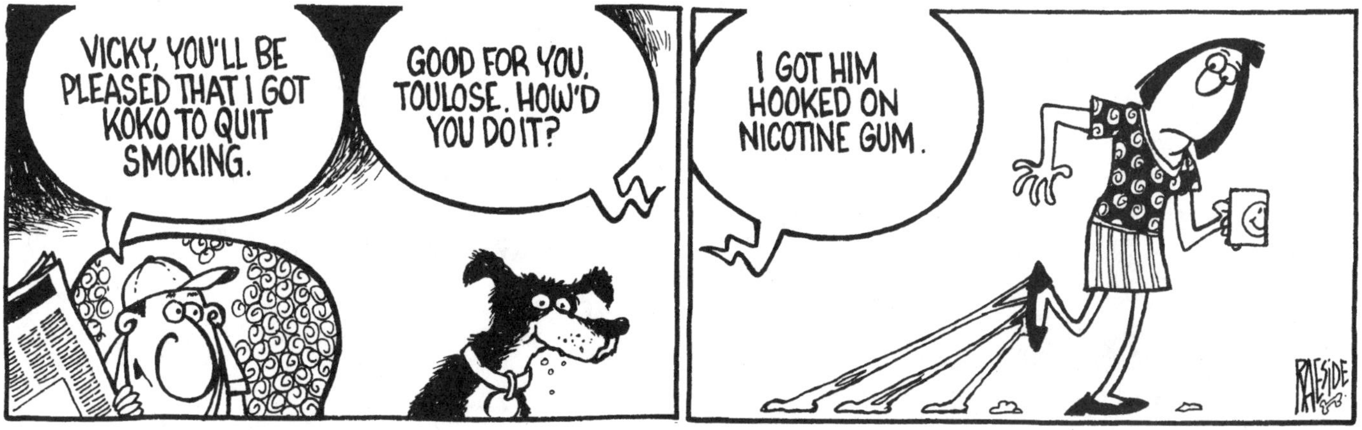
VICKY, YOU'LL BE PLEASED THAT I GOT KOKO TO QUIT SMOKING.
GOOD FOR YOU, TOULOSE. HOW'D YOU DO IT?
I GOT HIM HOOKED ON NICOTINE GUM.
RAESIDE

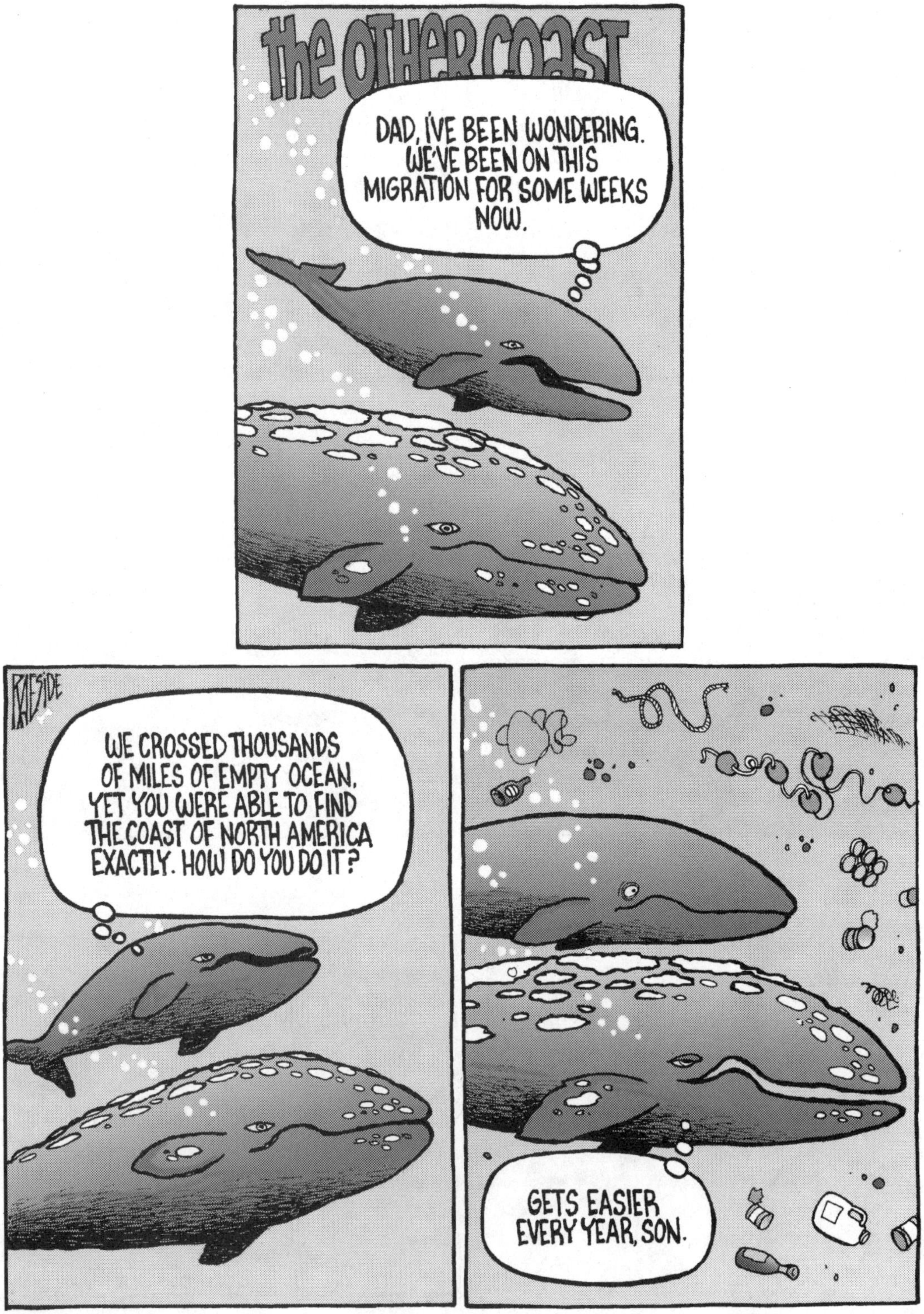
the OTHER COAST
DAD, I'VE BEEN WONDERING. WE'VE BEEN ON THIS MIGRATION FOR SOME WEEKS NOW.
WE CROSSED THOUSANDS OF MILES OF EMPTY OCEAN, YET YOU WERE ABLE TO FIND THE COAST OF NORTH AMERICA EXACTLY. HOW DO YOU DO IT?
GETS EASIER EVERY YEAR, SON.

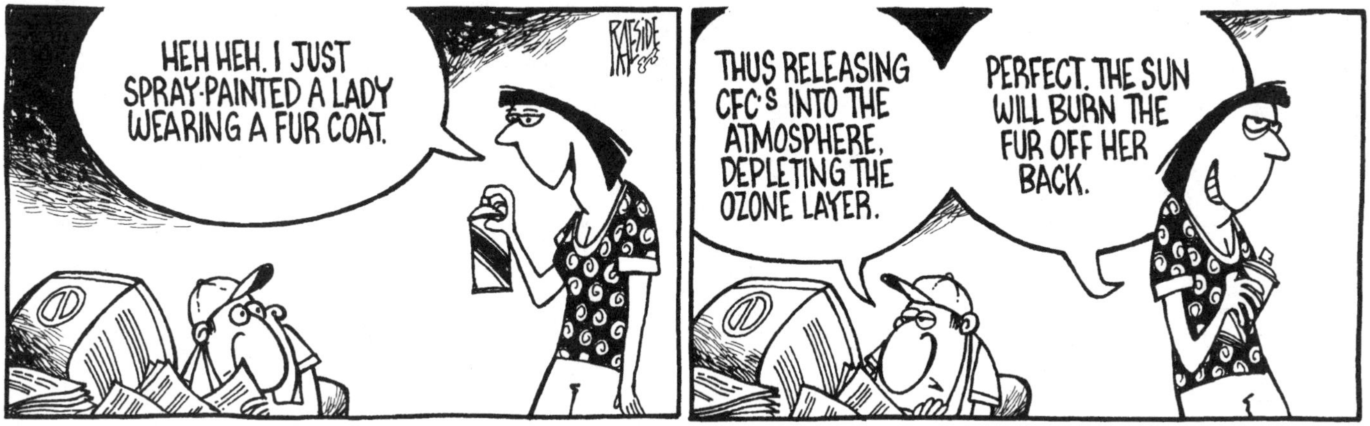
HEH HEH. I JUST SPRAY-PAINTED A LADY WEARING A FUR COAT.
THUS RELEASING CFC'S INTO THE ATMOSPHERE, DEPLETING THE OZONE LAYER.
PERFECT. THE SUN WILL BURN THE FUR OFF HER BACK.

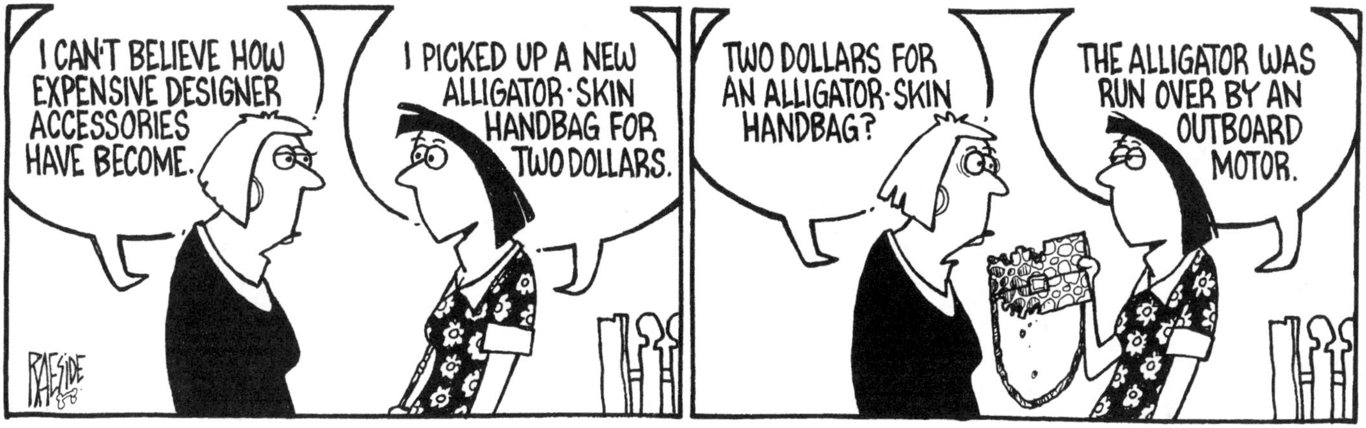
I CAN'T BELIEVE HOW EXPENSIVE DESIGNER ACCESSORIES HAVE BECOME.
I PICKED UP A NEW ALLIGATOR-SKIN HANDBAG FOR TWO DOLLARS.
TWO DOLLARS FOR AN ALLIGATOR-SKIN HANDBAG?
THE ALLIGATOR WAS RUN OVER BY AN OUTBOARD MOTOR.

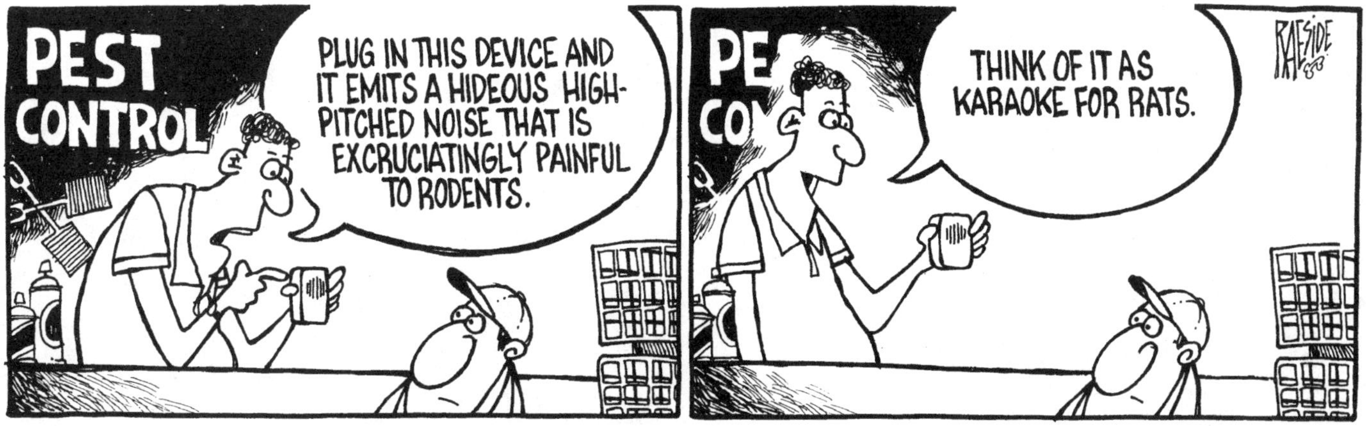
PEST CONTROL
PLUG IN THIS DEVICE AND IT EMITS A HIDEOUS HIGH-PITCHED NOISE THAT IS EXCRUCIATINGLY PAINFUL TO RODENTS.
THINK OF IT AS KARAOKE FOR RATS.

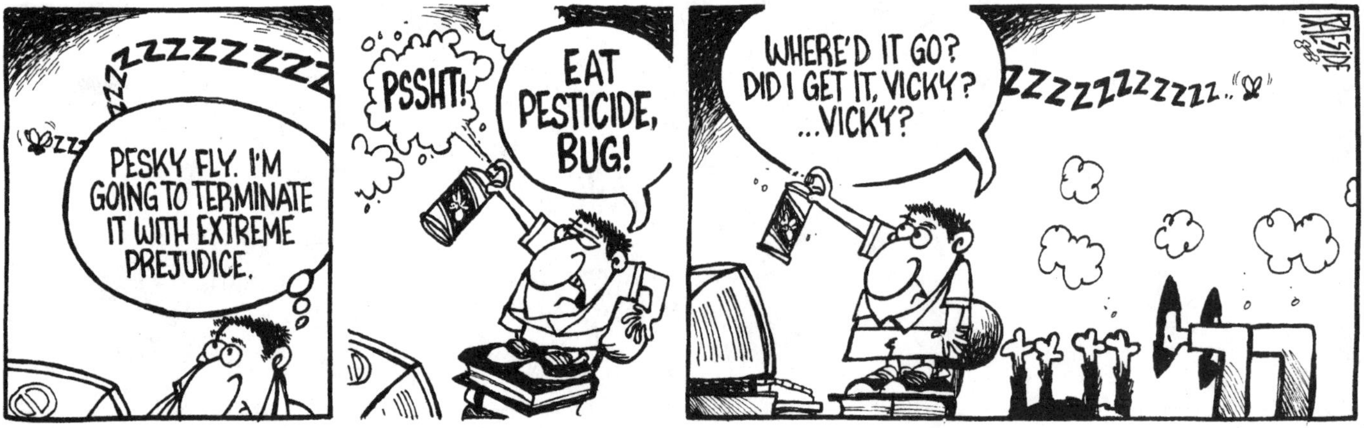
ZZZZZZZZZZZ
PESKY FLY. I'M GOING TO TERMINATE IT WITH EXTREME PREJUDICE.
PSSHT!
EAT PESTICIDE, BUG!
WHERE'D IT GO? DID I GET IT, VICKY? ...VICKY?
ZZZZZZZZZZZZ..

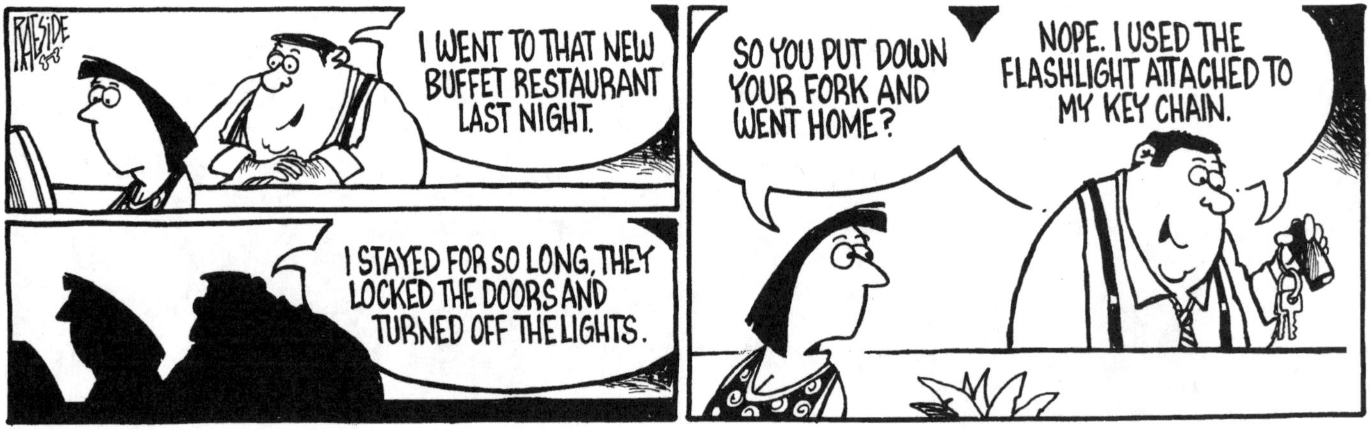
I WENT TO THAT NEW BUFFET RESTAURANT LAST NIGHT.
I STAYED FOR SO LONG, THEY LOCKED THE DOORS AND TURNED OFF THE LIGHTS.
SO YOU PUT DOWN YOUR FORK AND WENT HOME?
NOPE. I USED THE FLASHLIGHT ATTACHED TO MY KEY CHAIN.

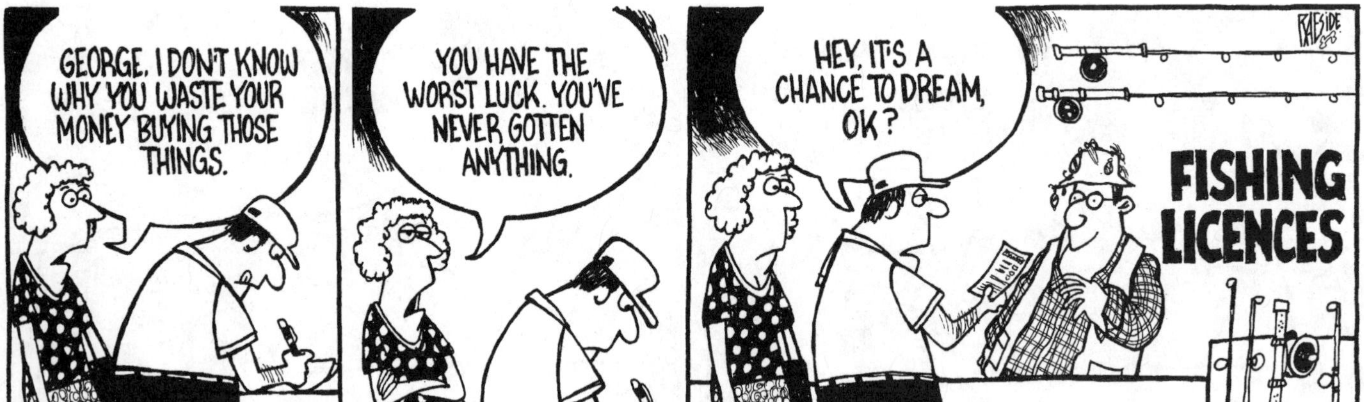
GEORGE, I DON'T KNOW WHY YOU WASTE YOUR MONEY BUYING THOSE THINGS.
YOU HAVE THE WORST LUCK. YOU'VE NEVER GOTTEN ANYTHING.
HEY, IT'S A CHANCE TO DREAM, OK?
FISHING LICENCES

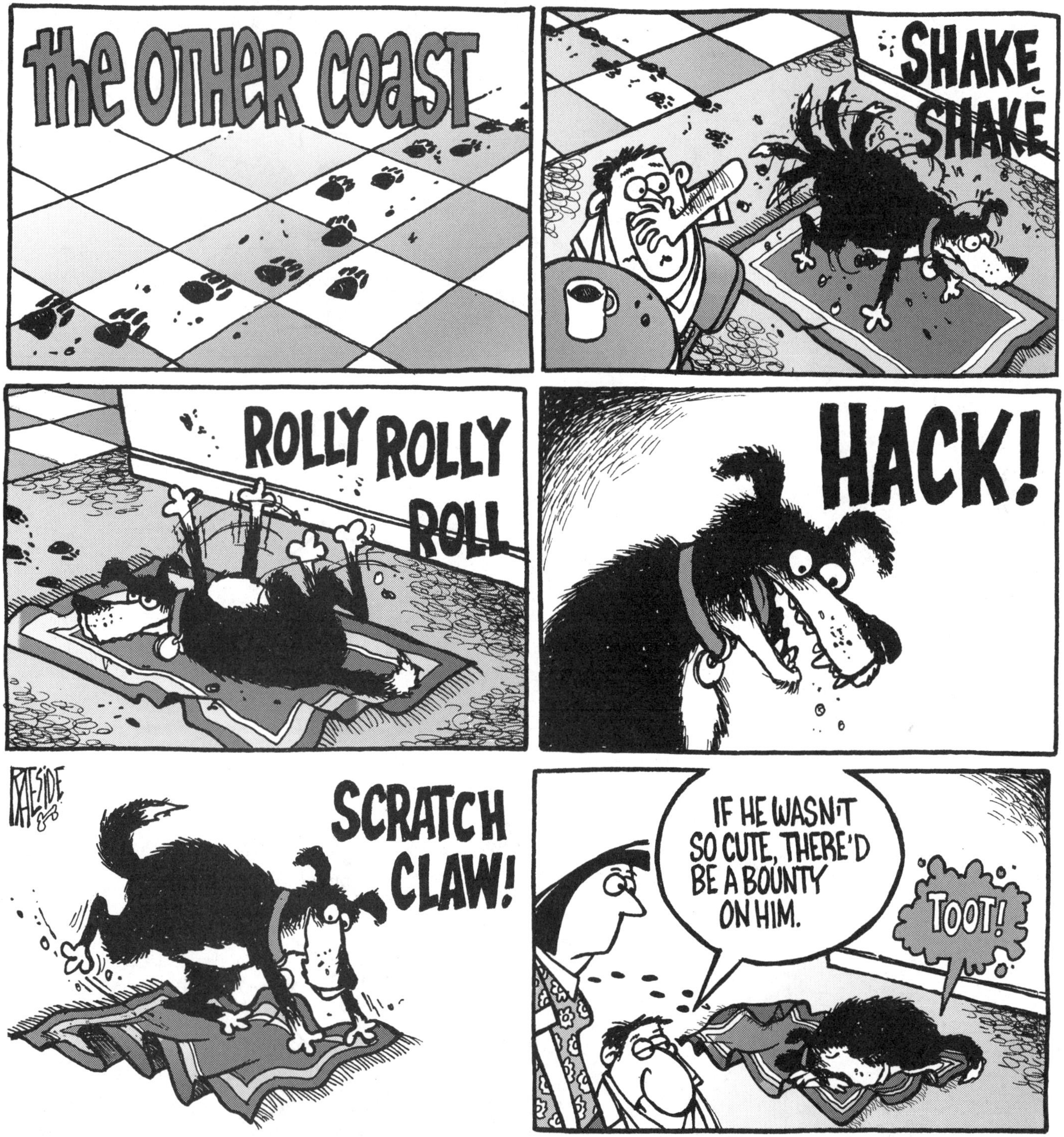
the OTHER COAST
SHAKE SHAKE
ROLLY ROLLY ROLL
HACK!
SCRATCH CLAW!
IF HE WASN'T SO CUTE, THERE'D BE A BOUNTY ON HIM.
TOOT!

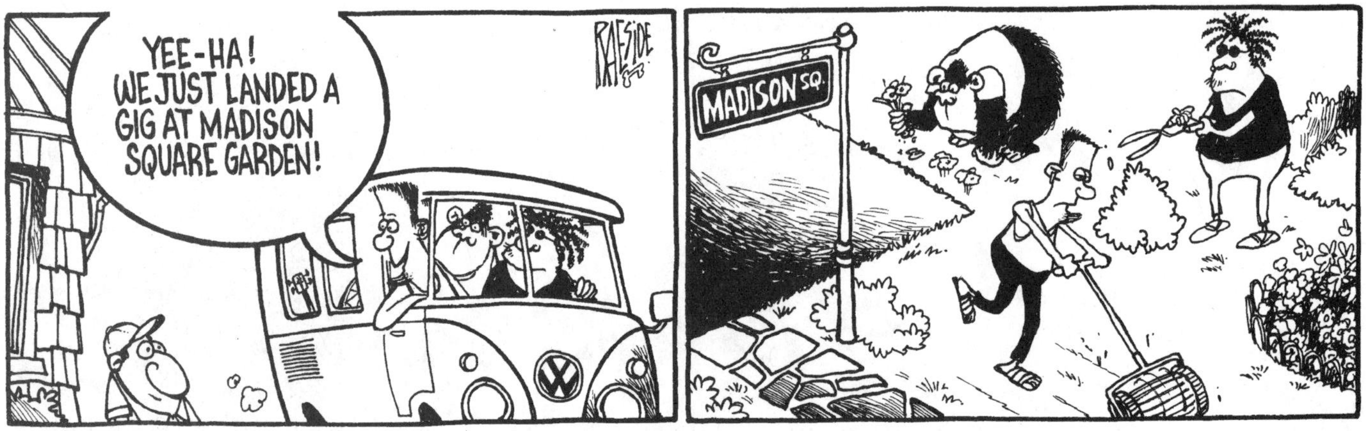
YEE-HA! WE JUST LANDED A GIG AT MADISON SQUARE GARDEN!
MADISON SQ.

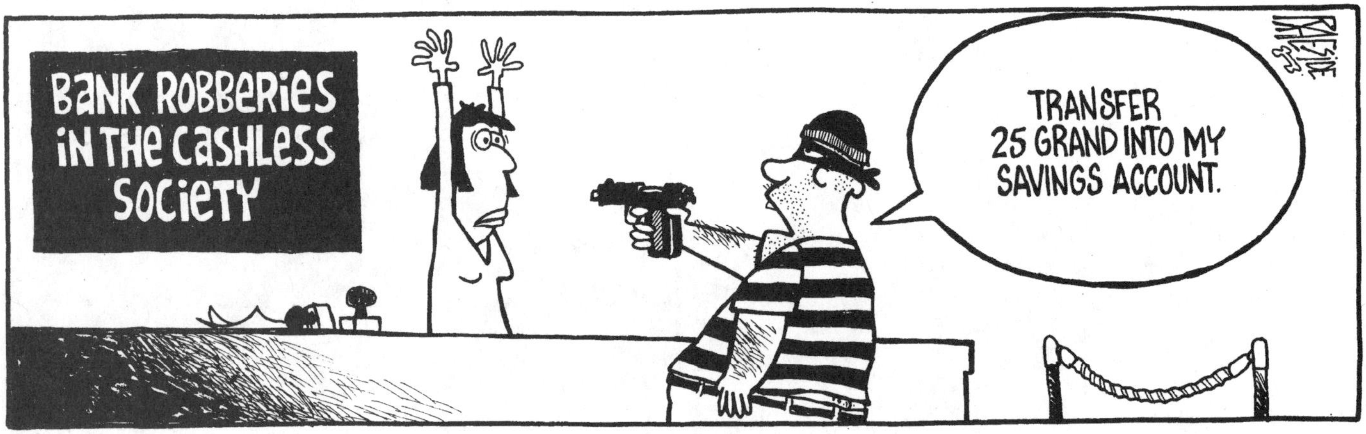
BANK ROBBERIES IN THE CASHLESS SOCIETY
TRANSFER 25 GRAND INTO MY SAVINGS ACCOUNT.

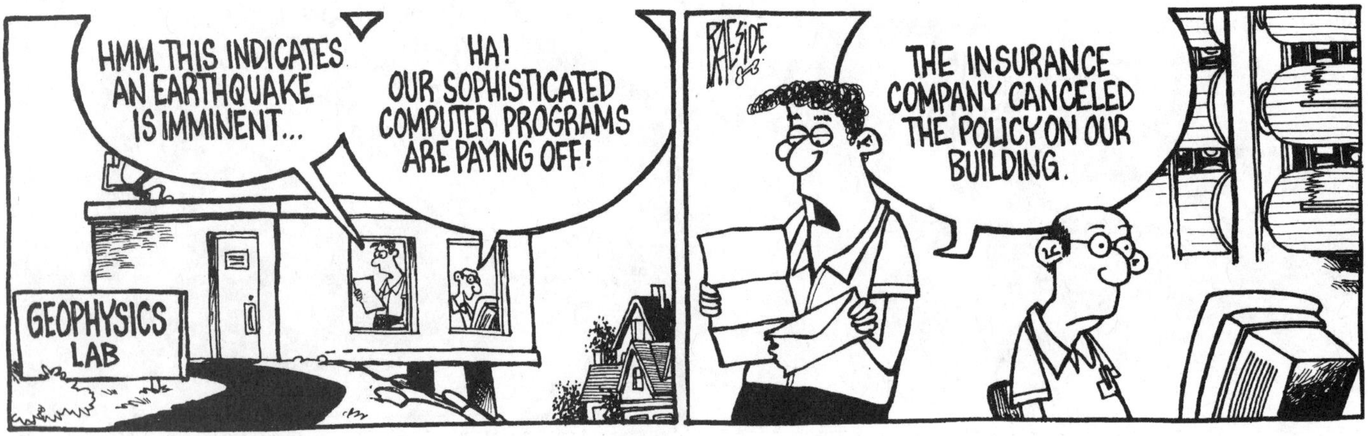
HMM, THIS INDICATES AN EARTHQUAKE IS IMMINENT...
HA! OUR SOPHISTICATED COMPUTER PROGRAMS ARE PAYING OFF!
GEOPHYSICS LAB
THE INSURANCE COMPANY CANCELED THE POLICY ON OUR BUILDING.

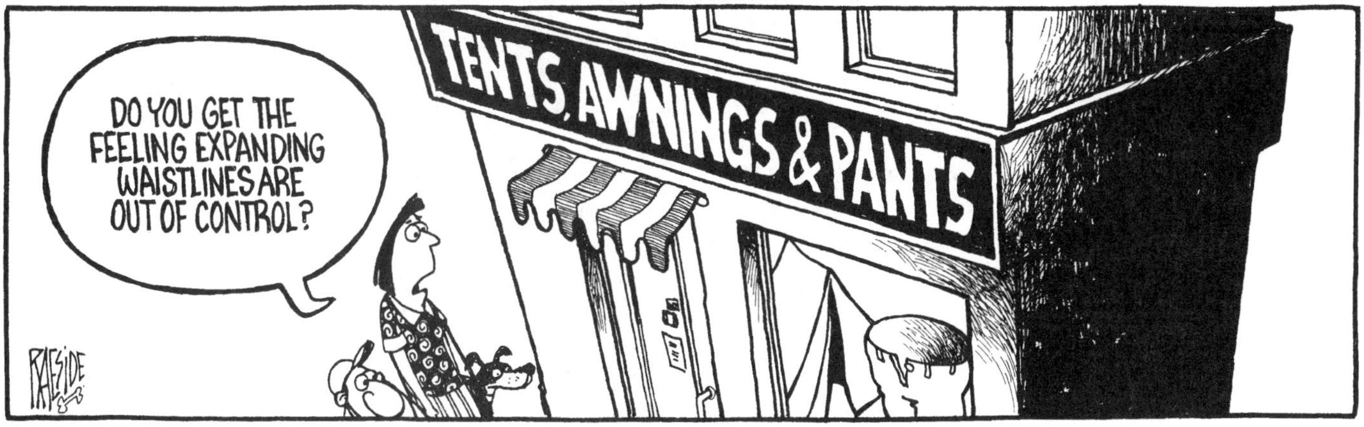
DO YOU GET THE FEELING EXPANDING WAISTLINES ARE OUT OF CONTROL?
TENTS, AWNINGS & PANTS

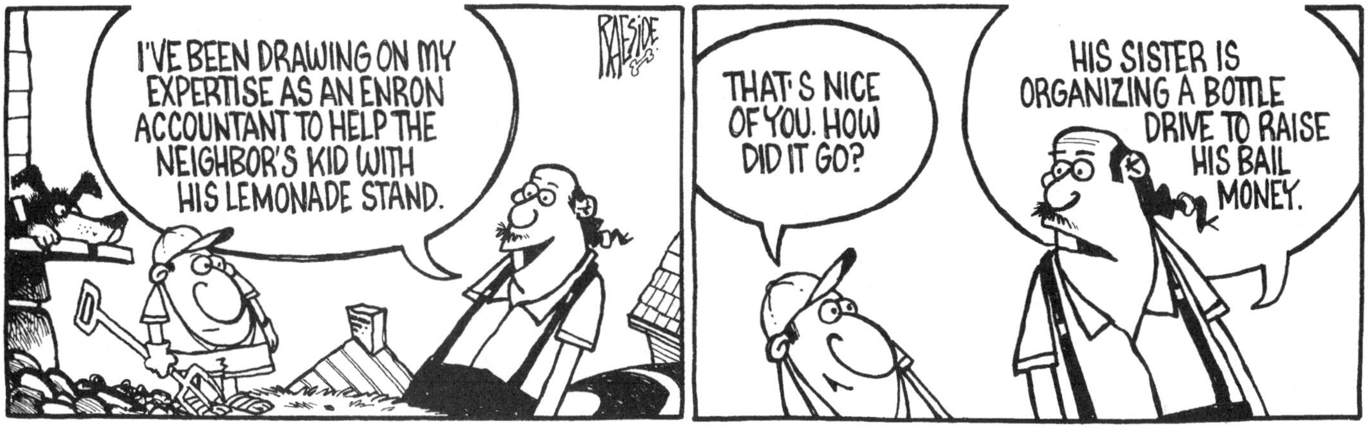
I'VE BEEN DRAWING ON MY EXPERTISE AS AN ENRON ACCOUNTANT TO HELP THE NEIGHBOR'S KID WITH HIS LEMONADE STAND.
THAT'S NICE OF YOU. HOW DID IT GO?
HIS SISTER IS ORGANIZING A BOTTLE DRIVE TO RAISE HIS BAIL MONEY.

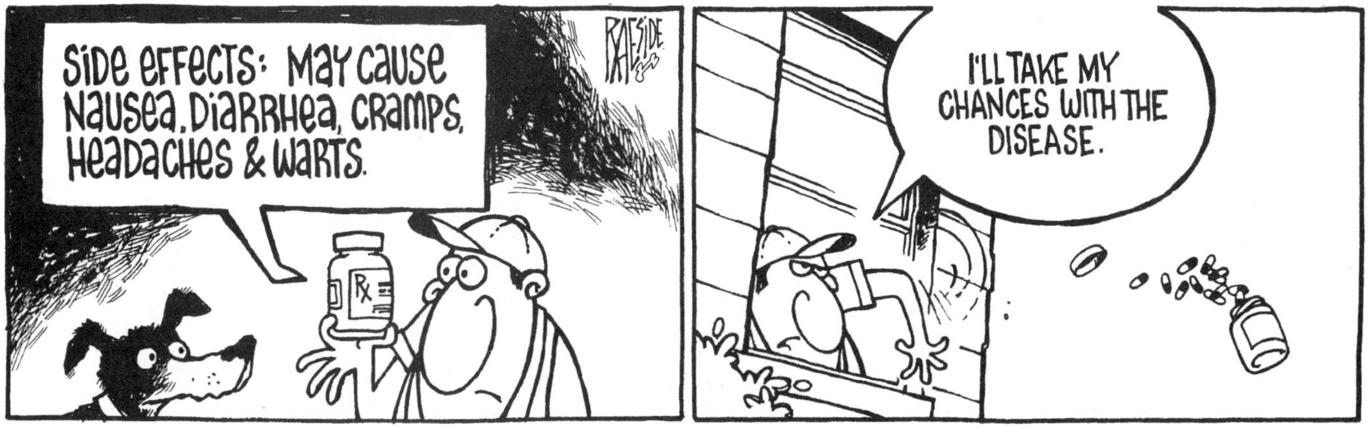
SIDE EFFECTS: MAY CAUSE NAUSEA, DIARRHEA, CRAMPS, HEADACHES & WARTS.
Rx
I'LL TAKE MY CHANCES WITH THE DISEASE.

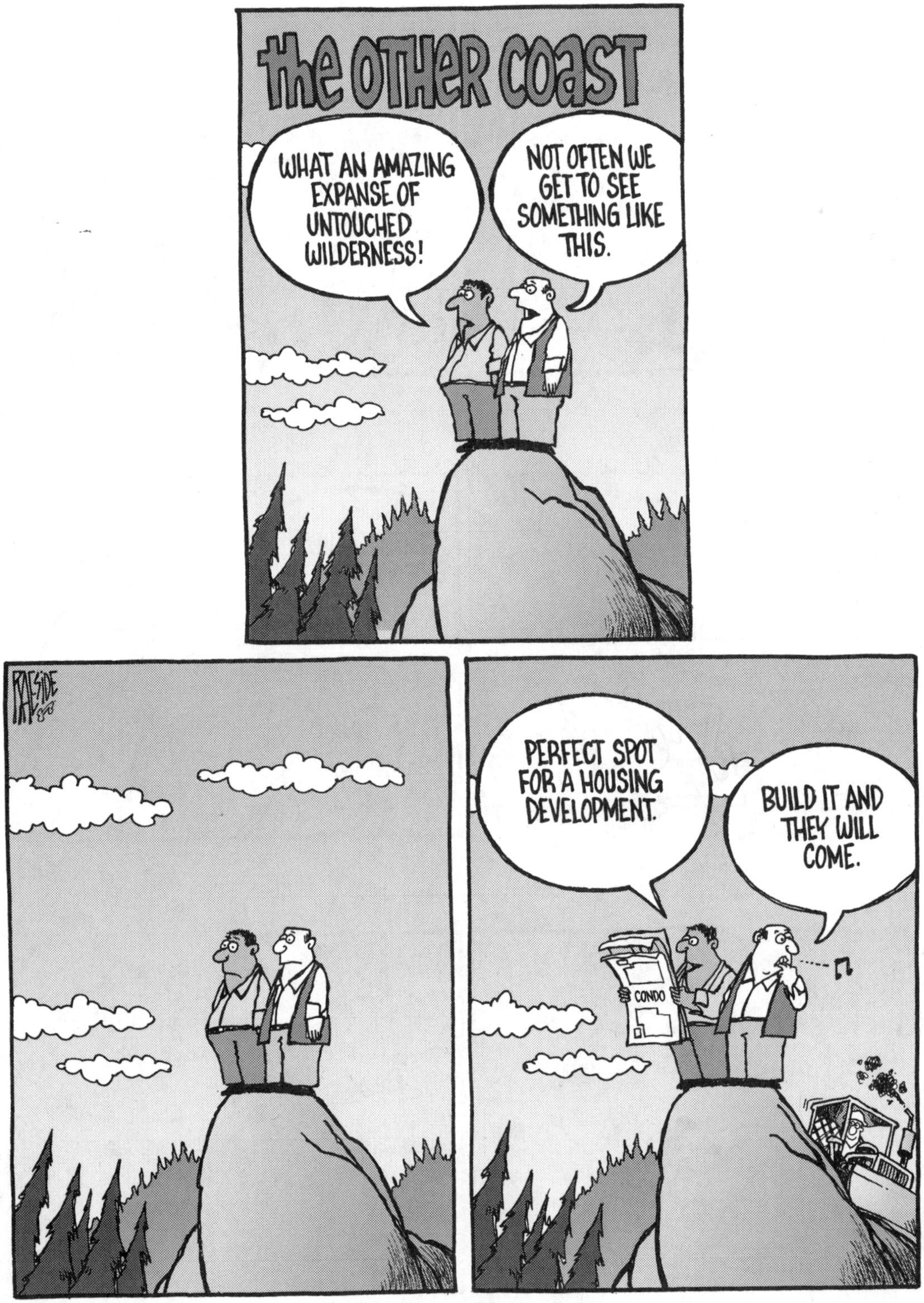
the OTHER COAST
WHAT AN AMAZING EXPANSE OF UNTOUCHED WILDERNESS!
NOT OFTEN WE GET TO SEE SOMETHING LIKE THIS.
PERFECT SPOT FOR A HOUSING DEVELOPMENT.
CONDO
BUILD IT AND THEY WILL COME.

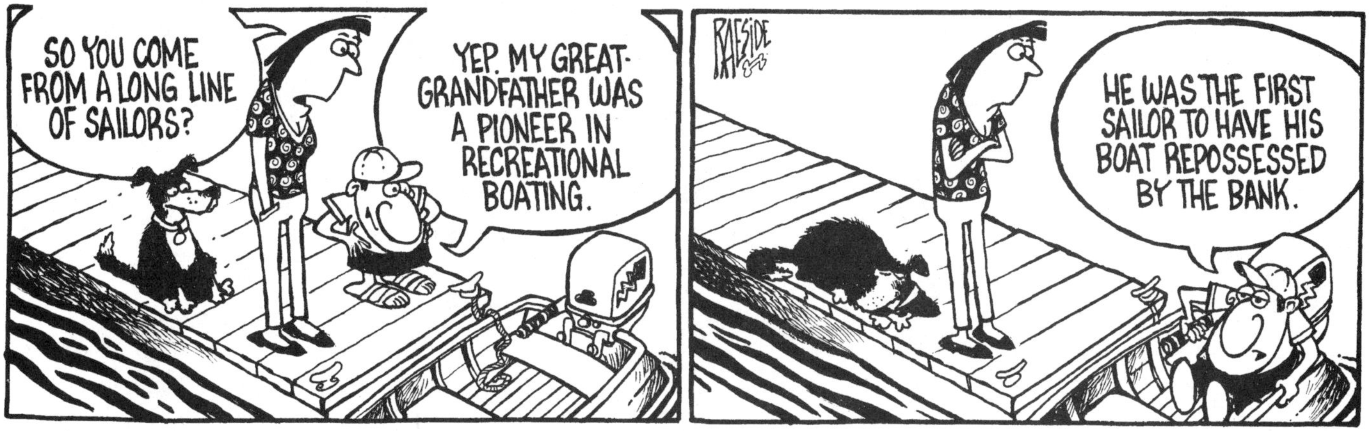
SO YOU COME FROM A LONG LINE OF SAILORS?
YEP. MY GREAT-GRANDFATHER WAS A PIONEER IN RECREATIONAL BOATING.
HE WAS THE FIRST SAILOR TO HAVE HIS BOAT REPOSSESSED BY THE BANK.

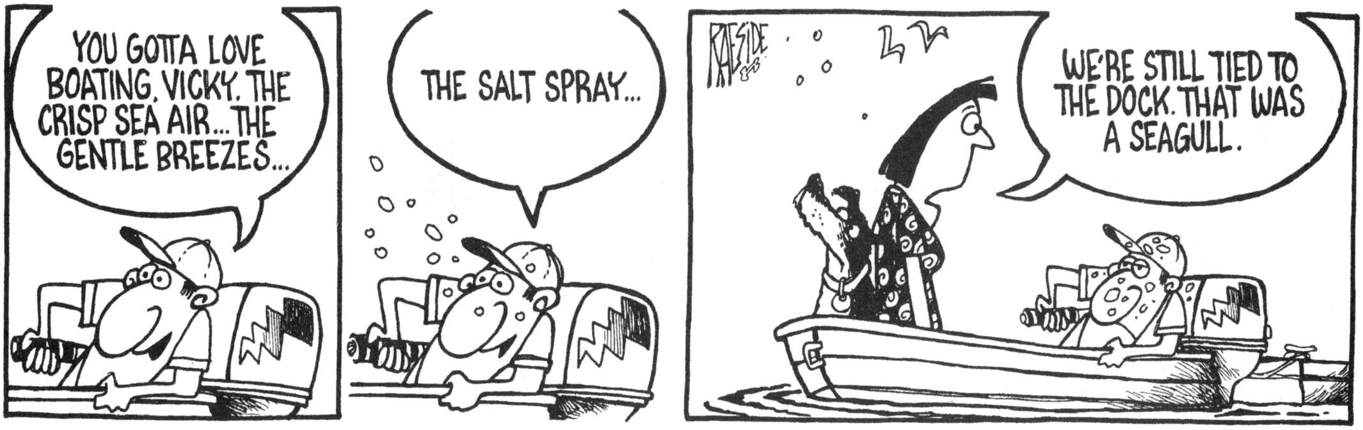
YOU GOTTA LOVE BOATING, VICKY. THE CRISP SEA AIR... THE GENTLE BREEZES...
THE SALT SPRAY...
WE'RE STILL TIED TO THE DOCK. THAT WAS A SEAGULL.

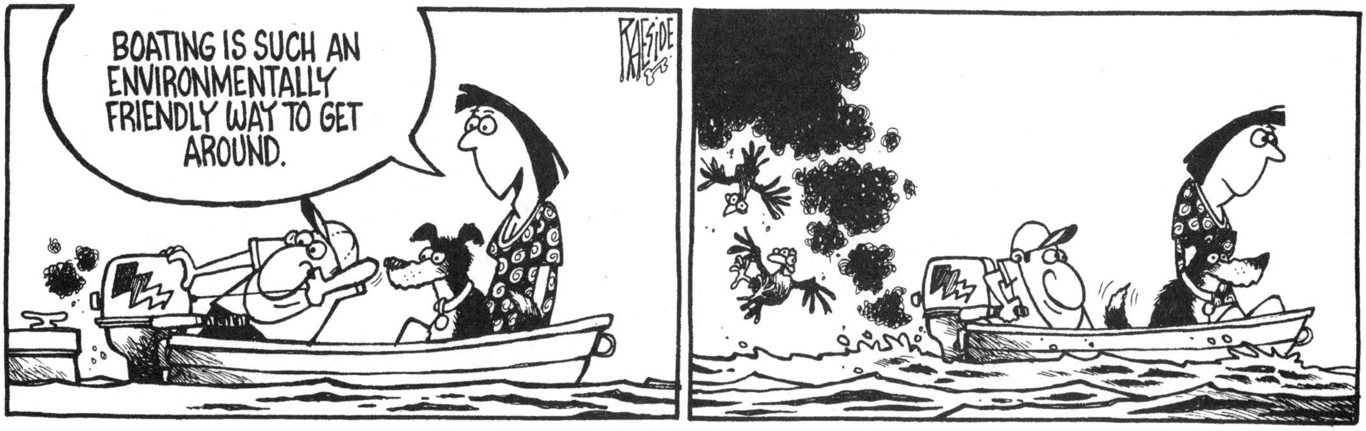
BOATING IS SUCH AN ENVIRONMENTALLY FRIENDLY WAY TO GET AROUND.

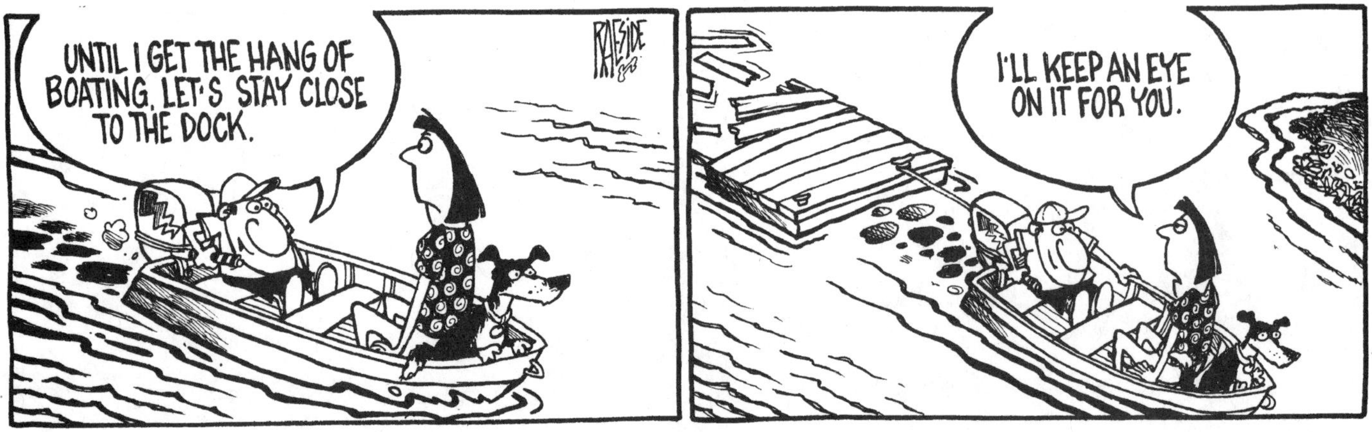
UNTIL I GET THE HANG OF BOATING, LET'S STAY CLOSE TO THE DOCK.
I'LL KEEP AN EYE ON IT FOR YOU.

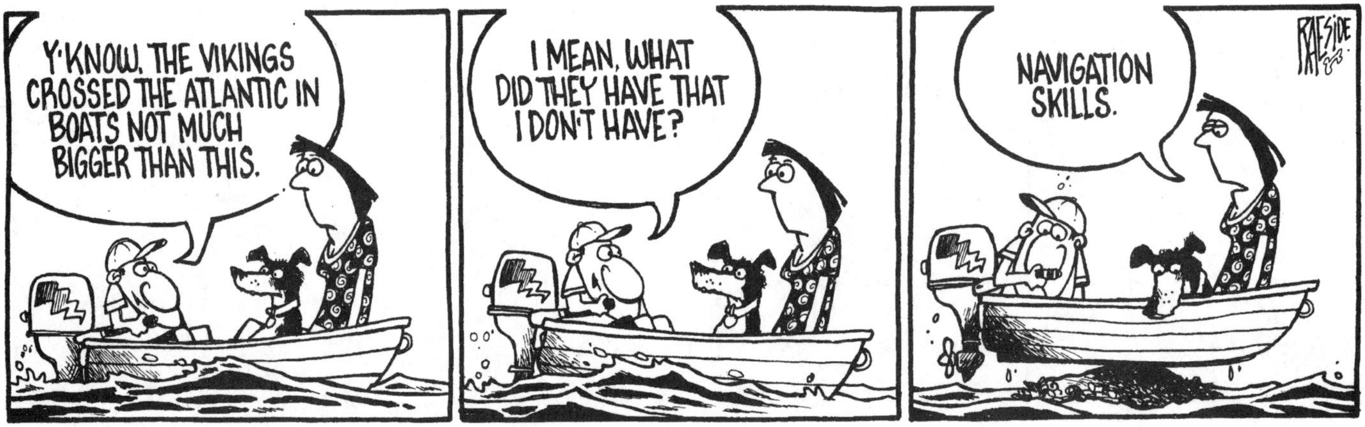
Y'KNOW, THE VIKINGS CROSSED THE ATLANTIC IN BOATS NOT MUCH BIGGER THAN THIS.
I MEAN, WHAT DID THEY HAVE THAT I DON'T HAVE?
NAVIGATION SKILLS.

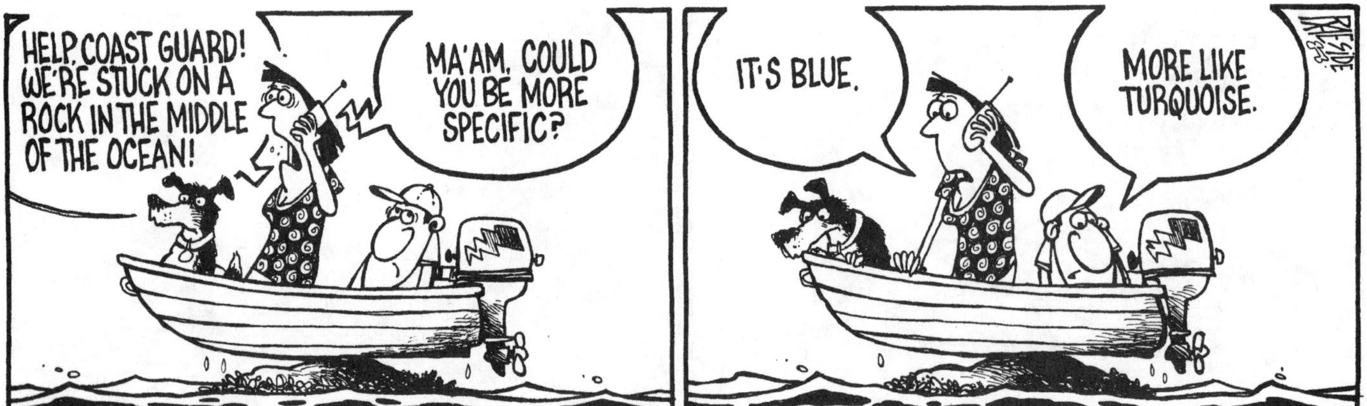
HELP, COAST GUARD! WE'RE STUCK ON A ROCK IN THE MIDDLE OF THE OCEAN!
MA'AM, COULD YOU BE MORE SPECIFIC?
IT'S BLUE.
MORE LIKE TURQUOISE.

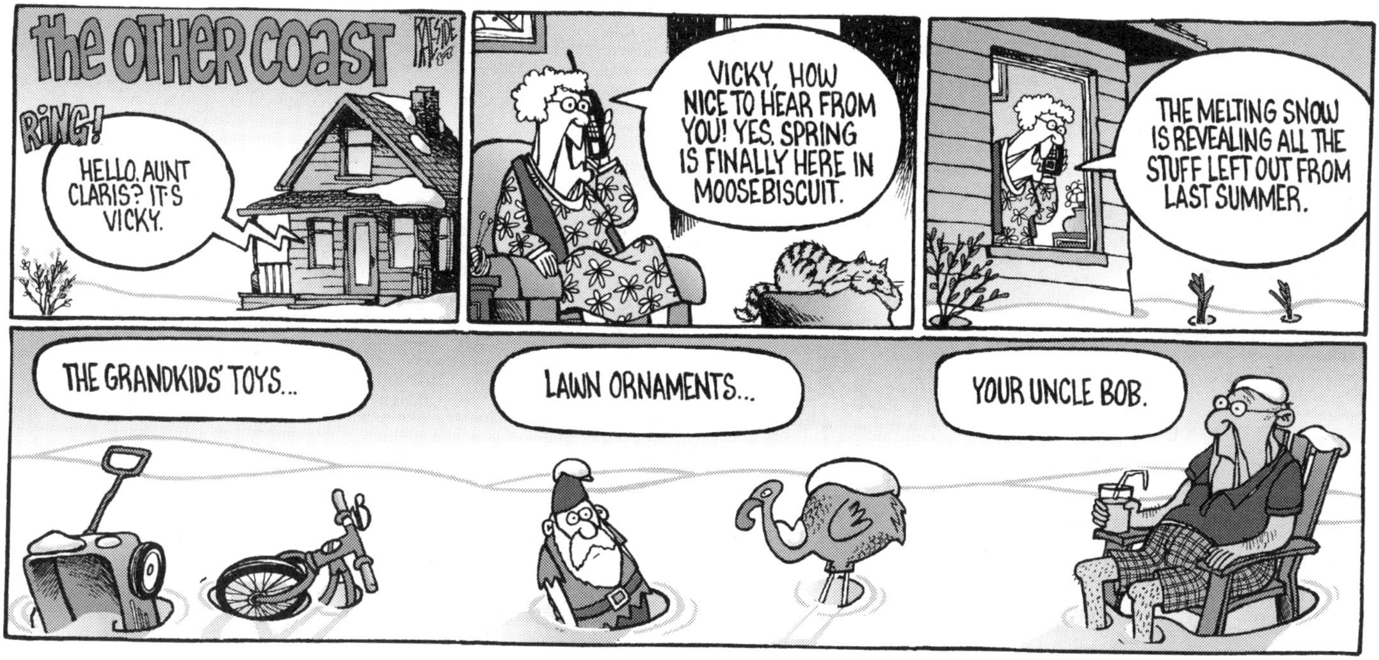
the OTHER COAST
RASIDE
RING!
HELLO, AUNT CLARIS? IT'S VICKY.
VICKY, HOW NICE TO HEAR FROM YOU! YES, SPRING IS FINALLY HERE IN MOOSEBISCUIT.
THE MELTING SNOW IS REVEALING ALL THE STUFF LEFT OUT FROM LAST SUMMER.
THE GRANDKIDS' TOYS...
LAWN ORNAMENTS...
YOUR UNCLE BOB.

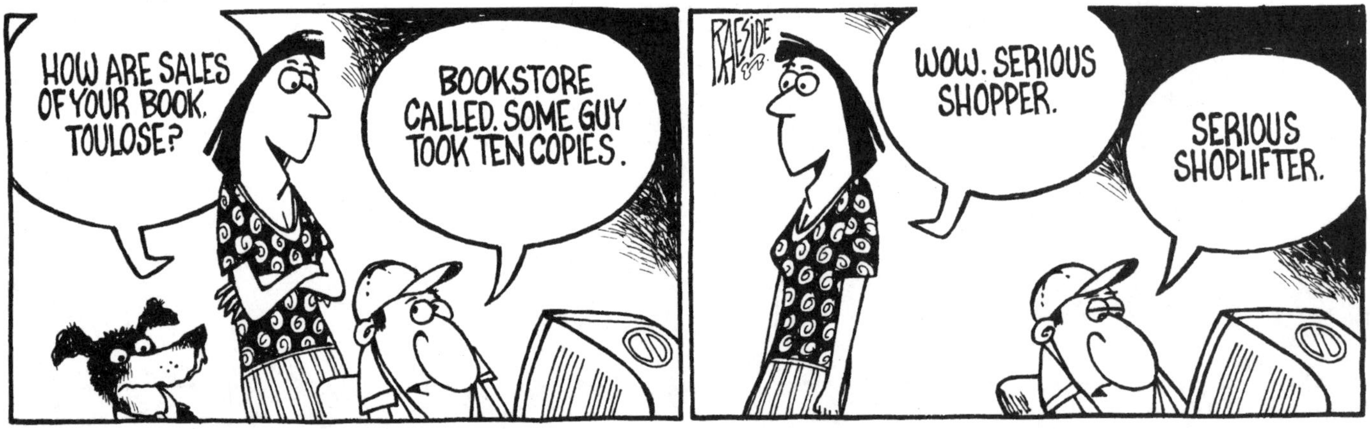
HOW ARE SALES OF YOUR BOOK, TOULOSE?
BOOKSTORE CALLED. SOME GUY TOOK TEN COPIES.
WOW. SERIOUS SHOPPER.
SERIOUS SHOPLIFTER.

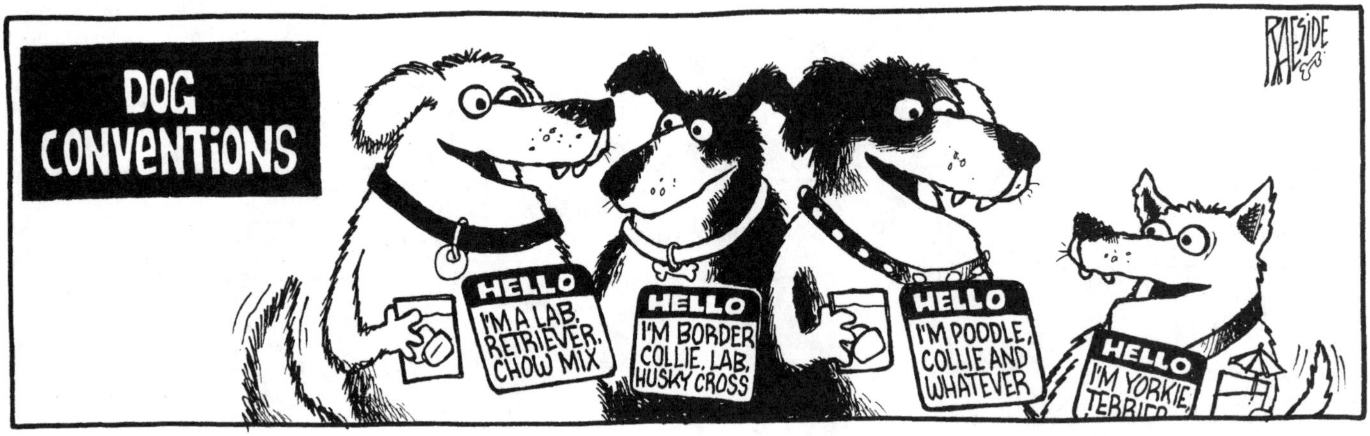
DOG CONVENTIONS
HELLO I'M A LAB, RETRIEVER, CHOW MIX
HELLO I'M BORDER COLLIE, LAB, HUSKY CROSS
HELLO I'M POODLE, COLLIE AND WHATEVER
HELLO I'M YORKIE,

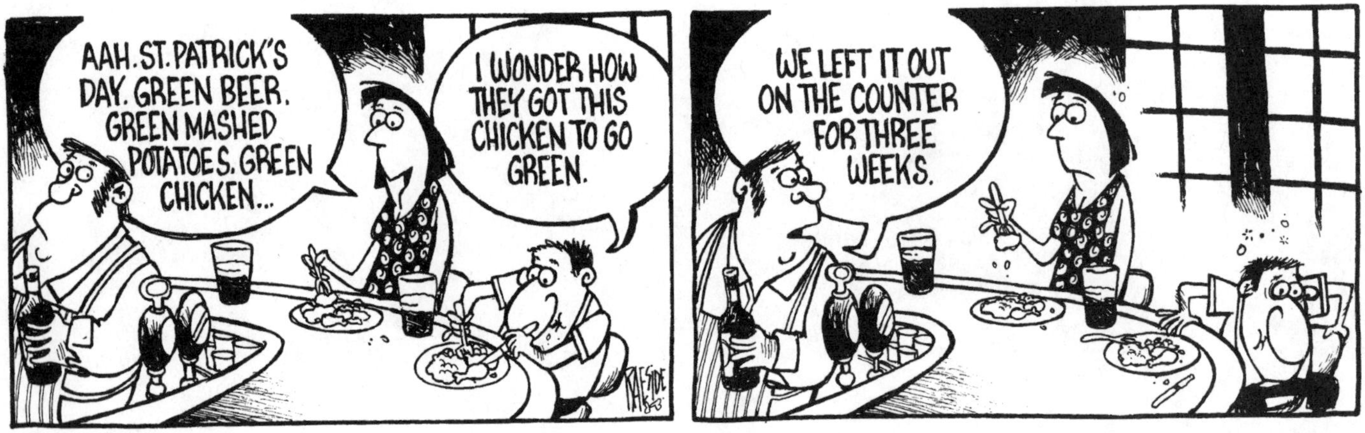
AAH. ST. PATRICK'S DAY. GREEN BEER. GREEN MASHED POTATOES. GREEN CHICKEN...
I WONDER HOW THEY GOT THIS CHICKEN TO GO GREEN.
WE LEFT IT OUT ON THE COUNTER FOR THREE WEEKS.

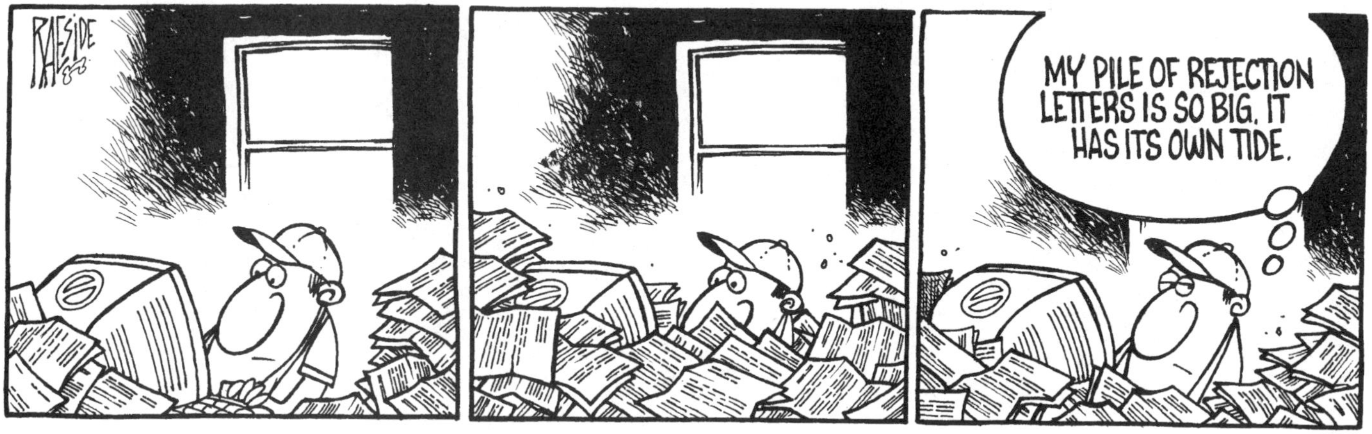
RAESIDE
MY PILE OF REJECTION LETTERS IS SO BIG, IT HAS ITS OWN TIDE.

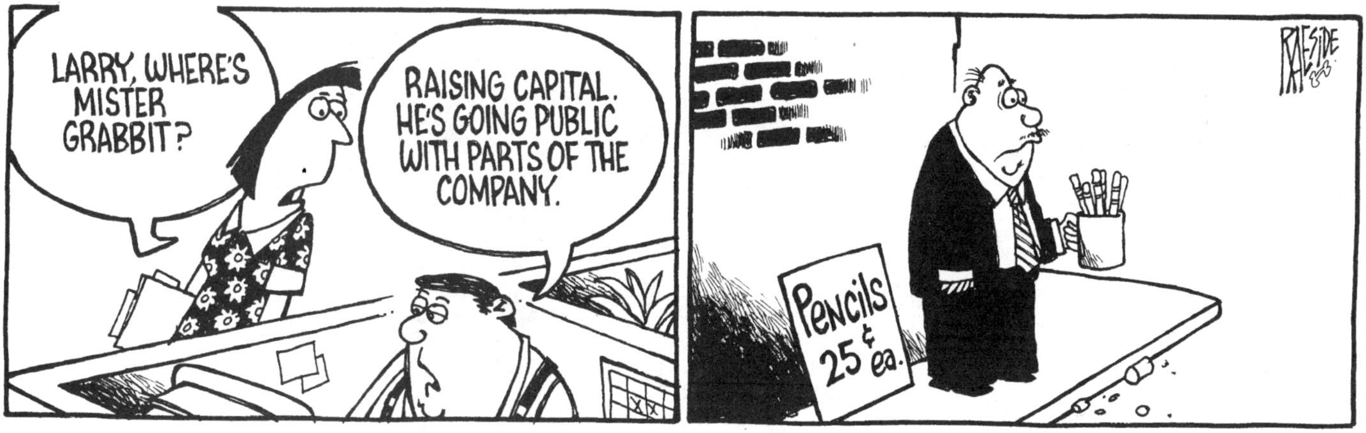
LARRY, WHERE'S MISTER GRABBIT?
RAISING CAPITAL. HE'S GOING PUBLIC WITH PARTS OF THE COMPANY.
RAESIDE
Pencils 25¢ ea.

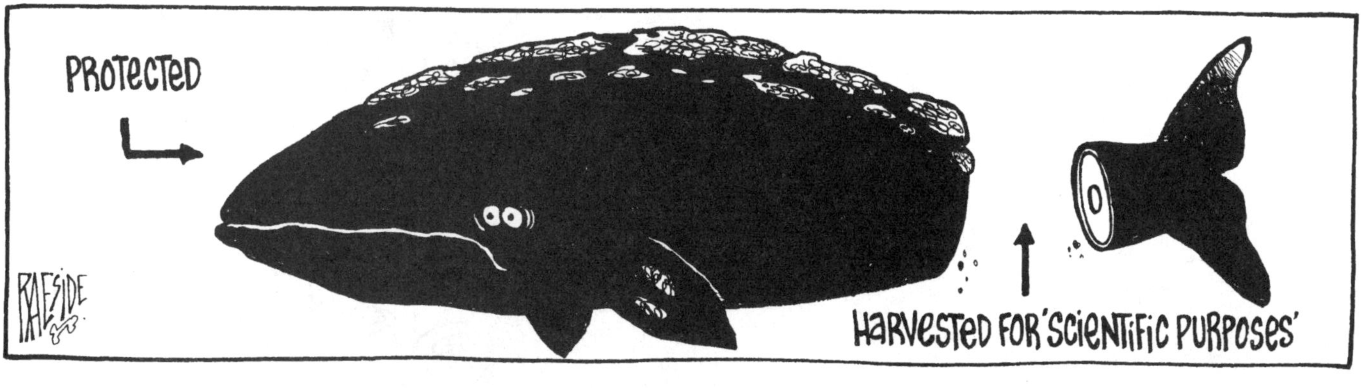
PROTECTED
HARVESTED FOR 'SCIENTIFIC PURPOSES'
RAESIDE

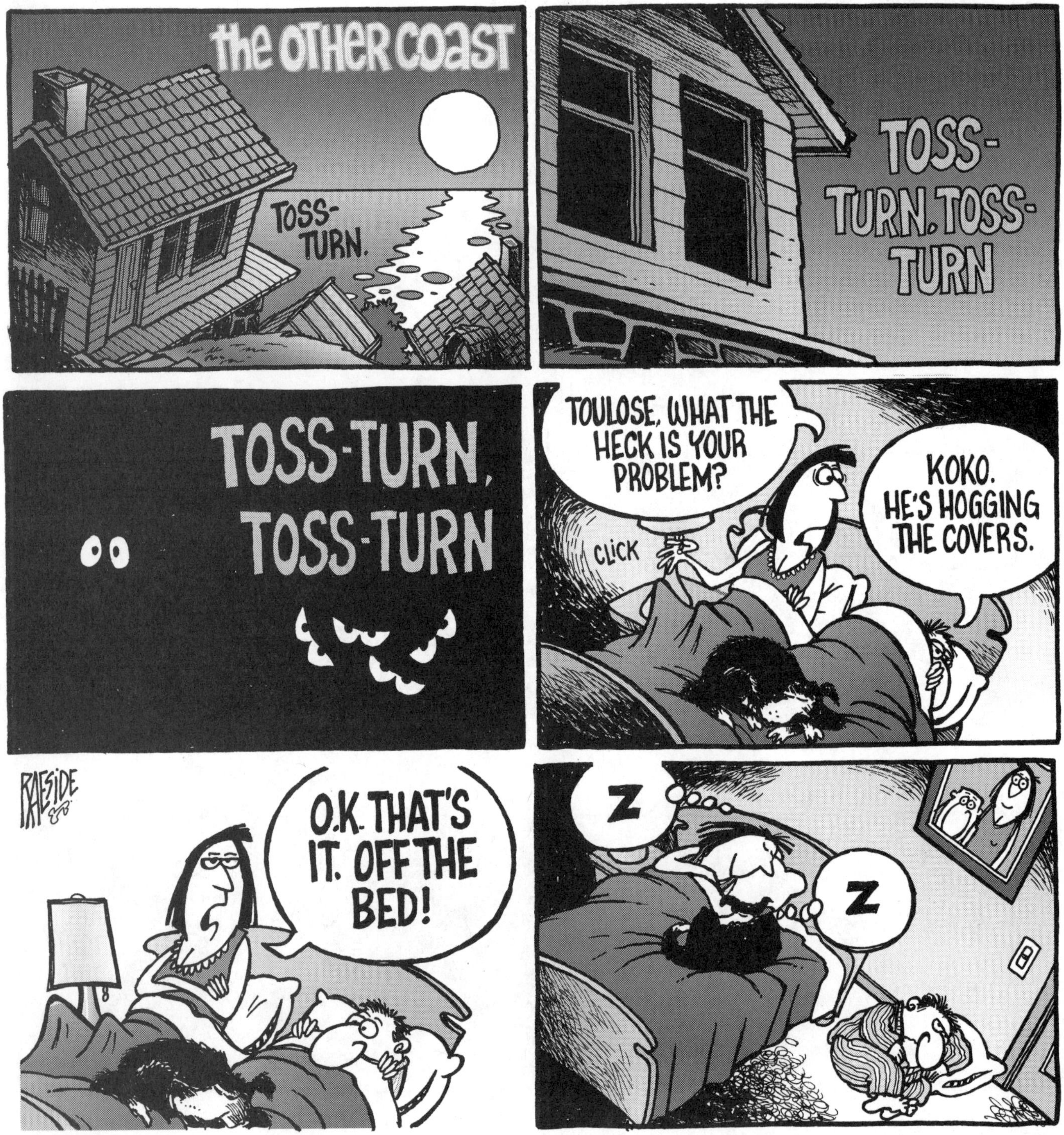
the OTHER COAST
TOSS-TURN.
TOSS-TURN. TOSS-TURN
TOSS-TURN, TOSS-TURN, TOSS-TURN
TOULOSE, WHAT THE HECK IS YOUR PROBLEM?
CLICK
KOKO. HE'S HOGGING THE COVERS.
RAESIDE
O.K. THAT'S IT. OFF THE BED!
Z
Z

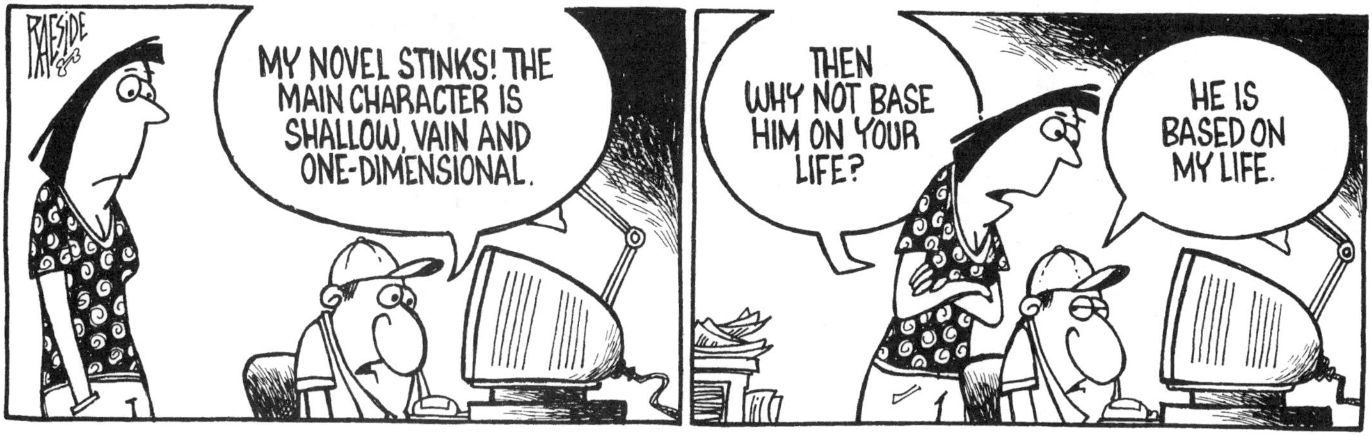
RAESIDE
MY NOVEL STINKS! THE MAIN CHARACTER IS SHALLOW, VAIN AND ONE-DIMENSIONAL.
THEN WHY NOT BASE HIM ON YOUR LIFE?
HE IS BASED ON MY LIFE.

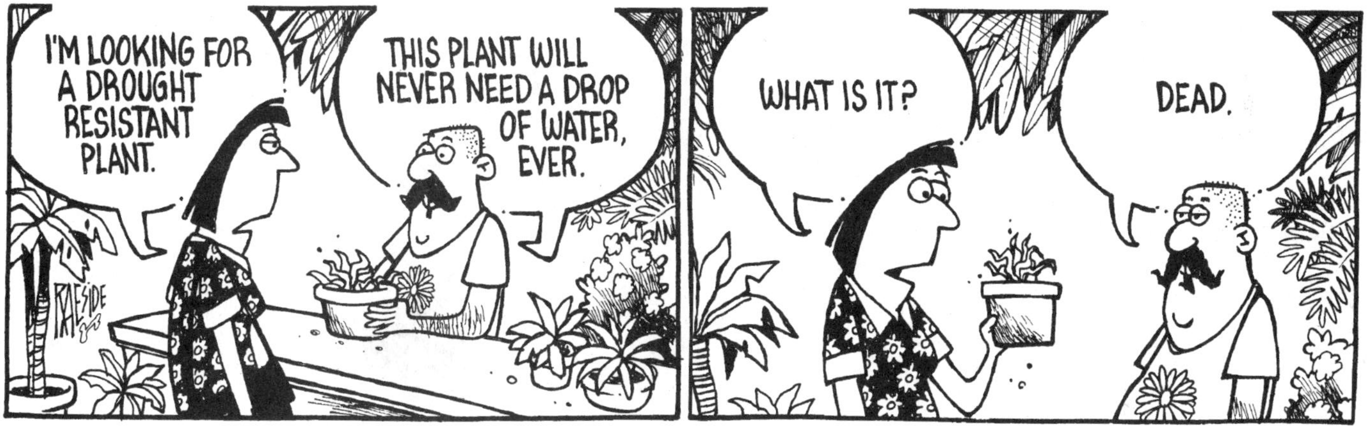
I'M LOOKING FOR A DROUGHT RESISTANT PLANT.
THIS PLANT WILL NEVER NEED A DROP OF WATER, EVER.
RAESIDE
WHAT IS IT?
DEAD.

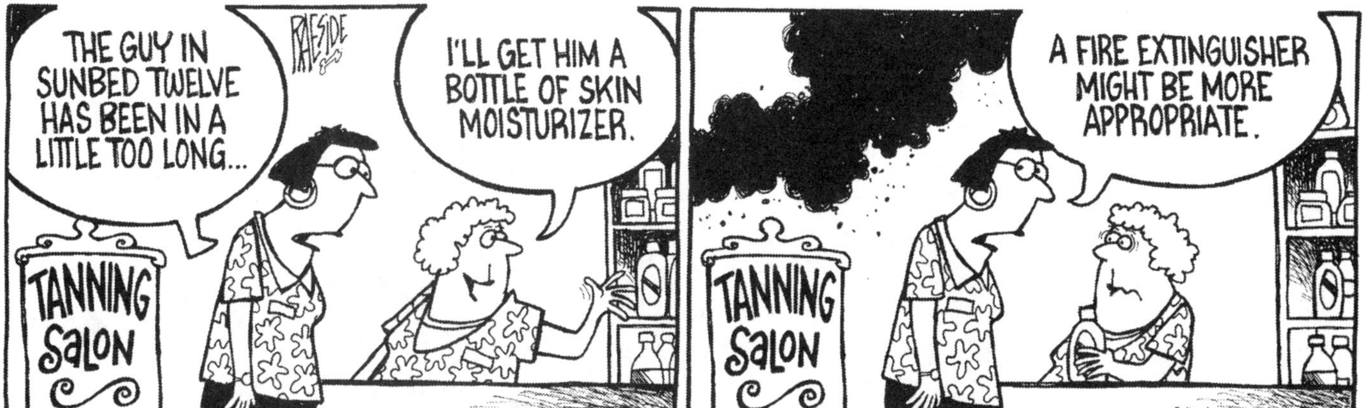
THE GUY IN SUNBED TWELVE HAS BEEN IN A LITTLE TOO LONG...
RAESIDE
I'LL GET HIM A BOTTLE OF SKIN MOISTURIZER.
TANNING SaLON
A FIRE EXTINGUISHER MIGHT BE MORE APPROPRIATE.
TANNING SaLON

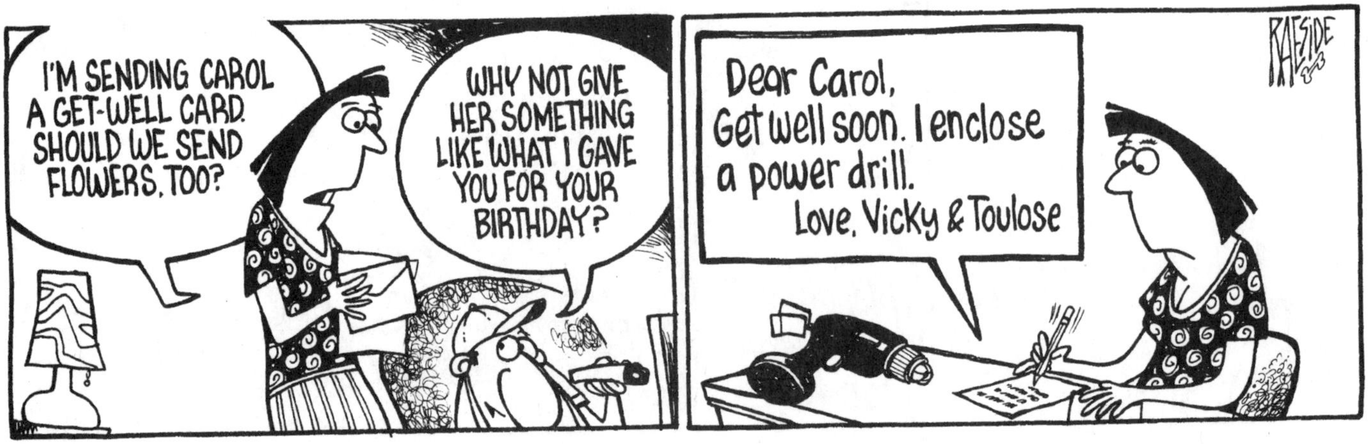
I'M SENDING CAROL A GET-WELL CARD. SHOULD WE SEND FLOWERS, TOO?
WHY NOT GIVE HER SOMETHING LIKE WHAT I GAVE YOU FOR YOUR BIRTHDAY?
RAESIDE
Dear Carol,
Get well soon. I enclose a power drill.
Love, Vicky & Toulose

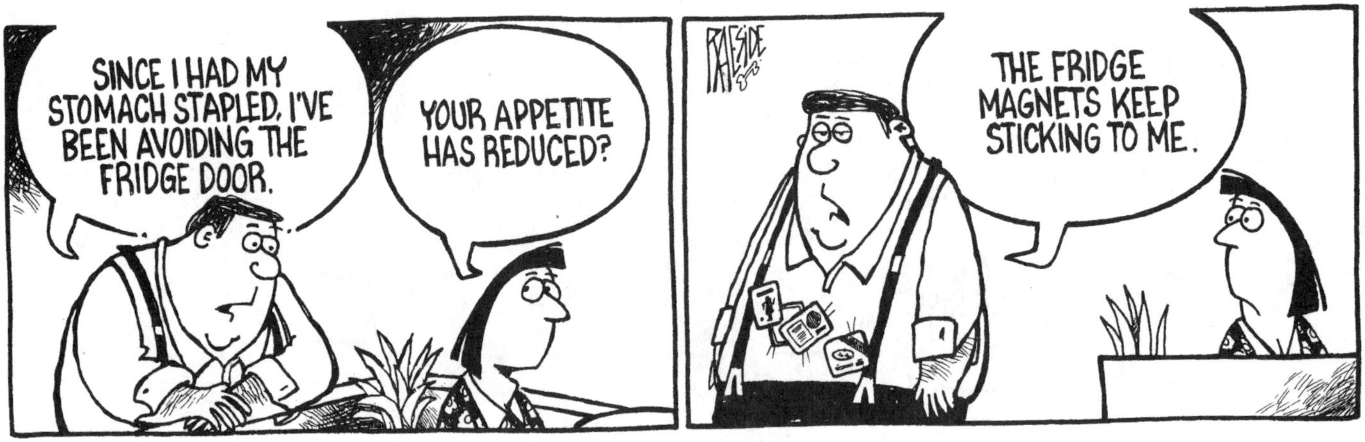
SINCE I HAD MY STOMACH STAPLED, I'VE BEEN AVOIDING THE FRIDGE DOOR.
YOUR APPETITE HAS REDUCED?
RAESIDE
THE FRIDGE MAGNETS KEEP STICKING TO ME.

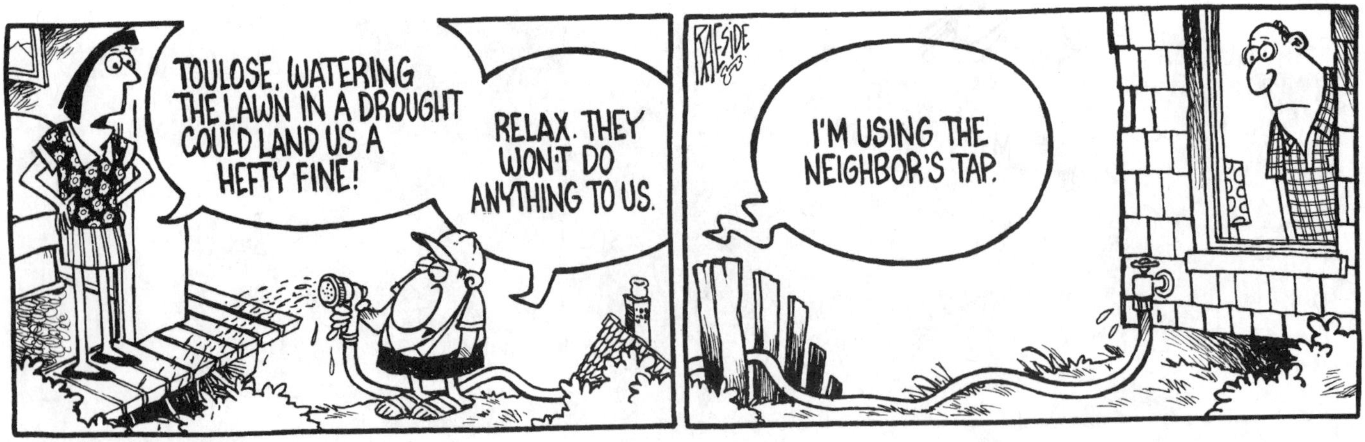
TOULOSE, WATERING THE LAWN IN A DROUGHT COULD LAND US A HEFTY FINE!
RELAX. THEY WON'T DO ANYTHING TO US.
RAESIDE
I'M USING THE NEIGHBOR'S TAP.

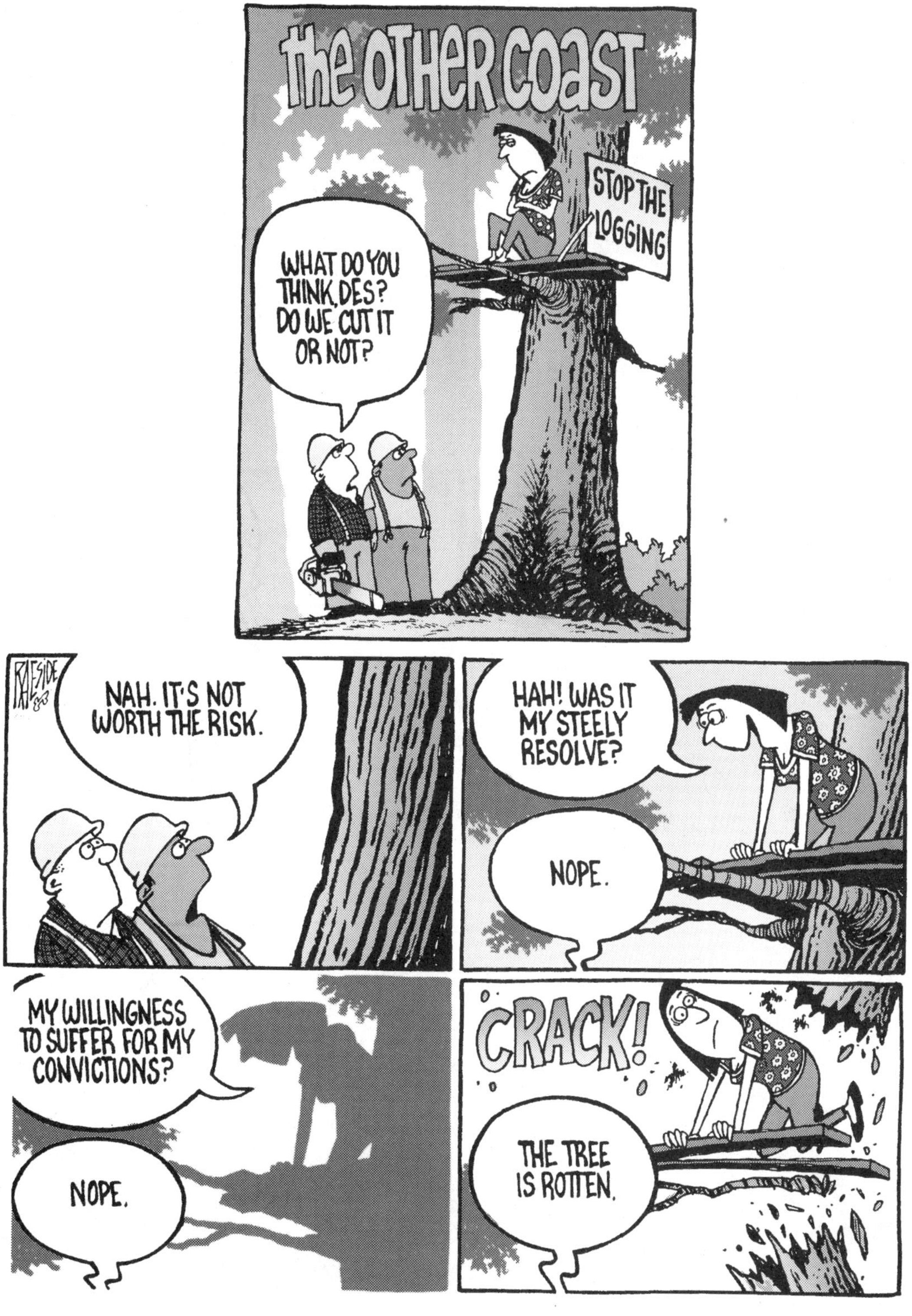
the OTHER COAST
STOP THE LOGGING
WHAT DO YOU THINK, DES? DO WE CUT IT OR NOT?
NAH. IT'S NOT WORTH THE RISK.
HAH! WAS IT MY STEELY RESOLVE?
NOPE.
MY WILLINGNESS TO SUFFER FOR MY CONVICTIONS?
NOPE.
CRACK!
THE TREE IS ROTTEN.

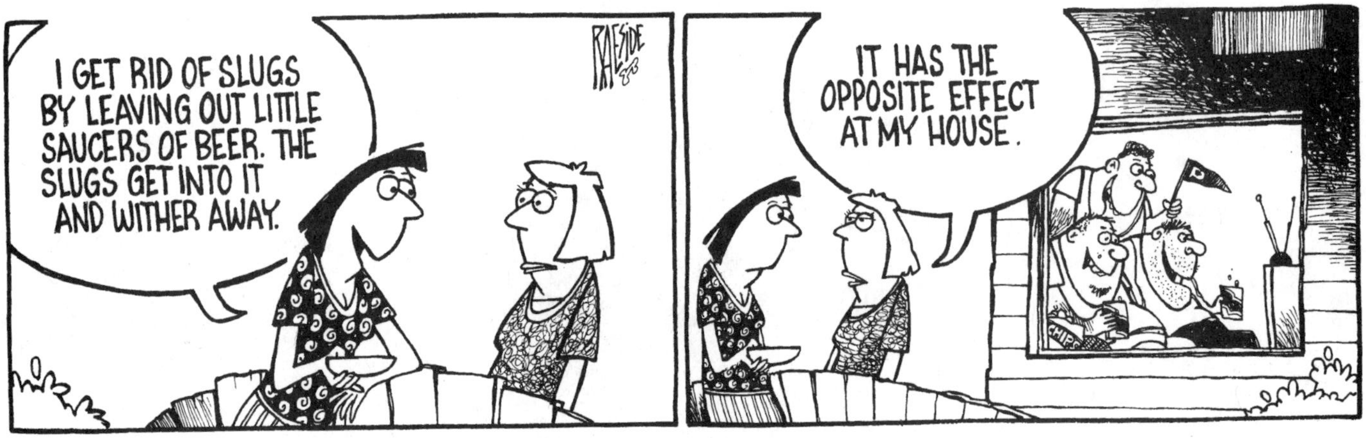
I GET RID OF SLUGS BY LEAVING OUT LITTLE SAUCERS OF BEER. THE SLUGS GET INTO IT AND WITHER AWAY.
IT HAS THE OPPOSITE EFFECT AT MY HOUSE.

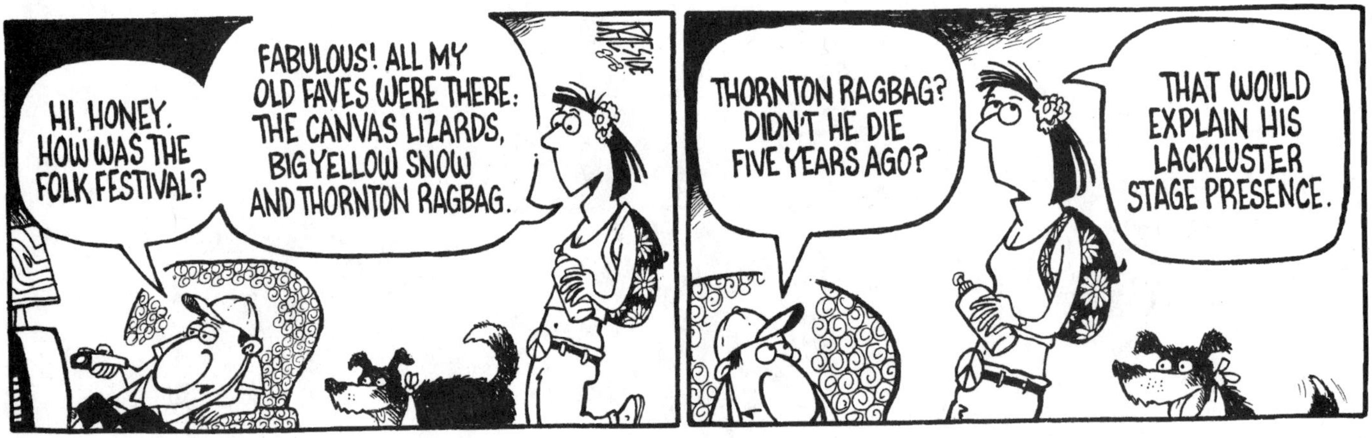
HI, HONEY. HOW WAS THE FOLK FESTIVAL?
FABULOUS! ALL MY OLD FAVES WERE THERE: THE CANVAS LIZARDS, BIG YELLOW SNOW AND THORNTON RAGBAG.
THORNTON RAGBAG? DIDN'T HE DIE FIVE YEARS AGO?
THAT WOULD EXPLAIN HIS LACKLUSTER STAGE PRESENCE.

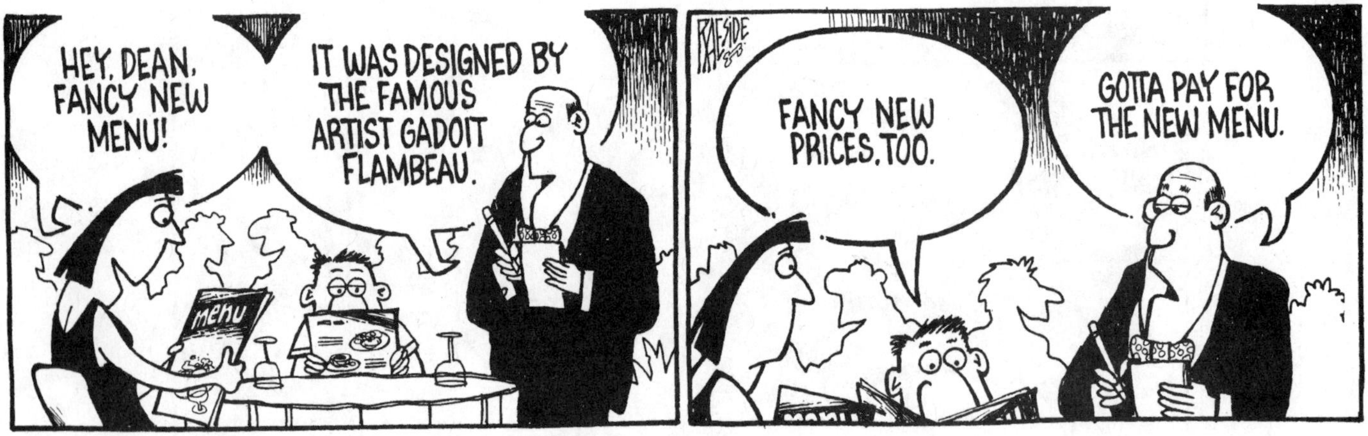
HEY, DEAN, FANCY NEW MENU!
IT WAS DESIGNED BY THE FAMOUS ARTIST GADOIT FLAMBEAU.
MENU
FANCY NEW PRICES, TOO.
GOTTA PAY FOR THE NEW MENU.

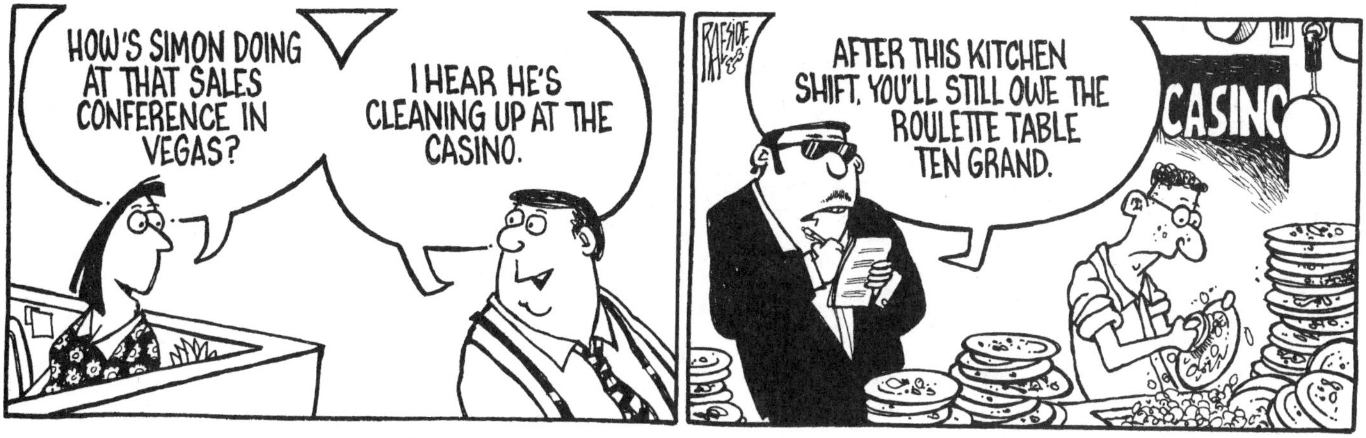
HOW'S SIMON DOING AT THAT SALES CONFERENCE IN VEGAS?
I HEAR HE'S CLEANING UP AT THE CASINO.
AFTER THIS KITCHEN SHIFT, YOU'LL STILL OWE THE ROULETTE TABLE TEN GRAND.
CASINO
RAESIDE

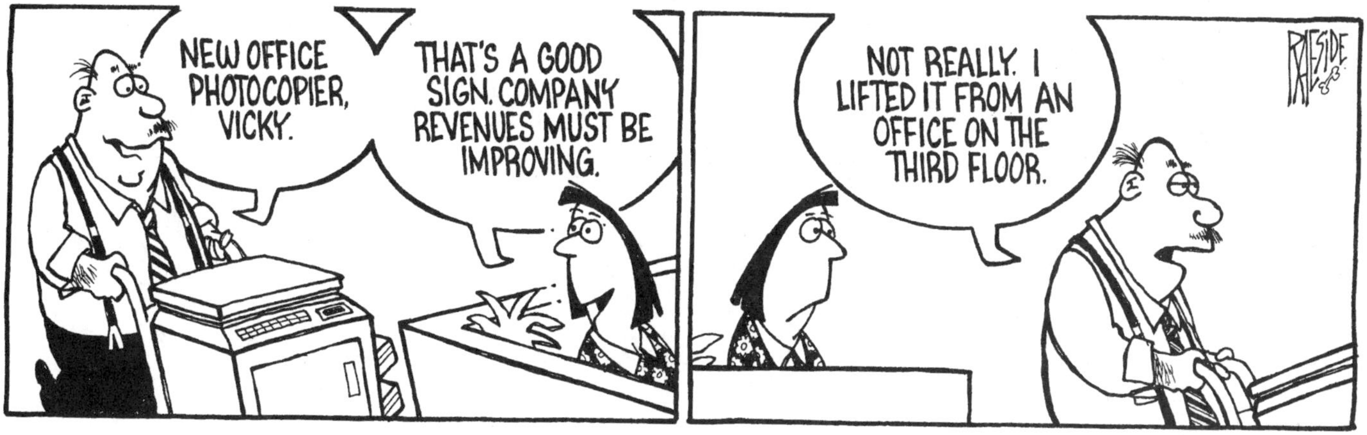
NEW OFFICE PHOTOCOPIER, VICKY.
THAT'S A GOOD SIGN. COMPANY REVENUES MUST BE IMPROVING.
NOT REALLY. I LIFTED IT FROM AN OFFICE ON THE THIRD FLOOR.
RAESIDE

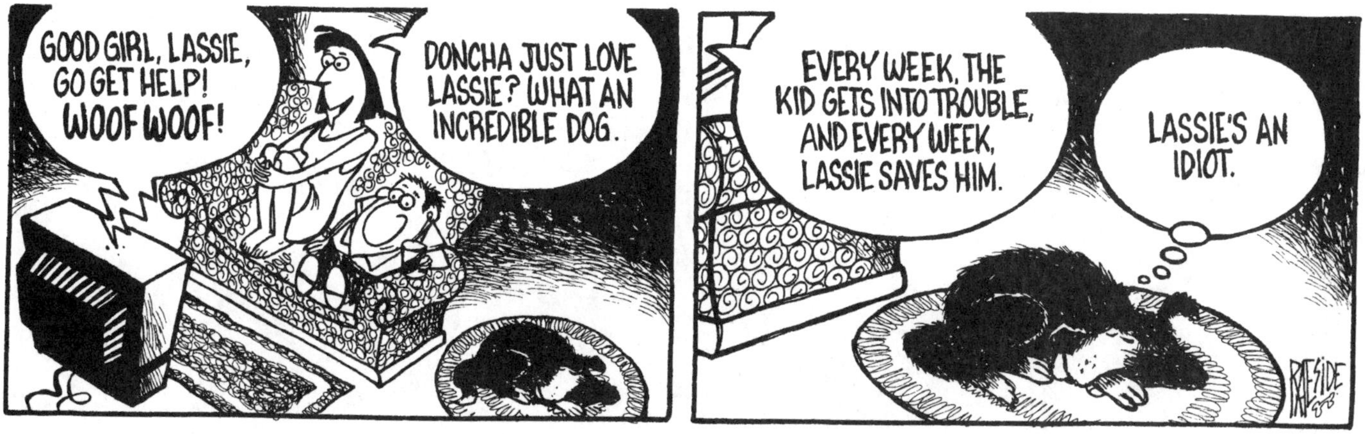
GOOD GIRL, LASSIE, GO GET HELP! WOOF WOOF!
DONCHA JUST LOVE LASSIE? WHAT AN INCREDIBLE DOG.
EVERY WEEK, THE KID GETS INTO TROUBLE, AND EVERY WEEK, LASSIE SAVES HIM.
LASSIE'S AN IDIOT.
RAESIDE

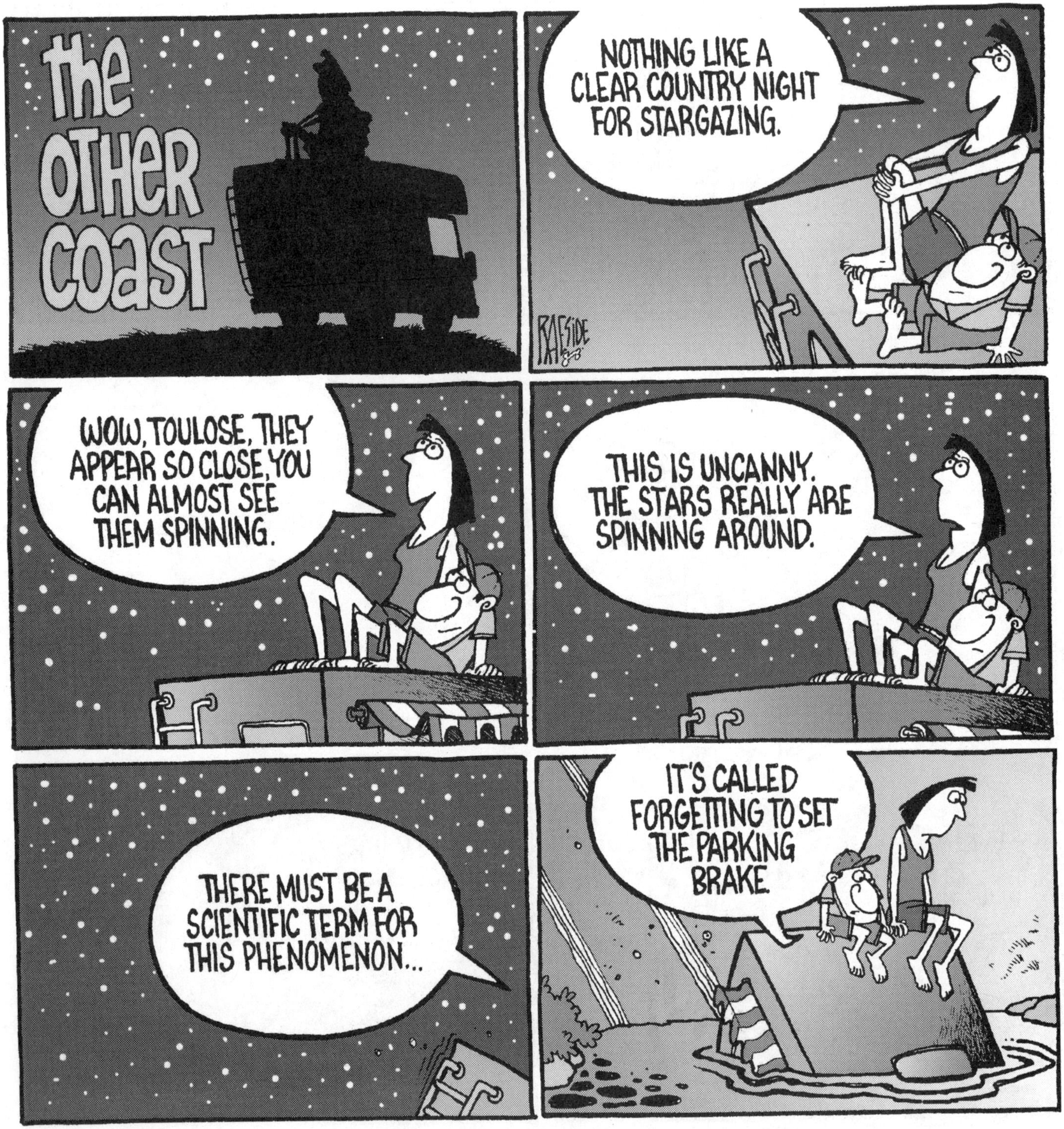

the OTHER COAST
RASIDE
NOTHING LIKE A CLEAR COUNTRY NIGHT FOR STARGAZING.
WOW, TOULOSE, THEY APPEAR SO CLOSE, YOU CAN ALMOST SEE THEM SPINNING.
THIS IS UNCANNY. THE STARS REALLY ARE SPINNING AROUND.
THERE MUST BE A SCIENTIFIC TERM FOR THIS PHENOMENON...
IT'S CALLED FORGETTING TO SET THE PARKING BRAKE.

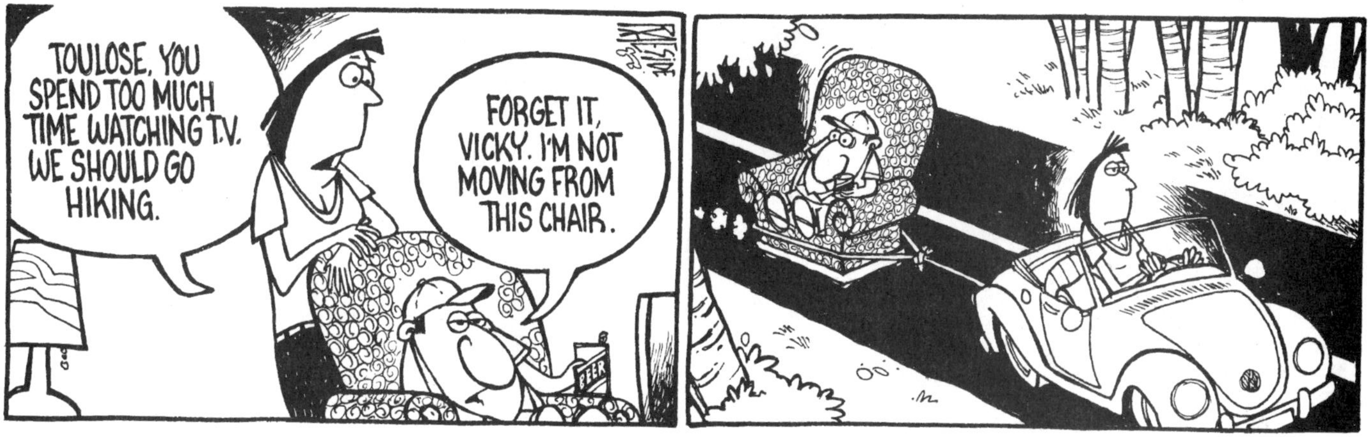
TOULOSE, YOU SPEND TOO MUCH TIME WATCHING T.V. WE SHOULD GO HIKING.
FORGET IT, VICKY. I'M NOT MOVING FROM THIS CHAIR.
BEER

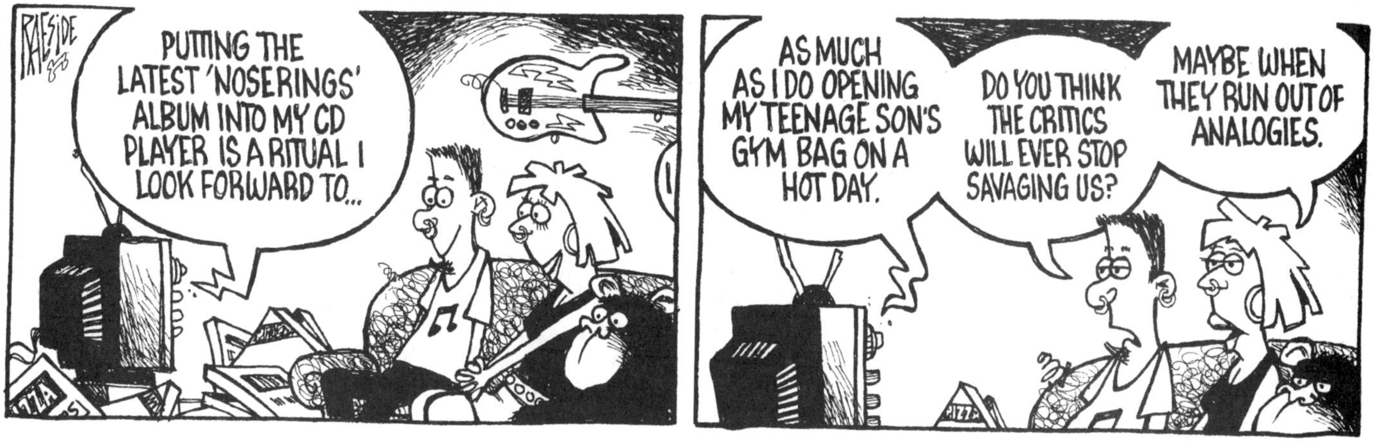
PUTTING THE LATEST 'NOSERINGS' ALBUM INTO MY CD PLAYER IS A RITUAL I LOOK FORWARD TO...
AS MUCH AS I DO OPENING MY TEENAGE SON'S GYM BAG ON A HOT DAY.
DO YOU THINK THE CRITICS WILL EVER STOP SAVAGING US?
MAYBE WHEN THEY RUN OUT OF ANALOGIES.

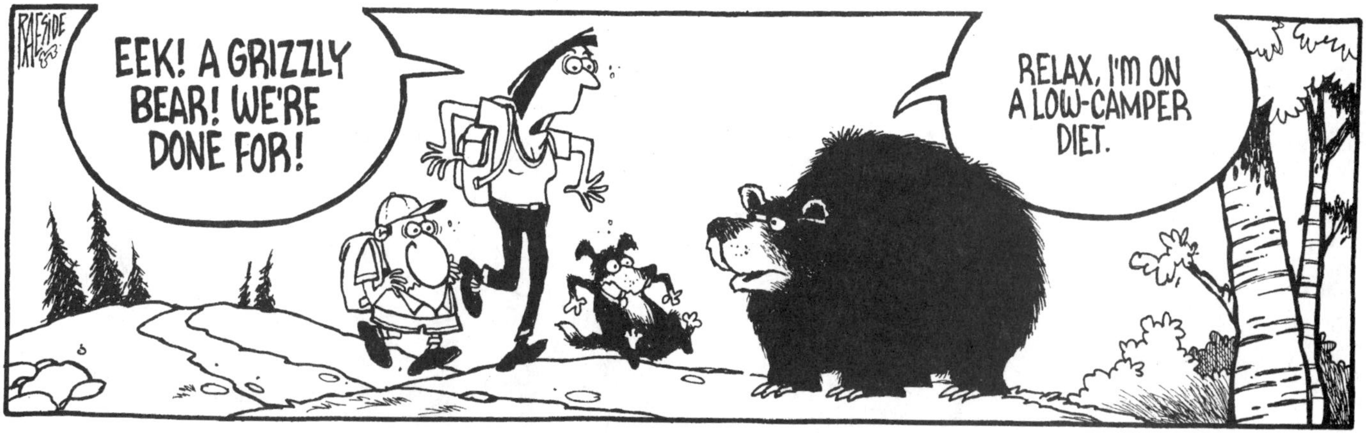
EEK! A GRIZZLY BEAR! WE'RE DONE FOR!
RELAX, I'M ON A LOW-CAMPER DIET.

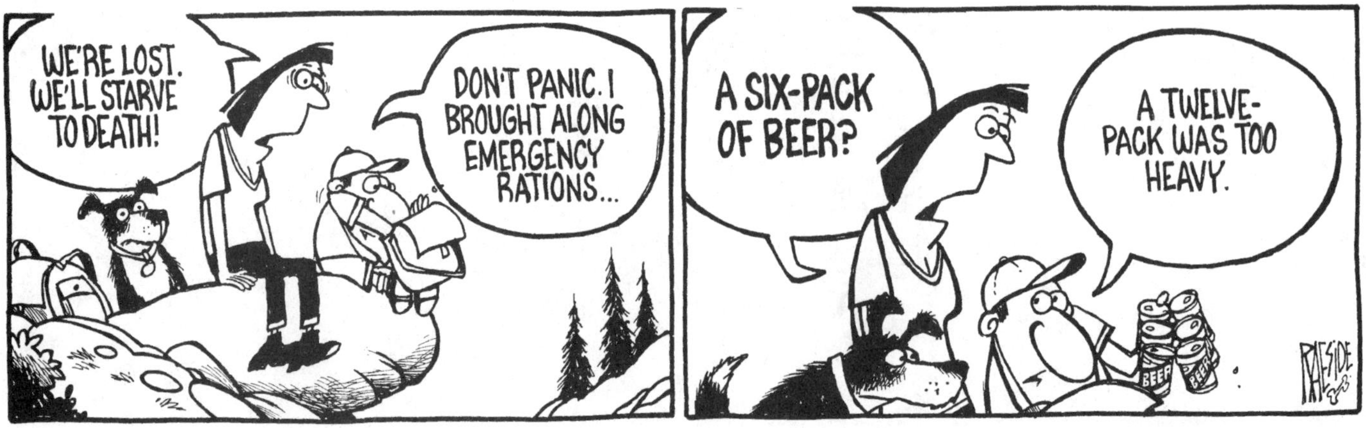
WE'RE LOST. WE'LL STARVE TO DEATH!
DON'T PANIC. I BROUGHT ALONG EMERGENCY RATIONS...
A SIX-PACK OF BEER?
A TWELVE-PACK WAS TOO HEAVY.

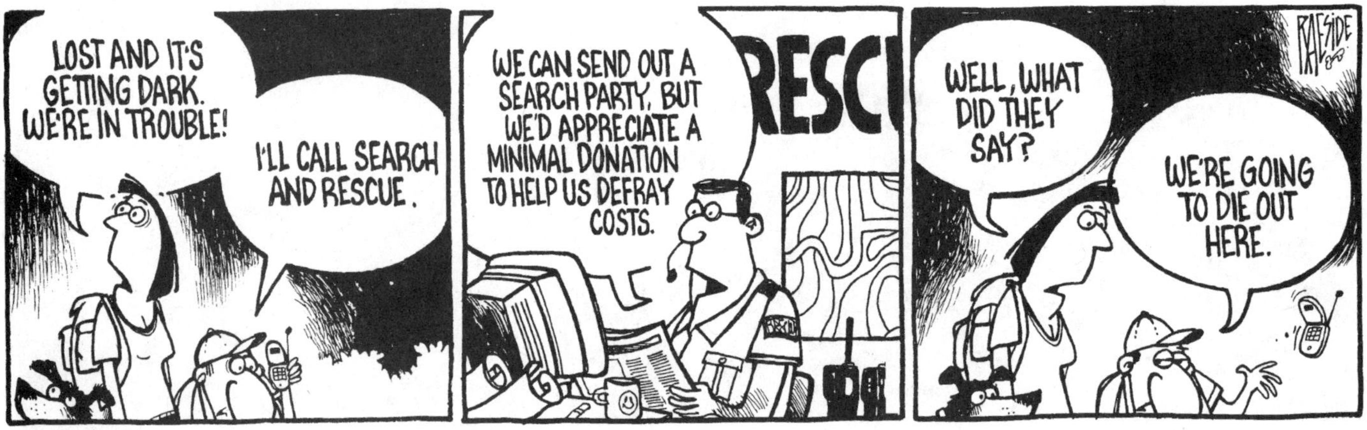
LOST AND IT'S GETTING DARK. WE'RE IN TROUBLE!
I'LL CALL SEARCH AND RESCUE.
WE CAN SEND OUT A SEARCH PARTY, BUT WE'D APPRECIATE A MINIMAL DONATION TO HELP US DEFRAY COSTS.
RESC
WELL, WHAT DID THEY SAY?
WE'RE GOING TO DIE OUT HERE.

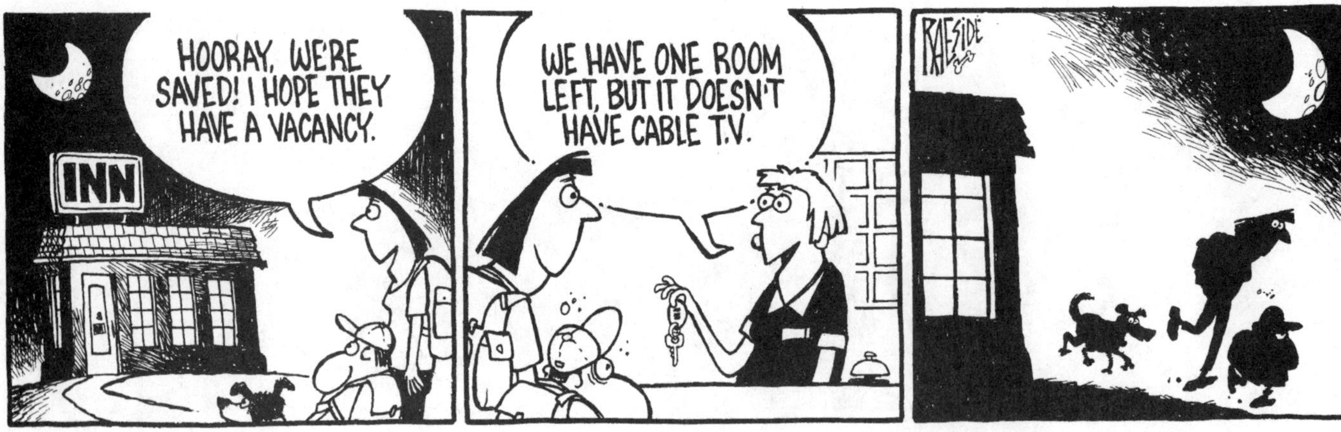
HOORAY, WE'RE SAVED! I HOPE THEY HAVE A VACANCY.
INN
WE HAVE ONE ROOM LEFT, BUT IT DOESN'T HAVE CABLE T.V.

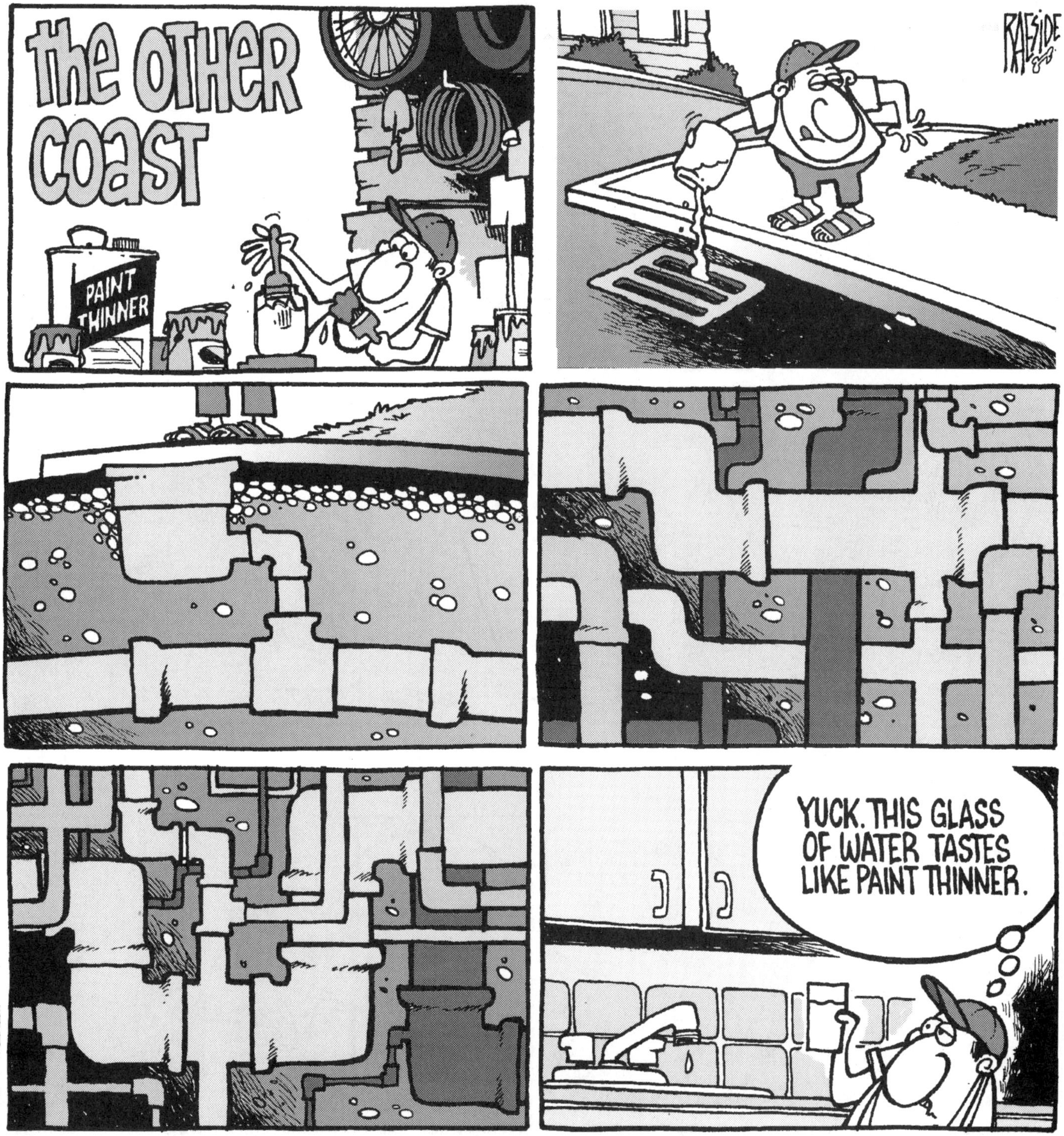
the OTHER COAST
PAINT THINNER
RAESIDE
YUCK. THIS GLASS OF WATER TASTES LIKE PAINT THINNER.

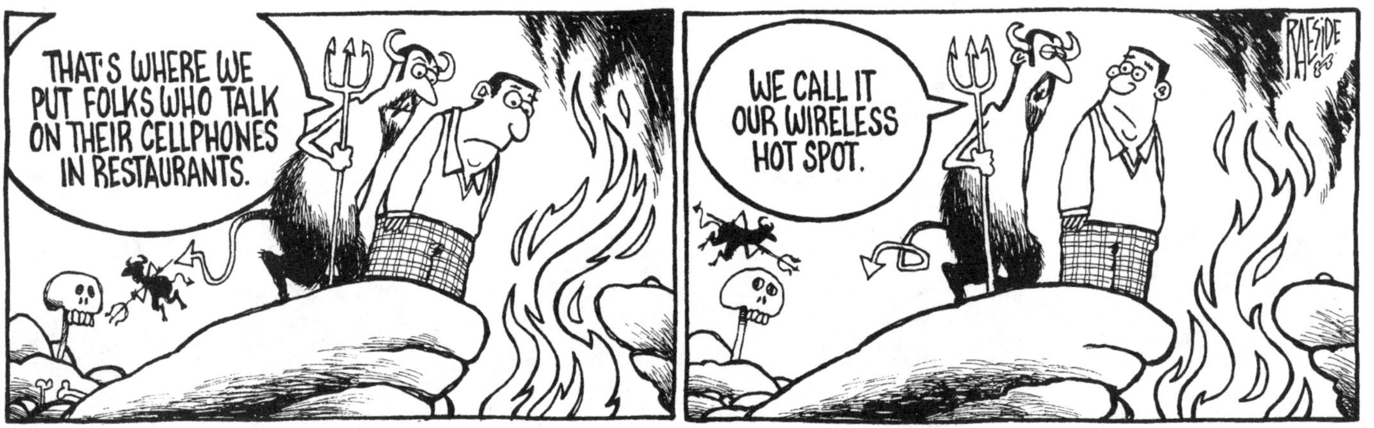
THAT'S WHERE WE PUT FOLKS WHO TALK ON THEIR CELLPHONES IN RESTAURANTS.
WE CALL IT OUR WIRELESS HOT SPOT.

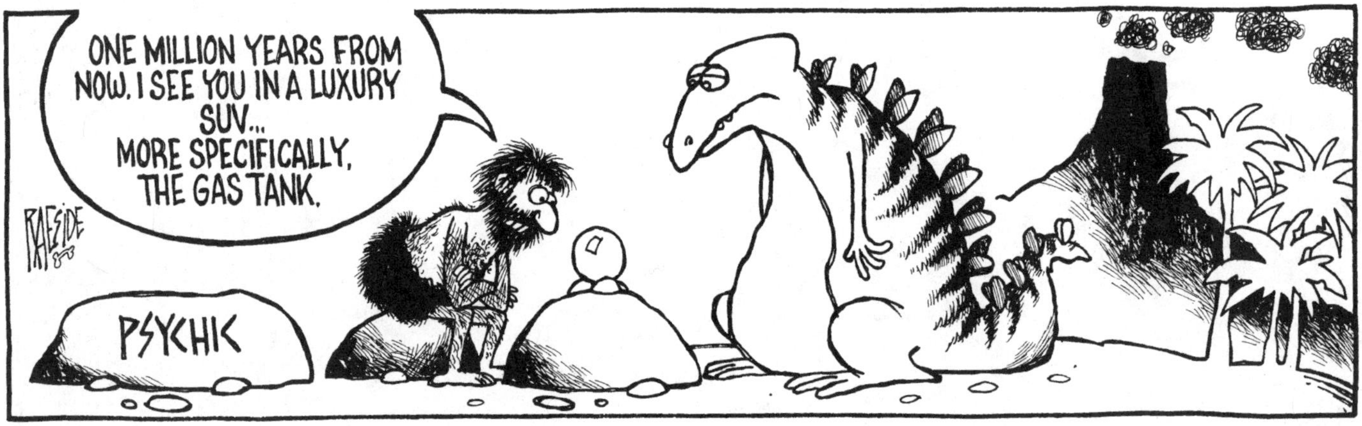
ONE MILLION YEARS FROM NOW. I SEE YOU IN A LUXURY SUV... MORE SPECIFICALLY, THE GAS TANK.
PSYCHIC

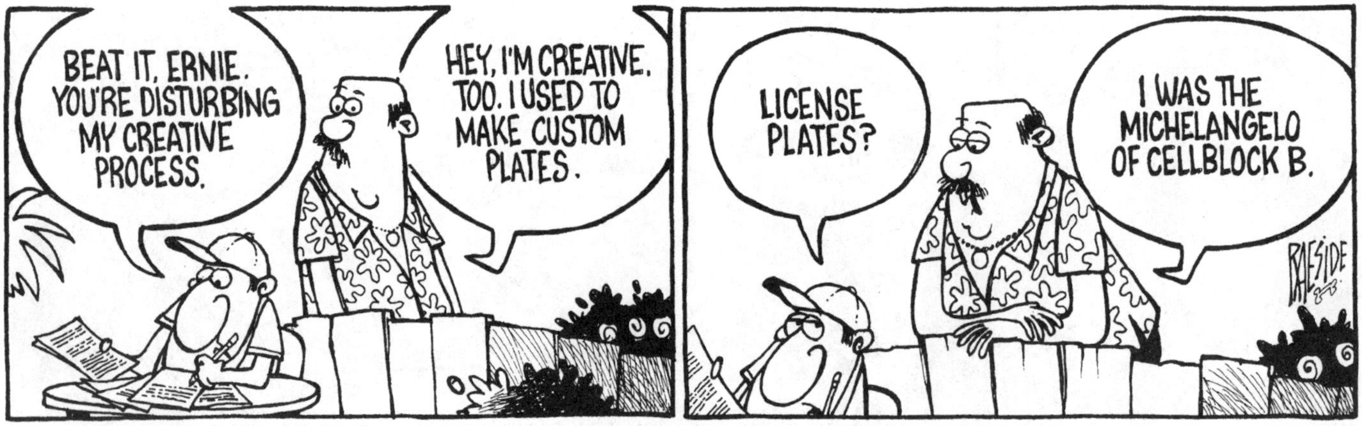
BEAT IT, ERNIE. YOU'RE DISTURBING MY CREATIVE PROCESS.
HEY, I'M CREATIVE, TOO. I USED TO MAKE CUSTOM PLATES.
LICENSE PLATES?
I WAS THE MICHELANGELO OF CELLBLOCK B.

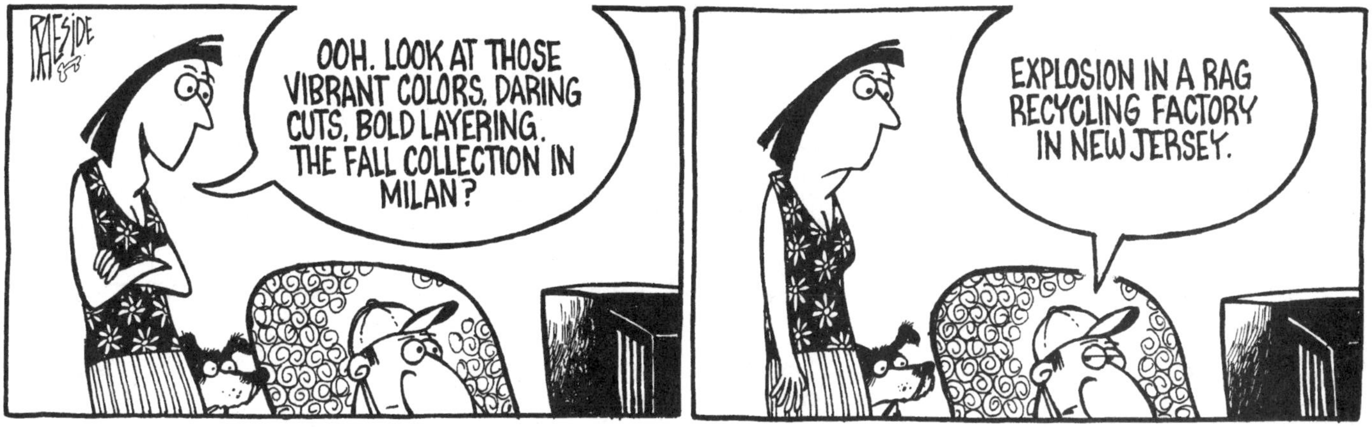
OOH. LOOK AT THOSE VIBRANT COLORS, DARING CUTS, BOLD LAYERING. THE FALL COLLECTION IN MILAN?
EXPLOSION IN A RAG RECYCLING FACTORY IN NEW JERSEY.

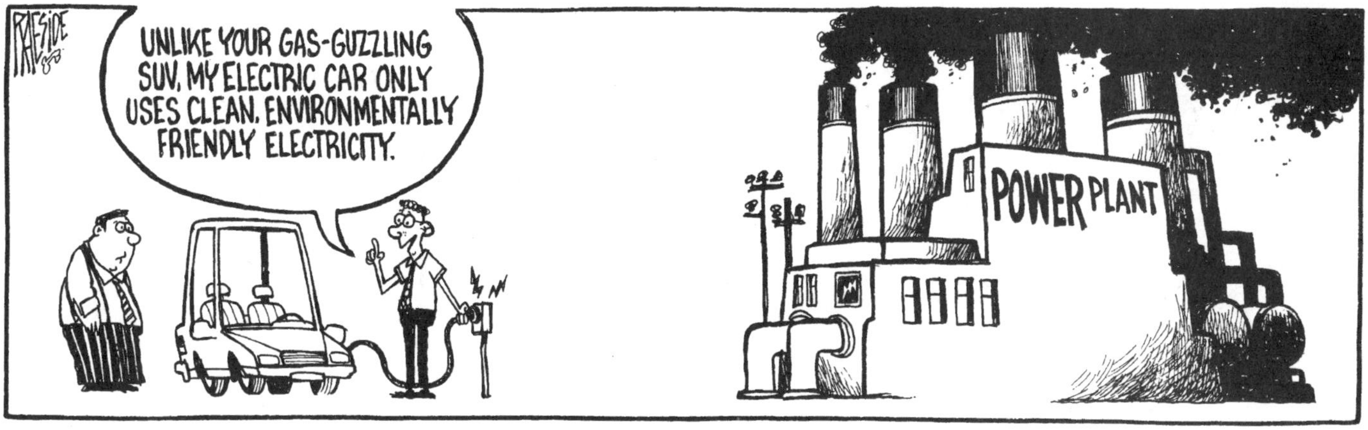
UNLIKE YOUR GAS-GUZZLING SUV, MY ELECTRIC CAR ONLY USES CLEAN, ENVIRONMENTALLY FRIENDLY ELECTRICITY.
POWER PLANT

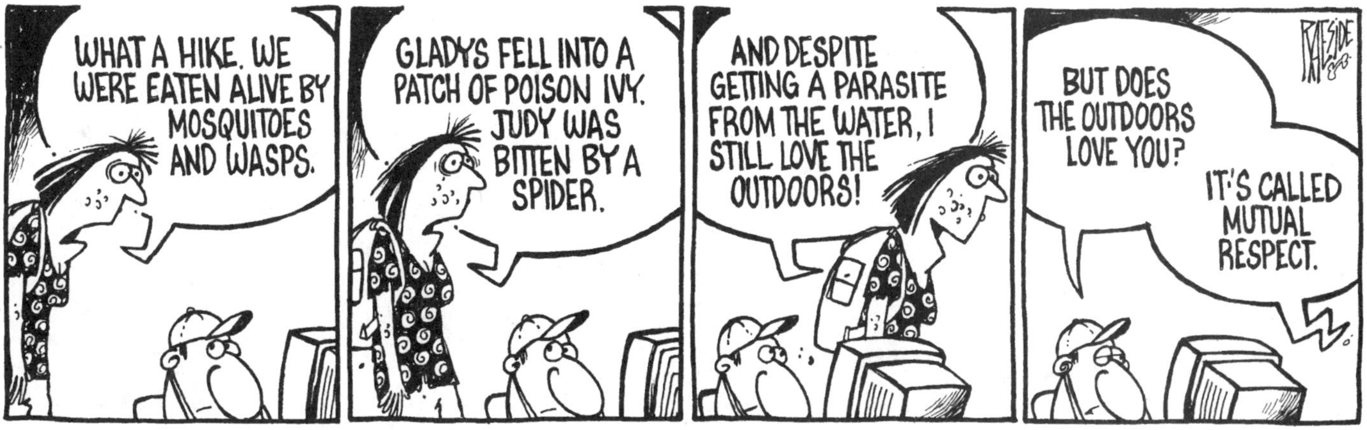
WHAT A HIKE. WE WERE EATEN ALIVE BY MOSQUITOES AND WASPS.
GLADYS FELL INTO A PATCH OF POISON IVY. JUDY WAS BITTEN BY A SPIDER.
AND DESPITE GETTING A PARASITE FROM THE WATER, I STILL LOVE THE OUTDOORS!
BUT DOES THE OUTDOORS LOVE YOU?
IT'S CALLED MUTUAL RESPECT.

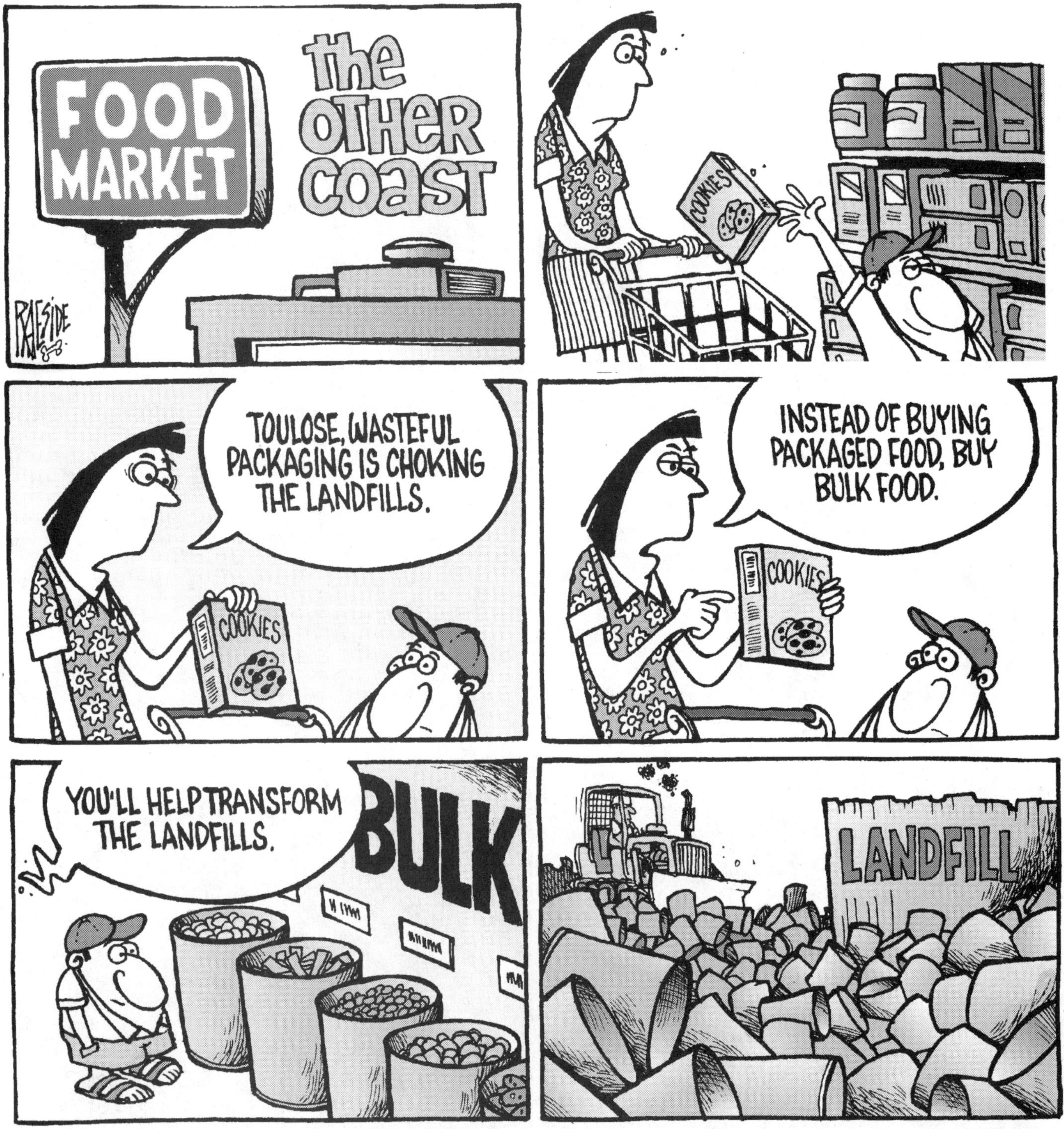
FOOD MARKET
the OTHER COAST
RAESIDE
COOKIES
TOULOSE, WASTEFUL PACKAGING IS CHOKING THE LANDFILLS.
INSTEAD OF BUYING PACKAGED FOOD, BUY BULK FOOD.
YOU'LL HELP TRANSFORM THE LANDFILLS.
BULK
LANDFILL

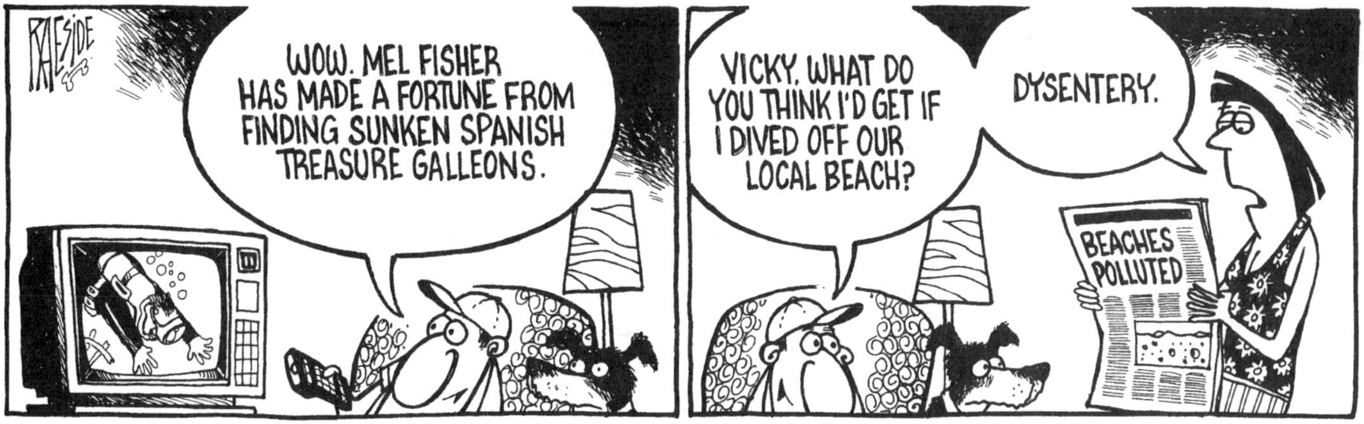
WOW. MEL FISHER HAS MADE A FORTUNE FROM FINDING SUNKEN SPANISH TREASURE GALLEONS.
VICKY, WHAT DO YOU THINK I'D GET IF I DIVED OFF OUR LOCAL BEACH?
DYSENTERY.
BEACHES POLLUTED

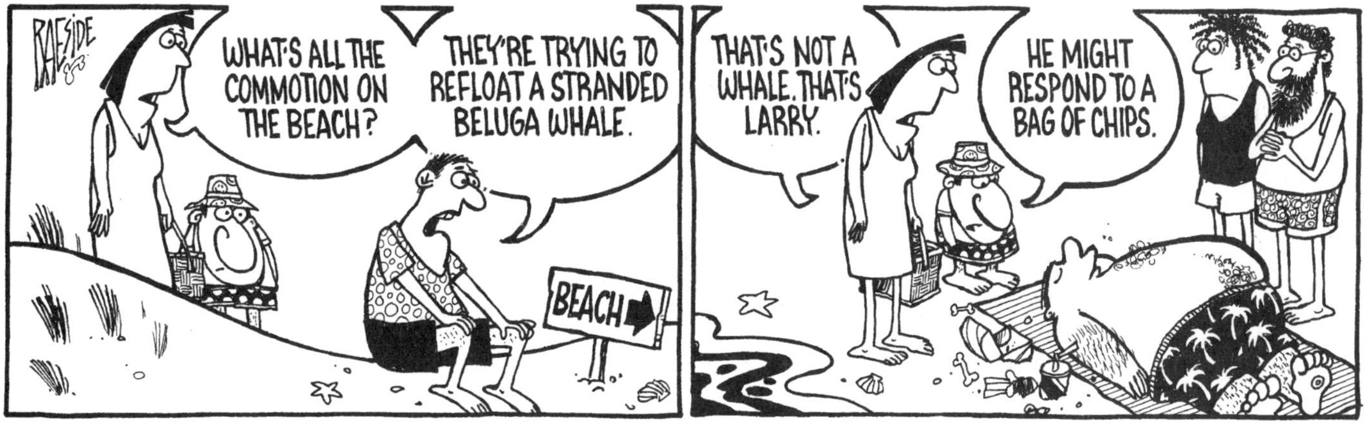
WHAT'S ALL THE COMMOTION ON THE BEACH?
THEY'RE TRYING TO REFLOAT A STRANDED BELUGA WHALE.
BEACH
THAT'S NOT A WHALE. THAT'S LARRY.
HE MIGHT RESPOND TO A BAG OF CHIPS.

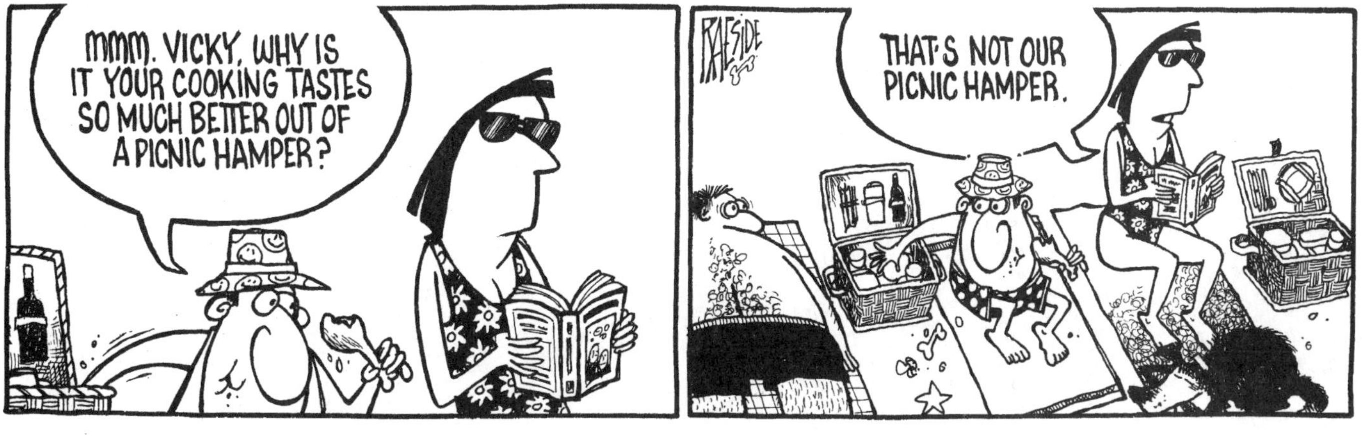
mmm. VICKY, WHY IS IT YOUR COOKING TASTES SO MUCH BETTER OUT OF A PICNIC HAMPER?
THAT'S NOT OUR PICNIC HAMPER.

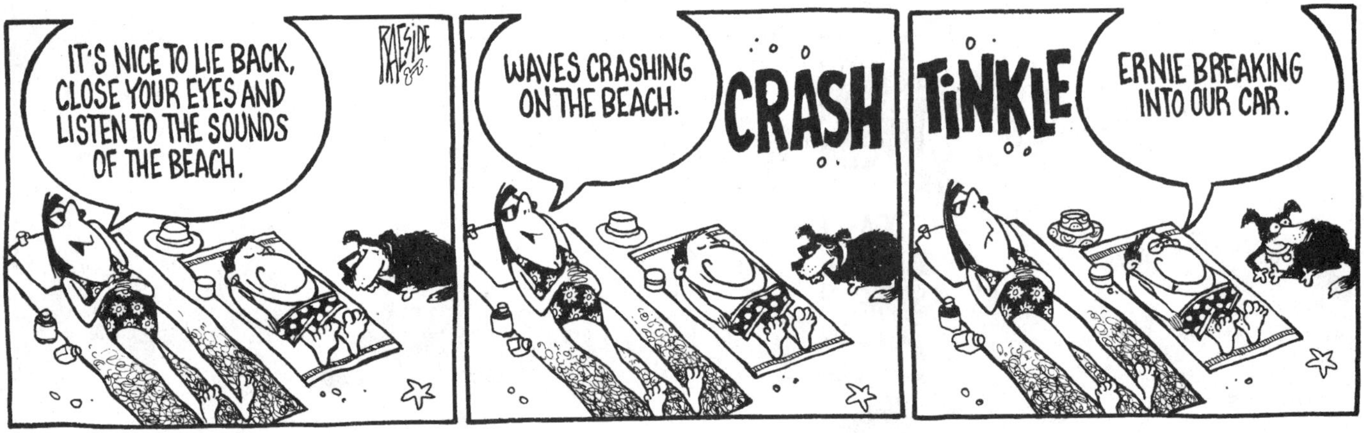
IT'S NICE TO LIE BACK, CLOSE YOUR EYES AND LISTEN TO THE SOUNDS OF THE BEACH.
WAVES CRASHING ON THE BEACH.
CRASH
TINKLE
ERNIE BREAKING INTO OUR CAR.

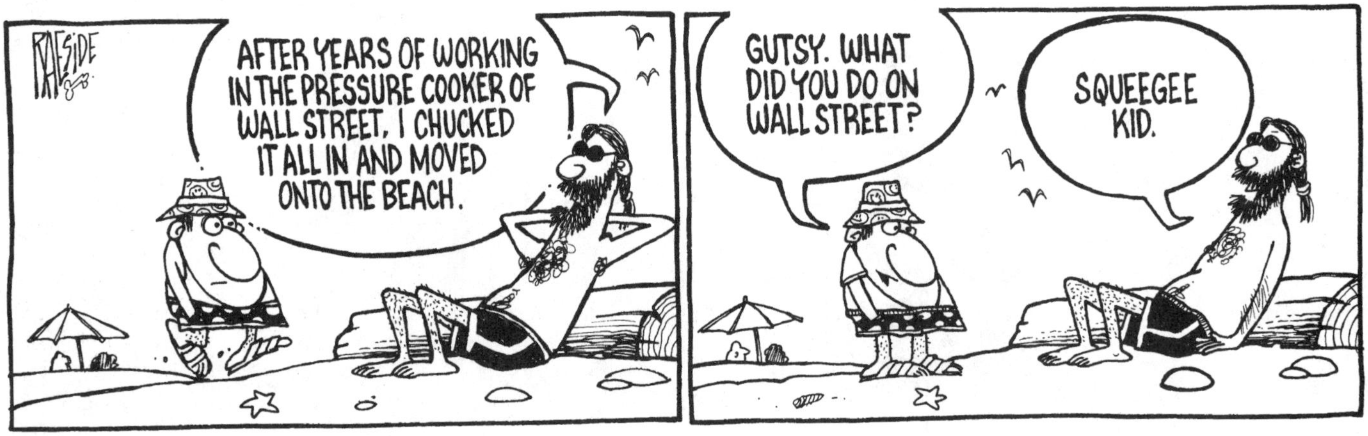
AFTER YEARS OF WORKING IN THE PRESSURE COOKER OF WALL STREET, I CHUCKED IT ALL IN AND MOVED ONTO THE BEACH.
GUTSY. WHAT DID YOU DO ON WALL STREET?
SQUEEGEE KID.

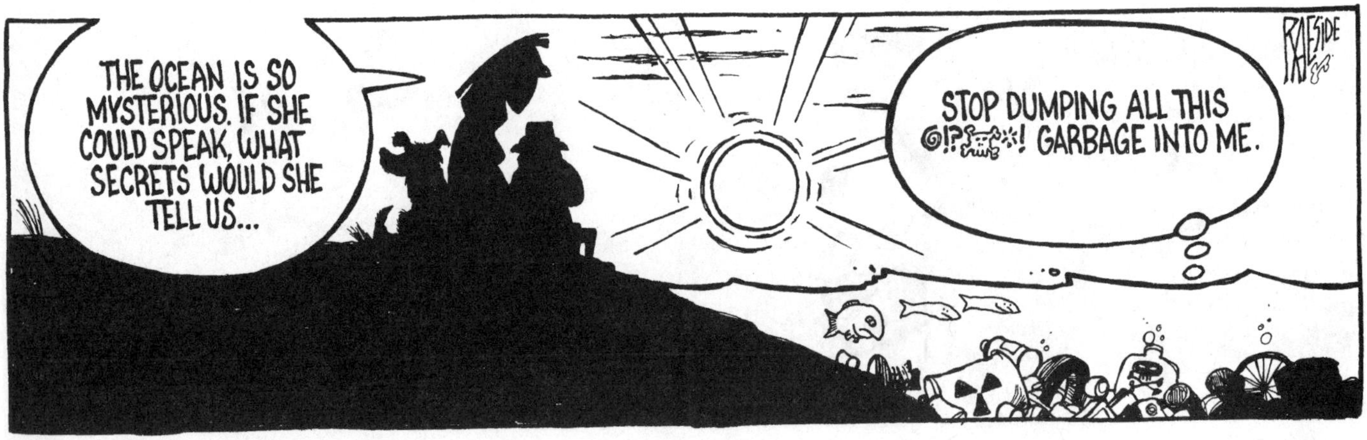
THE OCEAN IS SO MYSTERIOUS. IF SHE COULD SPEAK, WHAT SECRETS WOULD SHE TELL US...
STOP DUMPING ALL THIS
GARBAGE INTO ME.

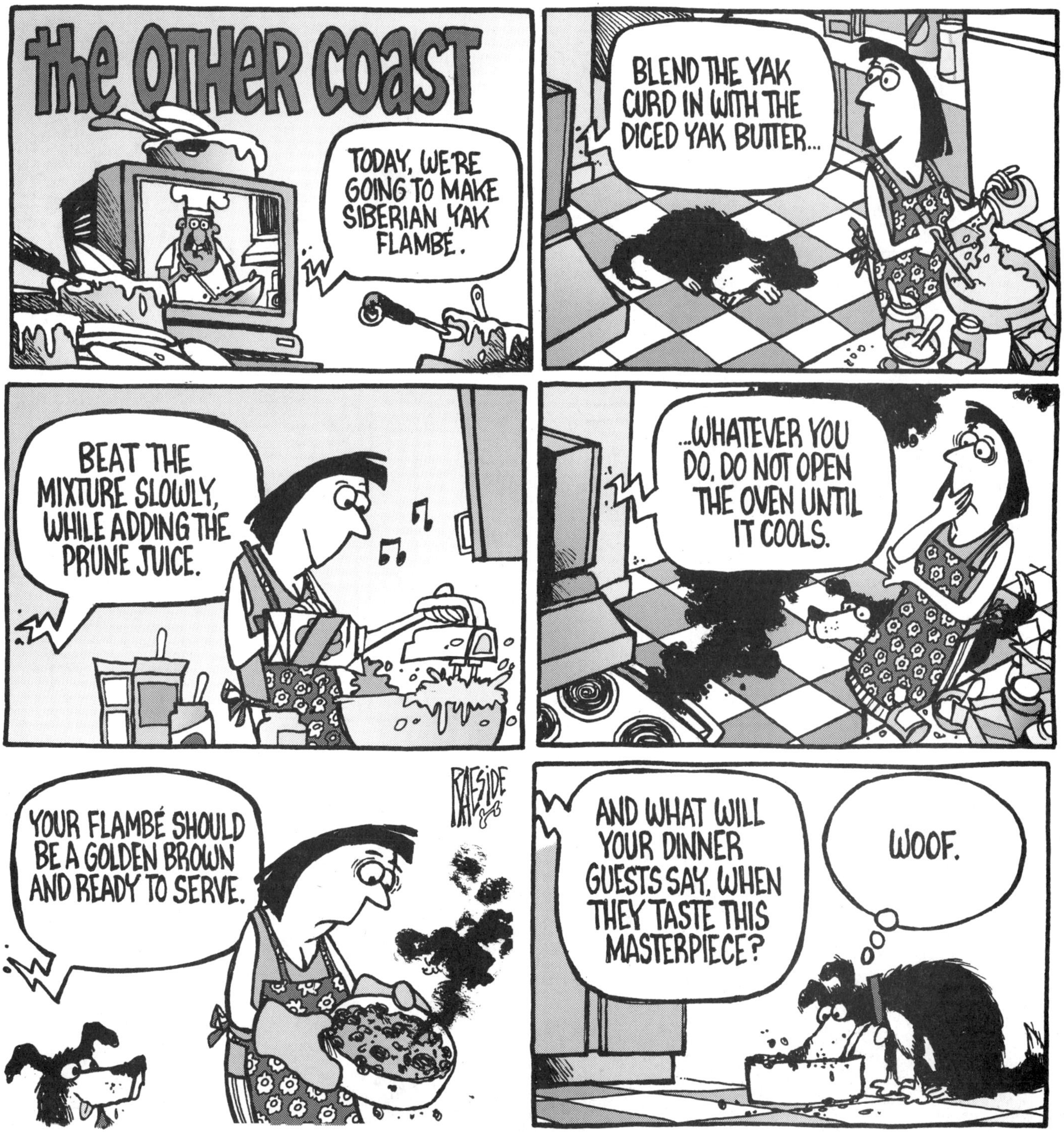
the OTHER COAST
TODAY, WE'RE GOING TO MAKE SIBERIAN YAK FLAMBÉ.
BLEND THE YAK CURD IN WITH THE DICED YAK BUTTER...
BEAT THE MIXTURE SLOWLY, WHILE ADDING THE PRUNE JUICE.
...WHATEVER YOU DO, DO NOT OPEN THE OVEN UNTIL IT COOLS.
YOUR FLAMBÉ SHOULD BE A GOLDEN BROWN AND READY TO SERVE.
RAESIDE
AND WHAT WILL YOUR DINNER GUESTS SAY, WHEN THEY TASTE THIS MASTERPIECE?
WOOF.

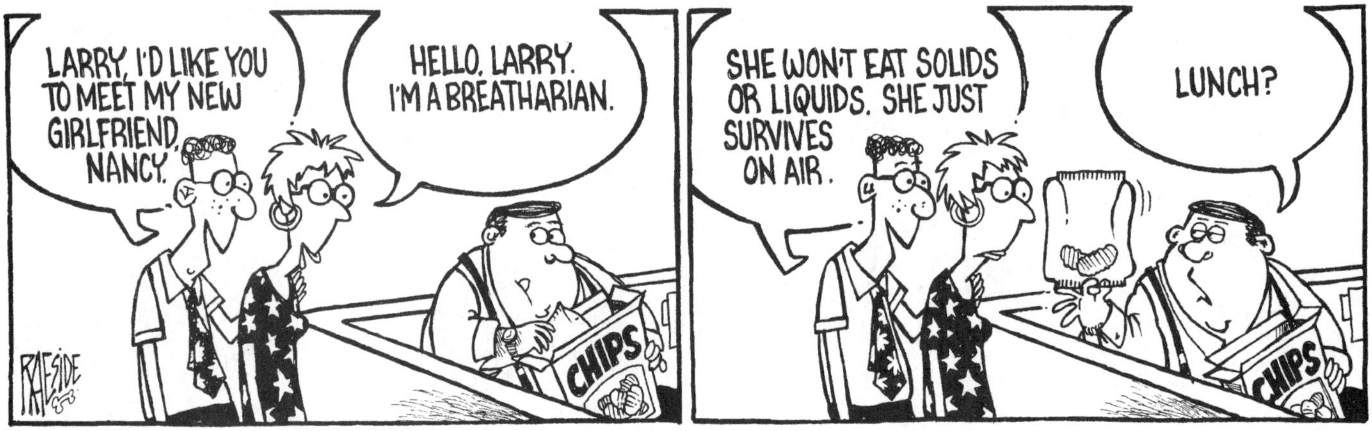
LARRY, I'D LIKE YOU TO MEET MY NEW GIRLFRIEND, NANCY.
HELLO, LARRY. I'M A BREATHARIAN.
CHIPS
SHE WON'T EAT SOLIDS OR LIQUIDS. SHE JUST SURVIVES ON AIR.
LUNCH?
CHIPS

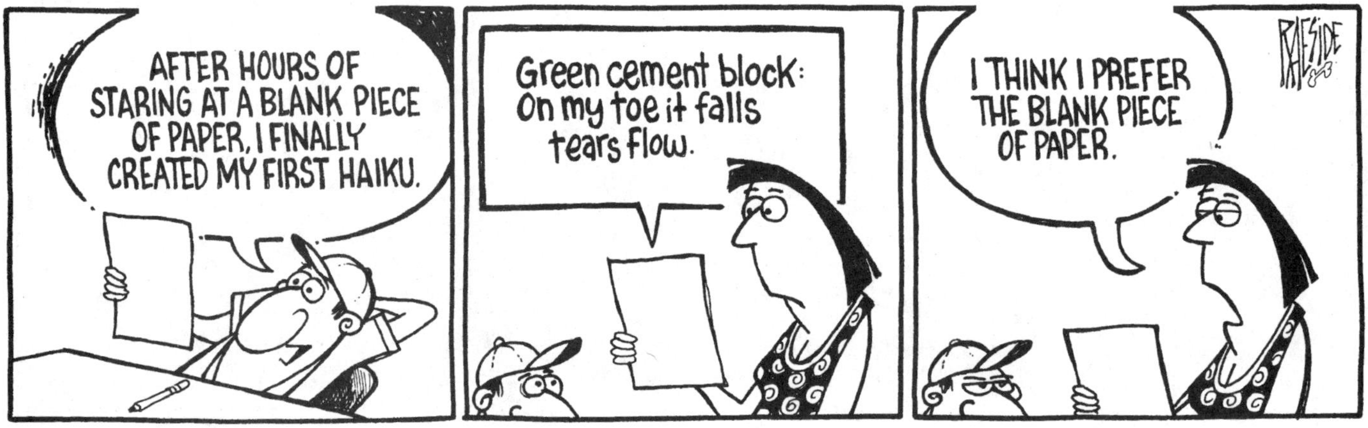
AFTER HOURS OF STARING AT A BLANK PIECE OF PAPER, I FINALLY CREATED MY FIRST HAIKU.
Green cement block:
On my toe it falls
tears flow.
I THINK I PREFER THE BLANK PIECE OF PAPER.

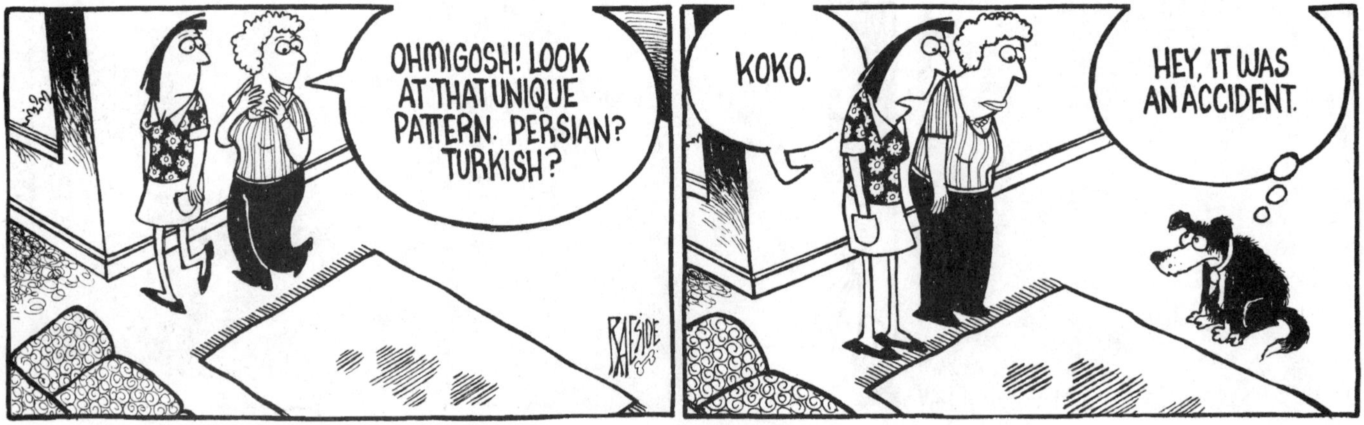
OHMIGOSH! LOOK AT THAT UNIQUE PATTERN. PERSIAN? TURKISH?
KOKO.
HEY, IT WAS AN ACCIDENT.

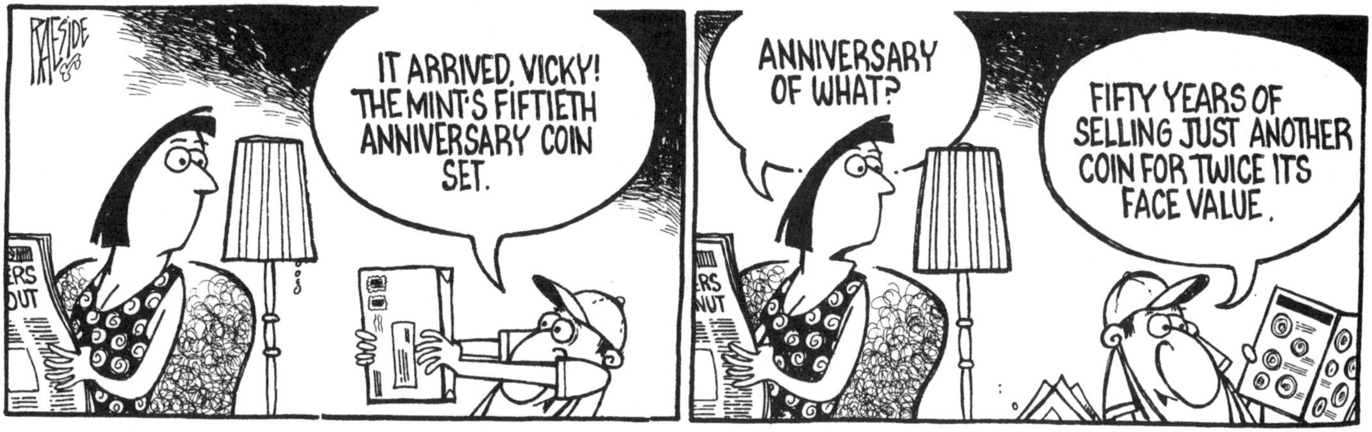
IT ARRIVED, VICKY! THE MINT'S FIFTIETH ANNIVERSARY COIN SET.
ANNIVERSARY OF WHAT?
FIFTY YEARS OF SELLING JUST ANOTHER COIN FOR TWICE ITS FACE VALUE.

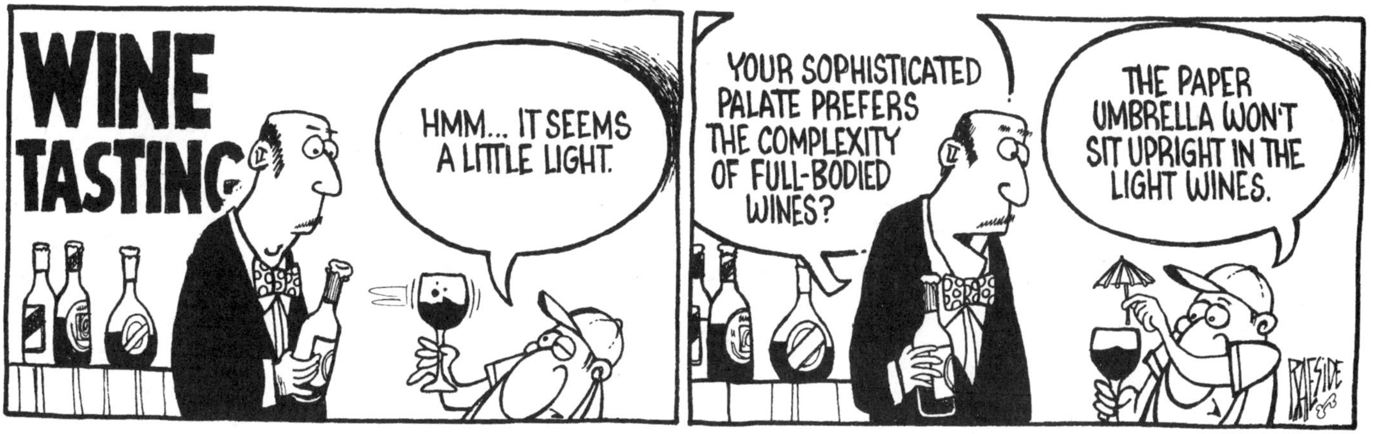
WINE TASTING
HMM... IT SEEMS A LITTLE LIGHT.
YOUR SOPHISTICATED PALATE PREFERS THE COMPLEXITY OF FULL-BODIED WINES?
THE PAPER UMBRELLA WON'T SIT UPRIGHT IN THE LIGHT WINES.

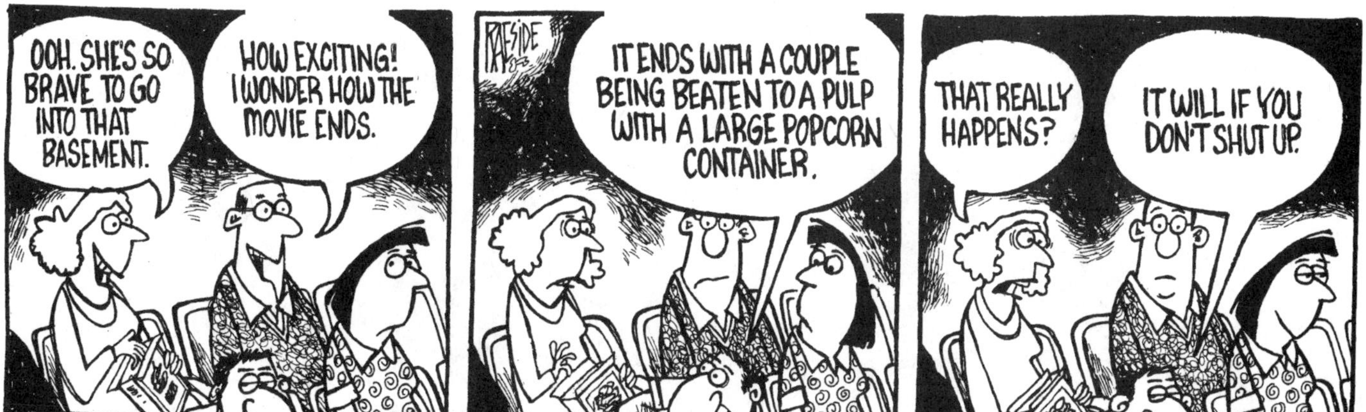
OOH. SHE'S SO BRAVE TO GO INTO THAT BASEMENT.
HOW EXCITING! I WONDER HOW THE MOVIE ENDS.
IT ENDS WITH A COUPLE BEING BEATEN TO A PULP WITH A LARGE POPCORN CONTAINER.
THAT REALLY HAPPENS?
IT WILL IF YOU DON'T SHUT UP.

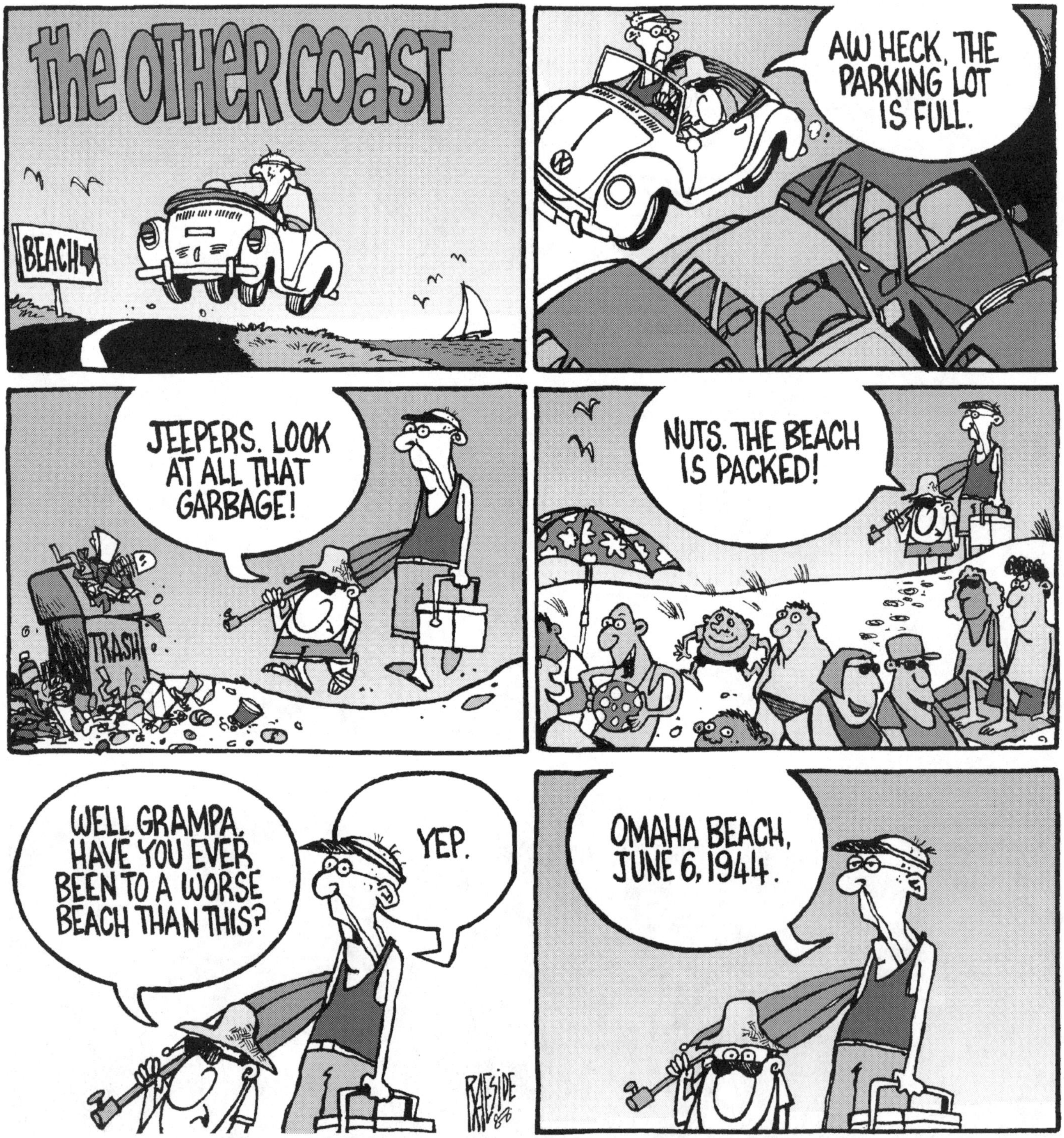
the OTHER COAST
BEACH
AW HECK, THE PARKING LOT IS FULL.
JEEPERS. LOOK AT ALL THAT GARBAGE!
TRASH
NUTS. THE BEACH IS PACKED!
WELL, GRAMPA, HAVE YOU EVER BEEN TO A WORSE BEACH THAN THIS?
YEP.
OMAHA BEACH, JUNE 6, 1944.
RAESIDE

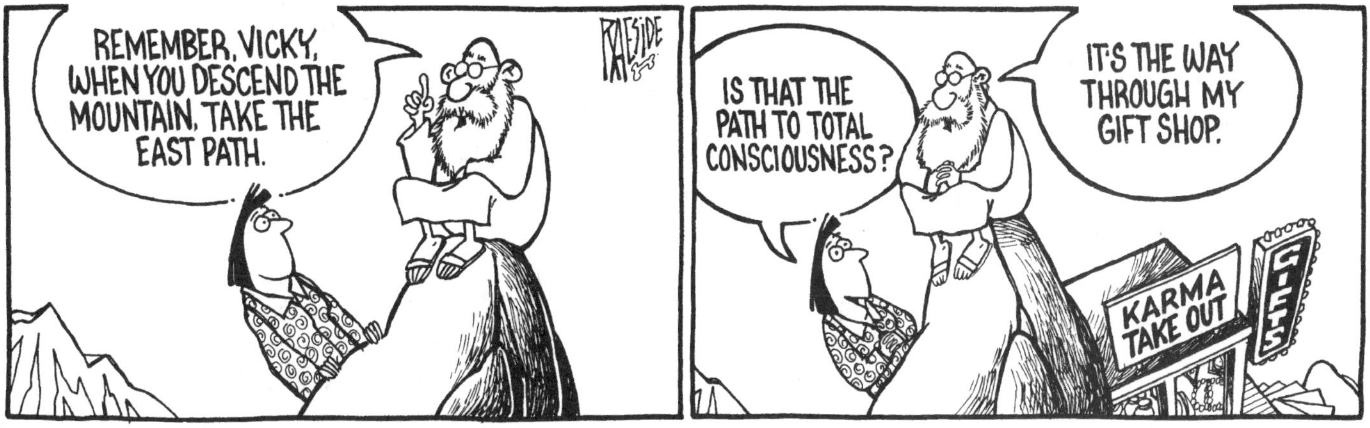
REMEMBER, VICKY, WHEN YOU DESCEND THE MOUNTAIN, TAKE THE EAST PATH.
IS THAT THE PATH TO TOTAL CONSCIOUSNESS?
IT'S THE WAY THROUGH MY GIFT SHOP.
KARMA TAKE OUT
GIFTS

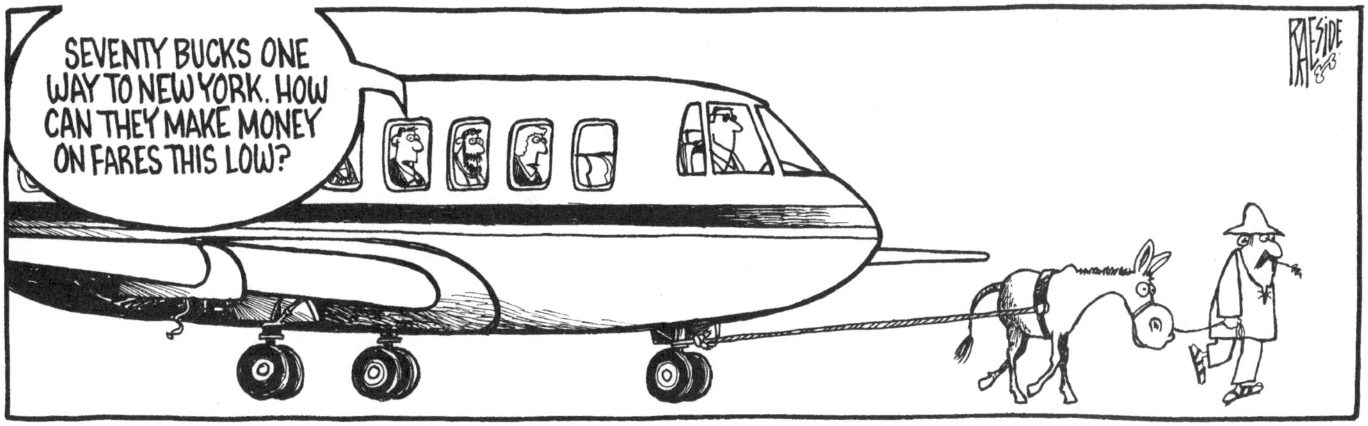
SEVENTY BUCKS ONE WAY TO NEW YORK. HOW CAN THEY MAKE MONEY ON FARES THIS LOW?

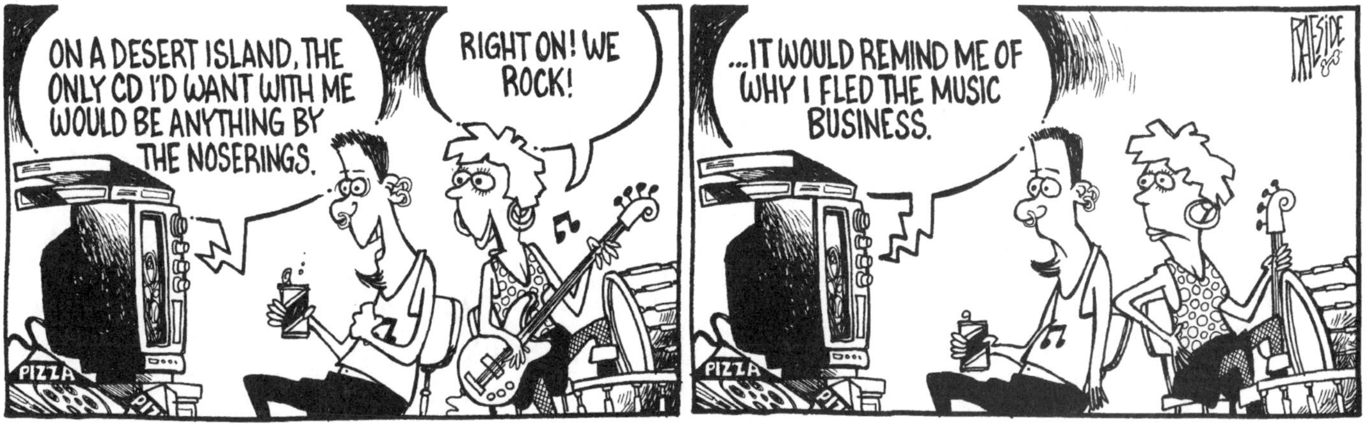
ON A DESERT ISLAND, THE ONLY CD I'D WANT WITH ME WOULD BE ANYTHING BY THE NOSERINGS.
RIGHT ON! WE ROCK!
...IT WOULD REMIND ME OF WHY I FLED THE MUSIC BUSINESS.
PIZZA

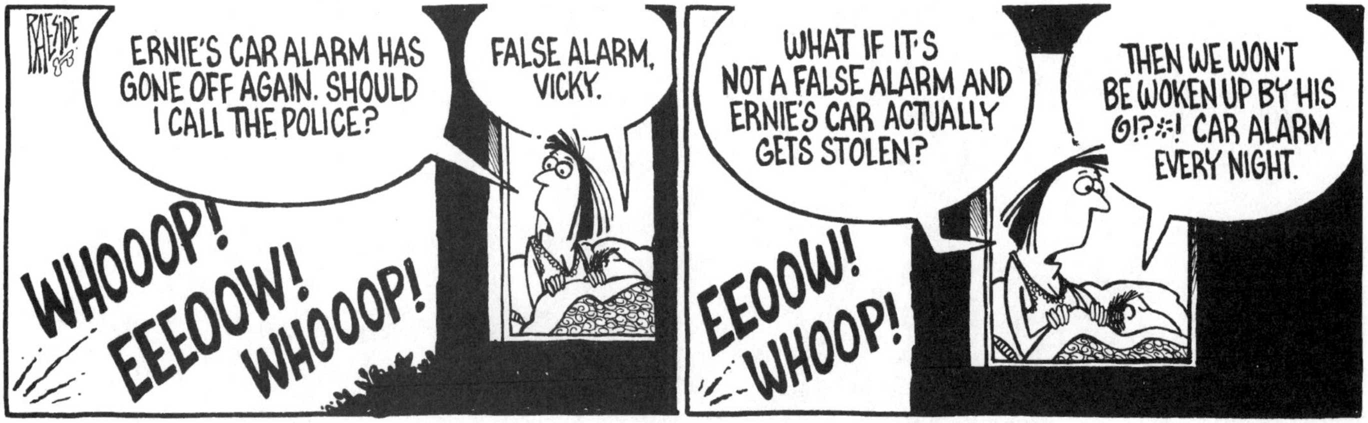
RAESIDE
ERNIE'S CAR ALARM HAS GONE OFF AGAIN. SHOULD I CALL THE POLICE?
FALSE ALARM, VICKY.
WHOOOP! EEEOOW! WHOOOP!
WHAT IF IT'S NOT A FALSE ALARM AND ERNIE'S CAR ACTUALLY GETS STOLEN?
THEN WE WON'T BE WOKEN UP BY HIS @!?*! CAR ALARM EVERY NIGHT.
EEOOW! WHOOP!

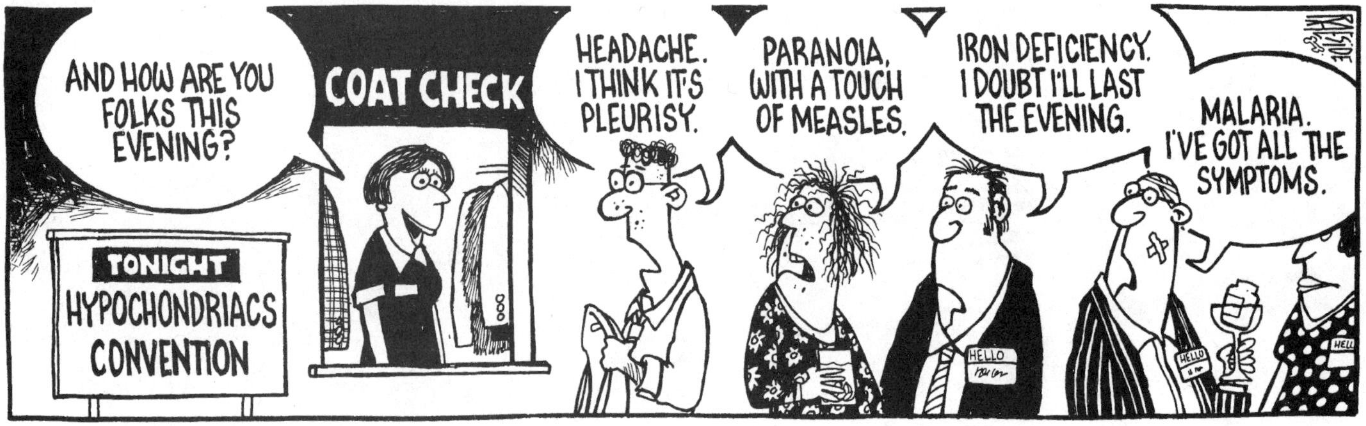
AND HOW ARE YOU FOLKS THIS EVENING?
COAT CHECK
TONIGHT
HYPOCHONDRIACS CONVENTION
HEADACHE. I THINK IT'S PLEURISY.
PARANOIA, WITH A TOUCH OF MEASLES.
IRON DEFICIENCY. I DOUBT I'LL LAST THE EVENING.
MALARIA. I'VE GOT ALL THE SYMPTOMS.
RAESIDE
HELLO

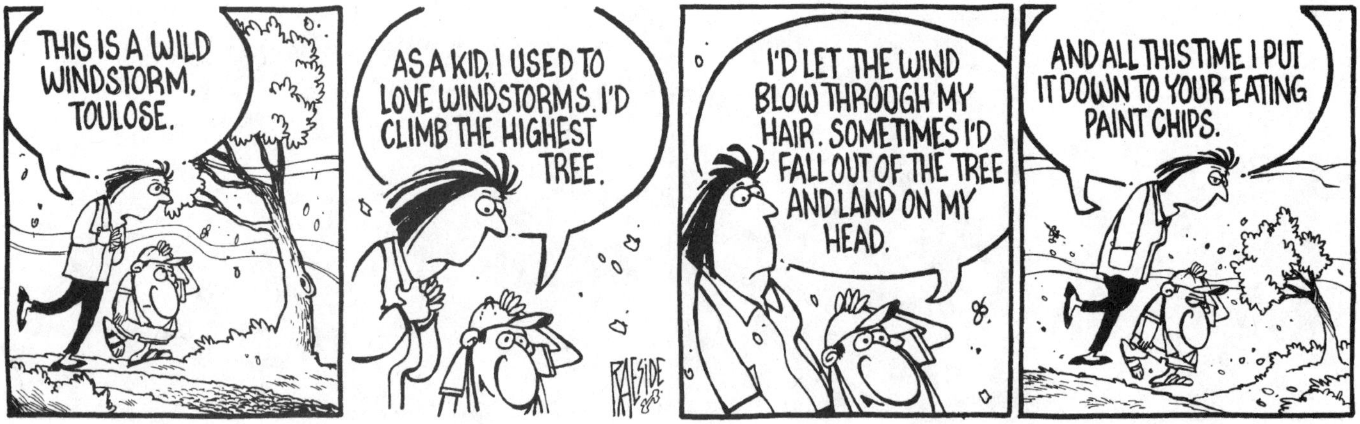
THIS IS A WILD WINDSTORM, TOULOSE.
AS A KID, I USED TO LOVE WINDSTORMS. I'D CLIMB THE HIGHEST TREE.
RAESIDE
I'D LET THE WIND BLOW THROUGH MY HAIR. SOMETIMES I'D FALL OUT OF THE TREE AND LAND ON MY HEAD.
AND ALL THIS TIME I PUT IT DOWN TO YOUR EATING PAINT CHIPS.

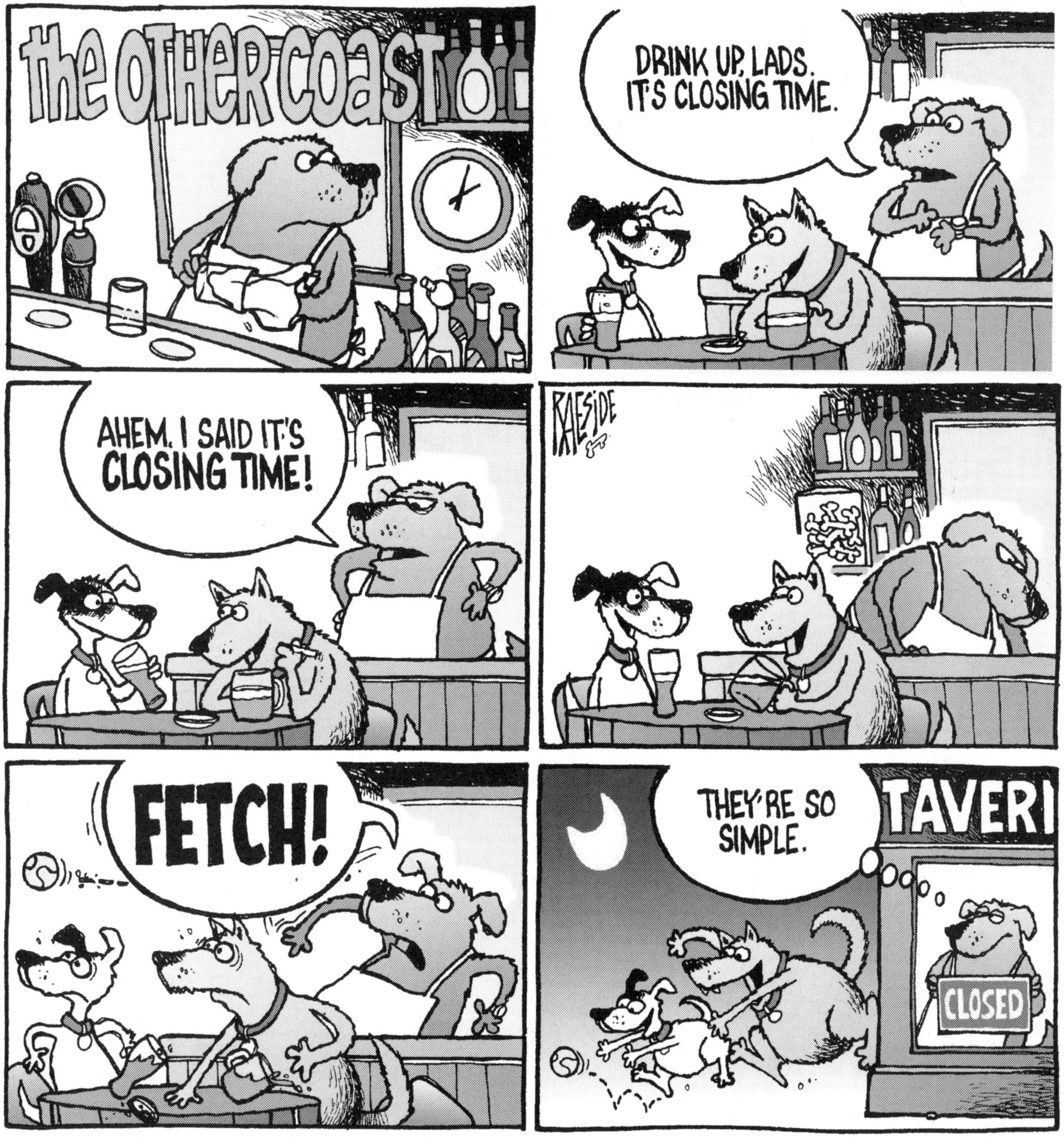
the OTHER COAST
DRINK UP, LADS. IT'S CLOSING TIME.
AHEM. I SAID IT'S CLOSING TIME!
RAESIDE
FETCH!
THEY'RE SO SIMPLE.
TAVERN
CLOSED

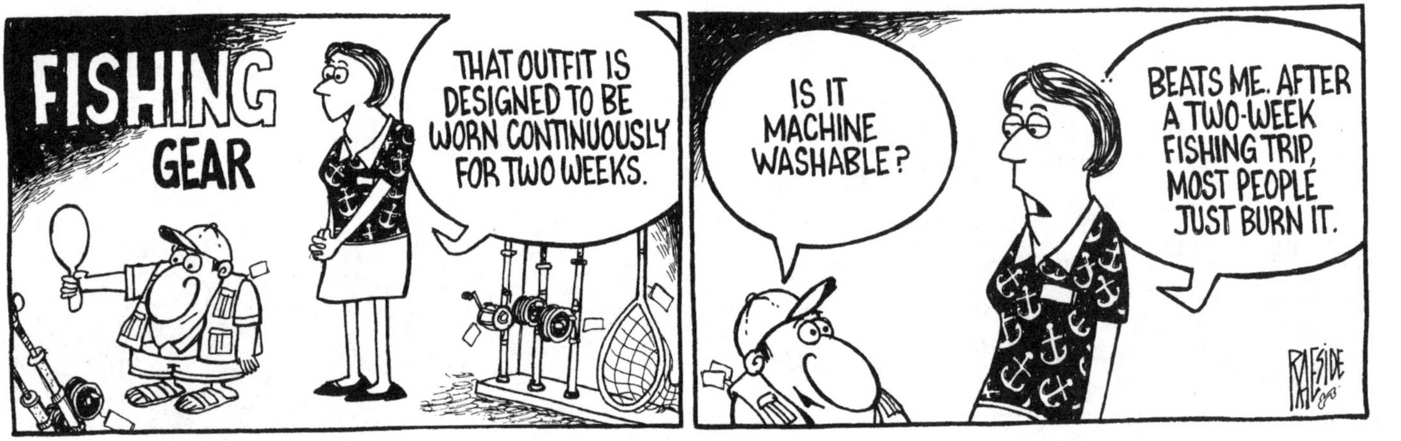
FISHING GEAR
THAT OUTFIT IS DESIGNED TO BE WORN CONTINUOUSLY FOR TWO WEEKS.
IS IT MACHINE WASHABLE?
BEATS ME. AFTER A TWO-WEEK FISHING TRIP, MOST PEOPLE JUST BURN IT.

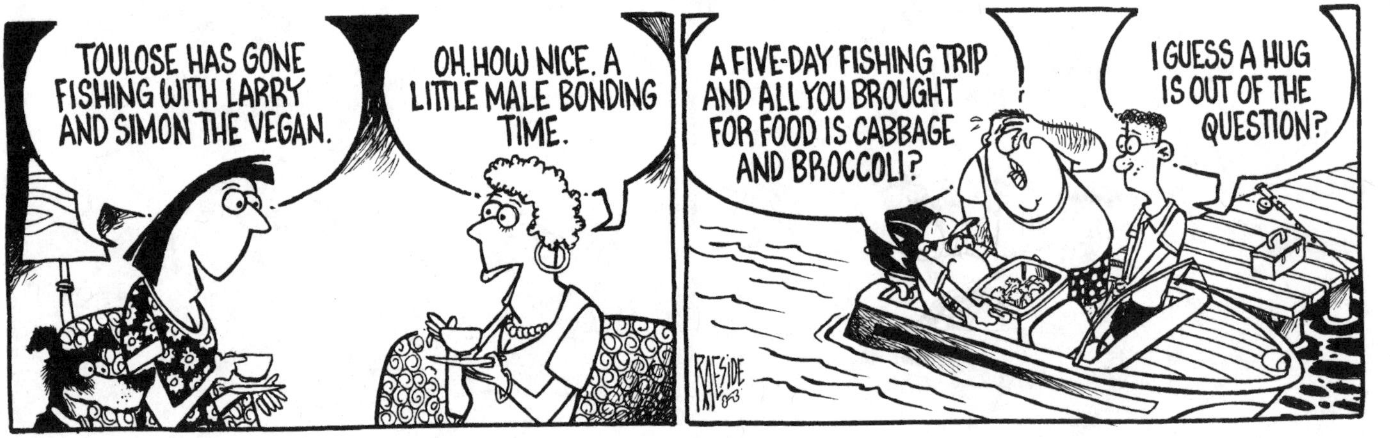
TOULOSE HAS GONE FISHING WITH LARRY AND SIMON THE VEGAN.
OH, HOW NICE. A LITTLE MALE BONDING TIME.
A FIVE-DAY FISHING TRIP AND ALL YOU BROUGHT FOR FOOD IS CABBAGE AND BROCCOLI?
I GUESS A HUG IS OUT OF THE QUESTION?

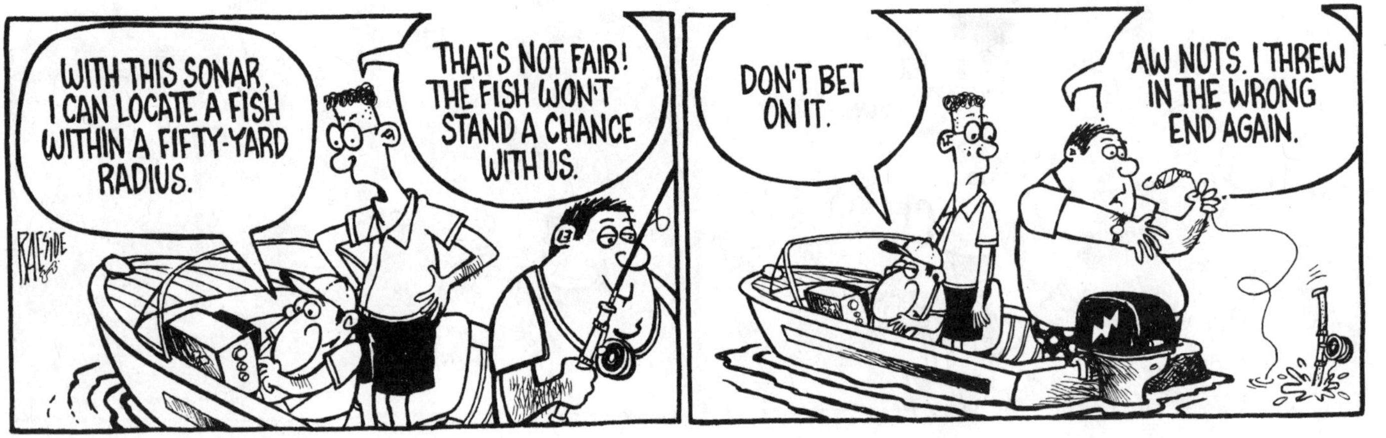
WITH THIS SONAR, I CAN LOCATE A FISH WITHIN A FIFTY-YARD RADIUS.
THAT'S NOT FAIR! THE FISH WON'T STAND A CHANCE WITH US.
DON'T BET ON IT.
AW NUTS. I THREW IN THE WRONG END AGAIN.

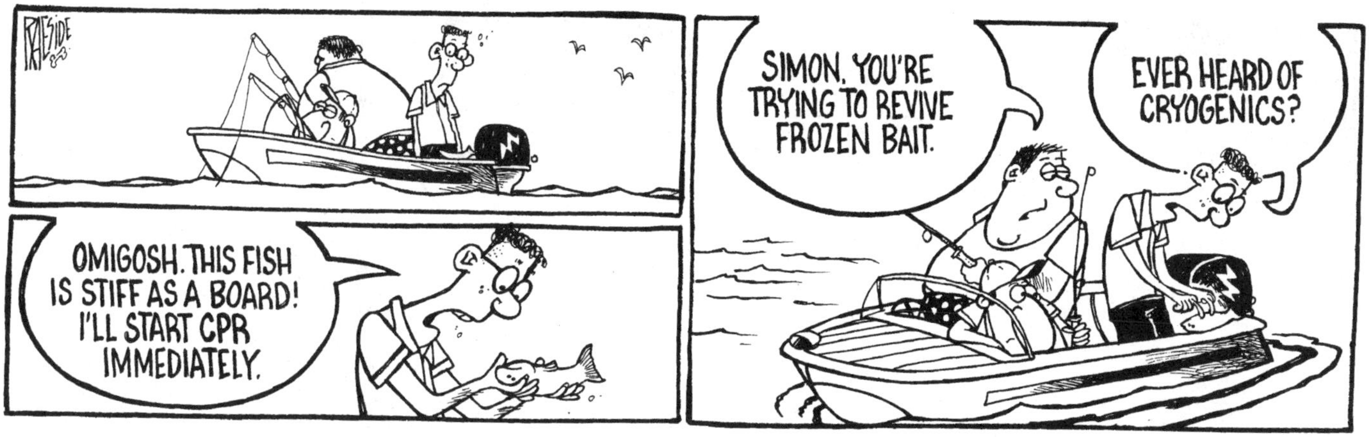
OMIGOSH. THIS FISH IS STIFF AS A BOARD! I'LL START CPR IMMEDIATELY.
SIMON, YOU'RE TRYING TO REVIVE FROZEN BAIT.
EVER HEARD OF CRYOGENICS?

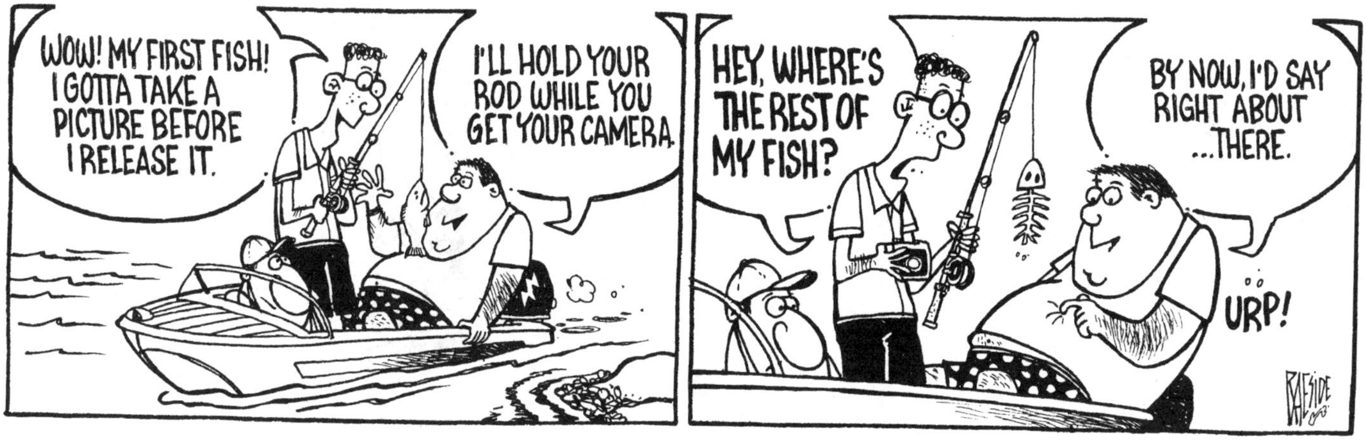
WOW! MY FIRST FISH! I GOTTA TAKE A PICTURE BEFORE I RELEASE IT.
I'LL HOLD YOUR ROD WHILE YOU GET YOUR CAMERA.
HEY, WHERE'S THE REST OF MY FISH?
BY NOW, I'D SAY RIGHT ABOUT ...THERE.
URP!

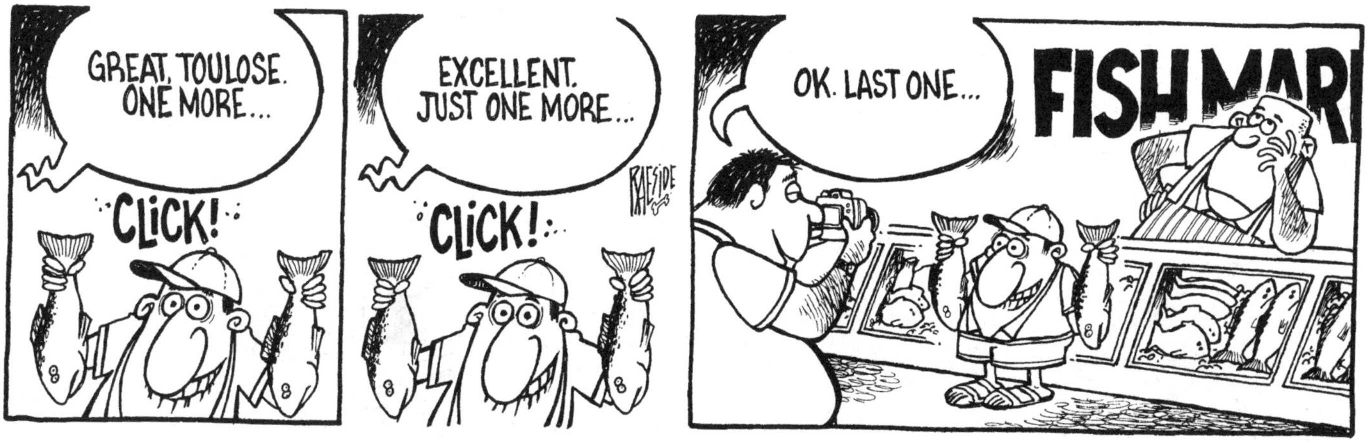
GREAT, TOULOSE. ONE MORE...
CLICK!
EXCELLENT. JUST ONE MORE...
CLICK!
OK. LAST ONE...
FISH MAR

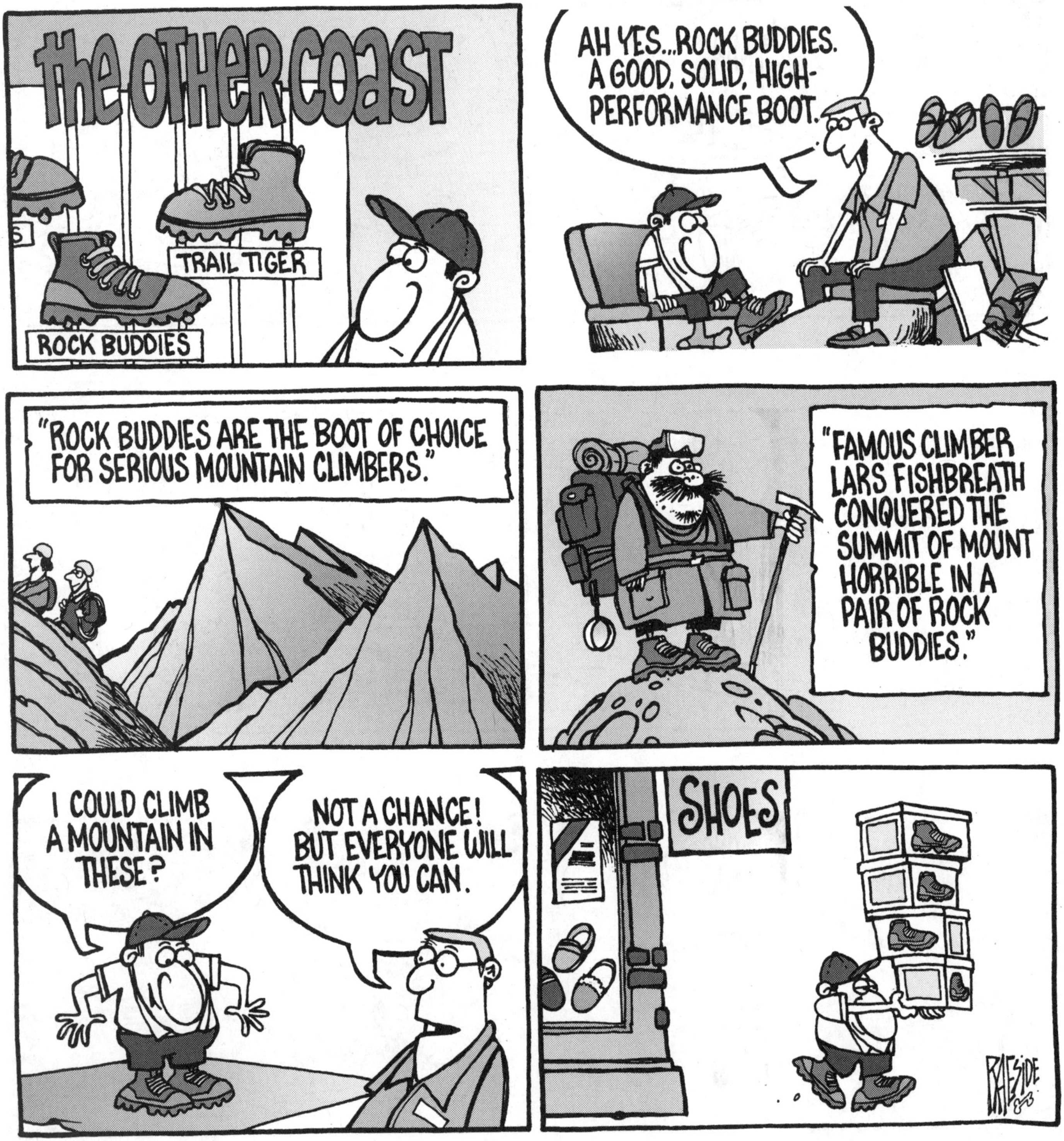
the OTHER COAST
TRAIL TIGER
ROCK BUDDIES
AH YES...ROCK BUDDIES. A GOOD, SOLID, HIGH-PERFORMANCE BOOT.
"ROCK BUDDIES ARE THE BOOT OF CHOICE FOR SERIOUS MOUNTAIN CLIMBERS."
"FAMOUS CLIMBER LARS FISHBREATH CONQUERED THE SUMMIT OF MOUNT HORRIBLE IN A PAIR OF ROCK BUDDIES."
I COULD CLIMB A MOUNTAIN IN THESE?
NOT A CHANCE! BUT EVERYONE WILL THINK YOU CAN.
SHOES
RAESIDE

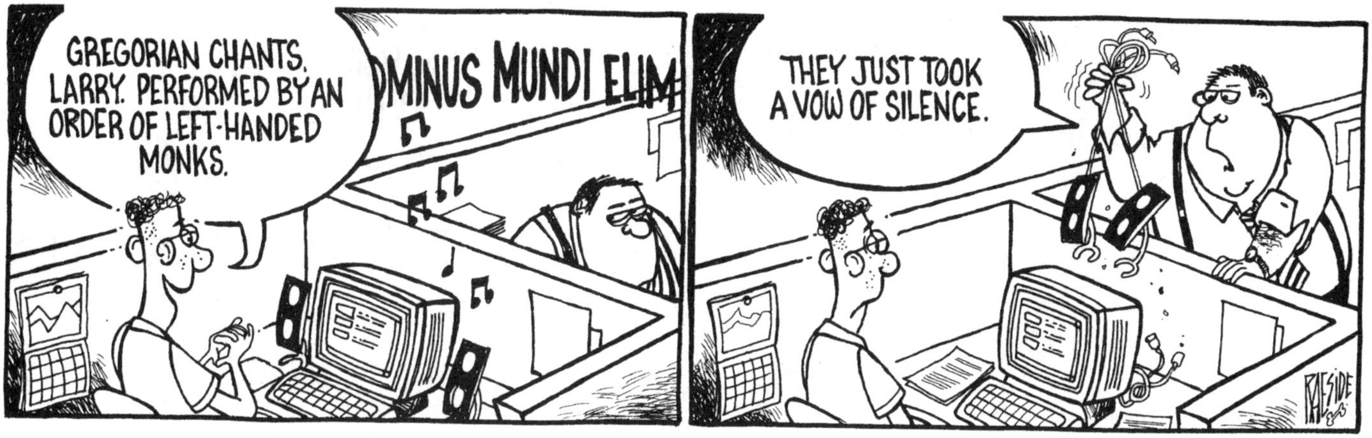
GREGORIAN CHANTS, LARRY. PERFORMED BY AN ORDER OF LEFT-HANDED MONKS.
THEY JUST TOOK A VOW OF SILENCE.

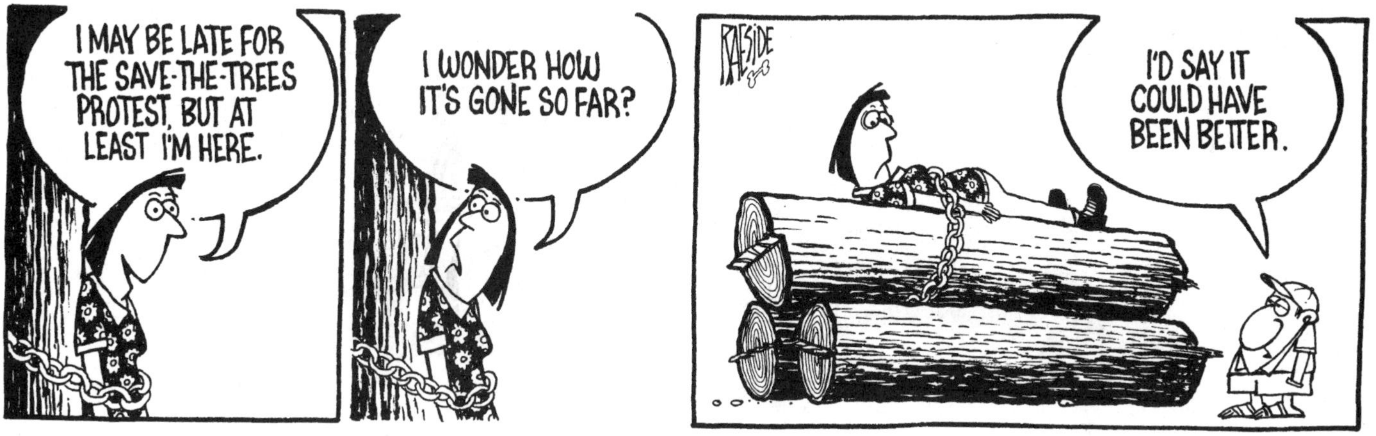
I MAY BE LATE FOR THE SAVE-THE-TREES PROTEST, BUT AT LEAST I'M HERE.
I WONDER HOW IT'S GONE SO FAR?
I'D SAY IT COULD HAVE BEEN BETTER.

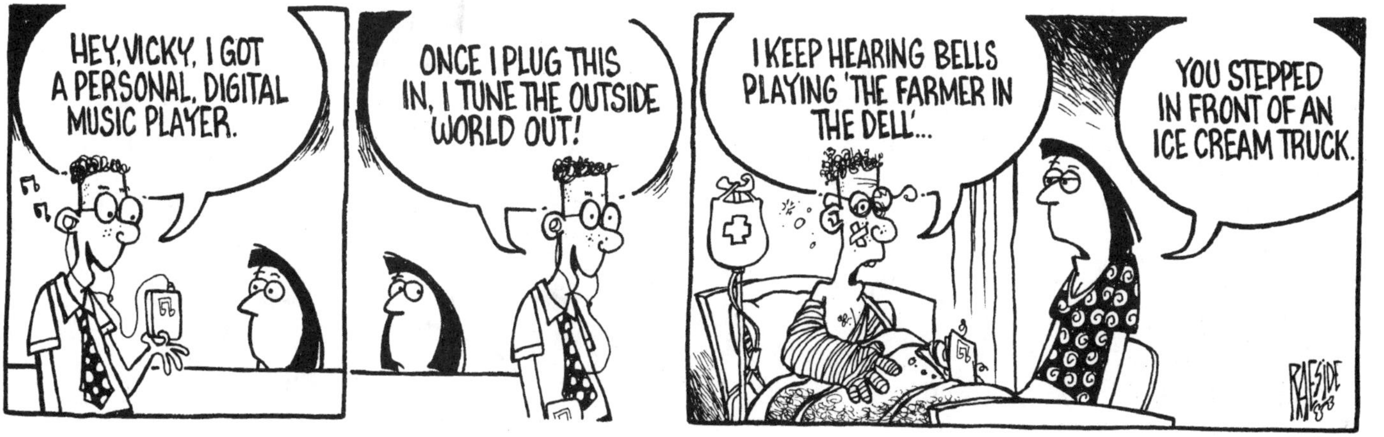
HEY, VICKY, I GOT A PERSONAL, DIGITAL MUSIC PLAYER.
ONCE I PLUG THIS IN, I TUNE THE OUTSIDE WORLD OUT!
I KEEP HEARING BELLS PLAYING 'THE FARMER IN THE DELL'...
YOU STEPPED IN FRONT OF AN ICE CREAM TRUCK.

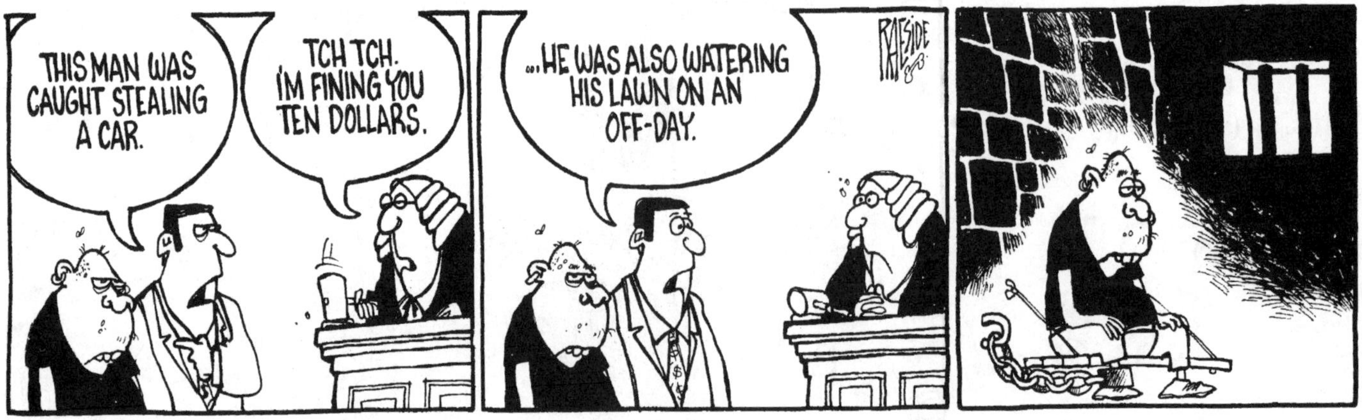
THIS MAN WAS CAUGHT STEALING A CAR.
TCH TCH. I'M FINING YOU TEN DOLLARS.
...HE WAS ALSO WATERING HIS LAWN ON AN OFF-DAY.
RAESIDE

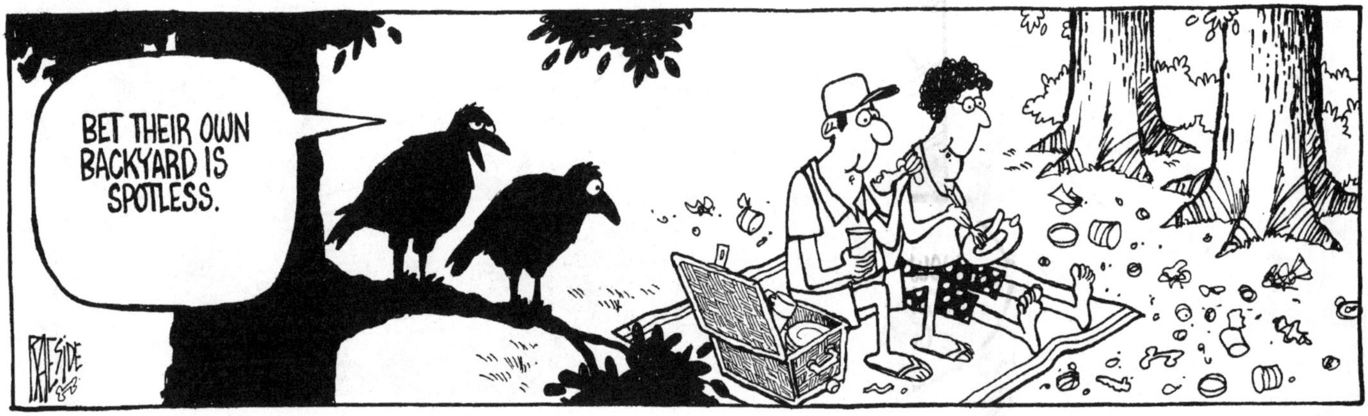
BET THEIR OWN BACKYARD IS SPOTLESS.
RAESIDE

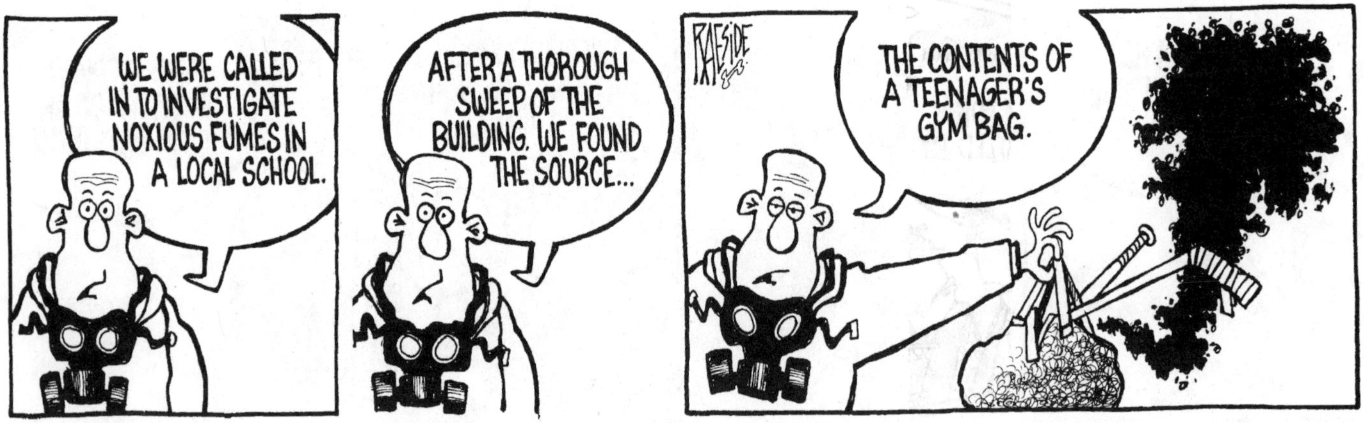
WE WERE CALLED IN TO INVESTIGATE NOXIOUS FUMES IN A LOCAL SCHOOL.
AFTER A THOROUGH SWEEP OF THE BUILDING, WE FOUND THE SOURCE...
RAESIDE
THE CONTENTS OF A TEENAGER'S GYM BAG.

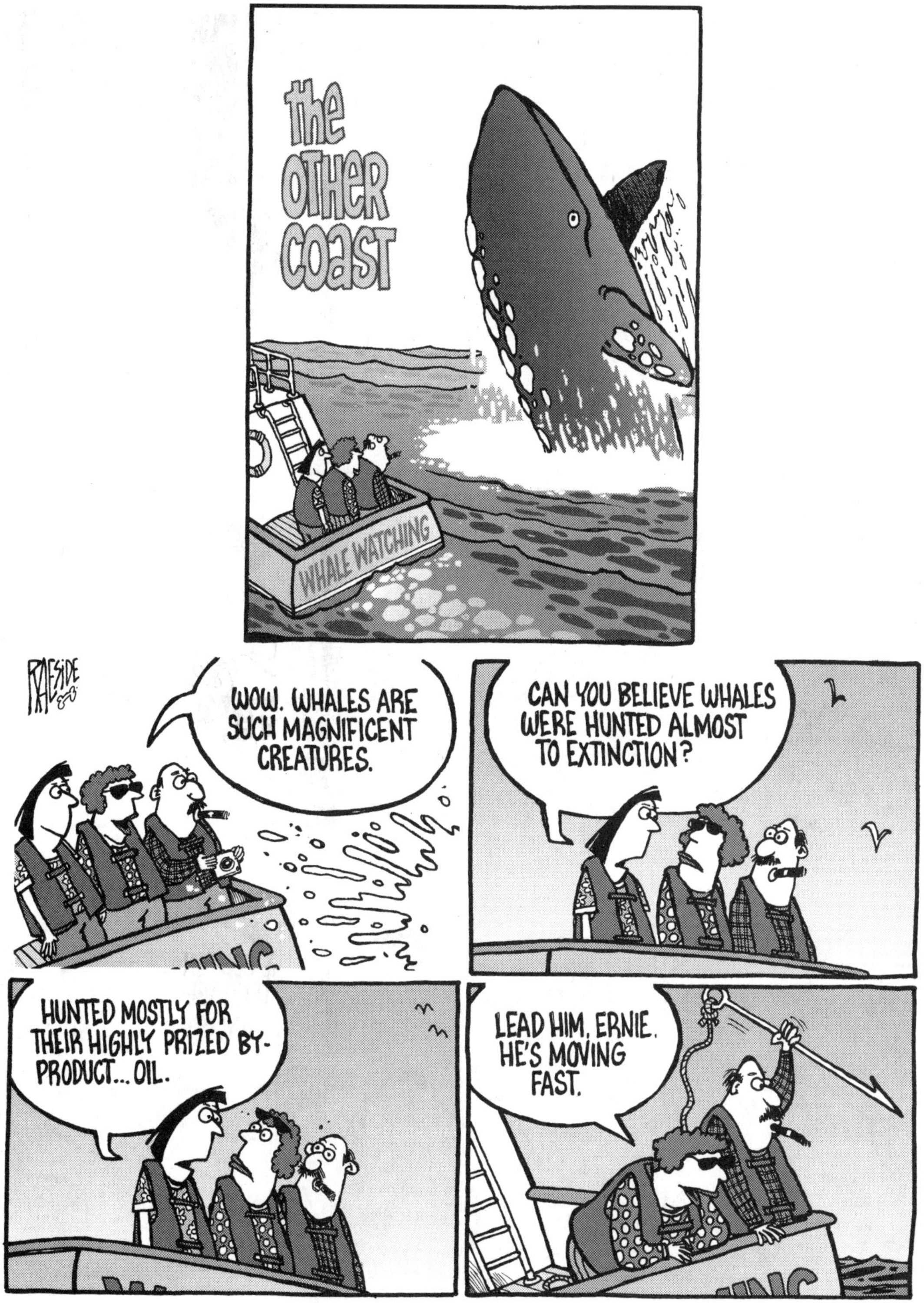
the OTHER COAST
WHALE WATCHING
RAESIDE
WOW. WHALES ARE SUCH MAGNIFICENT CREATURES.
CAN YOU BELIEVE WHALES WERE HUNTED ALMOST TO EXTINCTION?
HUNTED MOSTLY FOR THEIR HIGHLY PRIZED BY-PRODUCT... OIL.
LEAD HIM, ERNIE. HE'S MOVING FAST.

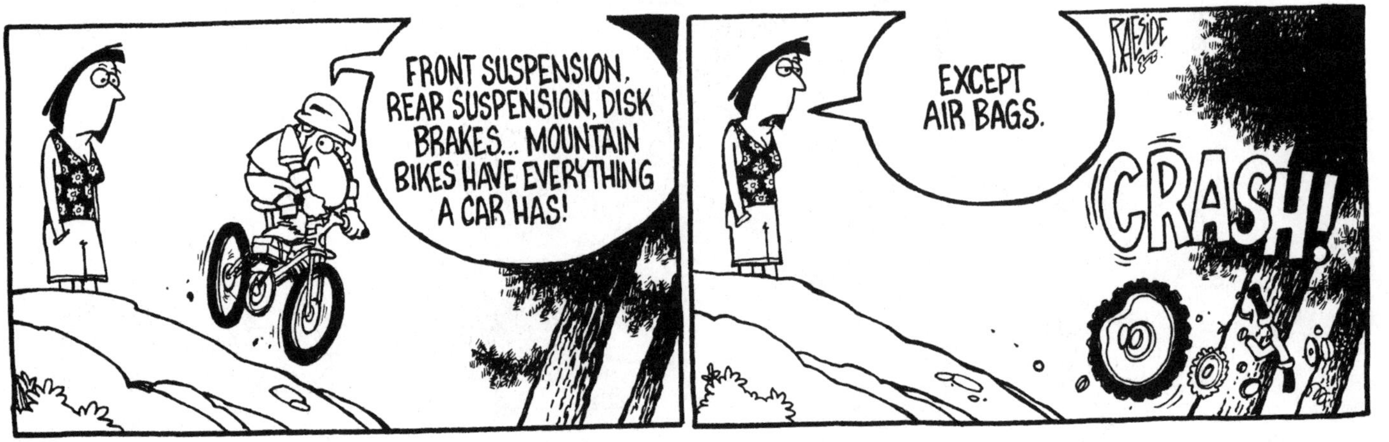
FRONT SUSPENSION, REAR SUSPENSION, DISK BRAKES... MOUNTAIN BIKES HAVE EVERYTHING A CAR HAS!
EXCEPT AIR BAGS.
CRASH!
RAESIDE

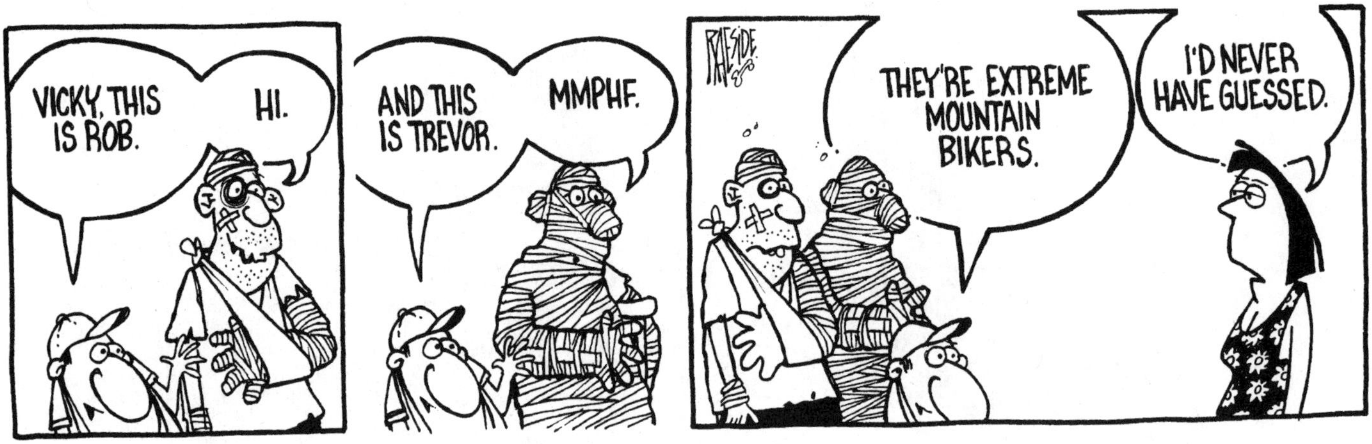
VICKY, THIS IS ROB.
HI.
AND THIS IS TREVOR.
MMPHF.
THEY'RE EXTREME MOUNTAIN BIKERS.
I'D NEVER HAVE GUESSED.
RAESIDE

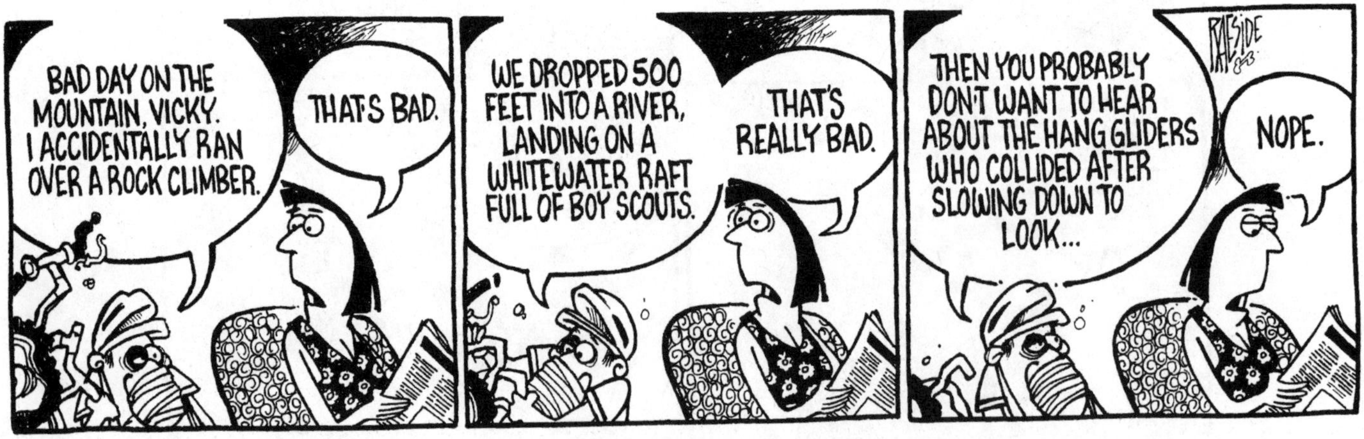
BAD DAY ON THE MOUNTAIN, VICKY. I ACCIDENTALLY RAN OVER A ROCK CLIMBER.
THAT'S BAD.
WE DROPPED 500 FEET INTO A RIVER, LANDING ON A WHITEWATER RAFT FULL OF BOY SCOUTS.
THAT'S REALLY BAD.
THEN YOU PROBABLY DON'T WANT TO HEAR ABOUT THE HANG GLIDERS WHO COLLIDED AFTER SLOWING DOWN TO LOOK...
NOPE.
RAESIDE

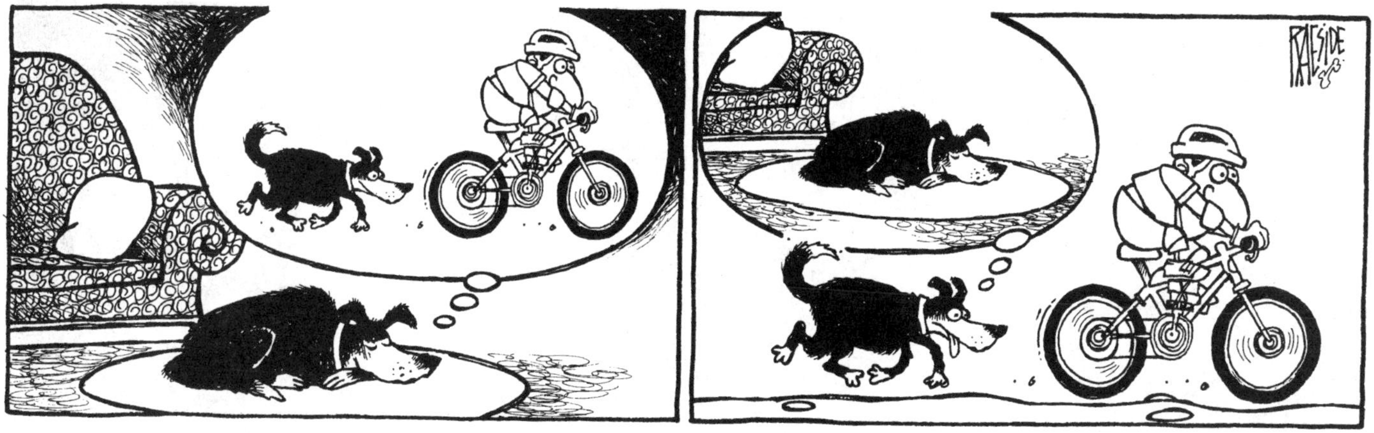

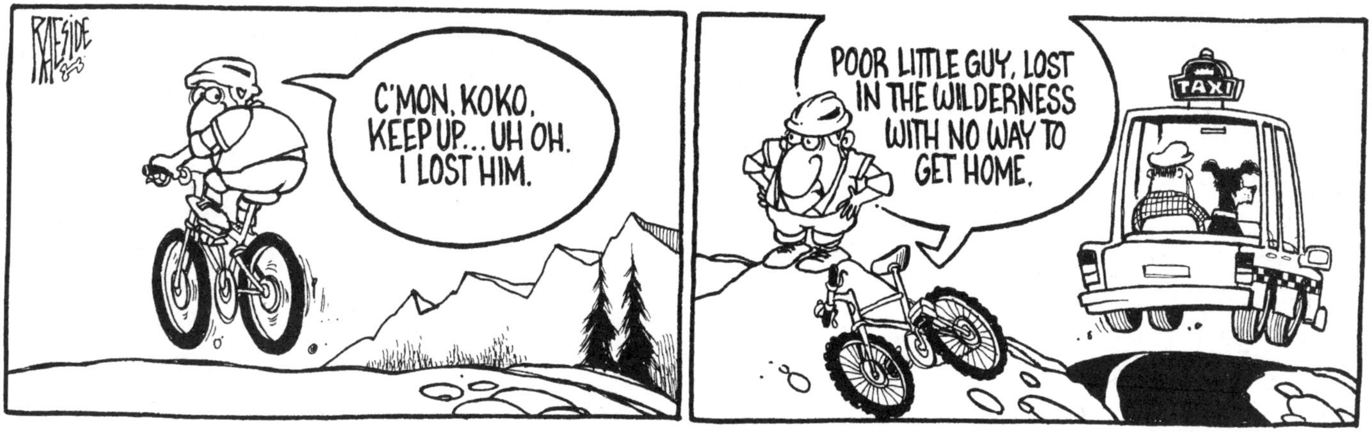
C'MON, KOKO, KEEP UP... UH OH. I LOST HIM.
POOR LITTLE GUY, LOST IN THE WILDERNESS WITH NO WAY TO GET HOME.
TAXI

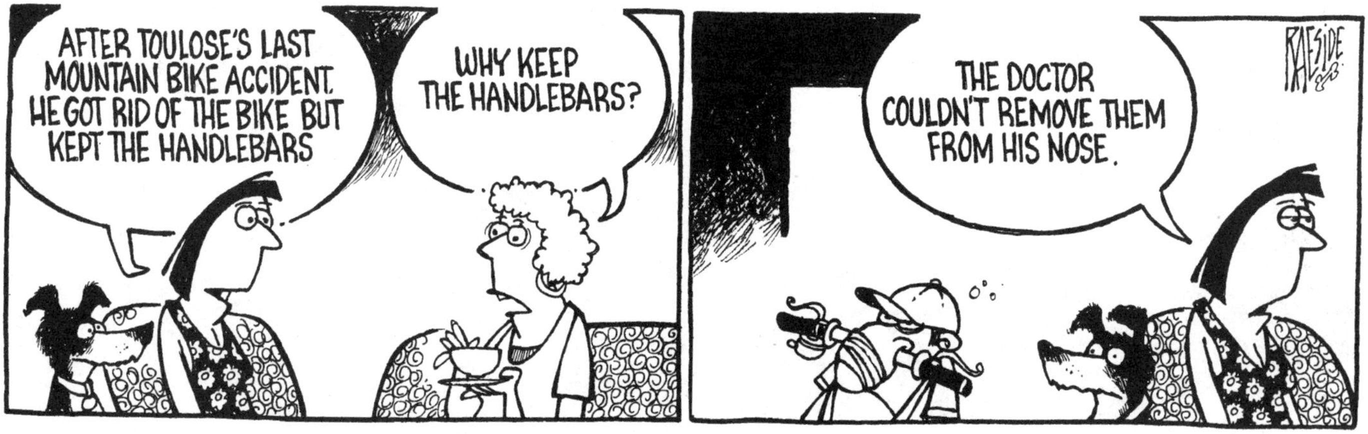
AFTER TOULOSE'S LAST MOUNTAIN BIKE ACCIDENT, HE GOT RID OF THE BIKE BUT KEPT THE HANDLEBARS
WHY KEEP THE HANDLEBARS?
THE DOCTOR COULDN'T REMOVE THEM FROM HIS NOSE.

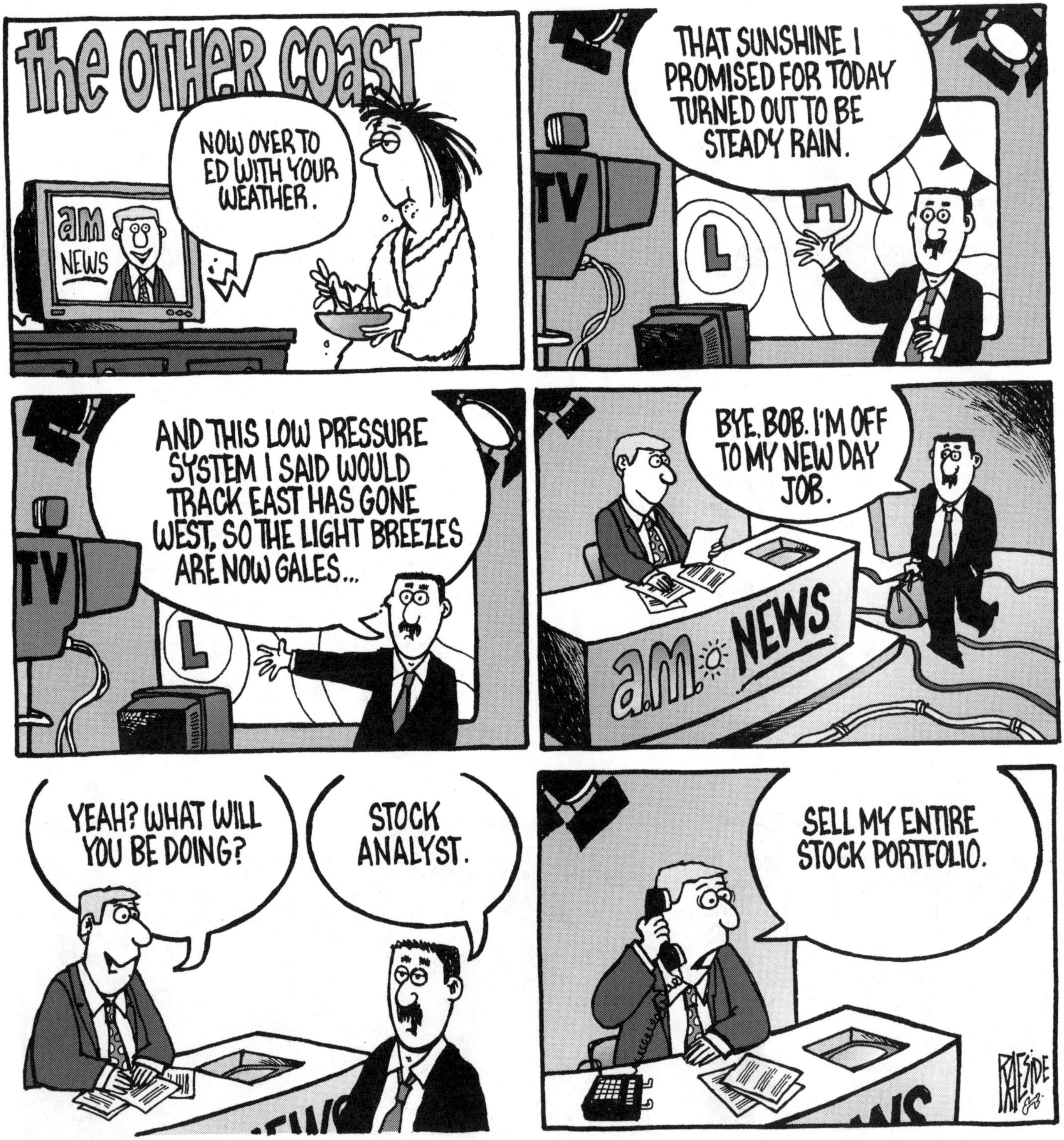
the OTHER COAST
NOW OVER TO ED WITH YOUR WEATHER.
am NEWS
THAT SUNSHINE I PROMISED FOR TODAY TURNED OUT TO BE STEADY RAIN.
TV
AND THIS LOW PRESSURE SYSTEM I SAID WOULD TRACK EAST HAS GONE WEST, SO THE LIGHT BREEZES ARE NOW GALES...
BYE, BOB. I'M OFF TO MY NEW DAY JOB.
a.m. NEWS
YEAH? WHAT WILL YOU BE DOING?
STOCK ANALYST.
SELL MY ENTIRE STOCK PORTFOLIO.
RAESIDE

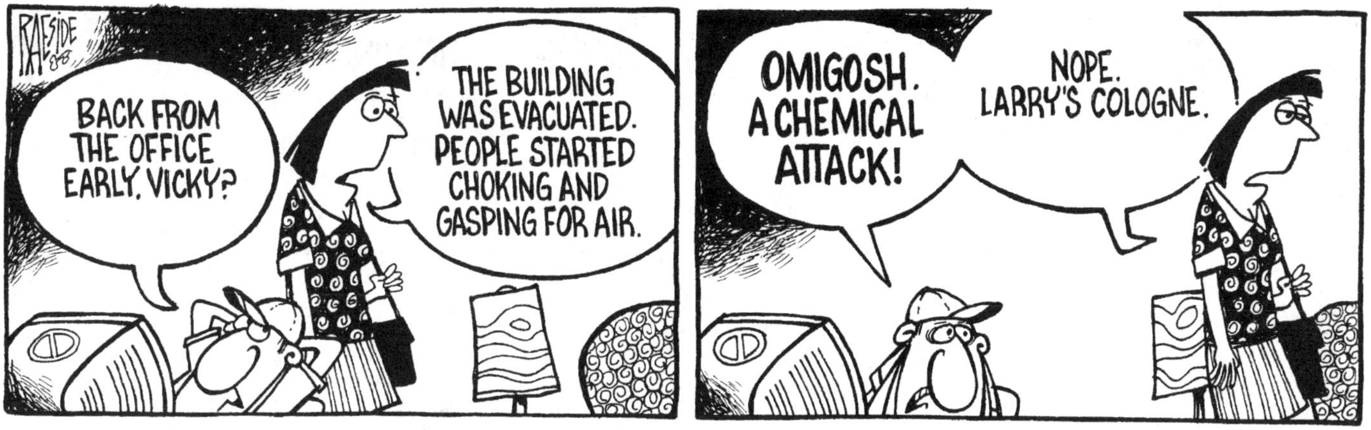
BACK FROM THE OFFICE EARLY, VICKY?
THE BUILDING WAS EVACUATED. PEOPLE STARTED CHOKING AND GASPING FOR AIR.
OMIGOSH. A CHEMICAL ATTACK!
NOPE. LARRY'S COLOGNE.

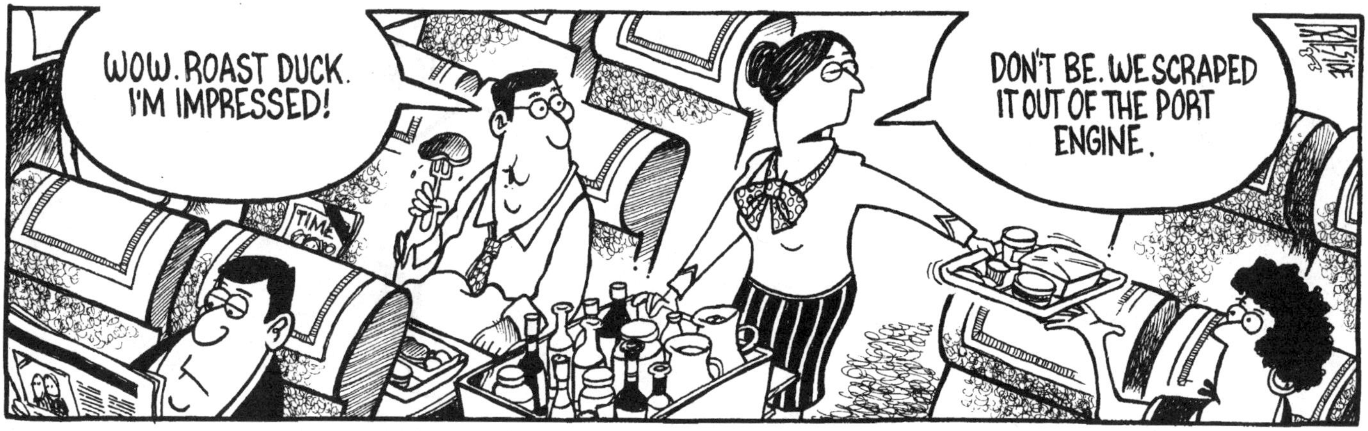
WOW. ROAST DUCK. I'M IMPRESSED!
DON'T BE. WE SCRAPED IT OUT OF THE PORT ENGINE.
TIME

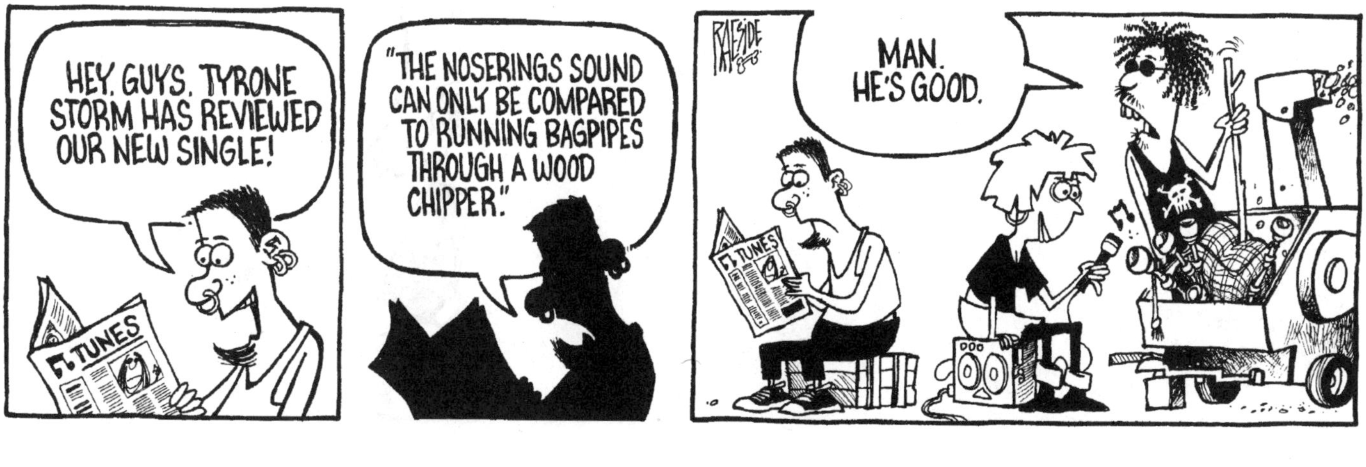
HEY, GUYS. TYRONE STORM HAS REVIEWED OUR NEW SINGLE!
TUNES
"THE NOSERINGS SOUND CAN ONLY BE COMPARED TO RUNNING BAGPIPES THROUGH A WOOD CHIPPER."
MAN. HE'S GOOD.
TUNES

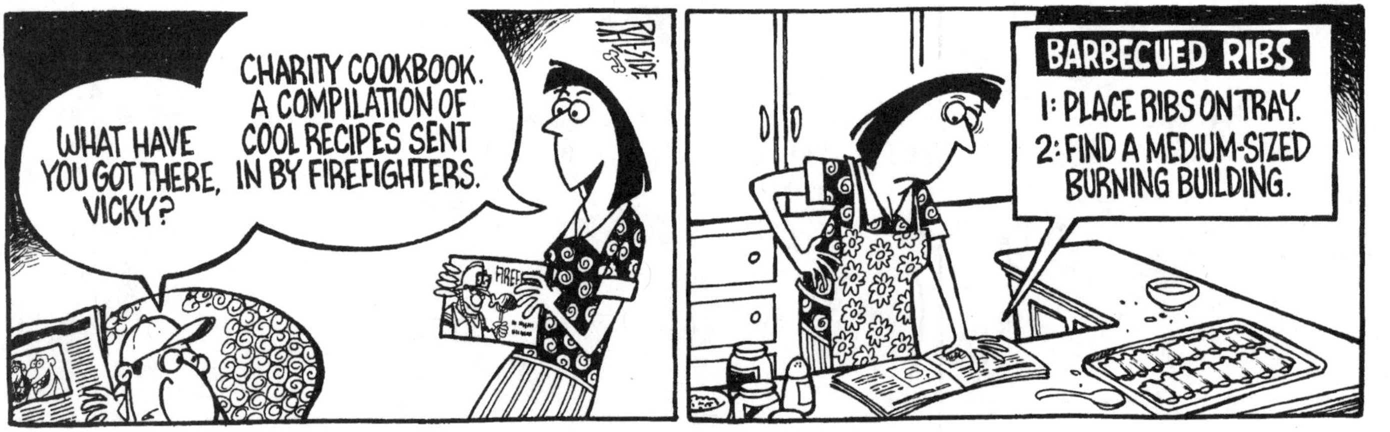
WHAT HAVE YOU GOT THERE, VICKY?
CHARITY COOKBOOK. A COMPILATION OF COOL RECIPES SENT IN BY FIREFIGHTERS.
BARBECUED RIBS
1: PLACE RIBS ON TRAY.
2: FIND A MEDIUM-SIZED BURNING BUILDING.

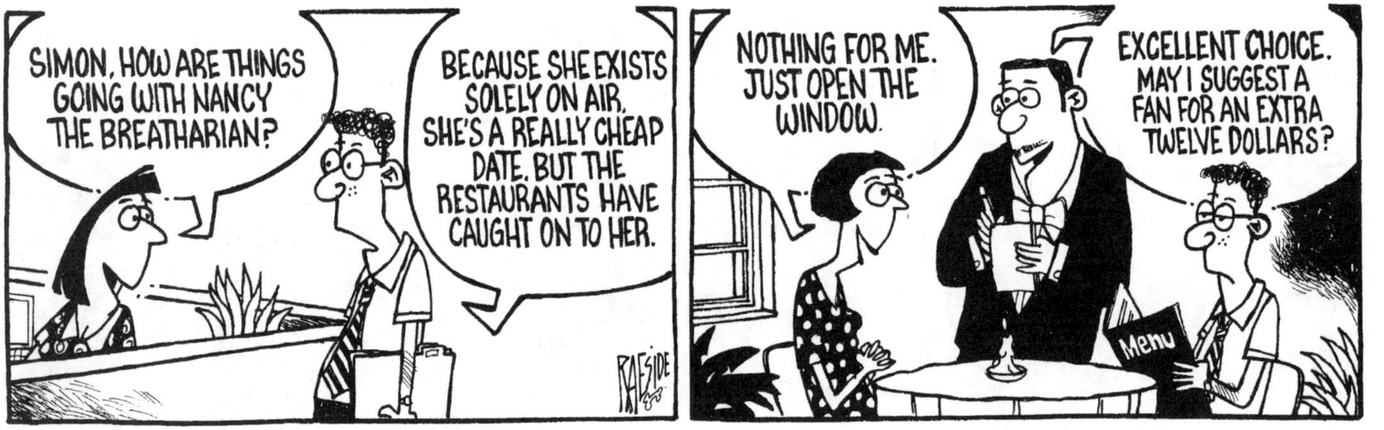
SIMON, HOW ARE THINGS GOING WITH NANCY THE BREATHARIAN?
BECAUSE SHE EXISTS SOLELY ON AIR, SHE'S A REALLY CHEAP DATE. BUT THE RESTAURANTS HAVE CAUGHT ON TO HER.
NOTHING FOR ME. JUST OPEN THE WINDOW.
EXCELLENT CHOICE. MAY I SUGGEST A FAN FOR AN EXTRA TWELVE DOLLARS?
Menu

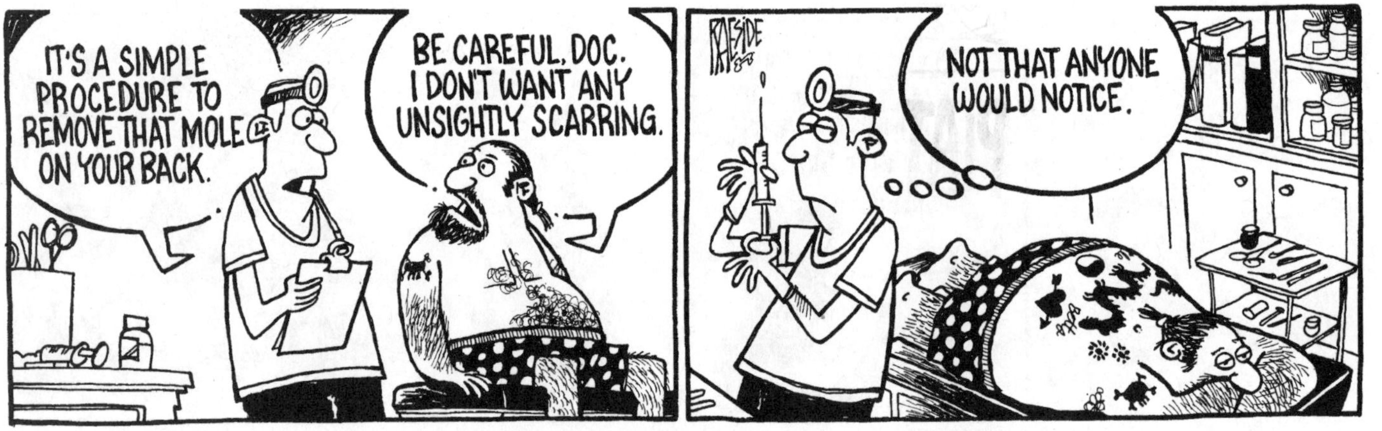
IT'S A SIMPLE PROCEDURE TO REMOVE THAT MOLE ON YOUR BACK.
BE CAREFUL, DOC. I DON'T WANT ANY UNSIGHTLY SCARRING.
NOT THAT ANYONE WOULD NOTICE.

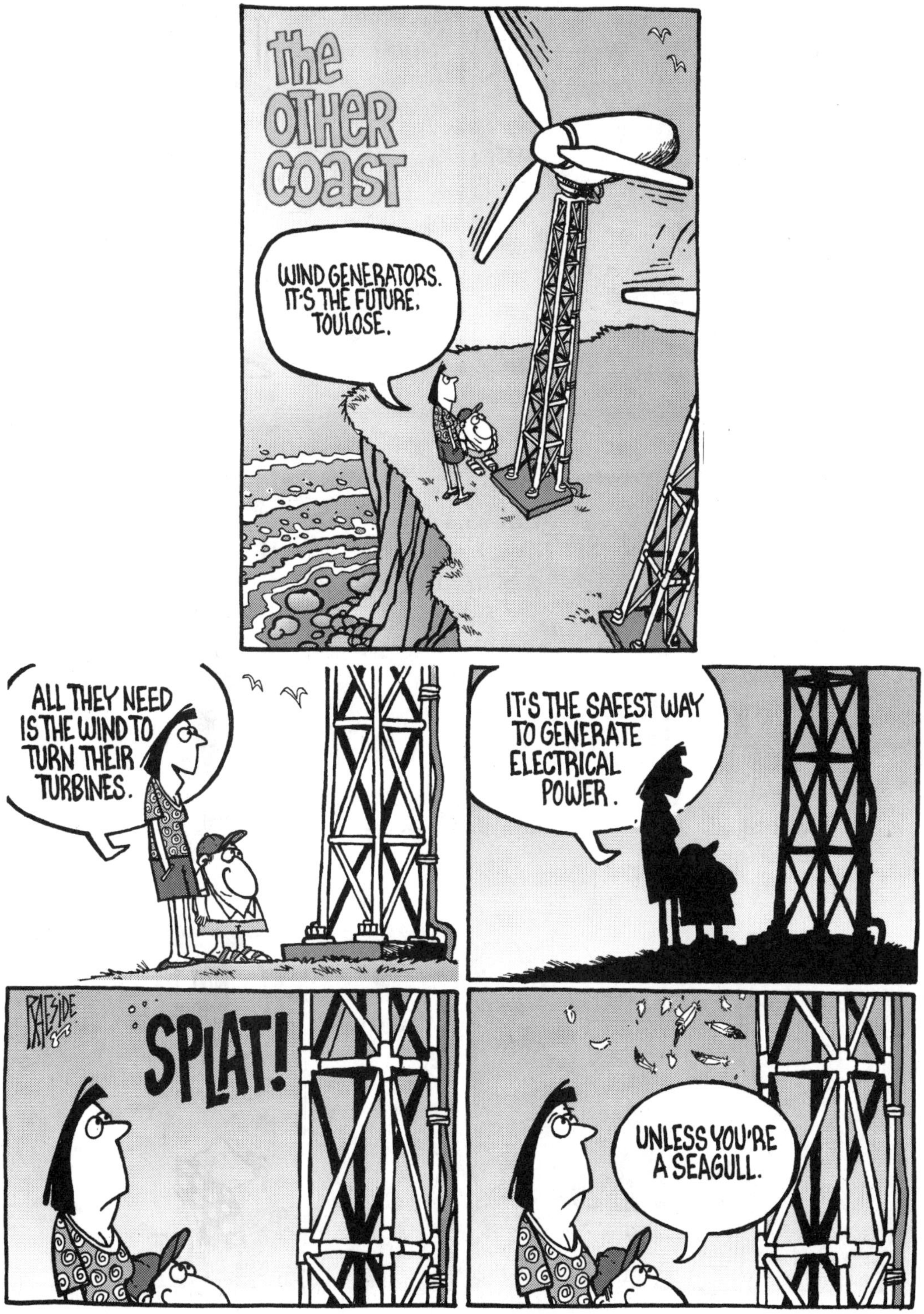
the OTHER COAST
WIND GENERATORS. IT'S THE FUTURE, TOULOSE.
ALL THEY NEED IS THE WIND TO TURN THEIR TURBINES.
IT'S THE SAFEST WAY TO GENERATE ELECTRICAL POWER.
SPLAT!
UNLESS YOU'RE A SEAGULL.

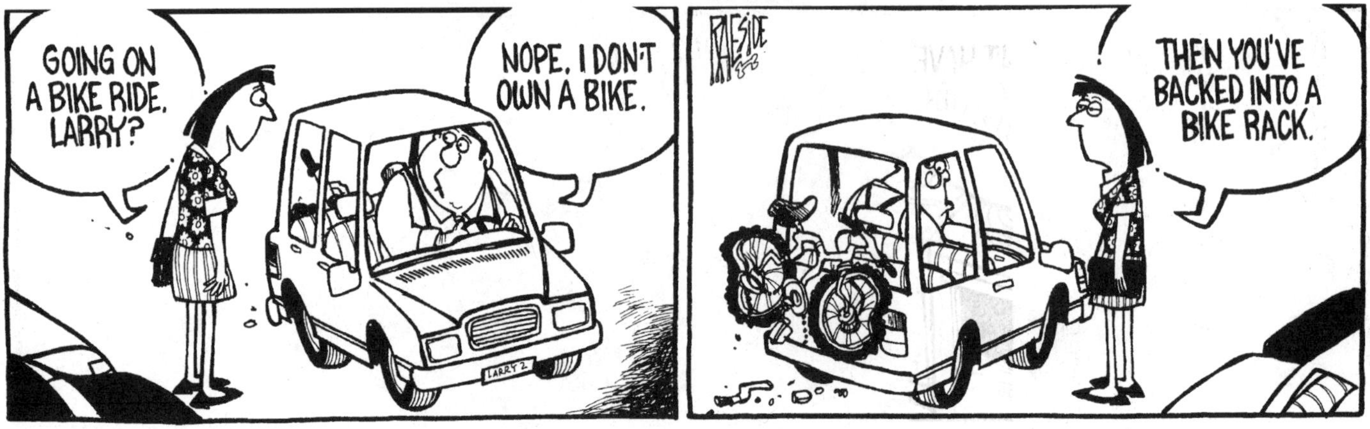
GOING ON A BIKE RIDE, LARRY?
NOPE, I DON'T OWN A BIKE.
THEN YOU'VE BACKED INTO A BIKE RACK.

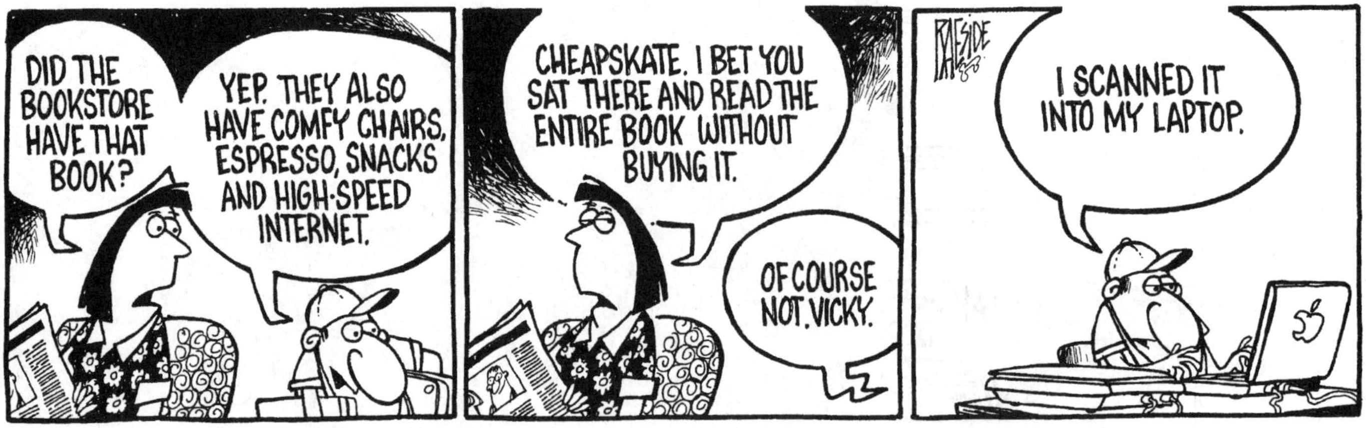
DID THE BOOKSTORE HAVE THAT BOOK?
YEP. THEY ALSO HAVE COMFY CHAIRS, ESPRESSO, SNACKS AND HIGH-SPEED INTERNET.
CHEAPSKATE. I BET YOU SAT THERE AND READ THE ENTIRE BOOK WITHOUT BUYING IT.
OF COURSE NOT, VICKY.
I SCANNED IT INTO MY LAPTOP.

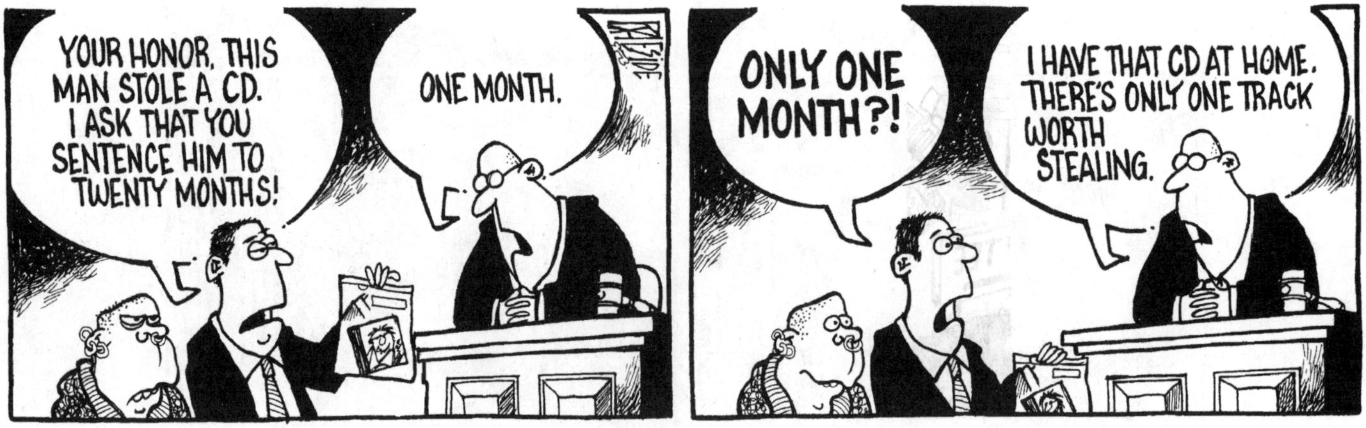
YOUR HONOR, THIS MAN STOLE A CD. I ASK THAT YOU SENTENCE HIM TO TWENTY MONTHS!
ONE MONTH.
ONLY ONE MONTH?!
I HAVE THAT CD AT HOME. THERE'S ONLY ONE TRACK WORTH STEALING.

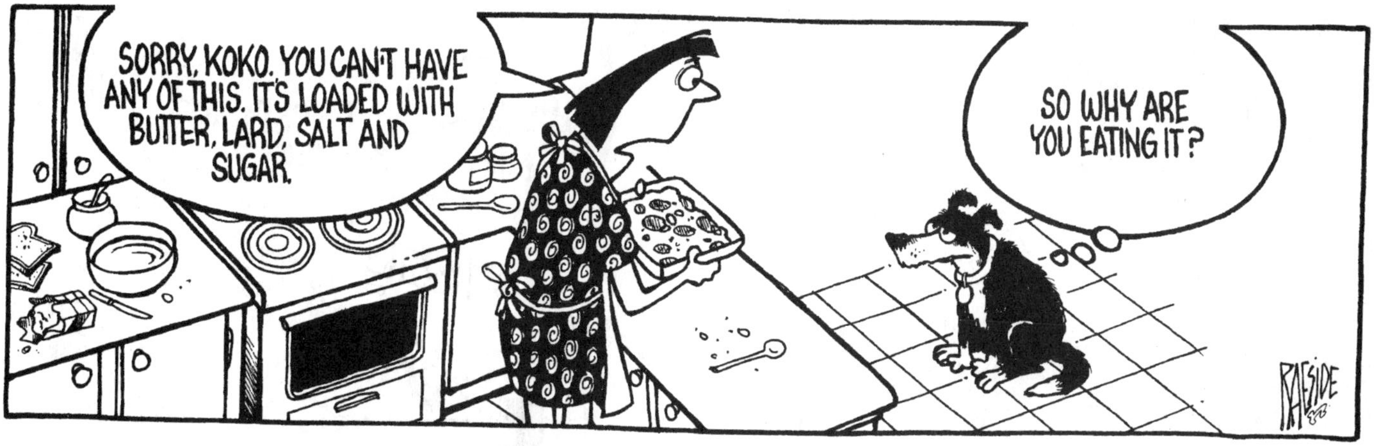
SORRY, KOKO. YOU CAN'T HAVE ANY OF THIS. IT'S LOADED WITH BUTTER, LARD, SALT AND SUGAR.
SO WHY ARE YOU EATING IT?

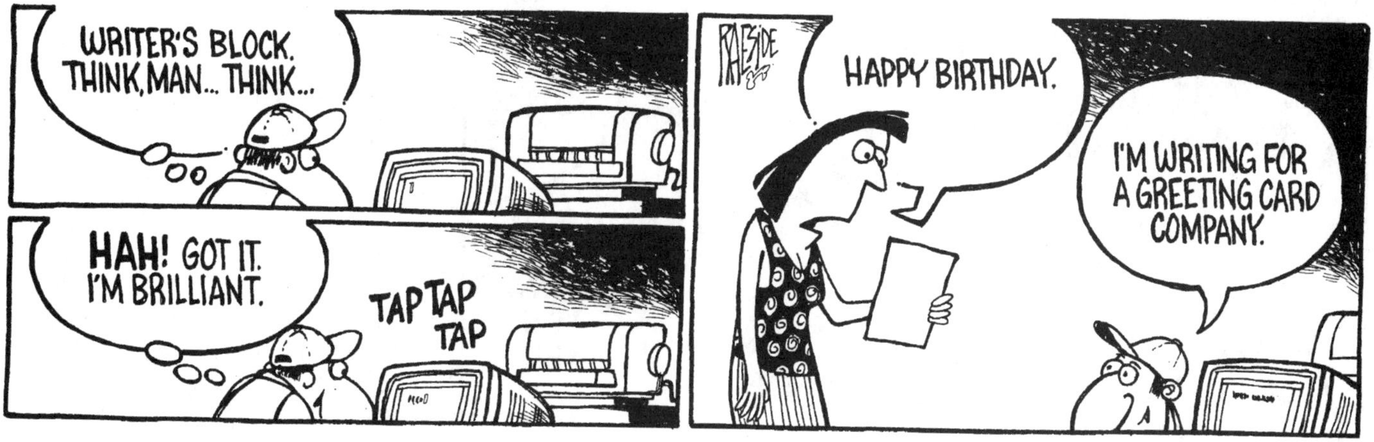
WRITER'S BLOCK. THINK, MAN... THINK...
HAH! GOT IT. I'M BRILLIANT.
TAP TAP TAP
HAPPY BIRTHDAY.
I'M WRITING FOR A GREETING CARD COMPANY.

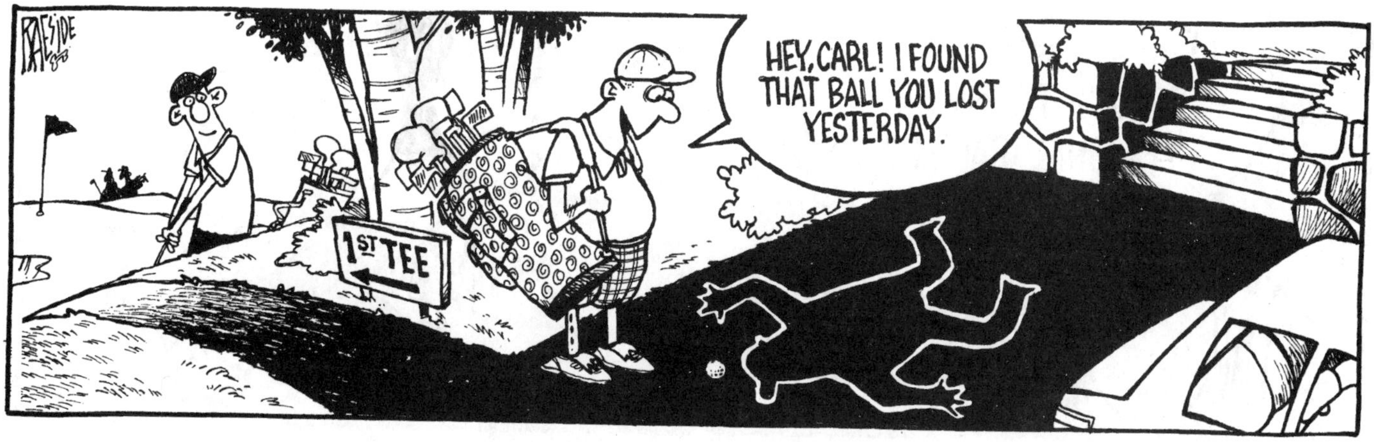
1ST TEE
HEY, CARL! I FOUND THAT BALL YOU LOST YESTERDAY.

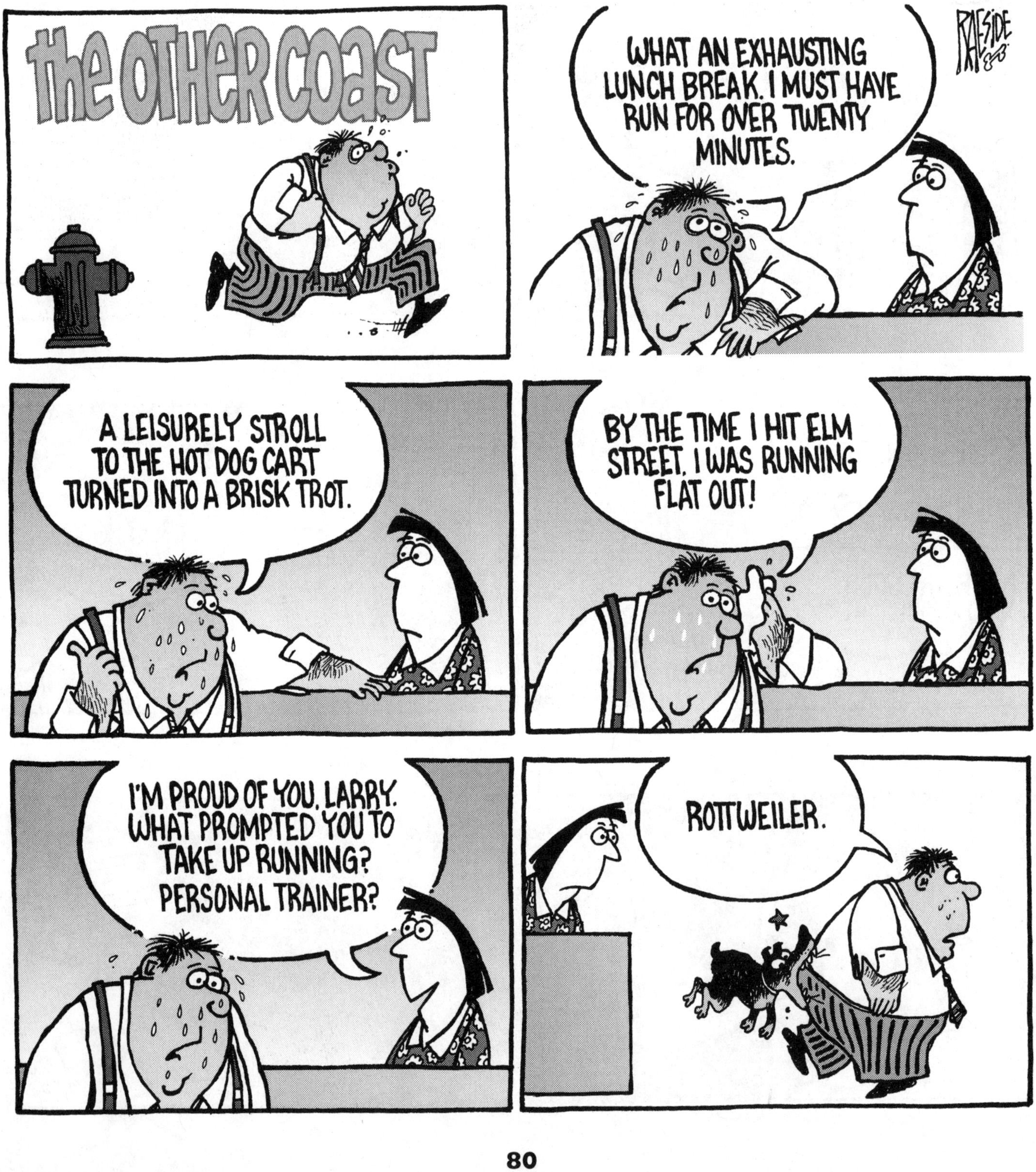
the OTHER COAST
RAESIDE
WHAT AN EXHAUSTING LUNCH BREAK. I MUST HAVE RUN FOR OVER TWENTY MINUTES.
A LEISURELY STROLL TO THE HOT DOG CART TURNED INTO A BRISK TROT.
BY THE TIME I HIT ELM STREET, I WAS RUNNING FLAT OUT!
I'M PROUD OF YOU, LARRY. WHAT PROMPTED YOU TO TAKE UP RUNNING? PERSONAL TRAINER?
ROTTWEILER.

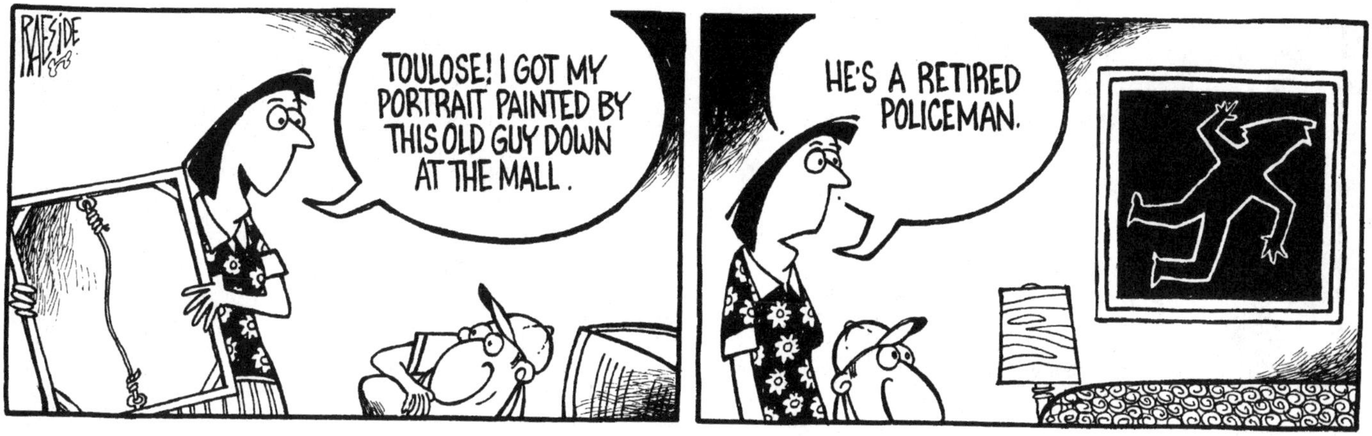
RAESIDE
TOULOSE! I GOT MY PORTRAIT PAINTED BY THIS OLD GUY DOWN AT THE MALL.
HE'S A RETIRED POLICEMAN.

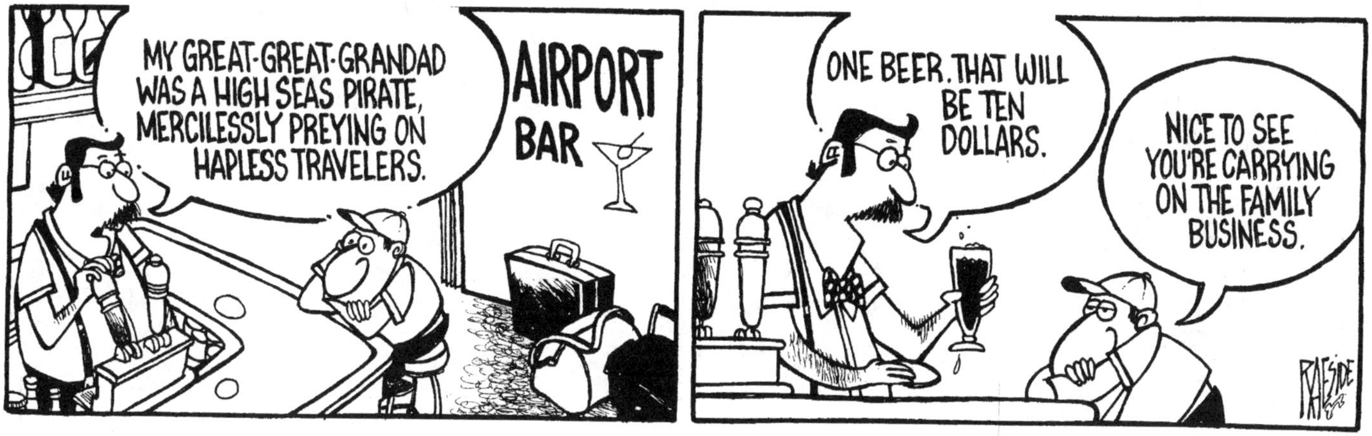
MY GREAT-GREAT-GRANDAD WAS A HIGH SEAS PIRATE, MERCILESSLY PREYING ON HAPLESS TRAVELERS.
AIRPORT BAR
ONE BEER. THAT WILL BE TEN DOLLARS.
NICE TO SEE YOU'RE CARRYING ON THE FAMILY BUSINESS.
RAESIDE

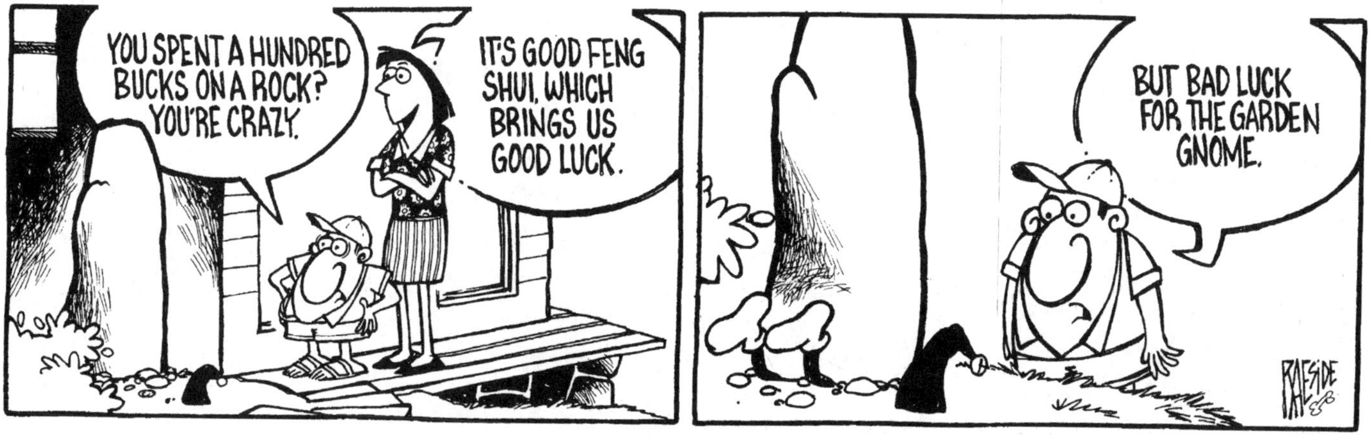
YOU SPENT A HUNDRED BUCKS ON A ROCK? YOU'RE CRAZY.
IT'S GOOD FENG SHUI, WHICH BRINGS US GOOD LUCK.
BUT BAD LUCK FOR THE GARDEN GNOME.
RAESIDE

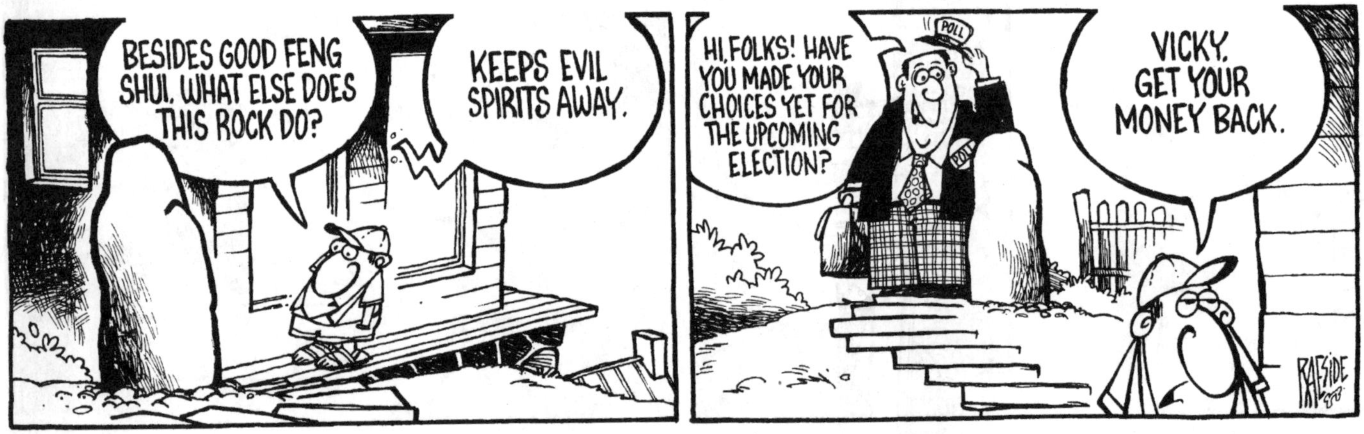
BESIDES GOOD FENG SHUI, WHAT ELSE DOES THIS ROCK DO?
KEEPS EVIL SPIRITS AWAY.
POLL
HI, FOLKS! HAVE YOU MADE YOUR CHOICES YET FOR THE UPCOMING ELECTION?
VICKY, GET YOUR MONEY BACK.
RAESIDE

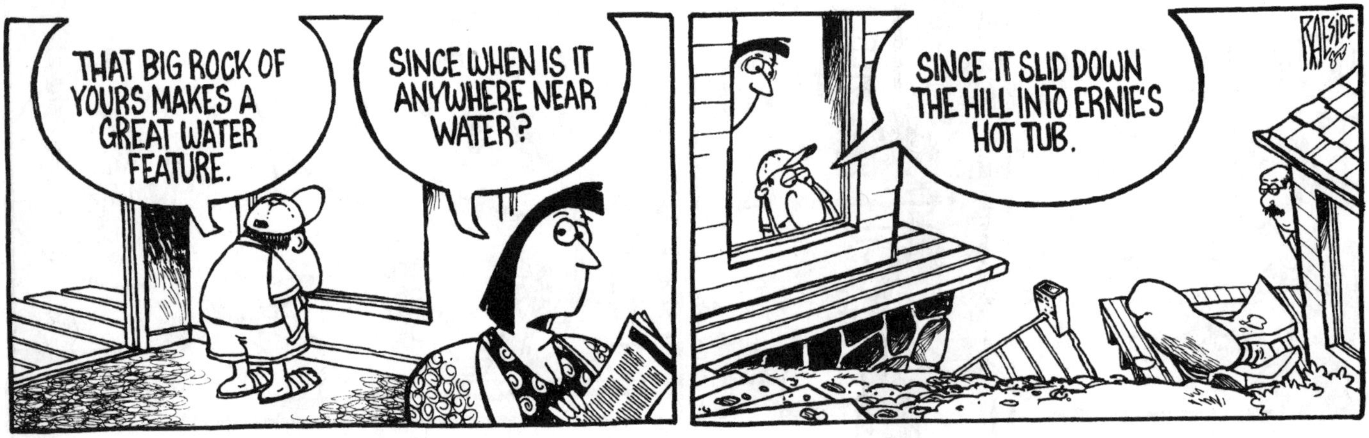
THAT BIG ROCK OF YOURS MAKES A GREAT WATER FEATURE.
SINCE WHEN IS IT ANYWHERE NEAR WATER?
SINCE IT SLID DOWN THE HILL INTO ERNIE'S HOT TUB.
RAESIDE

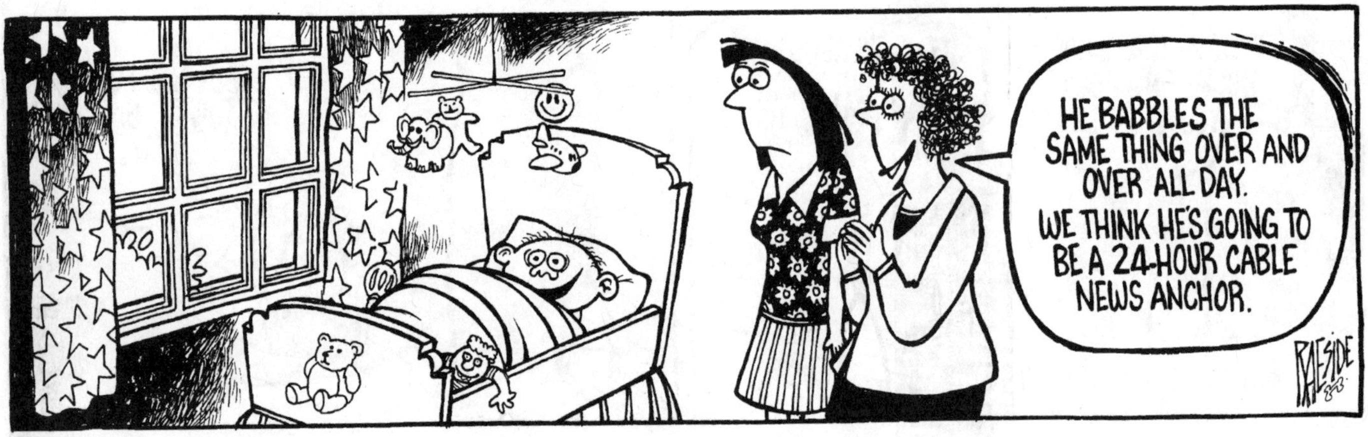
HE BABBLES THE SAME THING OVER AND OVER ALL DAY.
WE THINK HE'S GOING TO BE A 24-HOUR CABLE NEWS ANCHOR.
RAESIDE

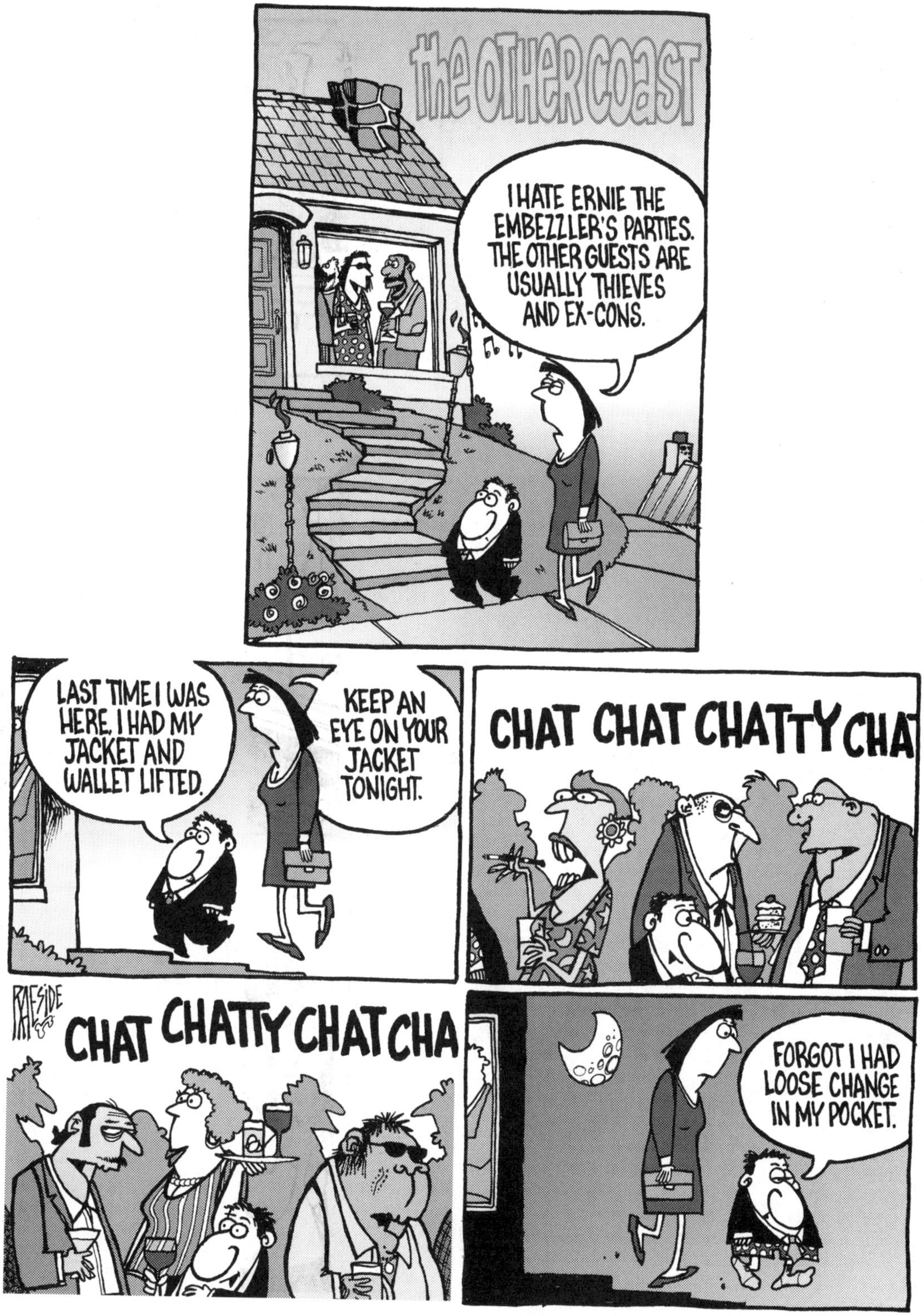
the OTHER COAST
I HATE ERNIE THE EMBEZZLER'S PARTIES. THE OTHER GUESTS ARE USUALLY THIEVES AND EX-CONS.
LAST TIME I WAS HERE, I HAD MY JACKET AND WALLET LIFTED.
KEEP AN EYE ON YOUR JACKET TONIGHT.
CHAT CHAT CHATTY CHA
RAFSIDE
CHAT CHATTY CHAT CHA
FORGOT I HAD LOOSE CHANGE IN MY POCKET.

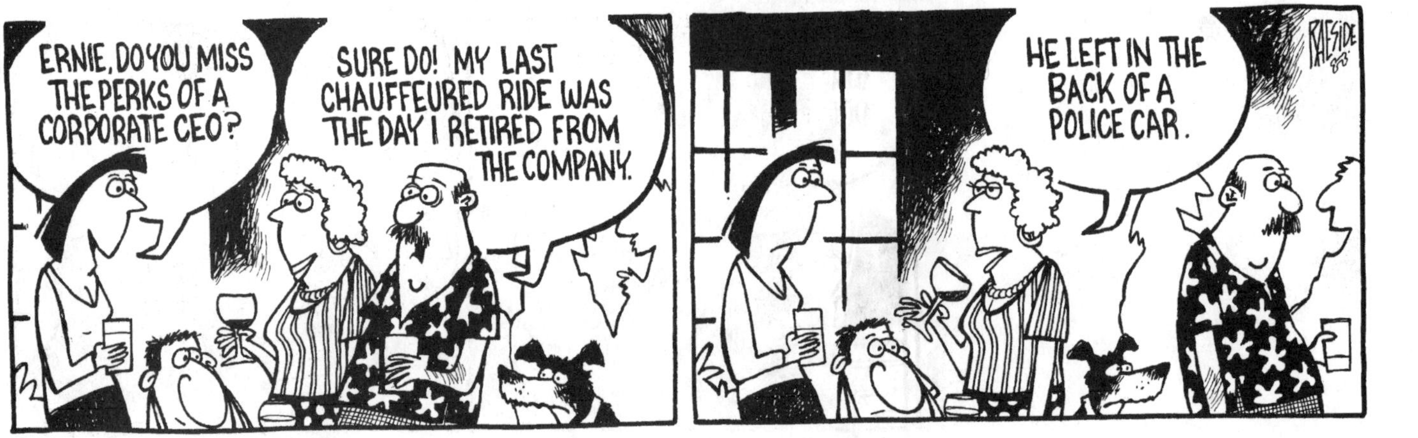
ERNIE, DO YOU MISS THE PERKS OF A CORPORATE CEO?
SURE DO! MY LAST CHAUFFEURED RIDE WAS THE DAY I RETIRED FROM THE COMPANY.
HE LEFT IN THE BACK OF A POLICE CAR.

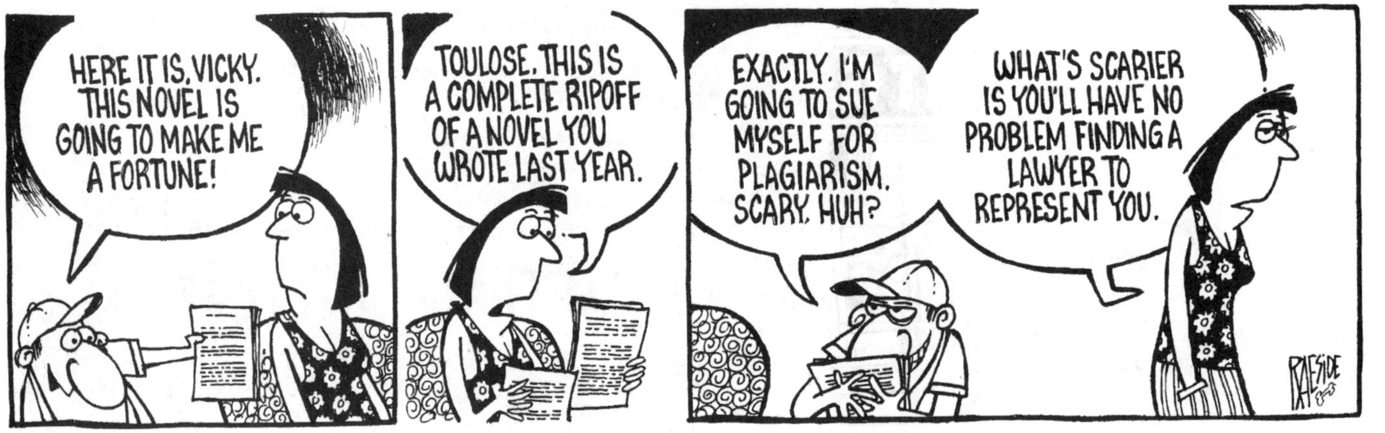
HERE IT IS, VICKY. THIS NOVEL IS GOING TO MAKE ME A FORTUNE!
TOULOSE, THIS IS A COMPLETE RIPOFF OF A NOVEL YOU WROTE LAST YEAR.
EXACTLY. I'M GOING TO SUE MYSELF FOR PLAGIARISM. SCARY, HUH?
WHAT'S SCARIER IS YOU'LL HAVE NO PROBLEM FINDING A LAWYER TO REPRESENT YOU.

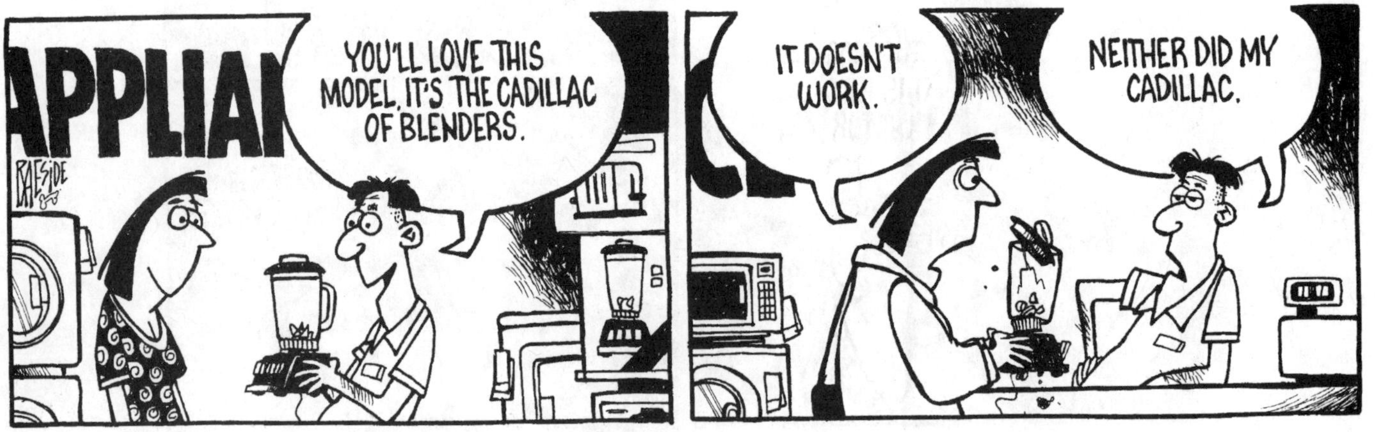
YOU'LL LOVE THIS MODEL. IT'S THE CADILLAC OF BLENDERS.
IT DOESN'T WORK.
NEITHER DID MY CADILLAC.

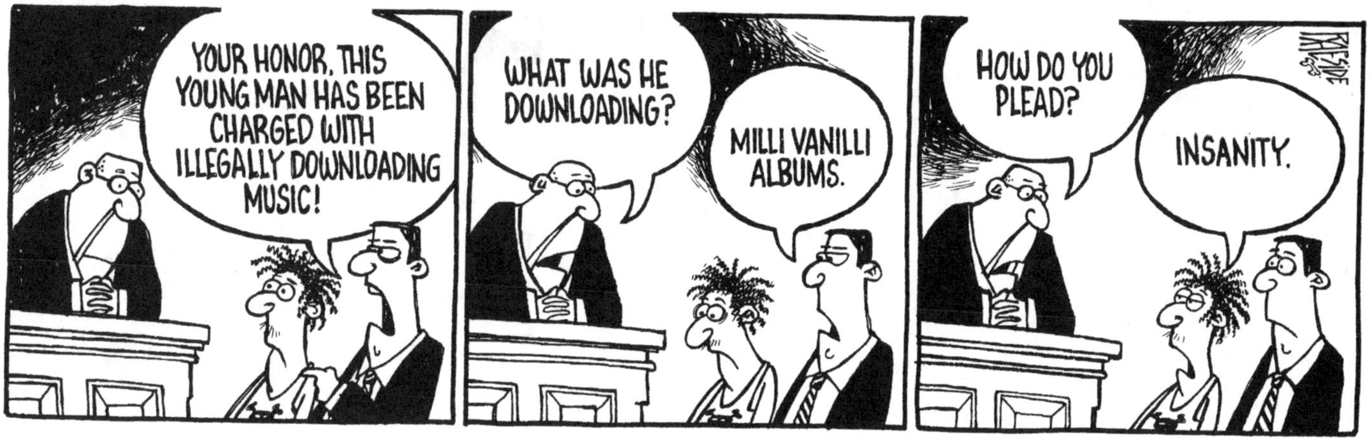
RAESIDE
YOUR HONOR, THIS YOUNG MAN HAS BEEN CHARGED WITH ILLEGALLY DOWNLOADING MUSIC!
WHAT WAS HE DOWNLOADING?
MILLI VANILLI ALBUMS.
HOW DO YOU PLEAD?
INSANITY.

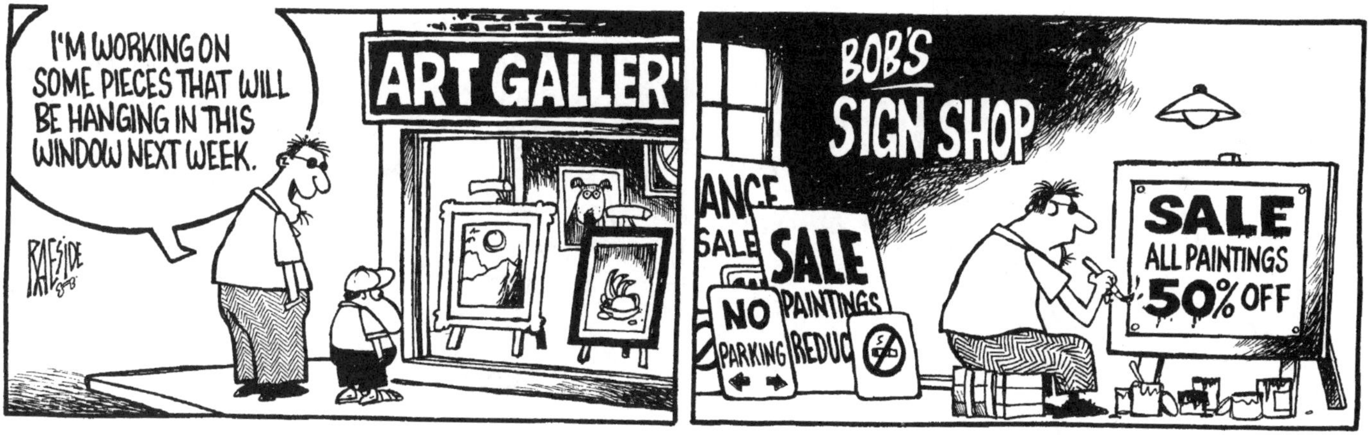
I'M WORKING ON SOME PIECES THAT WILL BE HANGING IN THIS WINDOW NEXT WEEK.
ART GALLER'
RAESIDE
BOB'S SIGN SHOP
ANCE
SALE
SALE
PAINTINGS
REDUC
NO PARKING
SALE ALL PAINTINGS 50% OFF

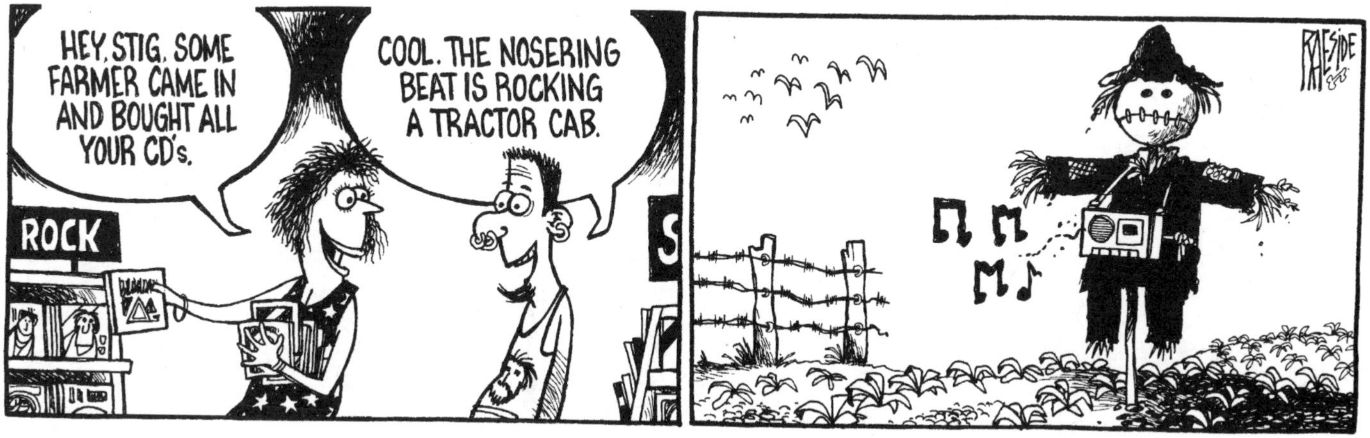
HEY, STIG, SOME FARMER CAME IN AND BOUGHT ALL YOUR CD's.
COOL. THE NOSERING BEAT IS ROCKING A TRACTOR CAB.
ROCK
RAESIDE

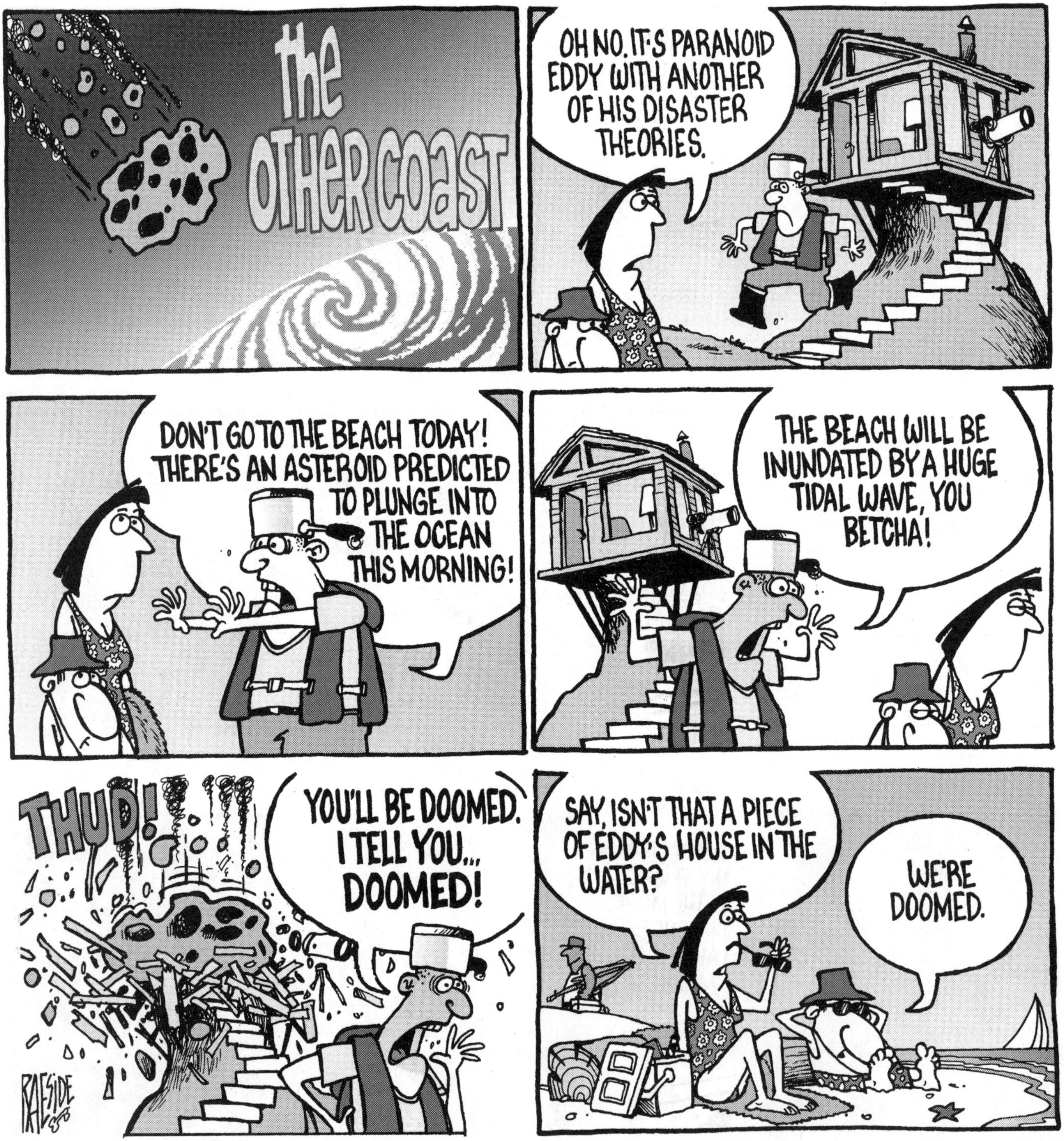
the OTHER COAST
OH NO. IT'S PARANOID EDDY WITH ANOTHER OF HIS DISASTER THEORIES.
DON'T GO TO THE BEACH TODAY! THERE'S AN ASTEROID PREDICTED TO PLUNGE INTO THE OCEAN THIS MORNING!
THE BEACH WILL BE INUNDATED BY A HUGE TIDAL WAVE, YOU BETCHA!
THUD!
YOU'LL BE DOOMED. I TELL YOU... DOOMED!
RAESIDE
SAY, ISN'T THAT A PIECE OF EDDY'S HOUSE IN THE WATER?
WE'RE DOOMED.

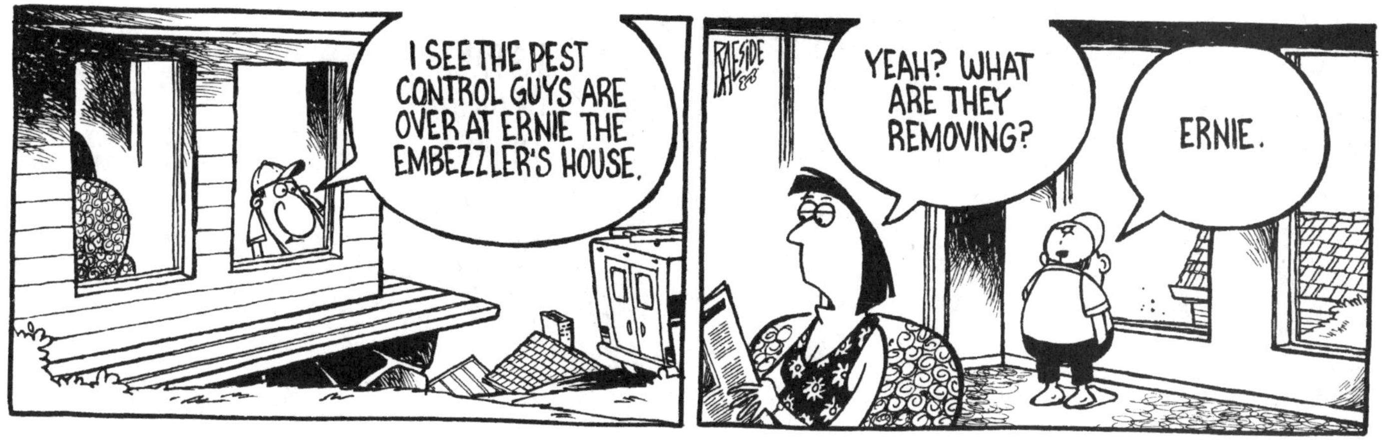
I SEE THE PEST CONTROL GUYS ARE OVER AT ERNIE THE EMBEZZLER'S HOUSE.
YEAH? WHAT ARE THEY REMOVING?
ERNIE.

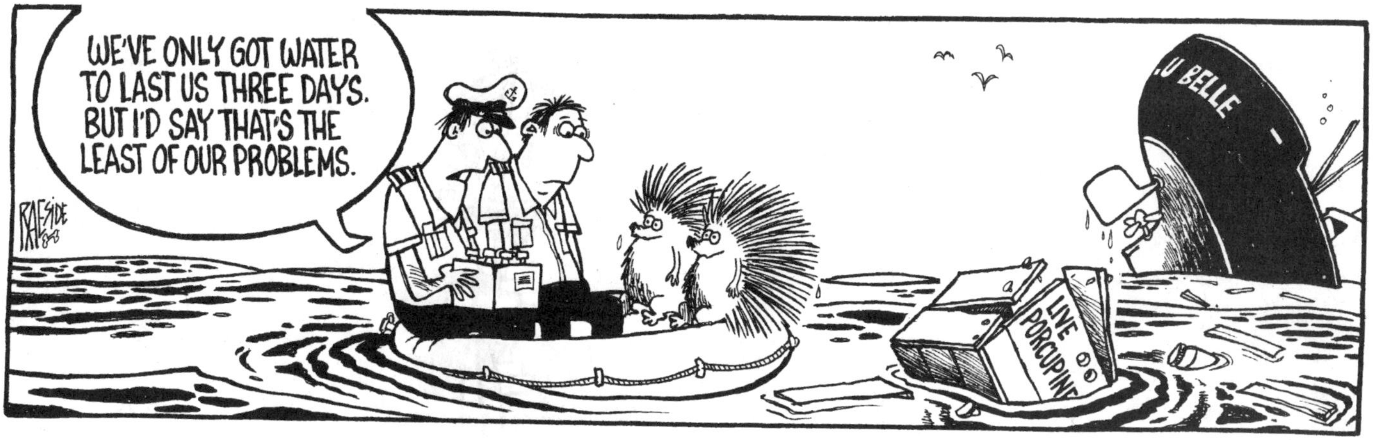
WE'VE ONLY GOT WATER TO LAST US THREE DAYS. BUT I'D SAY THAT'S THE LEAST OF OUR PROBLEMS.
LIVE

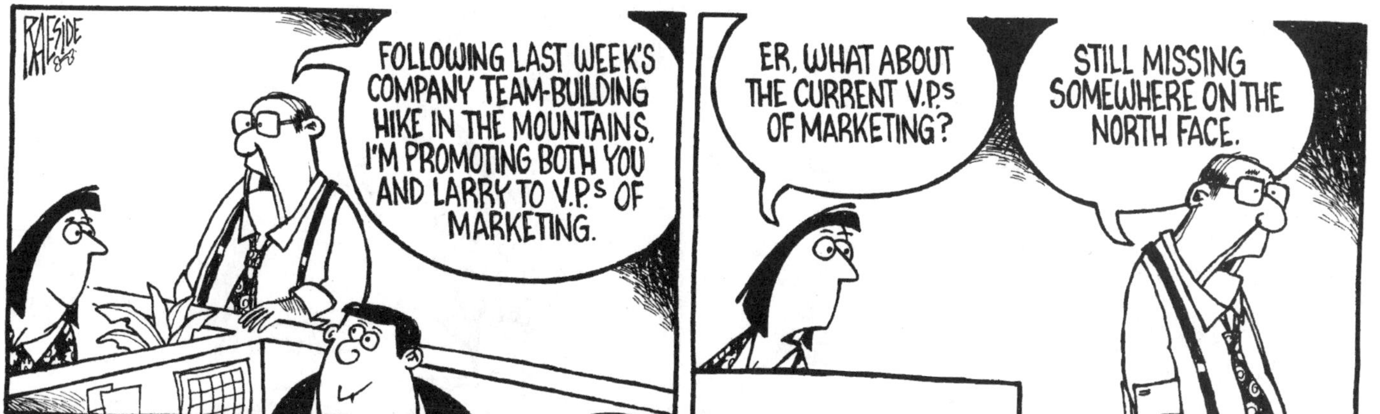
FOLLOWING LAST WEEK'S COMPANY TEAM-BUILDING HIKE IN THE MOUNTAINS, I'M PROMOTING BOTH YOU AND LARRY TO V.P.s OF MARKETING.
ER, WHAT ABOUT THE CURRENT V.P.s OF MARKETING?
STILL MISSING SOMEWHERE ON THE NORTH FACE.

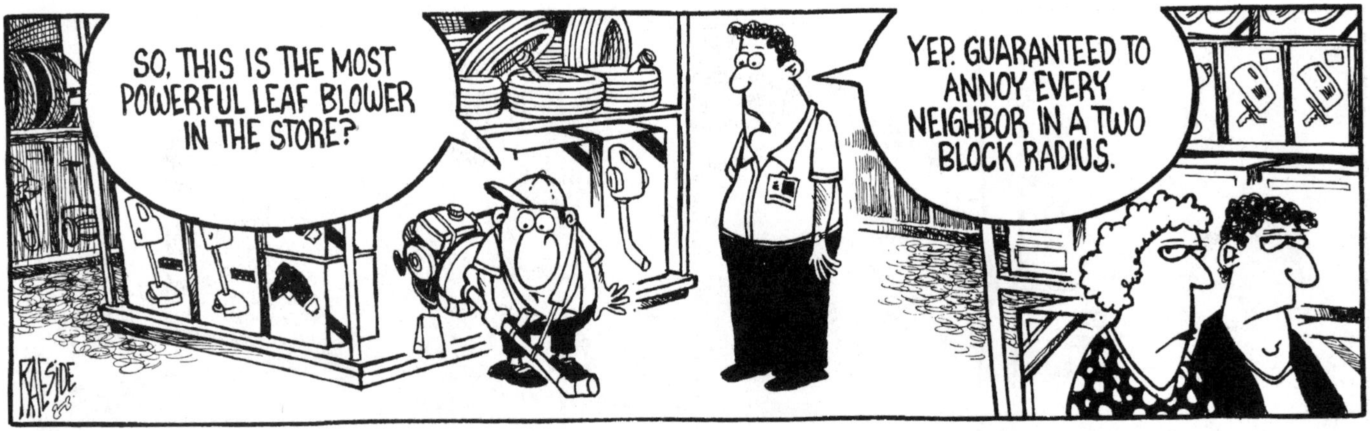
SO, THIS IS THE MOST POWERFUL LEAF BLOWER IN THE STORE?
YEP. GUARANTEED TO ANNOY EVERY NEIGHBOR IN A TWO BLOCK RADIUS.

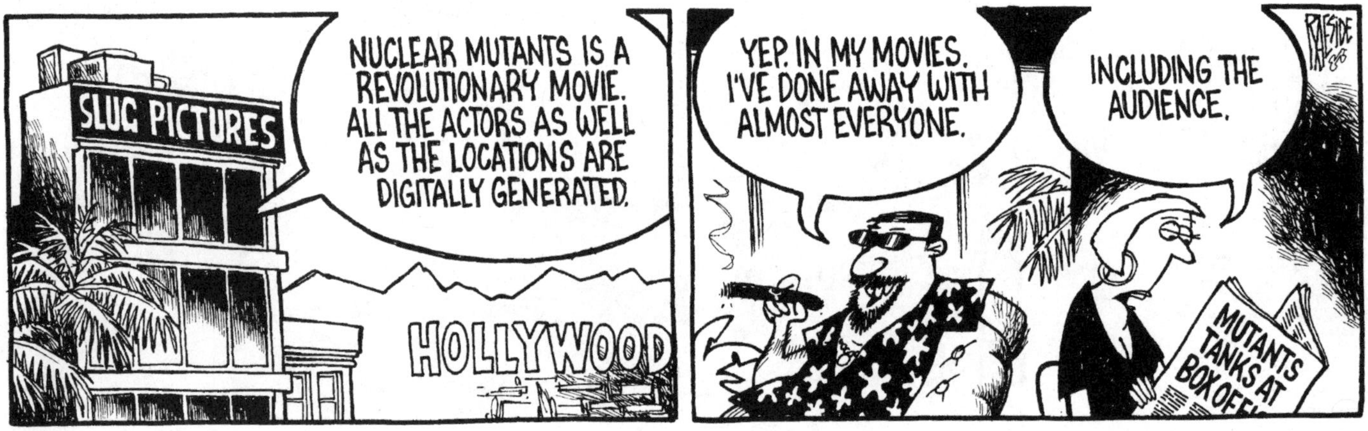
SLUG PICTURES
NUCLEAR MUTANTS IS A REVOLUTIONARY MOVIE. ALL THE ACTORS AS WELL AS THE LOCATIONS ARE DIGITALLY GENERATED.
HOLLYWOOD
YEP. IN MY MOVIES, I'VE DONE AWAY WITH ALMOST EVERYONE.
INCLUDING THE AUDIENCE.
MUTANTS TANKS AT

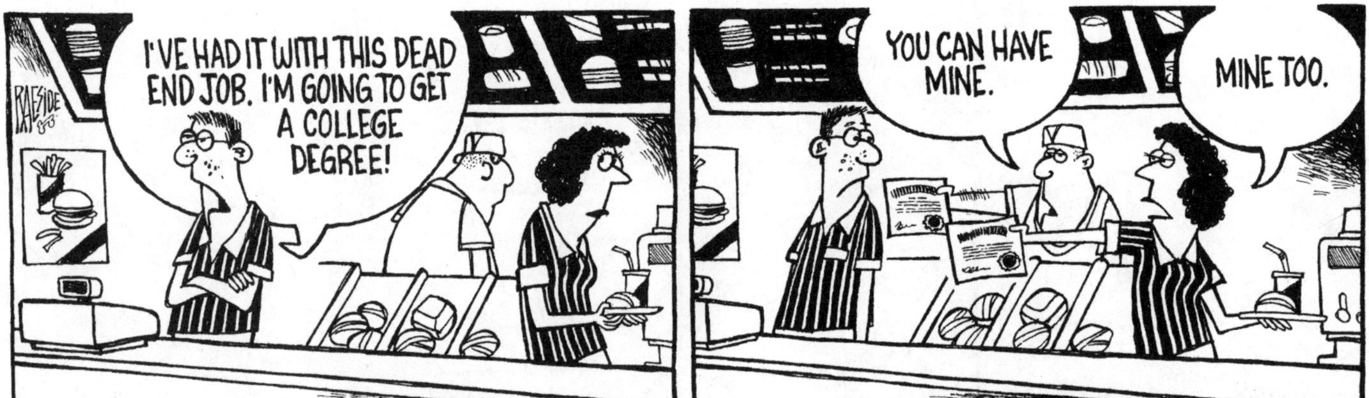
I'VE HAD IT WITH THIS DEAD END JOB. I'M GOING TO GET A COLLEGE DEGREE!
YOU CAN HAVE MINE.
MINE TOO.

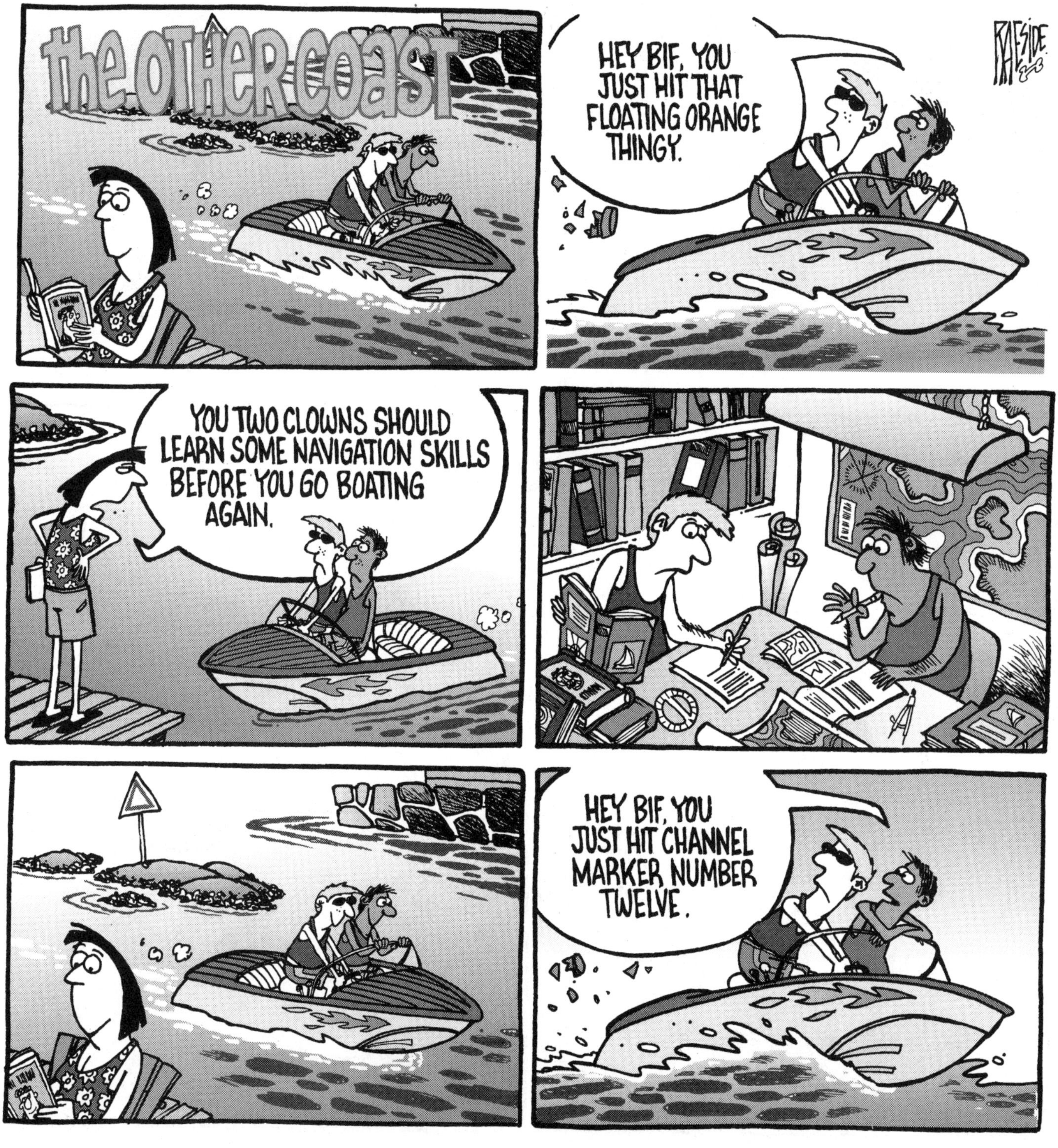
the OTHER COAST
RAESIDE
HEY BIF, YOU JUST HIT THAT FLOATING ORANGE THINGY.
YOU TWO CLOWNS SHOULD LEARN SOME NAVIGATION SKILLS BEFORE YOU GO BOATING AGAIN.
HEY BIF, YOU JUST HIT CHANNEL MARKER NUMBER TWELVE.

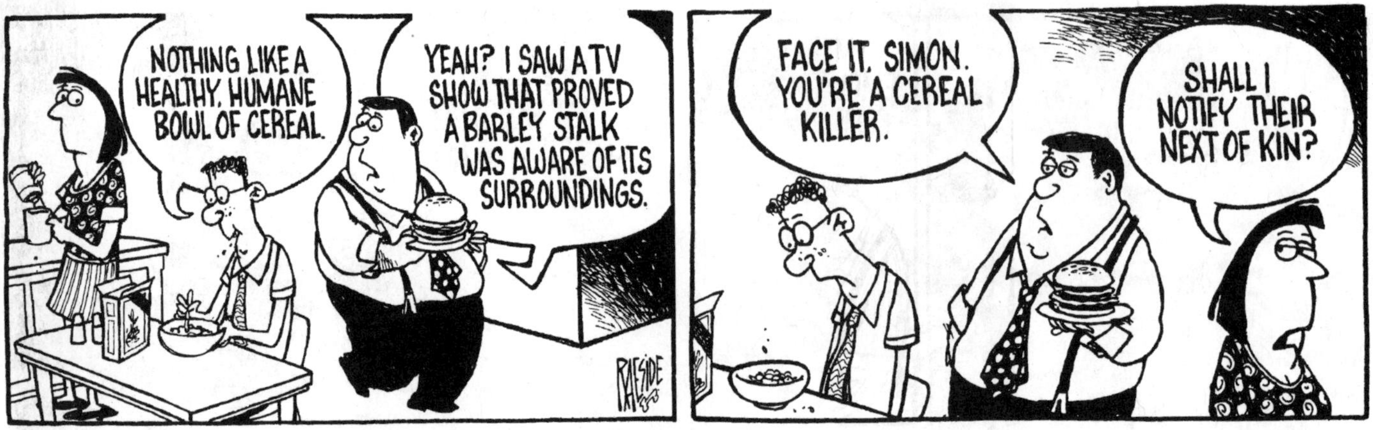
NOTHING LIKE A HEALTHY, HUMANE BOWL OF CEREAL.
YEAH? I SAW A TV SHOW THAT PROVED A BARLEY STALK WAS AWARE OF ITS SURROUNDINGS.
FACE IT, SIMON. YOU'RE A CEREAL KILLER.
SHALL I NOTIFY THEIR NEXT OF KIN?

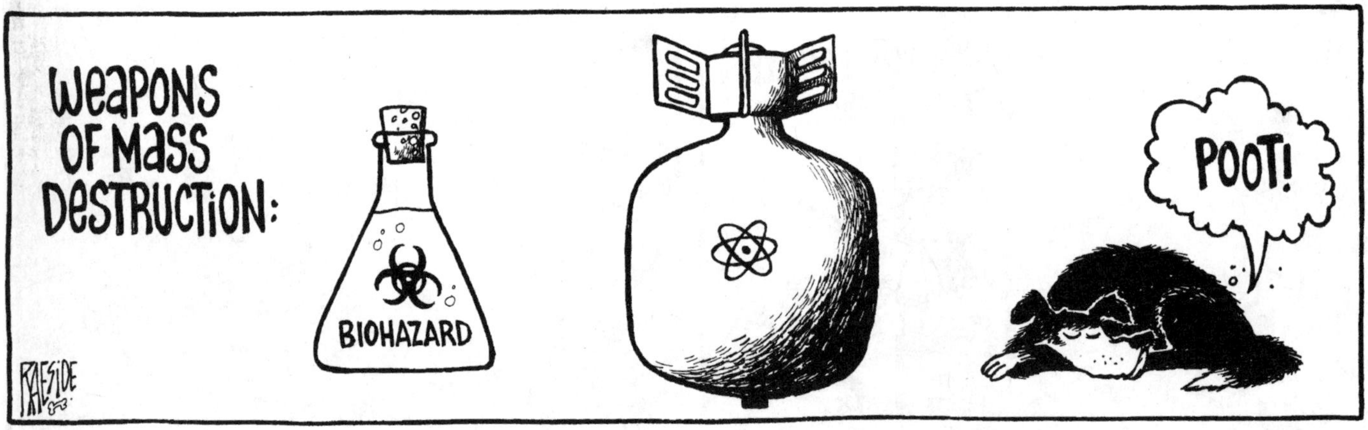
WEAPONS OF MASS DESTRUCTION:
BIOHAZARD
POOT!

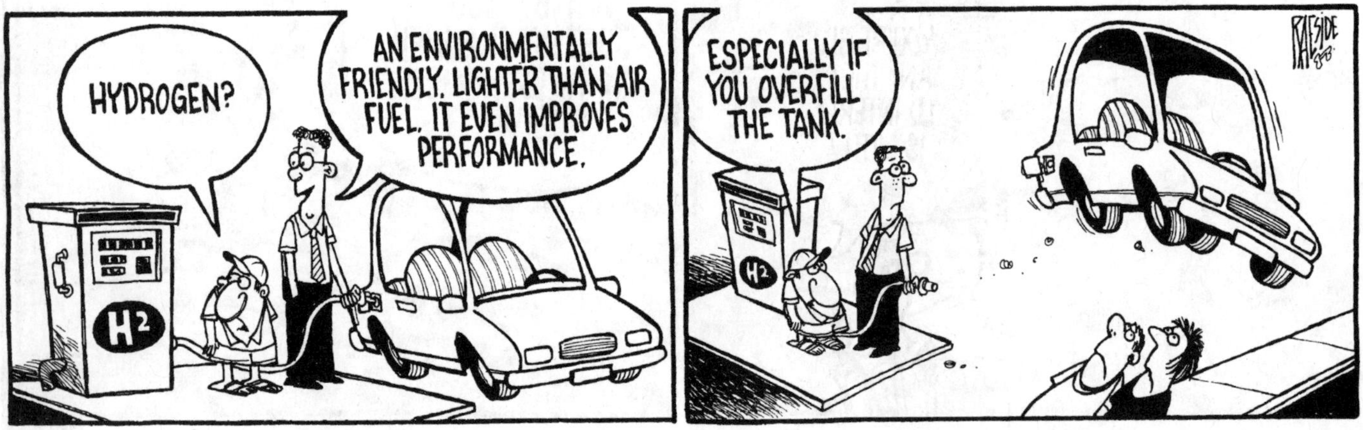
HYDROGEN?
AN ENVIRONMENTALLY FRIENDLY, LIGHTER THAN AIR FUEL. IT EVEN IMPROVES PERFORMANCE.
ESPECIALLY IF YOU OVERFILL THE TANK.

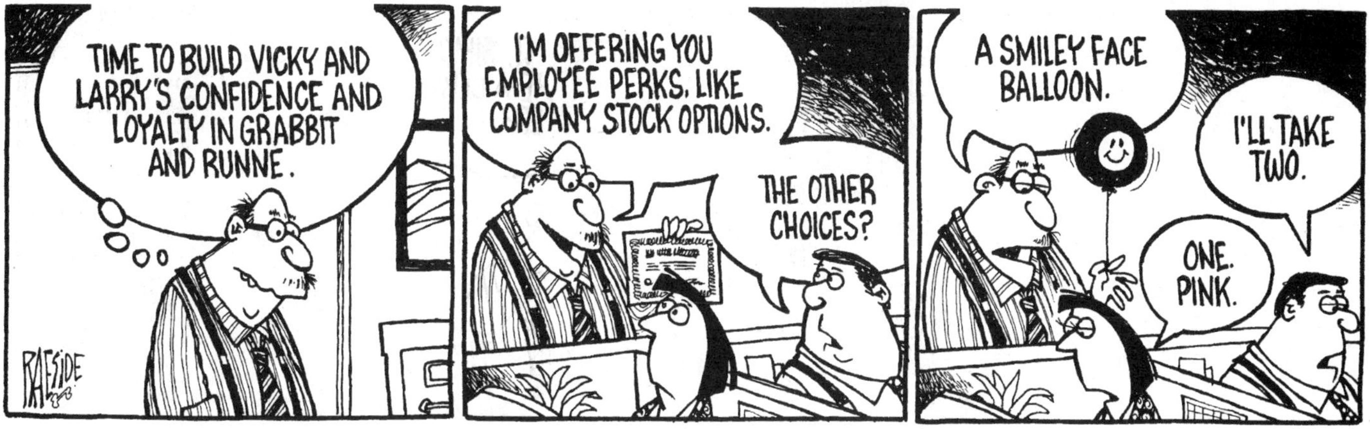
TIME TO BUILD VICKY AND LARRY'S CONFIDENCE AND LOYALTY IN GRABBIT AND RUNNE.
I'M OFFERING YOU EMPLOYEE PERKS, LIKE COMPANY STOCK OPTIONS.
THE OTHER CHOICES?
A SMILEY FACE BALLOON.
I'LL TAKE TWO.
ONE. PINK.

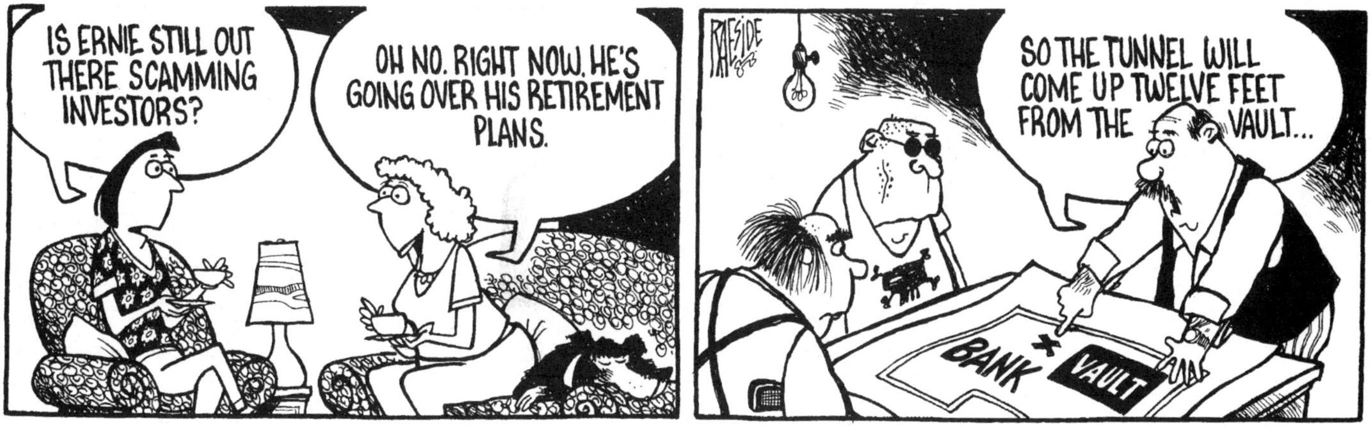
IS ERNIE STILL OUT THERE SCAMMING INVESTORS?
OH NO. RIGHT NOW, HE'S GOING OVER HIS RETIREMENT PLANS.
SO THE TUNNEL WILL COME UP TWELVE FEET FROM THE VAULT...
BANK
VAULT

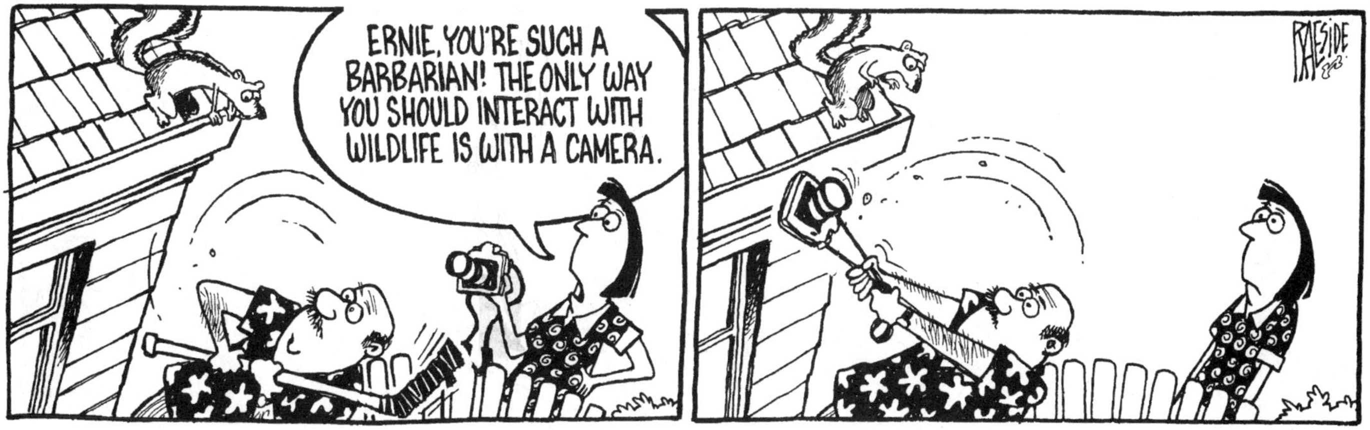
ERNIE, YOU'RE SUCH A BARBARIAN! THE ONLY WAY YOU SHOULD INTERACT WITH WILDLIFE IS WITH A CAMERA.

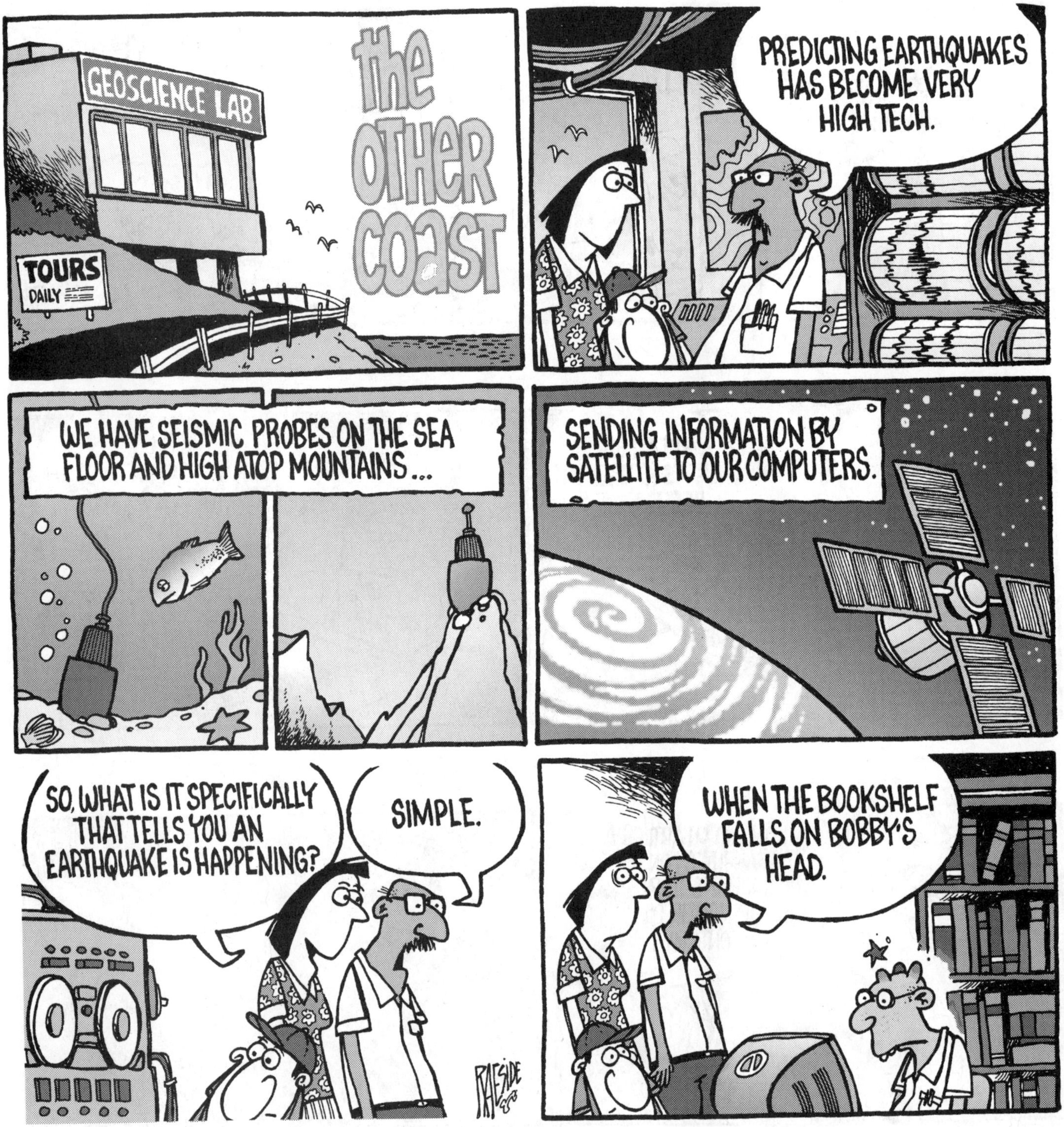
GEOSCIENCE LAB
the OTHER COAST
TOURS DAILY
PREDICTING EARTHQUAKES HAS BECOME VERY HIGH TECH.
WE HAVE SEISMIC PROBES ON THE SEA FLOOR AND HIGH ATOP MOUNTAINS...
SENDING INFORMATION BY SATELLITE TO OUR COMPUTERS.
SO, WHAT IS IT SPECIFICALLY THAT TELLS YOU AN EARTHQUAKE IS HAPPENING?
SIMPLE.
WHEN THE BOOKSHELF FALLS ON BOBBY'S HEAD.
RAESIDE

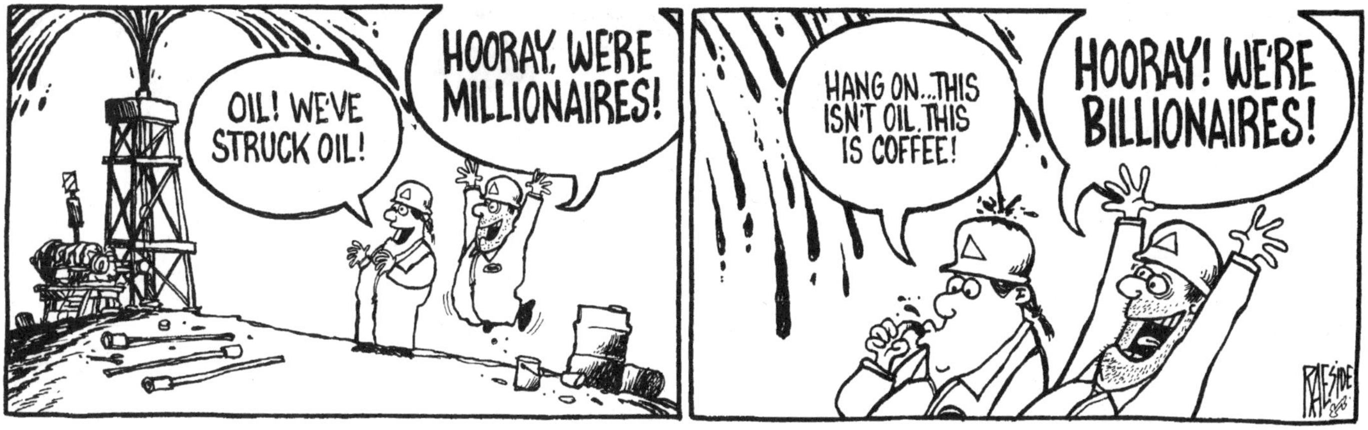
OIL! WE'VE STRUCK OIL!
HOORAY, WE'RE MILLIONAIRES!
HANG ON...THIS ISN'T OIL, THIS IS COFFEE!
HOORAY! WE'RE BILLIONAIRES!

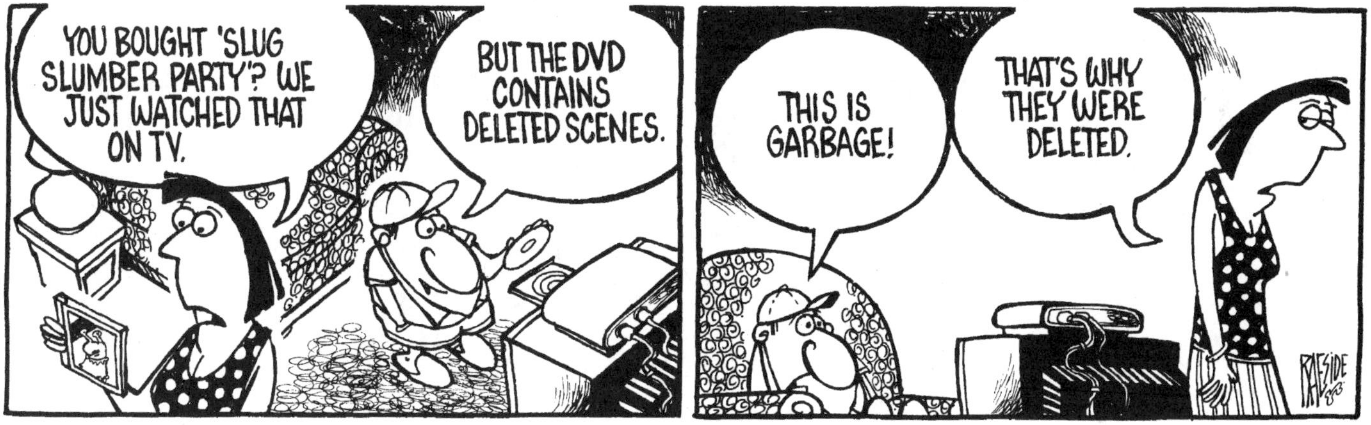
YOU BOUGHT 'SLUG SLUMBER PARTY'? WE JUST WATCHED THAT ON TV.
BUT THE DVD CONTAINS DELETED SCENES.
THIS IS GARBAGE!
THAT'S WHY THEY WERE DELETED.

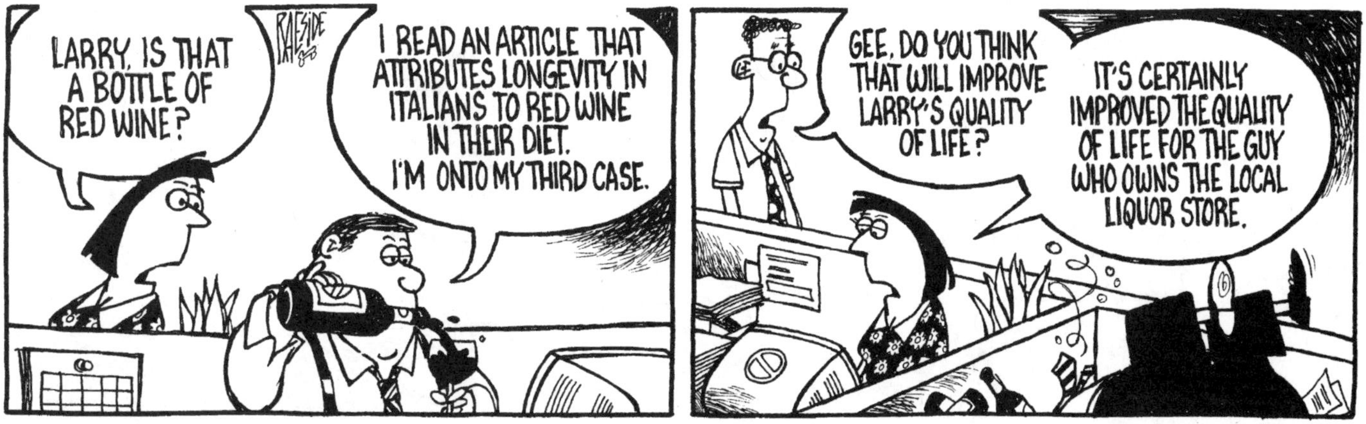
LARRY, IS THAT A BOTTLE OF RED WINE?
I READ AN ARTICLE THAT ATTRIBUTES LONGEVITY IN ITALIANS TO RED WINE IN THEIR DIET. I'M ONTO MY THIRD CASE.
GEE, DO YOU THINK THAT WILL IMPROVE LARRY'S QUALITY OF LIFE?
IT'S CERTAINLY IMPROVED THE QUALITY OF LIFE FOR THE GUY WHO OWNS THE LOCAL LIQUOR STORE.

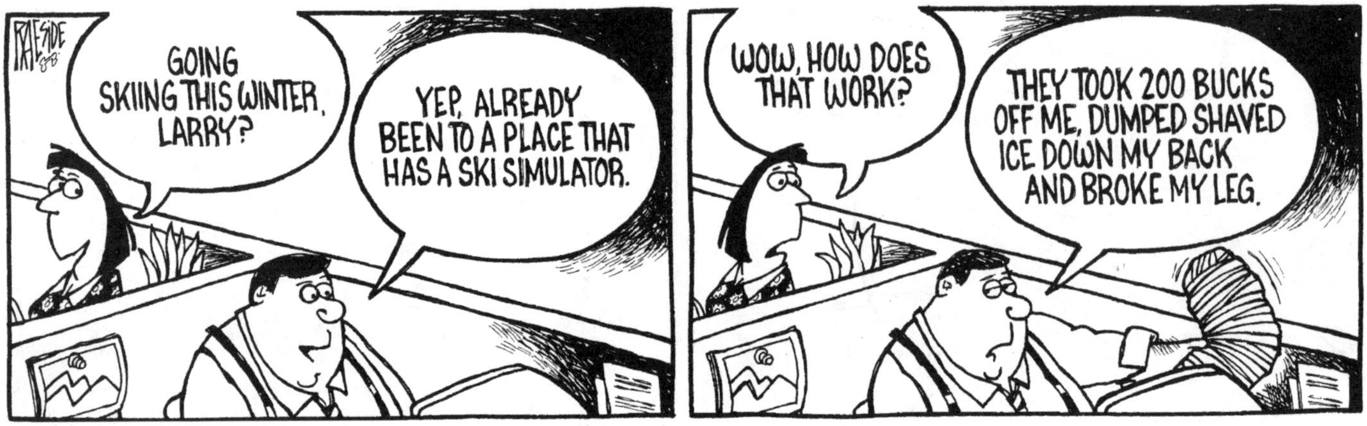
RAESIDE
GOING SKIING THIS WINTER, LARRY?
YEP, ALREADY BEEN TO A PLACE THAT HAS A SKI SIMULATOR.
WOW, HOW DOES THAT WORK?
THEY TOOK 200 BUCKS OFF ME, DUMPED SHAVED ICE DOWN MY BACK AND BROKE MY LEG.

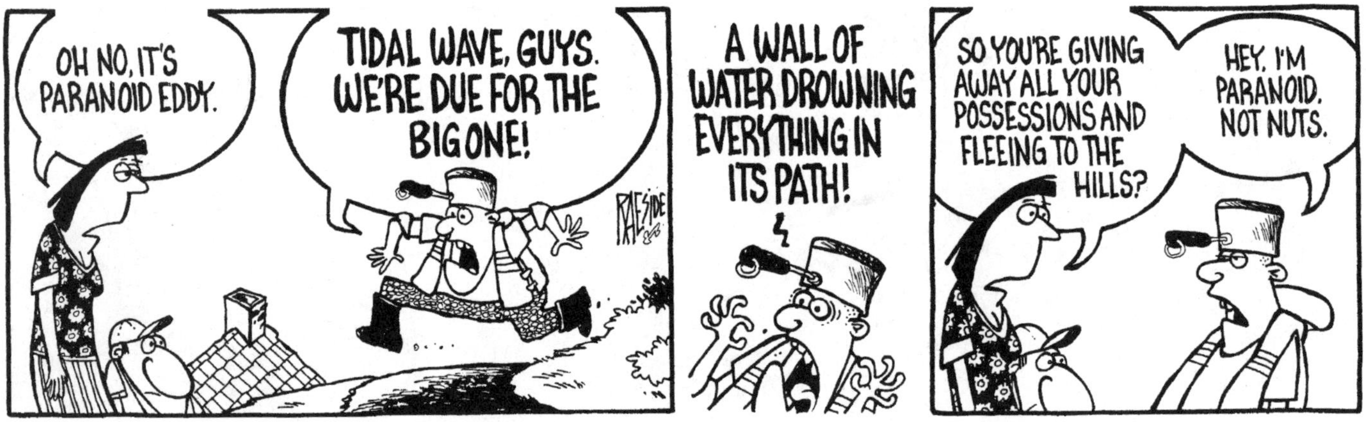
OH NO, IT'S PARANOID EDDY.
TIDAL WAVE, GUYS. WE'RE DUE FOR THE BIG ONE!
RAESIDE
A WALL OF WATER DROWNING EVERYTHING IN ITS PATH!
SO YOU'RE GIVING AWAY ALL YOUR POSSESSIONS AND FLEEING TO THE HILLS?
HEY, I'M PARANOID, NOT NUTS.

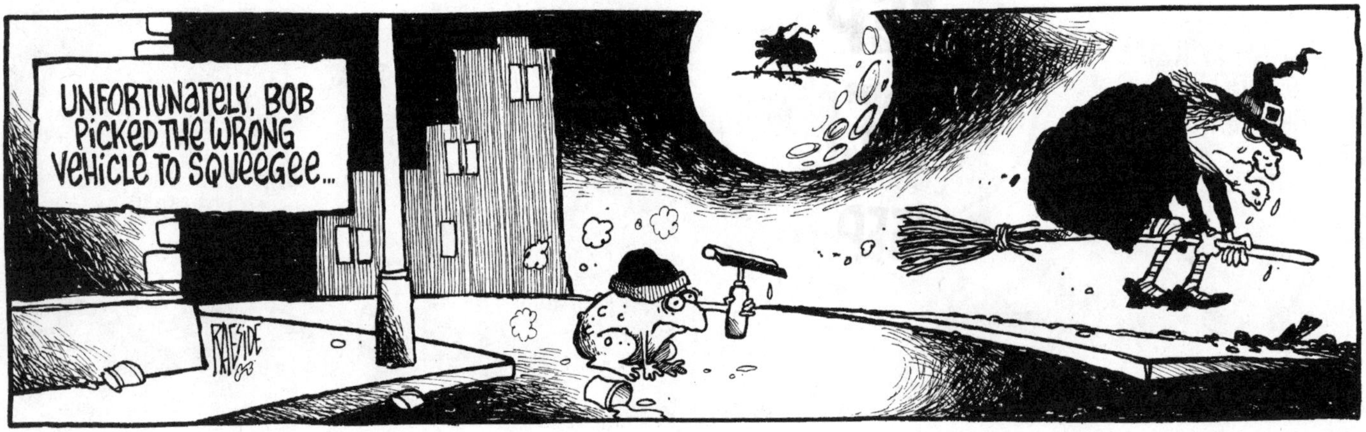
UNFORTUNATELY, BOB PICKED THE WRONG VEHICLE TO SQUEEGEE...
RAESIDE

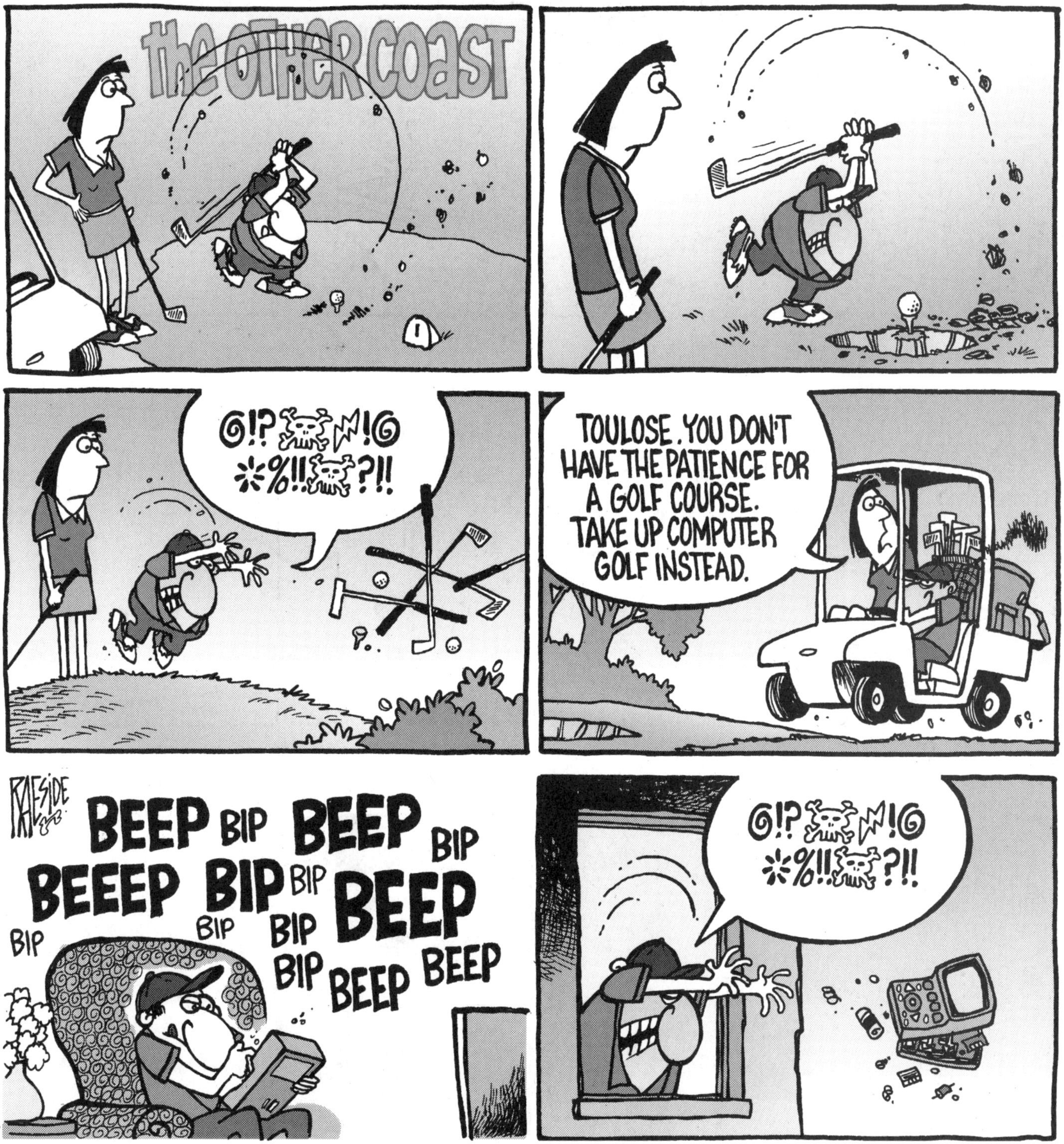
the OTHER COAST
6!? !6 *%!! ?!!
TOULOSE. YOU DON'T HAVE THE PATIENCE FOR A GOLF COURSE. TAKE UP COMPUTER GOLF INSTEAD.
RAESIDE
BEEP BIP BEEP BIP BEEEP BIP BIP BEEP BIP BIP BIP BIP BEEP BEEP
6!? !6 *%!! ?!!

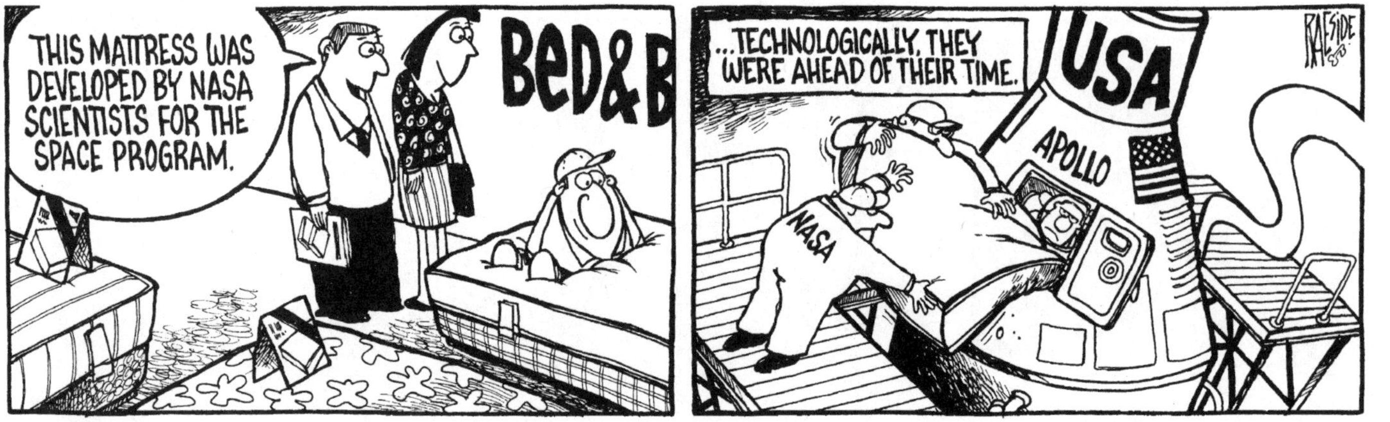
THIS MATTRESS WAS DEVELOPED BY NASA SCIENTISTS FOR THE SPACE PROGRAM.
Bed&B
...TECHNOLOGICALLY, THEY WERE AHEAD OF THEIR TIME.
USA
APOLLO
NASA
RAESIDE

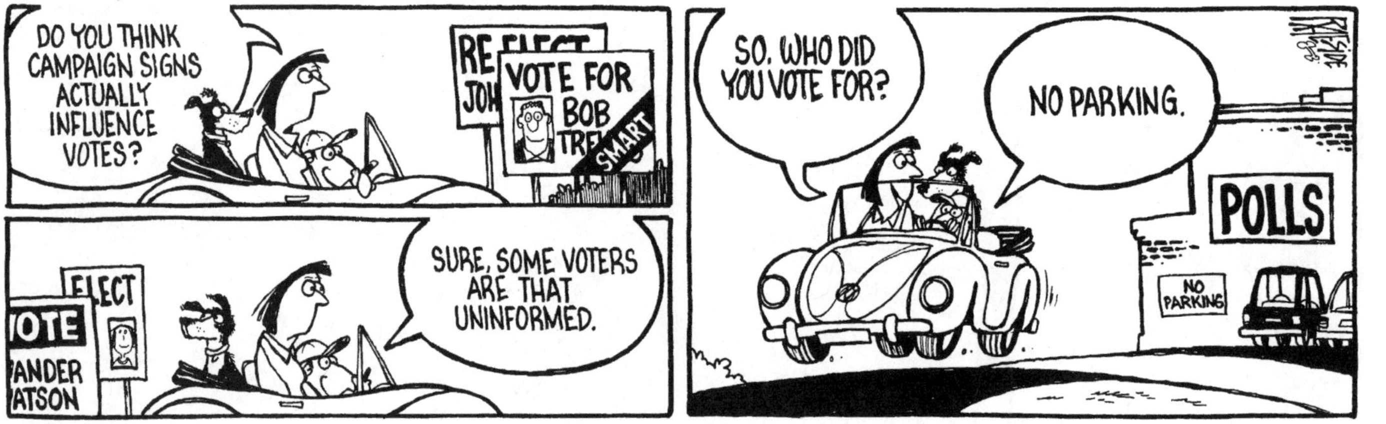
DO YOU THINK CAMPAIGN SIGNS ACTUALLY INFLUENCE VOTES?
VOTE FOR BOB
SMART
SURE, SOME VOTERS ARE THAT UNINFORMED.
ELECT
VOTE
SO. WHO DID YOU VOTE FOR?
NO PARKING.
POLLS
NO PARKING
RAESIDE

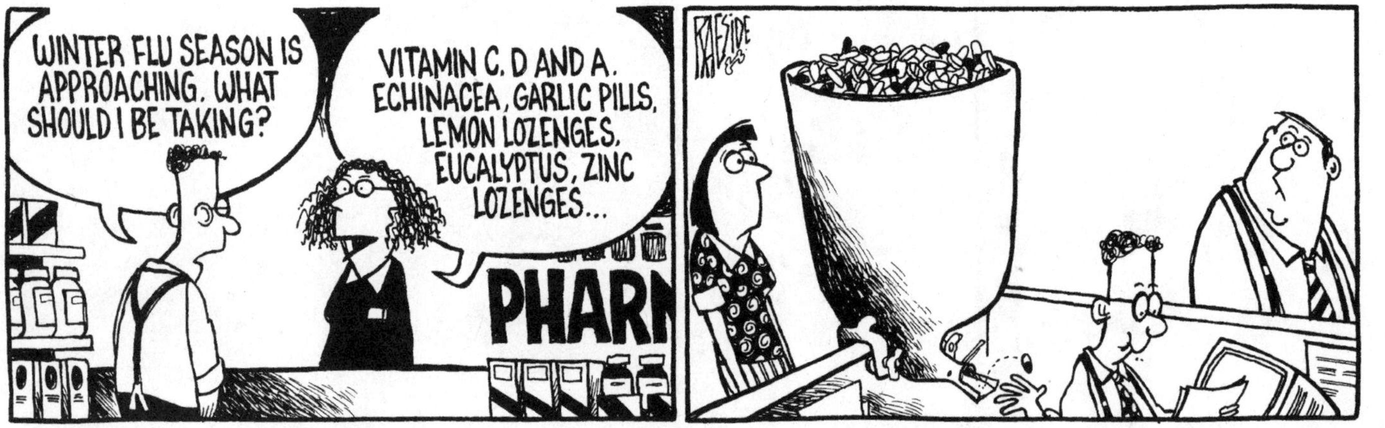
WINTER FLU SEASON IS APPROACHING. WHAT SHOULD I BE TAKING?
VITAMIN C, D AND A. ECHINACEA, GARLIC PILLS, LEMON LOZENGES, EUCALYPTUS, ZINC LOZENGES...
RAESIDE

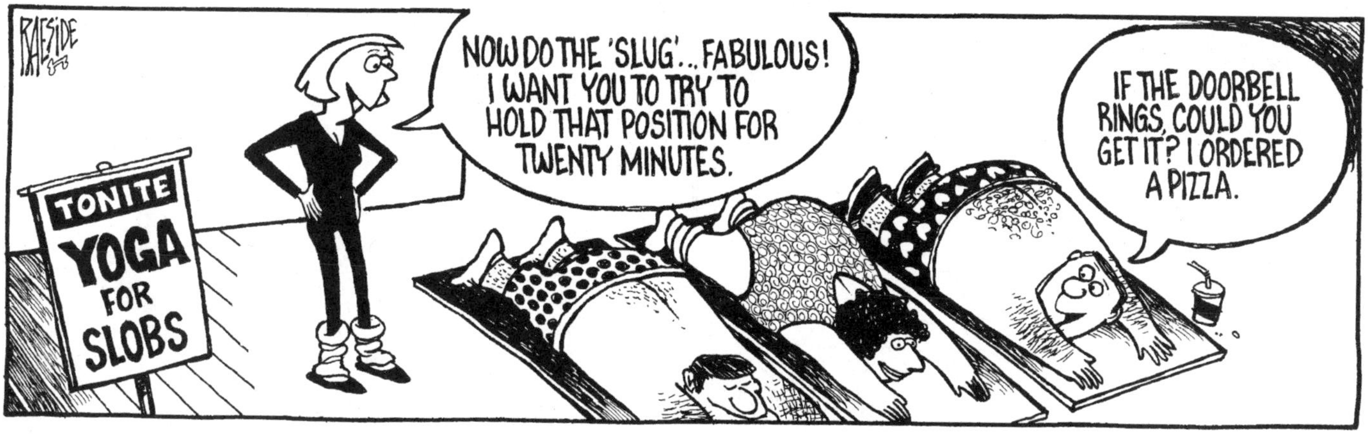
TONITE YOGA FOR SLOBS
NOW DO THE 'SLUG'... FABULOUS! I WANT YOU TO TRY TO HOLD THAT POSITION FOR TWENTY MINUTES.
IF THE DOORBELL RINGS, COULD YOU GET IT? I ORDERED A PIZZA.

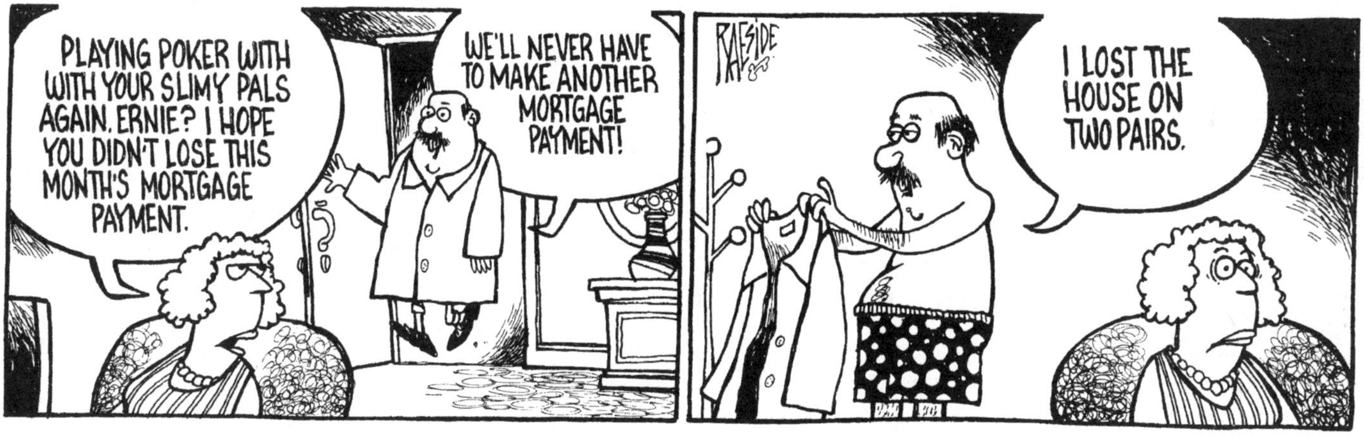
PLAYING POKER WITH WITH YOUR SLIMY PALS AGAIN, ERNIE? I HOPE YOU DIDN'T LOSE THIS MONTH'S MORTGAGE PAYMENT.
WE'LL NEVER HAVE TO MAKE ANOTHER MORTGAGE PAYMENT!
I LOST THE HOUSE ON TWO PAIRS.

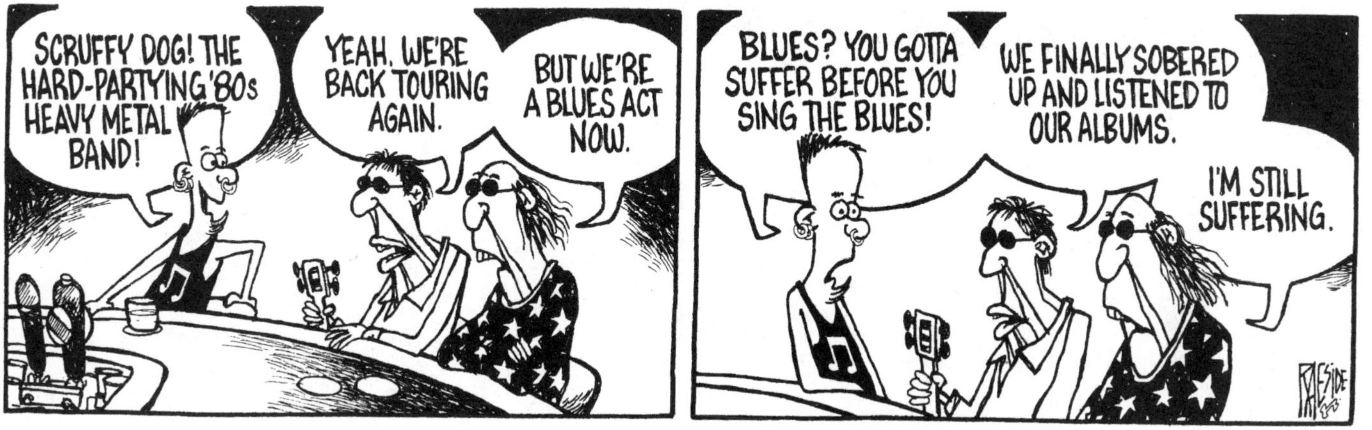
SCRUFFY DOG! THE HARD-PARTYING '80s HEAVY METAL BAND!
YEAH, WE'RE BACK TOURING AGAIN.
BUT WE'RE A BLUES ACT NOW.
BLUES? YOU GOTTA SUFFER BEFORE YOU SING THE BLUES!
WE FINALLY SOBERED UP AND LISTENED TO OUR ALBUMS.
I'M STILL SUFFERING.

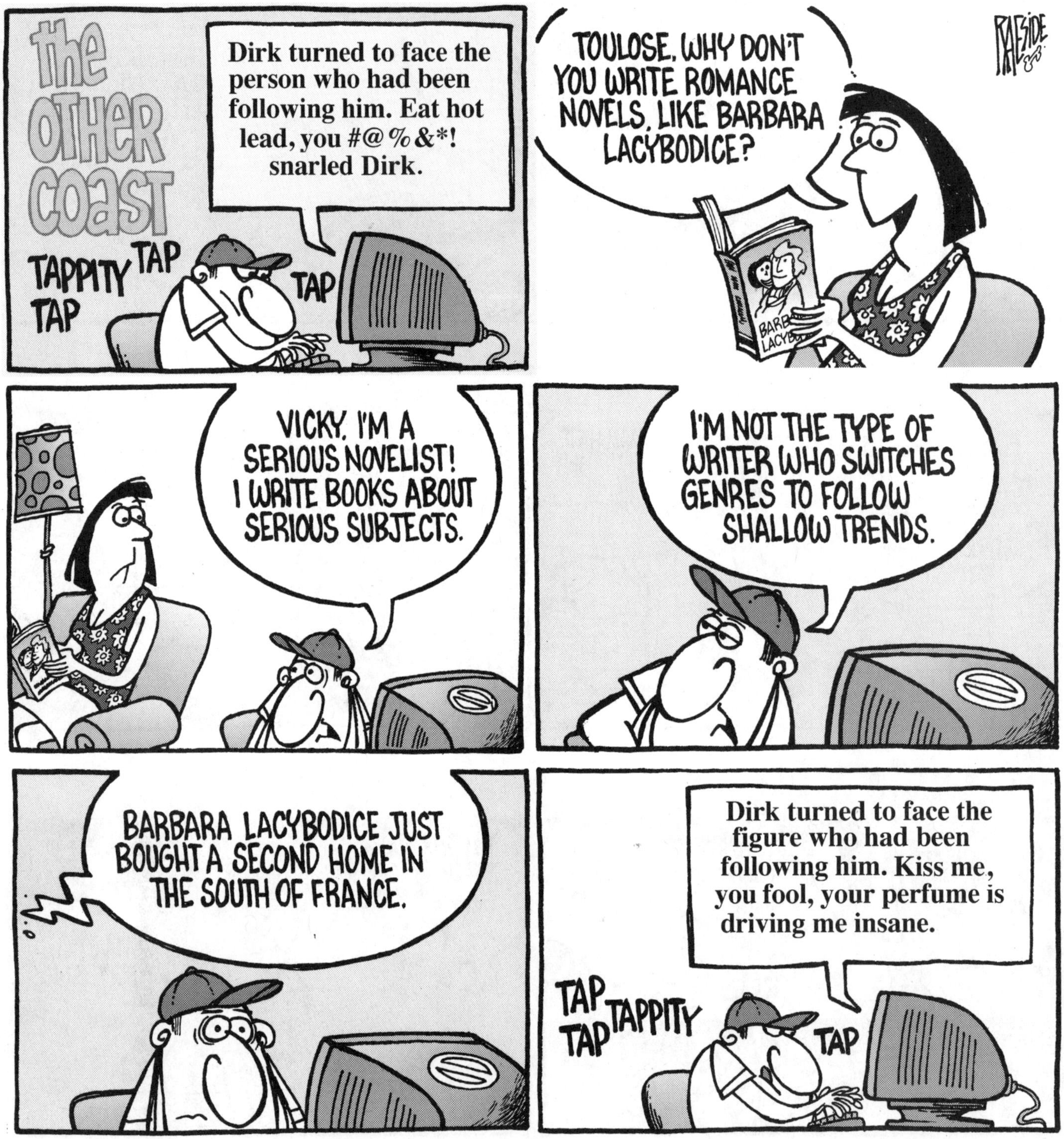
the OTHER COAST
RAESIDE
Dirk turned to face the person who had been following him. Eat hot lead, you #@%&*! snarled Dirk.
TAPPITY TAP TAP TAP
TOULOSE, WHY DON'T YOU WRITE ROMANCE NOVELS, LIKE BARBARA LACYBODICE?
VICKY, I'M A SERIOUS NOVELIST! I WRITE BOOKS ABOUT SERIOUS SUBJECTS.
I'M NOT THE TYPE OF WRITER WHO SWITCHES GENRES TO FOLLOW SHALLOW TRENDS.
BARBARA LACYBODICE JUST BOUGHT A SECOND HOME IN THE SOUTH OF FRANCE.
Dirk turned to face the figure who had been following him. Kiss me, you fool, your perfume is driving me insane.
TAP TAP TAPPITY TAP

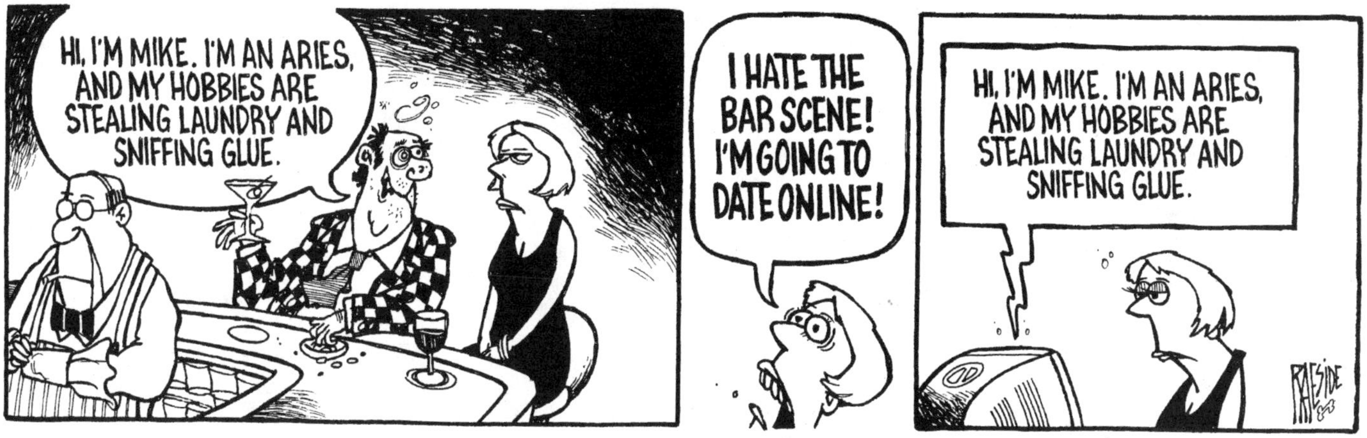
HI, I'M MIKE. I'M AN ARIES, AND MY HOBBIES ARE STEALING LAUNDRY AND SNIFFING GLUE.
I HATE THE BAR SCENE! I'M GOING TO DATE ONLINE!
HI, I'M MIKE. I'M AN ARIES, AND MY HOBBIES ARE STEALING LAUNDRY AND SNIFFING GLUE.
RAESIDE

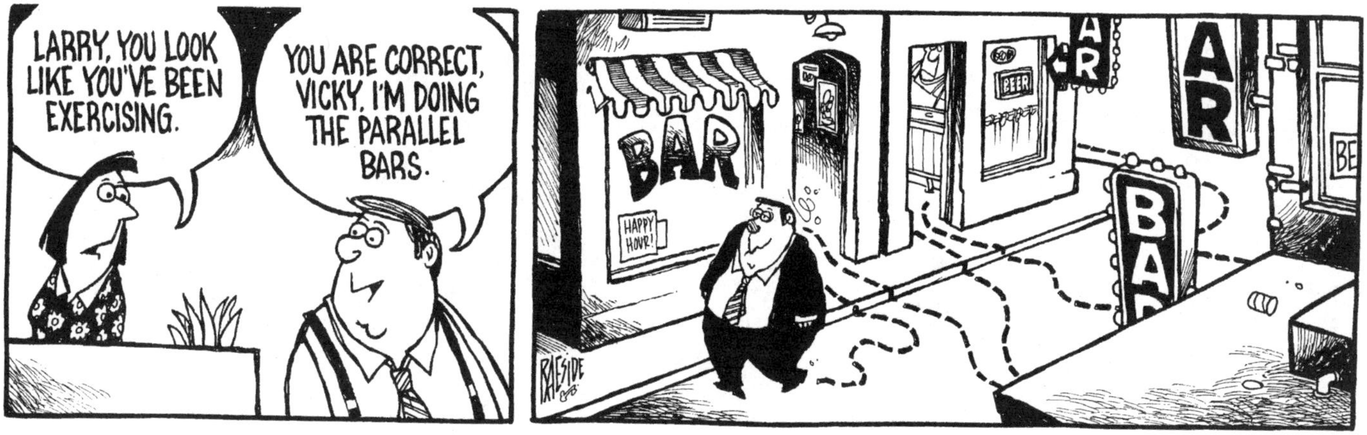
LARRY, YOU LOOK LIKE YOU'VE BEEN EXERCISING.
YOU ARE CORRECT, VICKY. I'M DOING THE PARALLEL BARS.
BAR
HAPPY HOUR!
BEER
RAESIDE

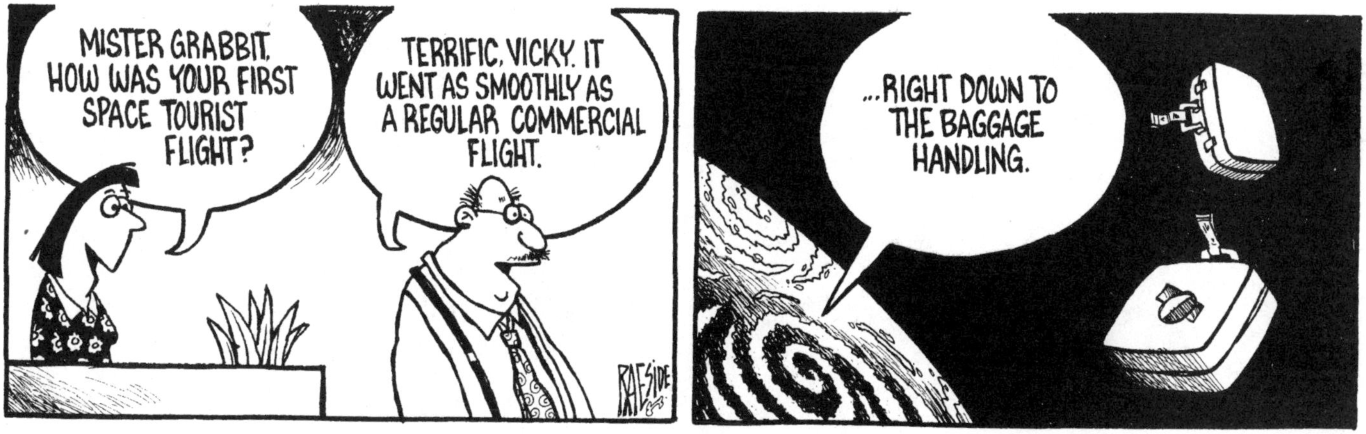
MISTER GRABBIT, HOW WAS YOUR FIRST SPACE TOURIST FLIGHT?
TERRIFIC, VICKY. IT WENT AS SMOOTHLY AS A REGULAR COMMERCIAL FLIGHT.
...RIGHT DOWN TO THE BAGGAGE HANDLING.
RAESIDE

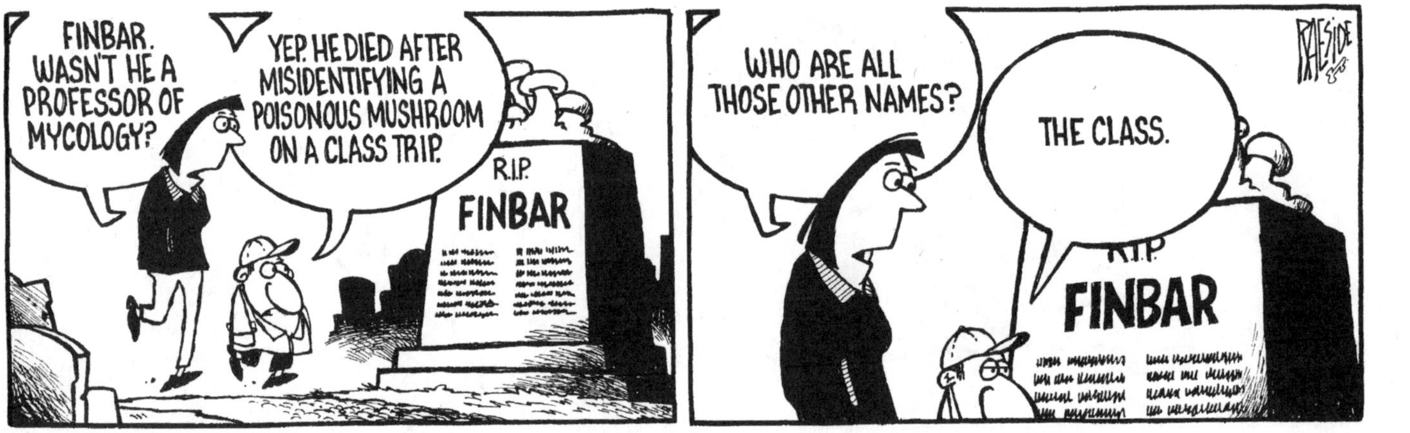
FINBAR. WASN'T HE A PROFESSOR OF MYCOLOGY?
YEP. HE DIED AFTER MISIDENTIFYING A POISONOUS MUSHROOM ON A CLASS TRIP.
R.I.P.
FINBAR
WHO ARE ALL THOSE OTHER NAMES?
THE CLASS.
R.I.P.
FINBAR
RAESIDE

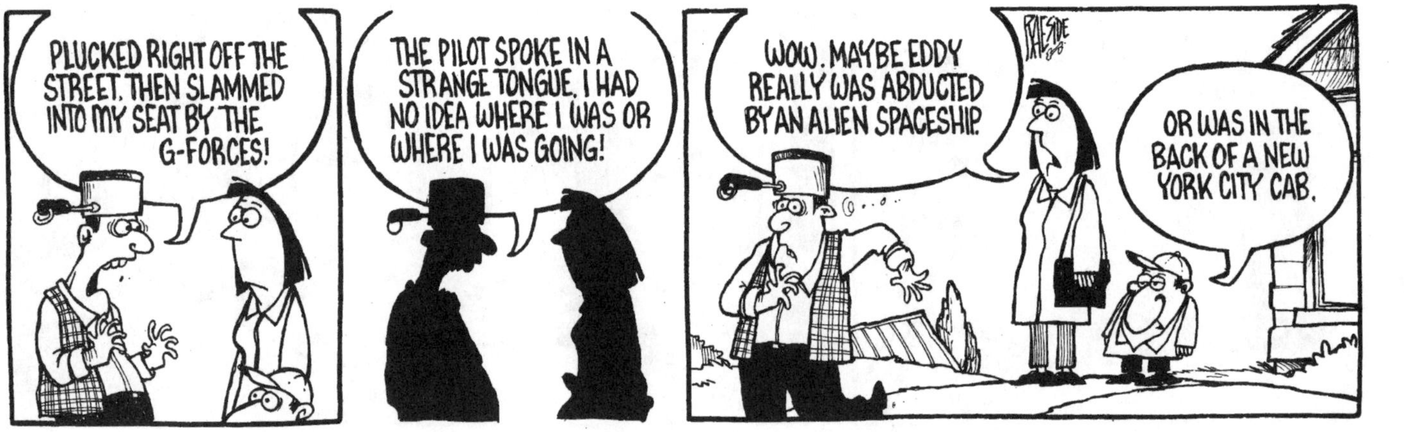
PLUCKED RIGHT OFF THE STREET, THEN SLAMMED INTO MY SEAT BY THE G-FORCES!
THE PILOT SPOKE IN A STRANGE TONGUE. I HAD NO IDEA WHERE I WAS OR WHERE I WAS GOING!
WOW. MAYBE EDDY REALLY WAS ABDUCTED BY AN ALIEN SPACESHIP.
OR WAS IN THE BACK OF A NEW YORK CITY CAB.
RAESIDE

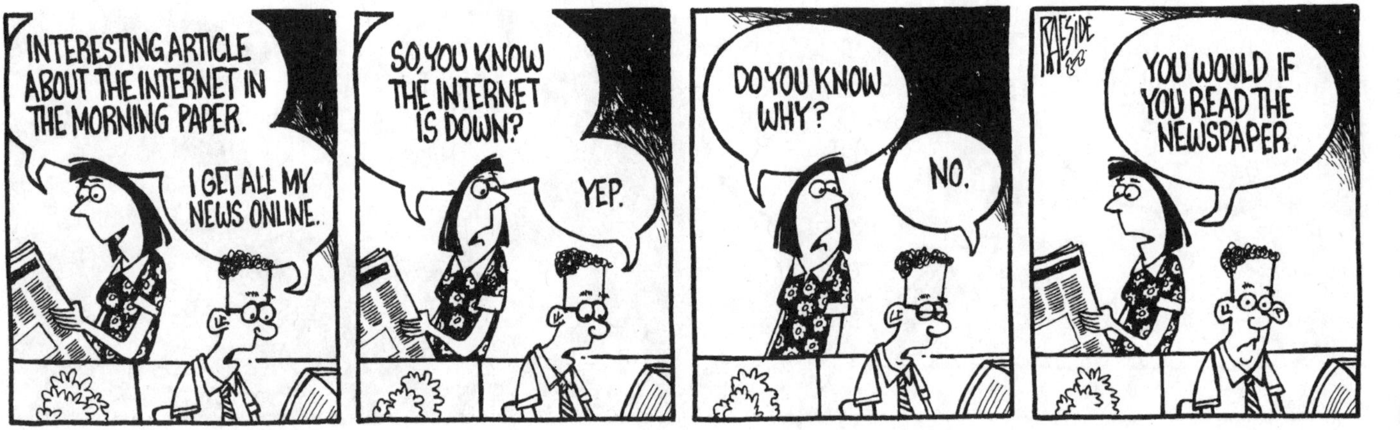
INTERESTING ARTICLE ABOUT THE INTERNET IN THE MORNING PAPER.
I GET ALL MY NEWS ONLINE.
SO, YOU KNOW THE INTERNET IS DOWN?
YEP.
DO YOU KNOW WHY?
NO.
YOU WOULD IF YOU READ THE NEWSPAPER.
RAESIDE

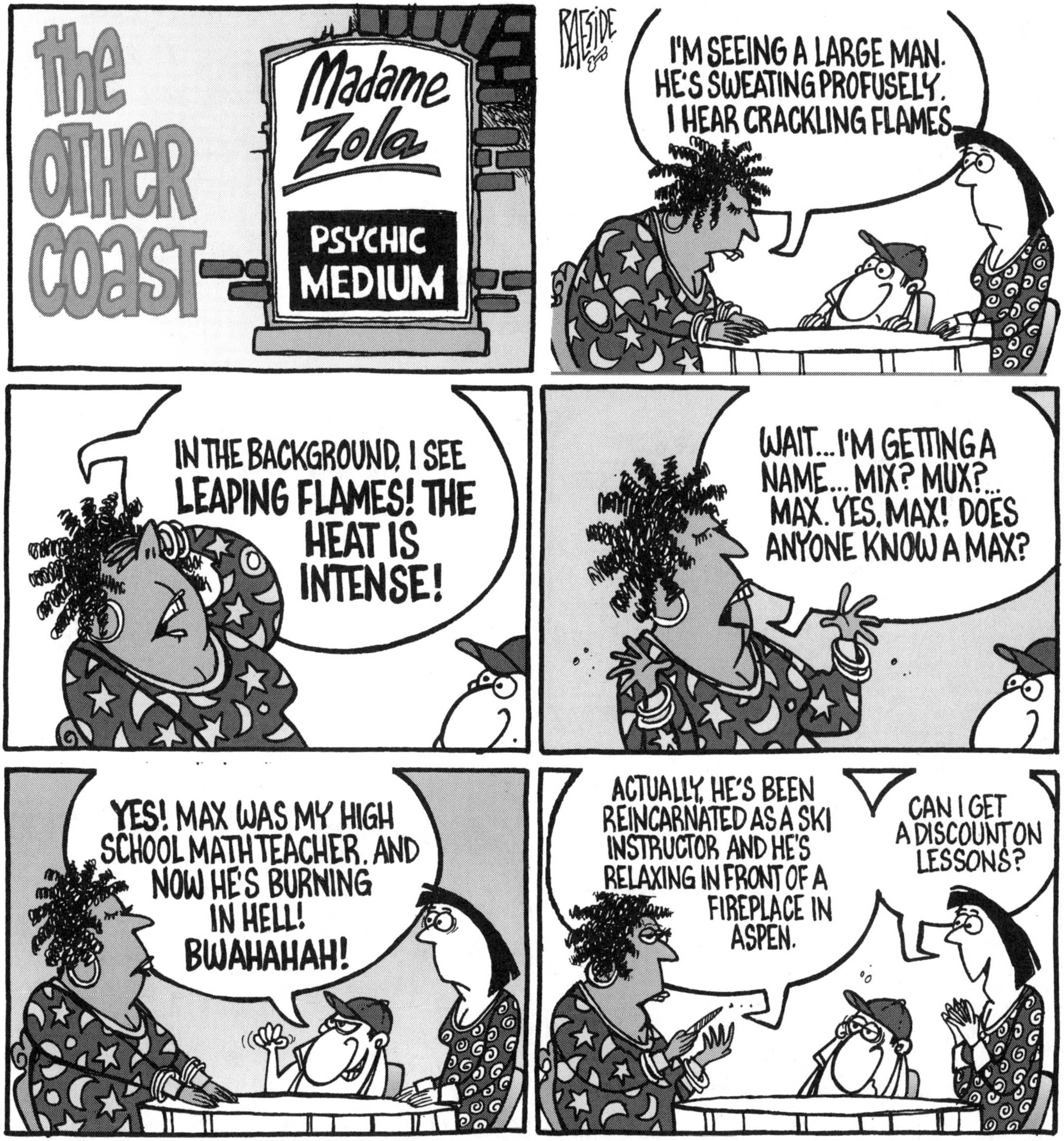
the OTHER COAST
Madame Zola
PSYCHIC MEDIUM
RAESIDE
I'M SEEING A LARGE MAN. HE'S SWEATING PROFUSELY. I HEAR CRACKLING FLAMES.
IN THE BACKGROUND, I SEE LEAPING FLAMES! THE HEAT IS INTENSE!
WAIT... I'M GETTING A NAME... MIX? MUX?... MAX. YES, MAX! DOES ANYONE KNOW A MAX?
YES! MAX WAS MY HIGH SCHOOL MATH TEACHER. AND NOW HE'S BURNING IN HELL! BWAHAHAH!
ACTUALLY, HE'S BEEN REINCARNATED AS A SKI INSTRUCTOR AND HE'S RELAXING IN FRONT OF A FIREPLACE IN ASPEN.
CAN I GET A DISCOUNT ON LESSONS?

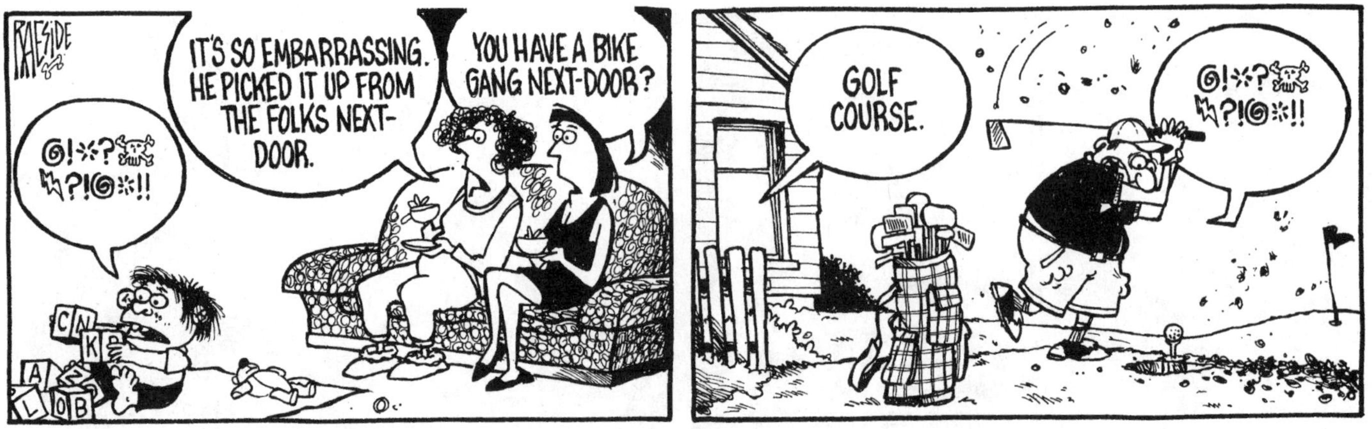
RAESIDE
IT'S SO EMBARRASSING. HE PICKED IT UP FROM THE FOLKS NEXT-DOOR.
YOU HAVE A BIKE GANG NEXT-DOOR?
GOLF COURSE.

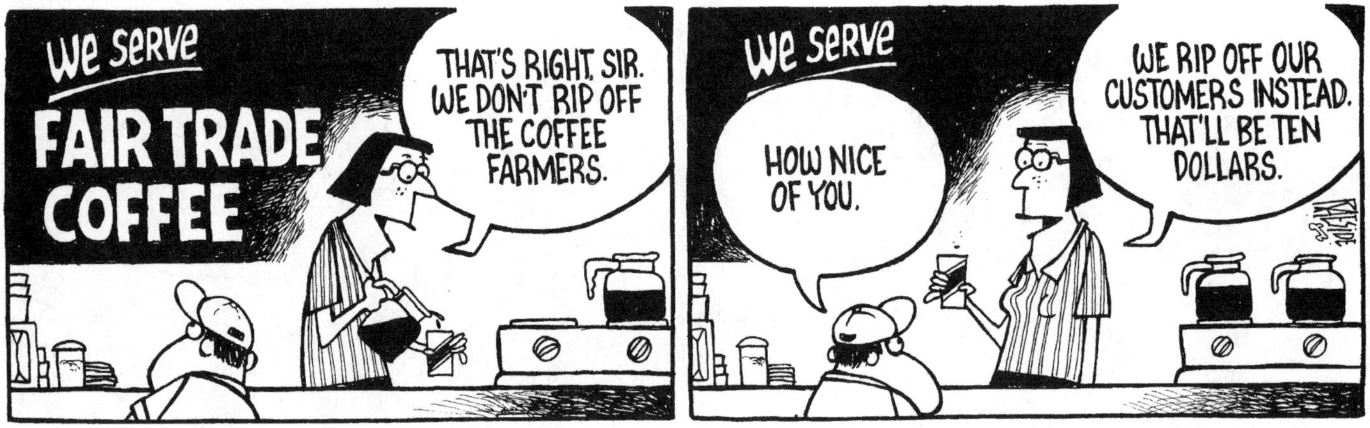
We serve
FAIR TRADE COFFEE
THAT'S RIGHT, SIR. WE DON'T RIP OFF THE COFFEE FARMERS.
We serve
HOW NICE OF YOU.
WE RIP OFF OUR CUSTOMERS INSTEAD. THAT'LL BE TEN DOLLARS.
RAESIDE

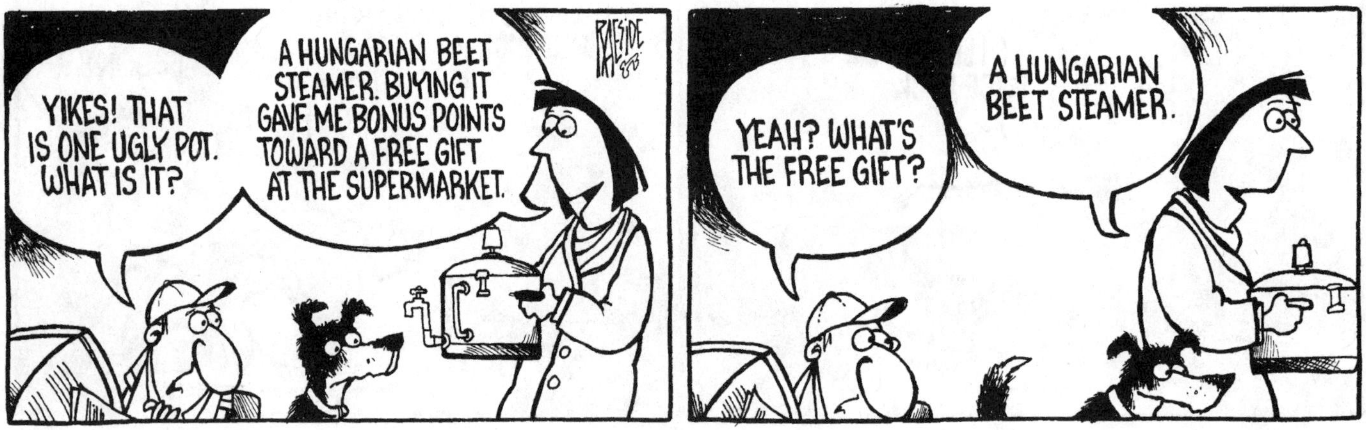
RAESIDE
YIKES! THAT IS ONE UGLY POT. WHAT IS IT?
A HUNGARIAN BEET STEAMER. BUYING IT GAVE ME BONUS POINTS TOWARD A FREE GIFT AT THE SUPERMARKET.
YEAH? WHAT'S THE FREE GIFT?
A HUNGARIAN BEET STEAMER.

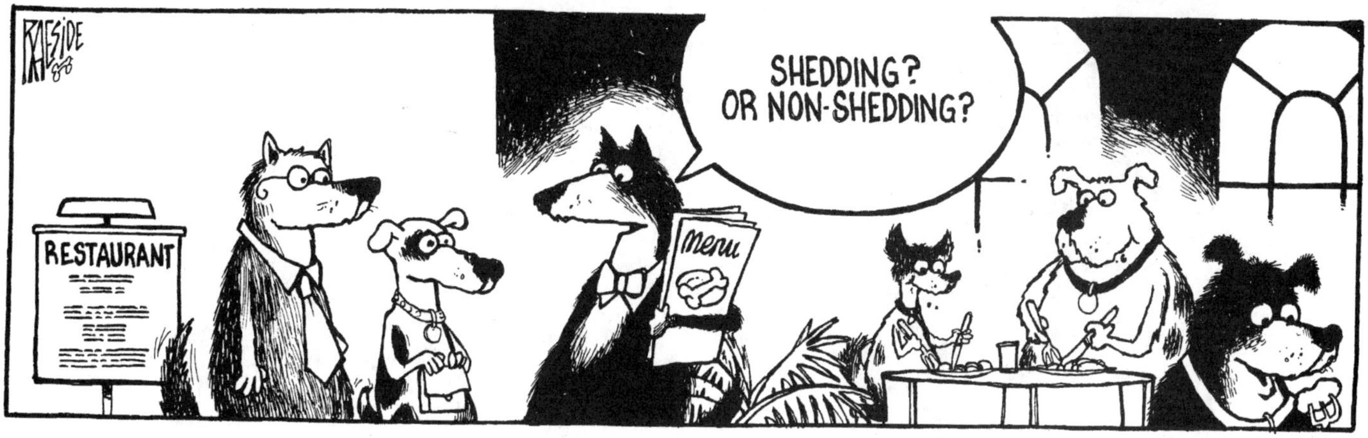
RAESIDE
RESTAURANT
SHEDDING? OR NON-SHEDDING?
Menu

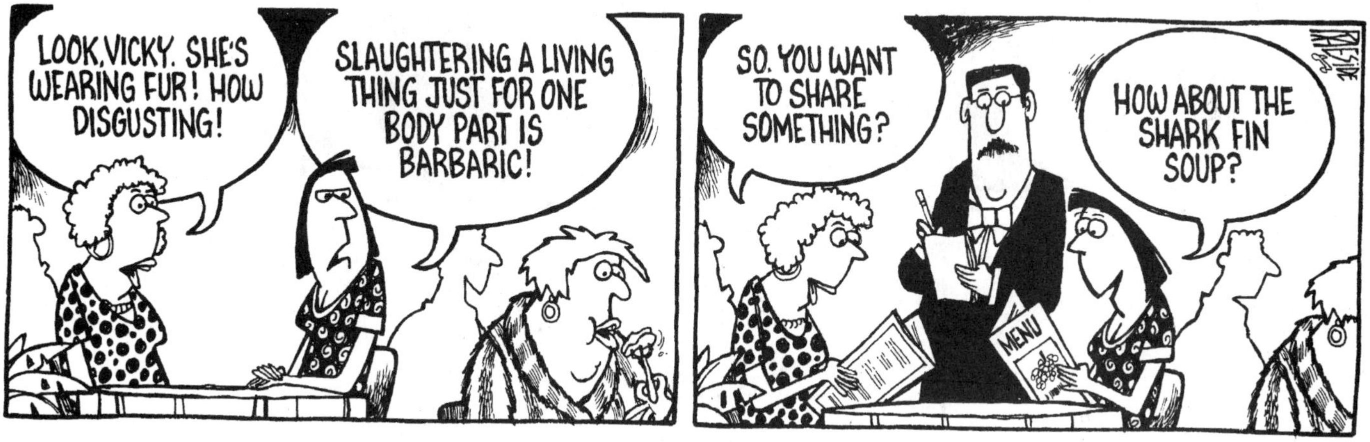
LOOK, VICKY. SHE'S WEARING FUR! HOW DISGUSTING!
SLAUGHTERING A LIVING THING JUST FOR ONE BODY PART IS BARBARIC!
SO. YOU WANT TO SHARE SOMETHING?
HOW ABOUT THE SHARK FIN SOUP?
MENU
RAESIDE

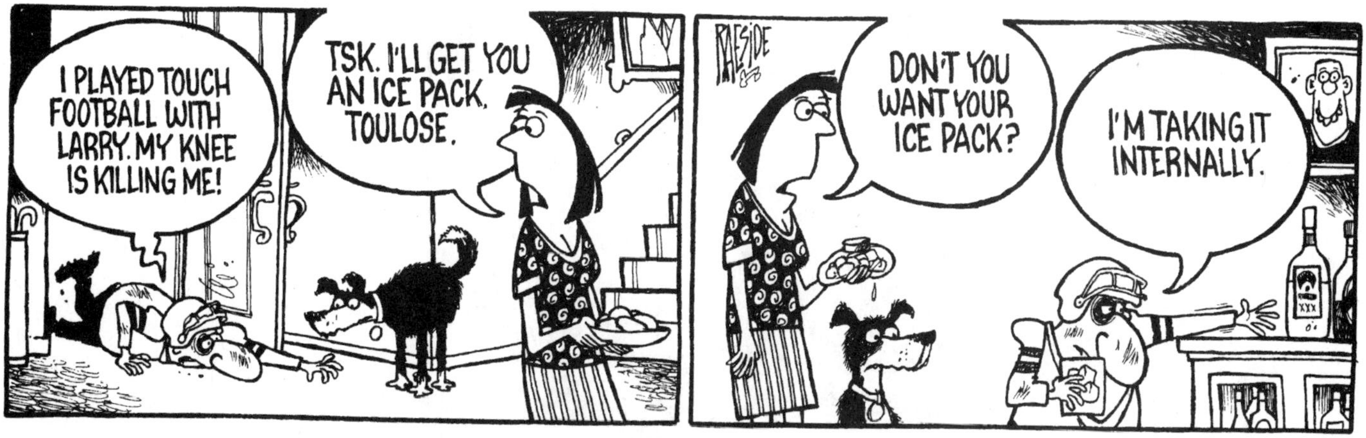
I PLAYED TOUCH FOOTBALL WITH LARRY. MY KNEE IS KILLING ME!
TSK. I'LL GET YOU AN ICE PACK, TOULOSE.
RAESIDE
DON'T YOU WANT YOUR ICE PACK?
I'M TAKING IT INTERNALLY.
XXX

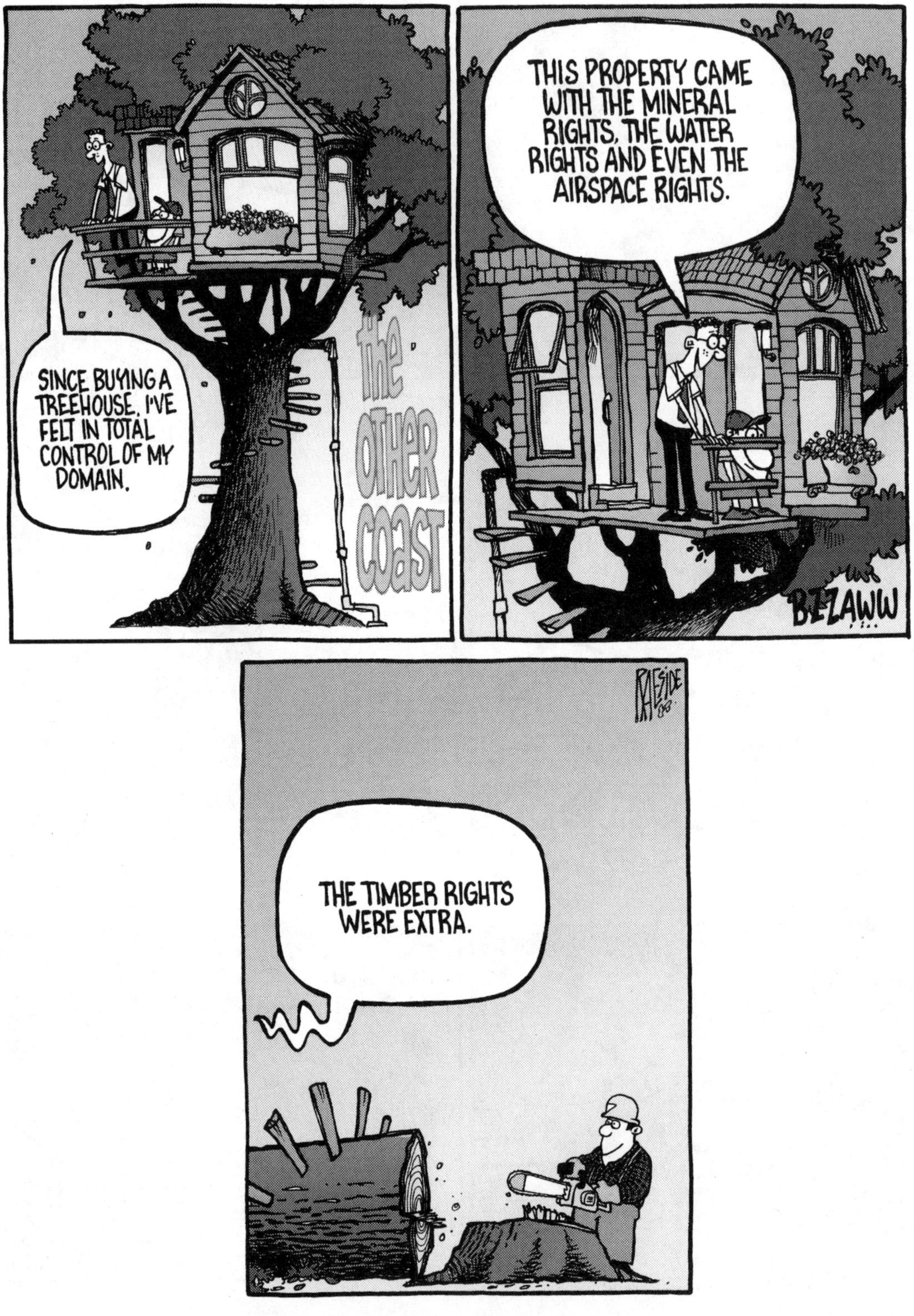

SINCE BUYING A TREEHOUSE, I'VE FELT IN TOTAL CONTROL OF MY DOMAIN.
the OTHER COAST
THIS PROPERTY CAME WITH THE MINERAL RIGHTS, THE WATER RIGHTS AND EVEN THE AIRSPACE RIGHTS.
BZZAWW
THE TIMBER RIGHTS WERE EXTRA.

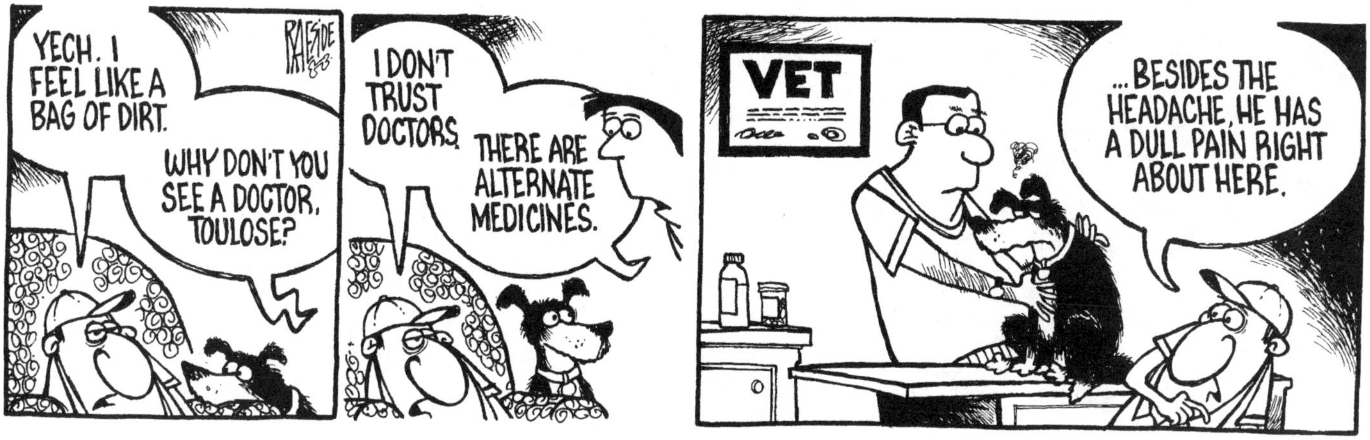
YECH. I FEEL LIKE A BAG OF DIRT.
WHY DON'T YOU SEE A DOCTOR, TOULOSE?
I DON'T TRUST DOCTORS.
THERE ARE ALTERNATE MEDICINES.
VET
... BESIDES THE HEADACHE, HE HAS A DULL PAIN RIGHT ABOUT HERE.

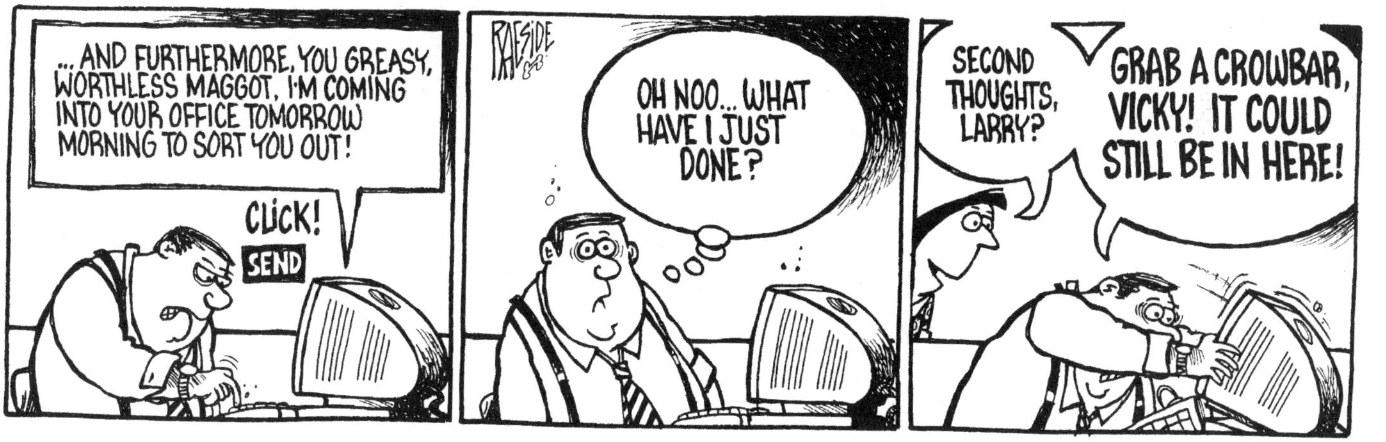
... AND FURTHERMORE, YOU GREASY, WORTHLESS MAGGOT, I'M COMING INTO YOUR OFFICE TOMORROW MORNING TO SORT YOU OUT!
CLICK!
SEND
OH NOO... WHAT HAVE I JUST DONE?
SECOND THOUGHTS, LARRY?
GRAB A CROWBAR, VICKY! IT COULD STILL BE IN HERE!

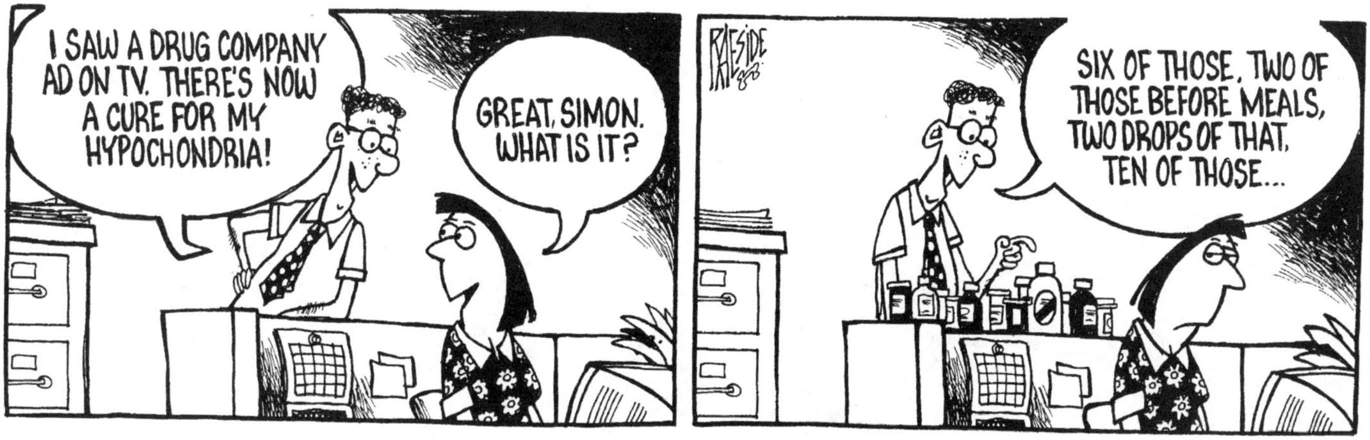
I SAW A DRUG COMPANY AD ON TV. THERE'S NOW A CURE FOR MY HYPOCHONDRIA!
GREAT, SIMON. WHAT IS IT?
SIX OF THOSE, TWO OF THOSE BEFORE MEALS, TWO DROPS OF THAT, TEN OF THOSE...

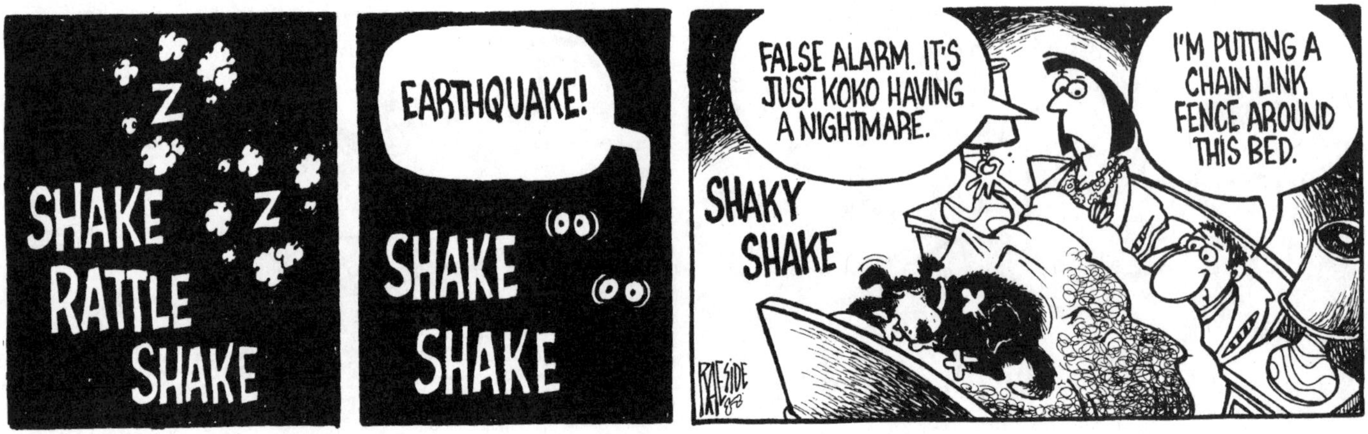
Z
SHAKE
RATTLE
SHAKE
Z
EARTHQUAKE!
SHAKE
SHAKE
FALSE ALARM. IT'S JUST KOKO HAVING A NIGHTMARE.
I'M PUTTING A CHAIN LINK FENCE AROUND THIS BED.
SHAKY
SHAKE

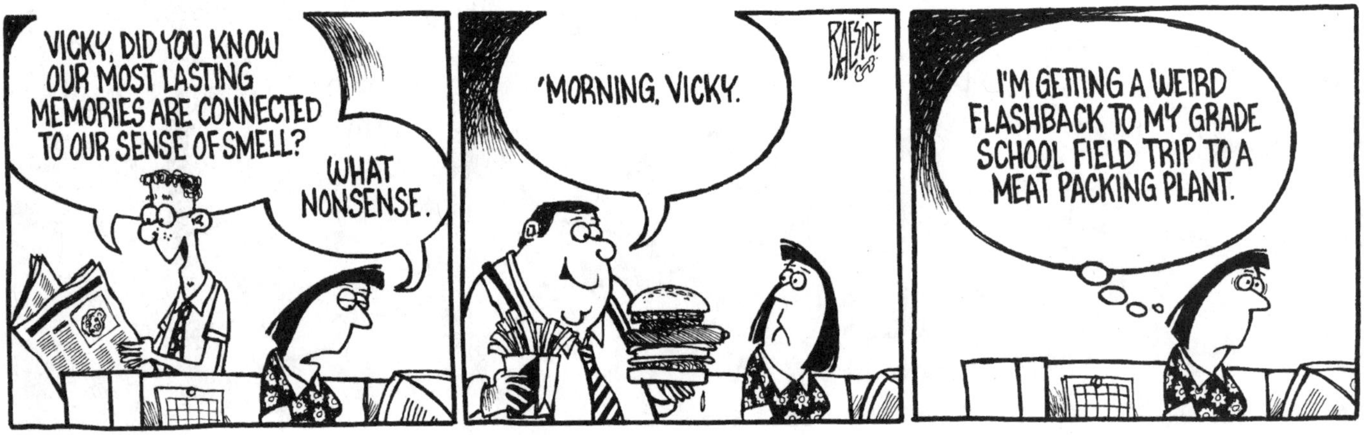
VICKY, DID YOU KNOW OUR MOST LASTING MEMORIES ARE CONNECTED TO OUR SENSE OF SMELL?
WHAT NONSENSE.
'MORNING, VICKY.
I'M GETTING A WEIRD FLASHBACK TO MY GRADE SCHOOL FIELD TRIP TO A MEAT PACKING PLANT.

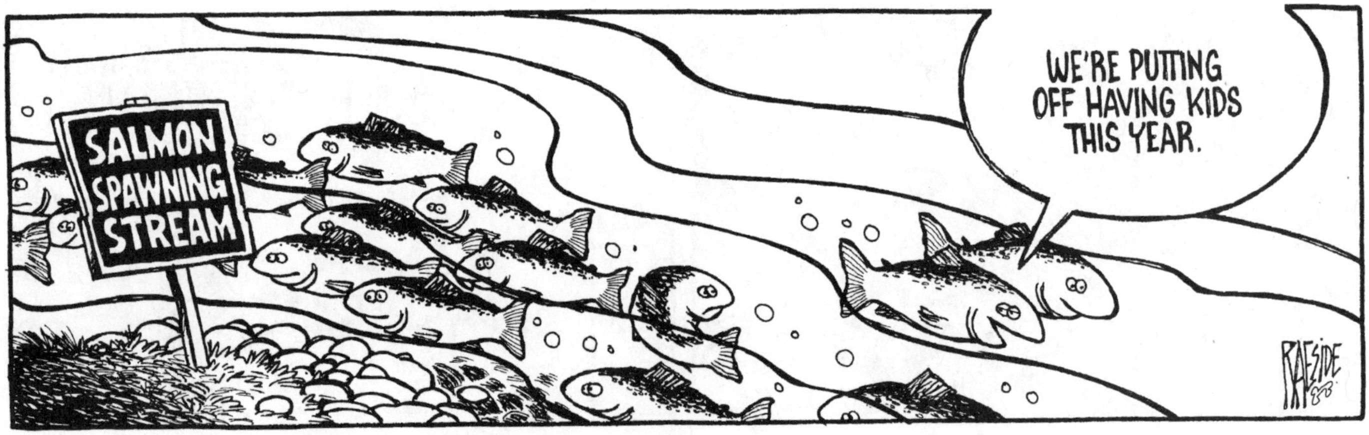
SALMON
SPAWNING
STREAM
WE'RE PUTTING OFF HAVING KIDS THIS YEAR.

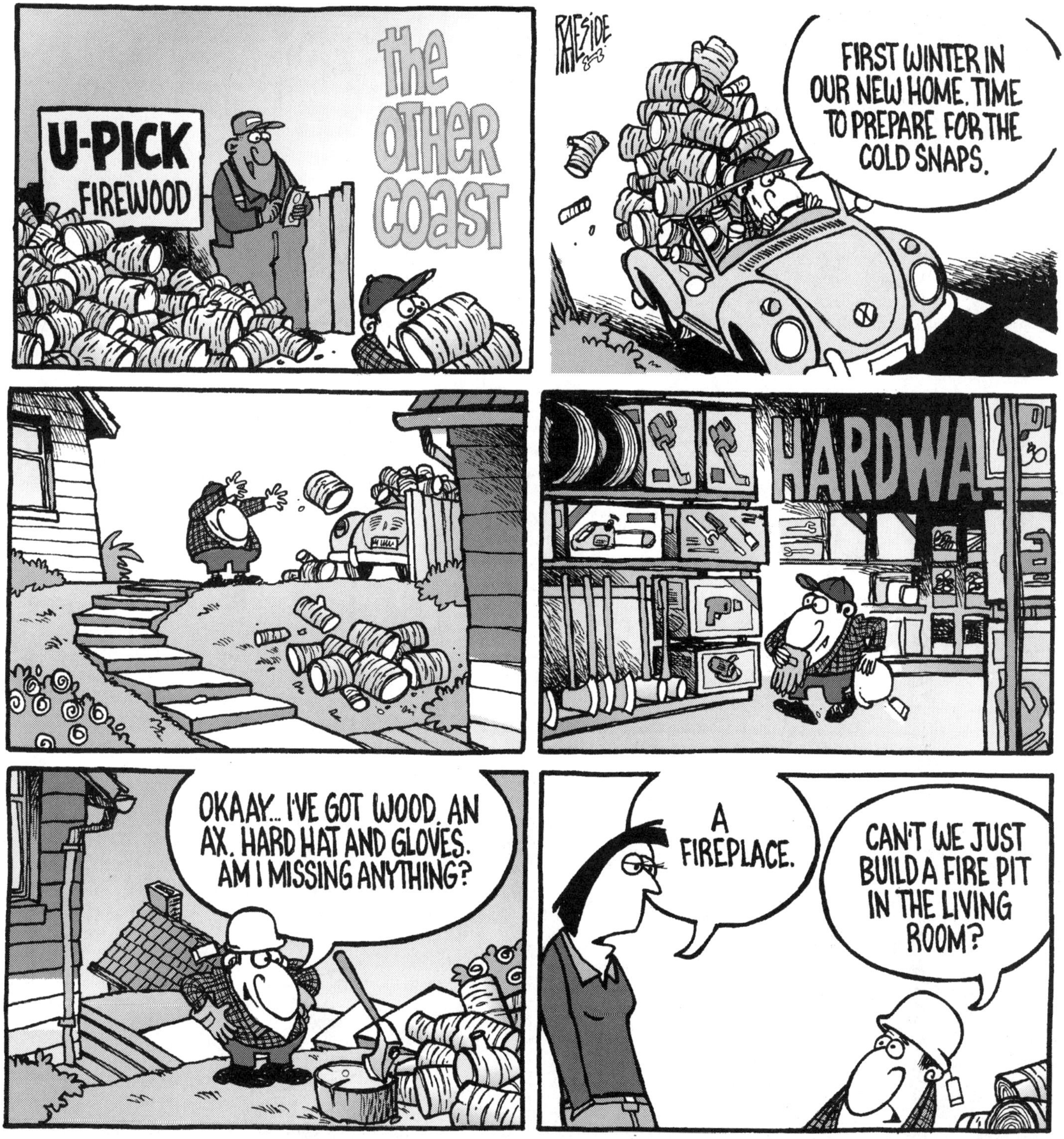
U-PICK
FIREWOOD
the OTHER COAST
RAESIDE
FIRST WINTER IN OUR NEW HOME. TIME TO PREPARE FOR THE COLD SNAPS.
HARDWA
OKAAY... I'VE GOT WOOD. AN AX. HARD HAT AND GLOVES. AM I MISSING ANYTHING?
A FIREPLACE.
CAN'T WE JUST BUILD A FIRE PIT IN THE LIVING ROOM?

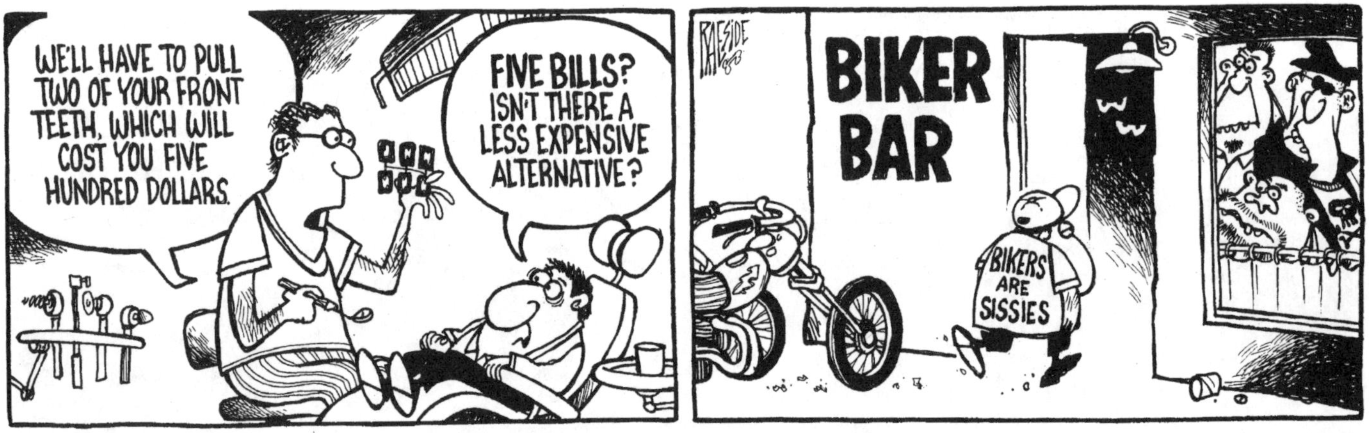
WE'LL HAVE TO PULL TWO OF YOUR FRONT TEETH, WHICH WILL COST YOU FIVE HUNDRED DOLLARS.
FIVE BILLS? ISN'T THERE A LESS EXPENSIVE ALTERNATIVE?
RAESIDE
BIKER BAR
BIKERS ARE SISSIES

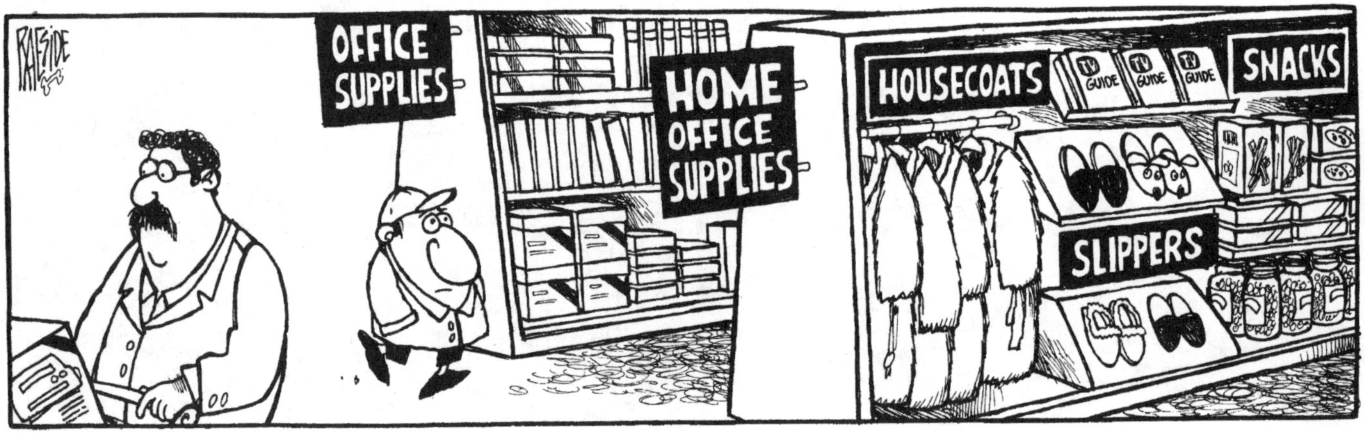
RAESIDE
OFFICE SUPPLIES
HOME OFFICE SUPPLIES
HOUSECOATS
TV GUIDE
SNACKS
SLIPPERS

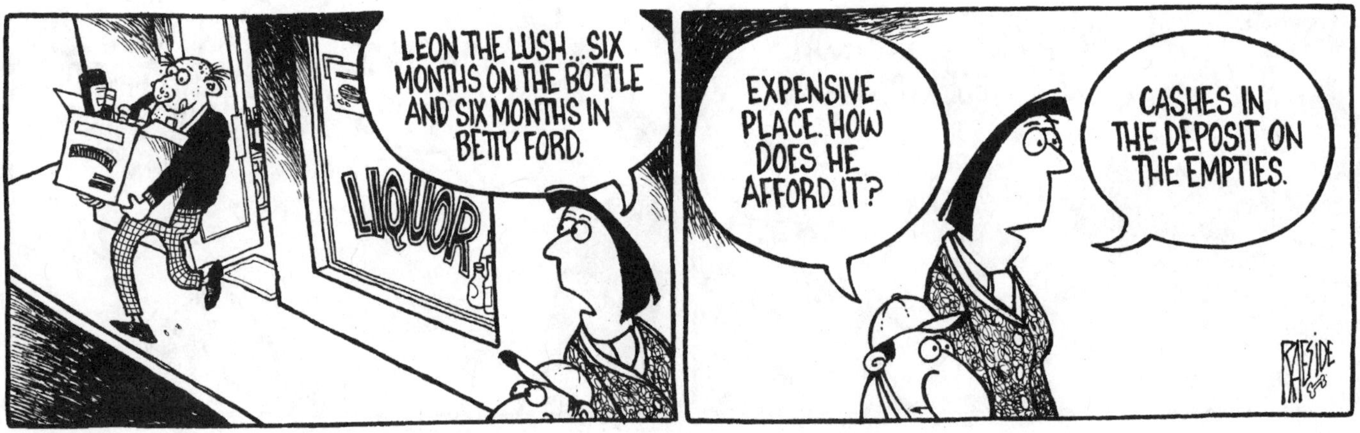
LEON THE LUSH...SIX MONTHS ON THE BOTTLE AND SIX MONTHS IN BETTY FORD.
LIQUOR
EXPENSIVE PLACE. HOW DOES HE AFFORD IT?
CASHES IN THE DEPOSIT ON THE EMPTIES.
RAESIDE

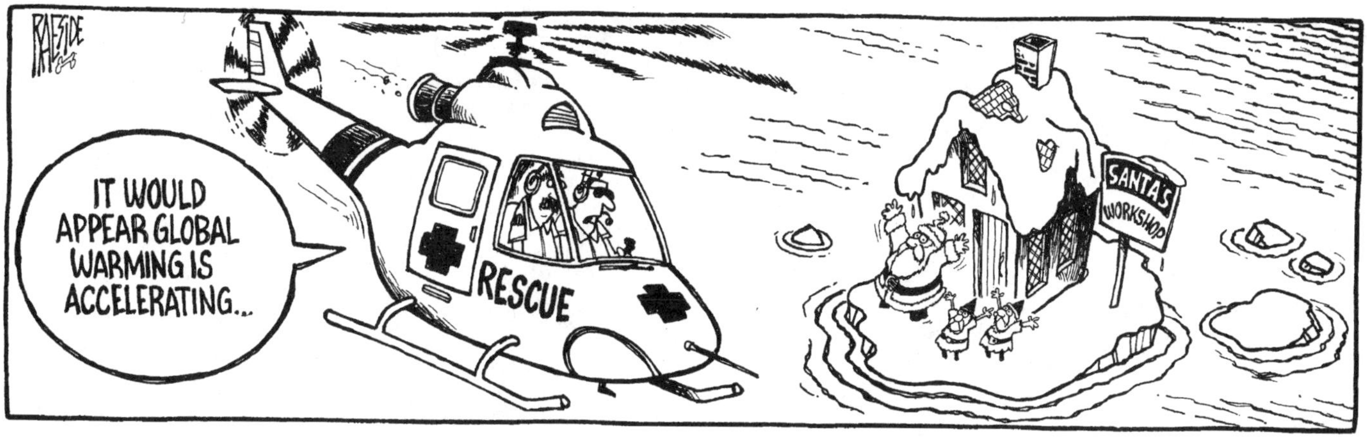
RAESIDE
IT WOULD APPEAR GLOBAL WARMING IS ACCELERATING...
RESCUE
SANTA'S WORKSHOP

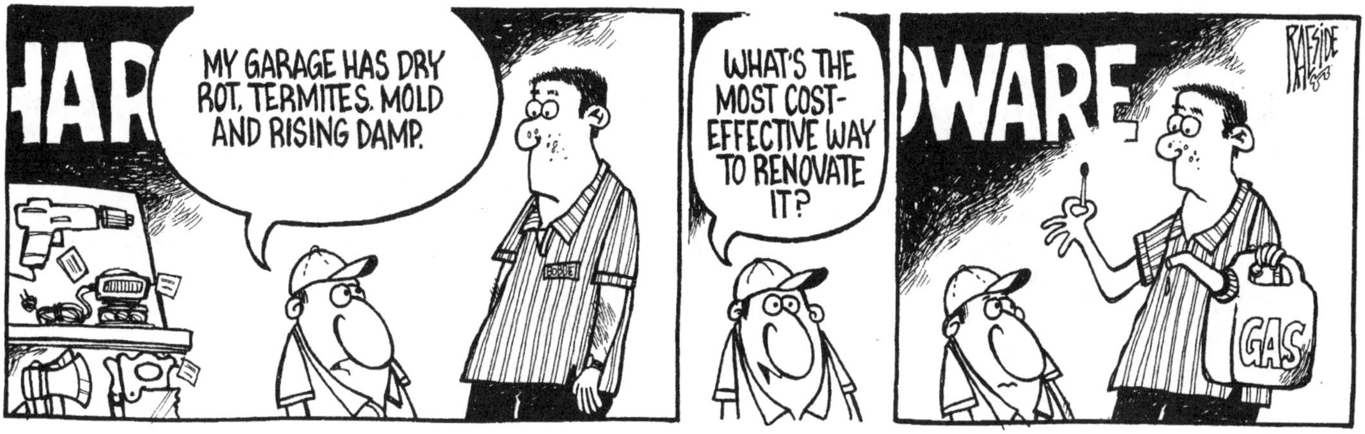
HAR
MY GARAGE HAS DRY ROT, TERMITES. MOLD AND RISING DAMP.
BOBBIE
WHAT'S THE MOST COST-EFFECTIVE WAY TO RENOVATE IT?
WARE
RAESIDE
GAS

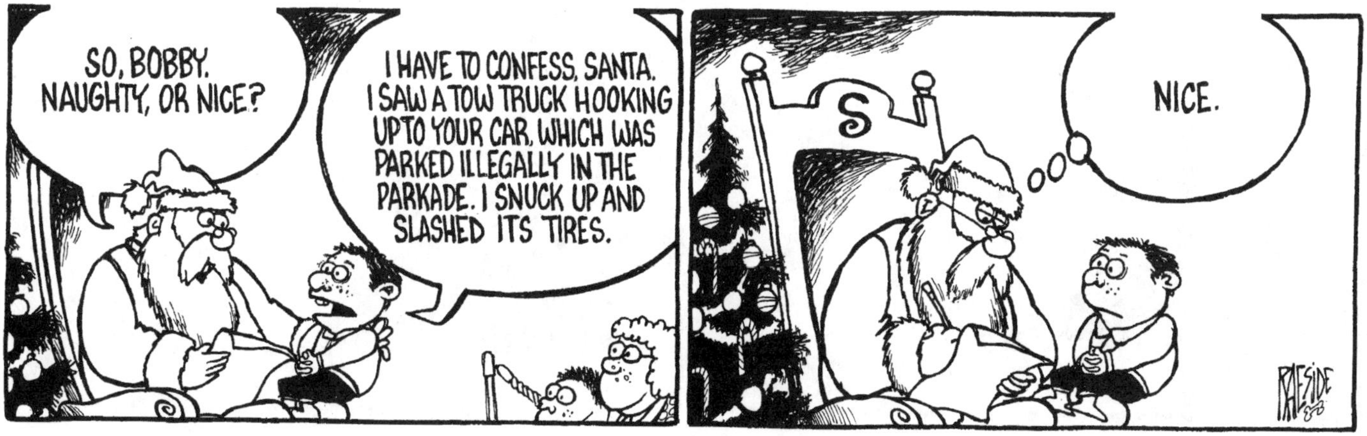
SO, BOBBY. NAUGHTY, OR NICE?
I HAVE TO CONFESS, SANTA. I SAW A TOW TRUCK HOOKING UP TO YOUR CAR, WHICH WAS PARKED ILLEGALLY IN THE PARKADE. I SNUCK UP AND SLASHED ITS TIRES.
S
NICE.
RAESIDE

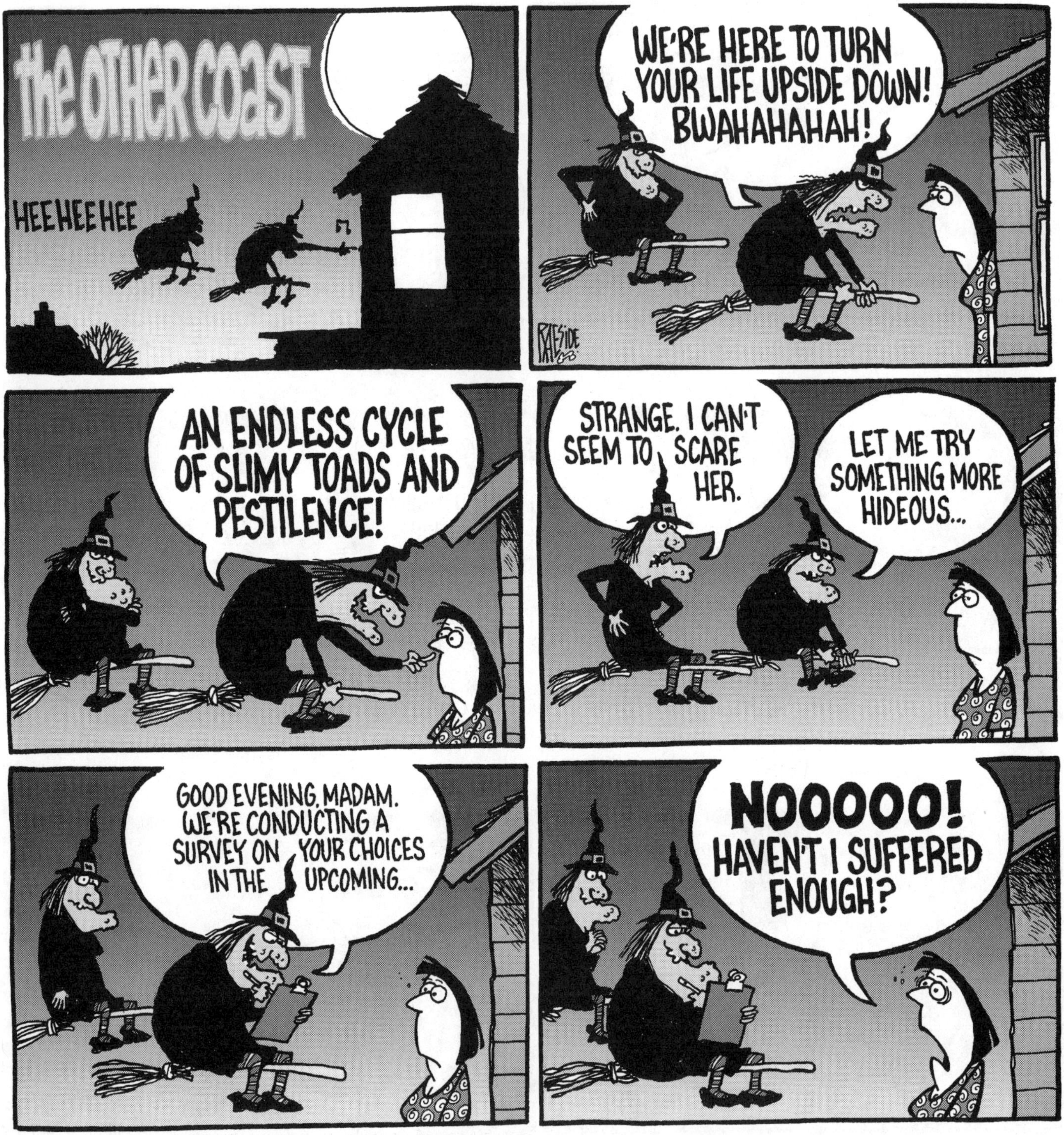
the OTHER COAST
HEE HEE HEE
RAESIDE
WE'RE HERE TO TURN YOUR LIFE UPSIDE DOWN! BWAHAHAHAH!
AN ENDLESS CYCLE OF SLIMY TOADS AND PESTILENCE!
STRANGE. I CAN'T SEEM TO SCARE HER.
LET ME TRY SOMETHING MORE HIDEOUS...
GOOD EVENING, MADAM. WE'RE CONDUCTING A SURVEY ON YOUR CHOICES IN THE UPCOMING...
NOOOOO! HAVEN'T I SUFFERED ENOUGH?

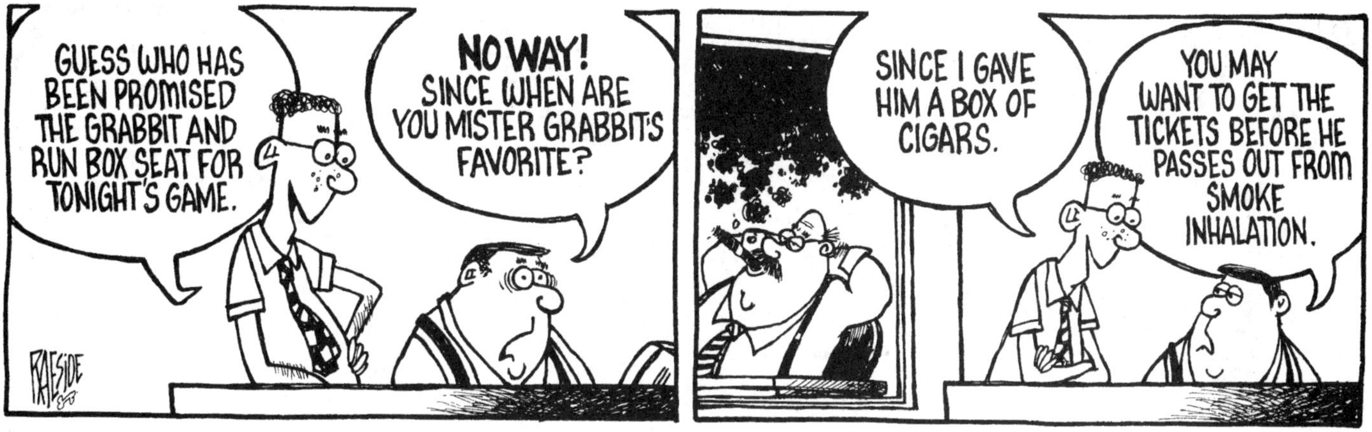
GUESS WHO HAS BEEN PROMISED THE GRABBIT AND RUN BOX SEAT FOR TONIGHT'S GAME.
NO WAY! SINCE WHEN ARE YOU MISTER GRABBIT'S FAVORITE?
SINCE I GAVE HIM A BOX OF CIGARS.
YOU MAY WANT TO GET THE TICKETS BEFORE HE PASSES OUT FROM SMOKE INHALATION.
RAESIDE

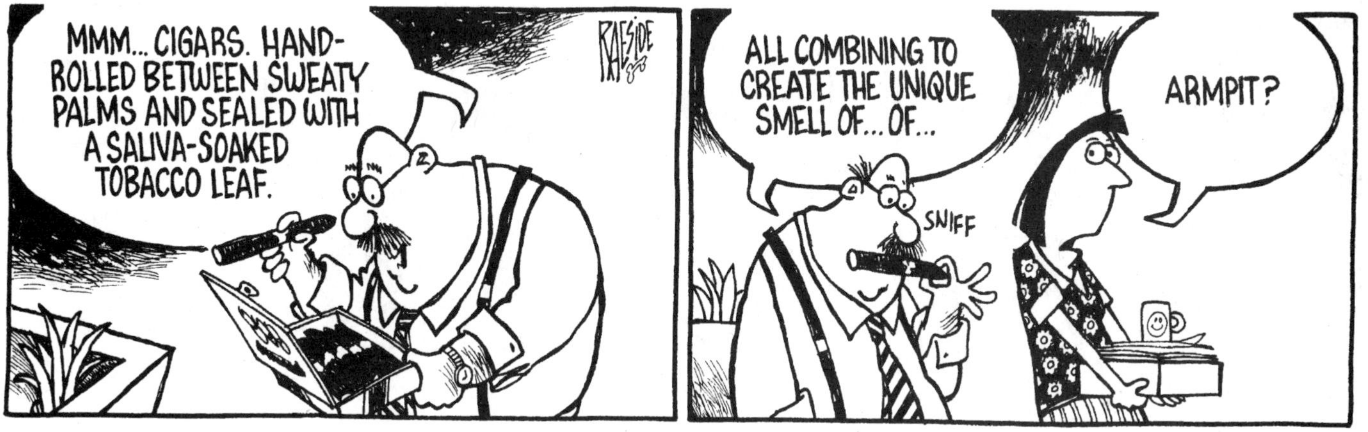
MMM... CIGARS. HAND-ROLLED BETWEEN SWEATY PALMS AND SEALED WITH A SALIVA-SOAKED TOBACCO LEAF.
RAESIDE
ALL COMBINING TO CREATE THE UNIQUE SMELL OF... OF...
SNIFF
ARMPIT?

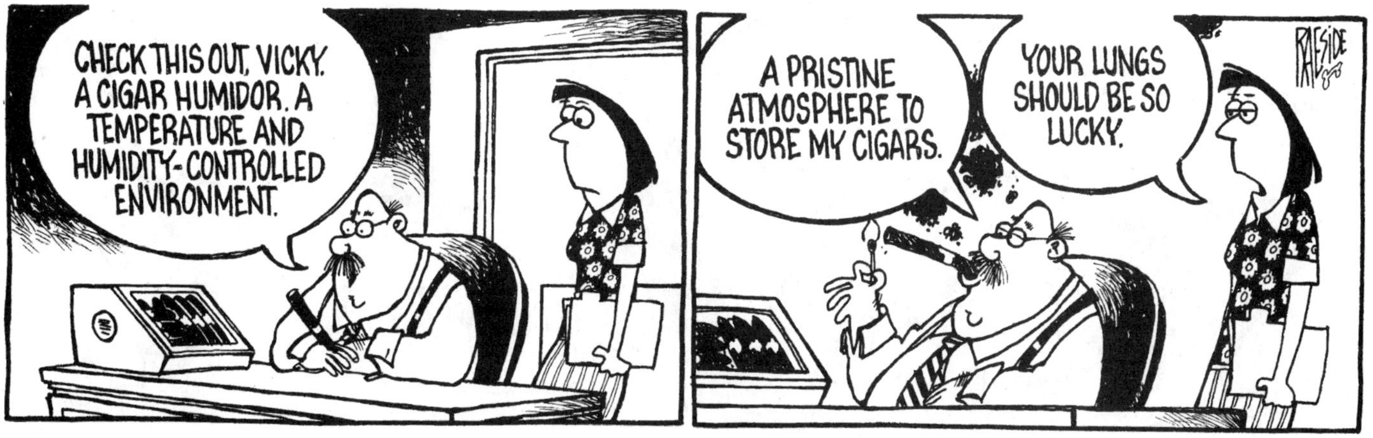
CHECK THIS OUT, VICKY. A CIGAR HUMIDOR. A TEMPERATURE AND HUMIDITY-CONTROLLED ENVIRONMENT.
A PRISTINE ATMOSPHERE TO STORE MY CIGARS.
YOUR LUNGS SHOULD BE SO LUCKY.
RAESIDE

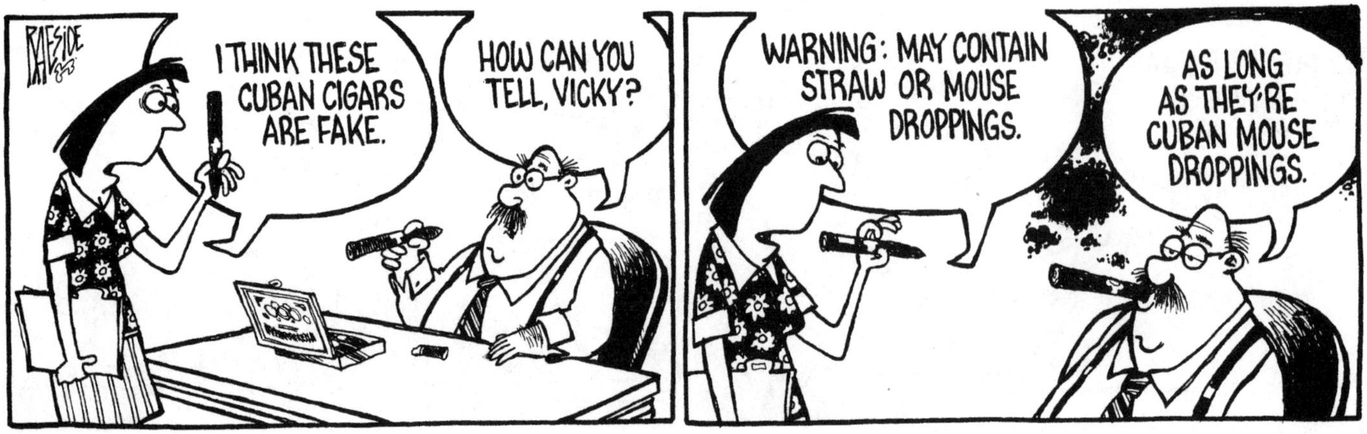
I THINK THESE CUBAN CIGARS ARE FAKE.
HOW CAN YOU TELL, VICKY?
WARNING: MAY CONTAIN STRAW OR MOUSE DROPPINGS.
AS LONG AS THEY'RE CUBAN MOUSE DROPPINGS.

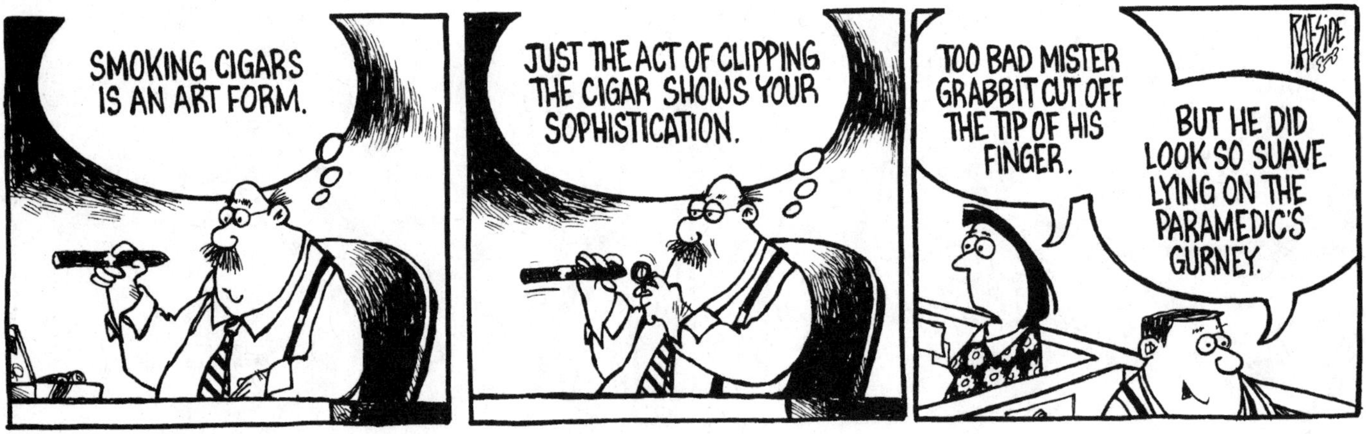
SMOKING CIGARS IS AN ART FORM.
JUST THE ACT OF CLIPPING THE CIGAR SHOWS YOUR SOPHISTICATION.
TOO BAD MISTER GRABBIT CUT OFF THE TIP OF HIS FINGER.
BUT HE DID LOOK SO SUAVE LYING ON THE PARAMEDIC'S GURNEY.

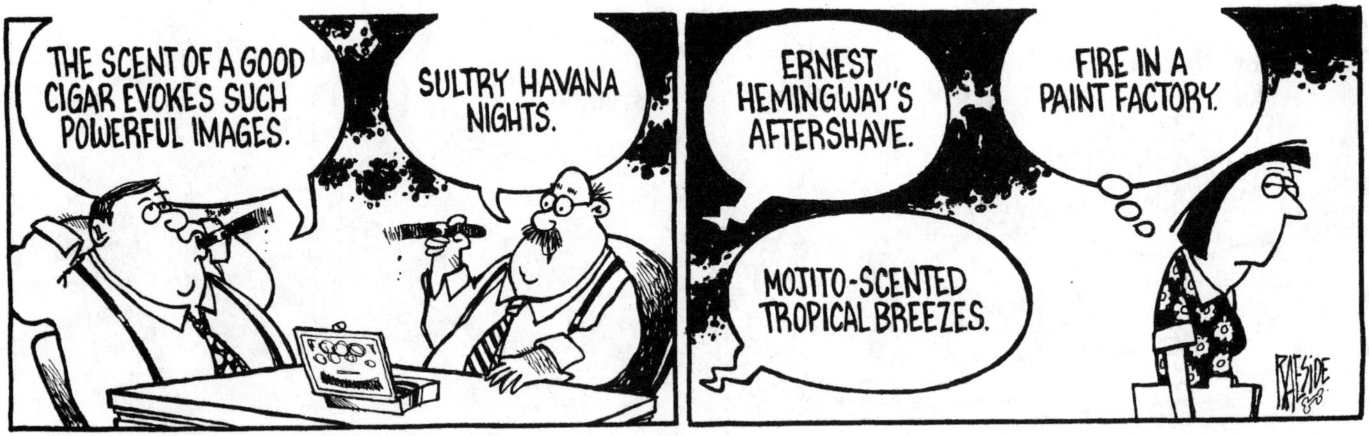
THE SCENT OF A GOOD CIGAR EVOKES SUCH POWERFUL IMAGES.
SULTRY HAVANA NIGHTS.
ERNEST HEMINGWAY'S AFTERSHAVE.
MOJITO-SCENTED TROPICAL BREEZES.
FIRE IN A PAINT FACTORY.

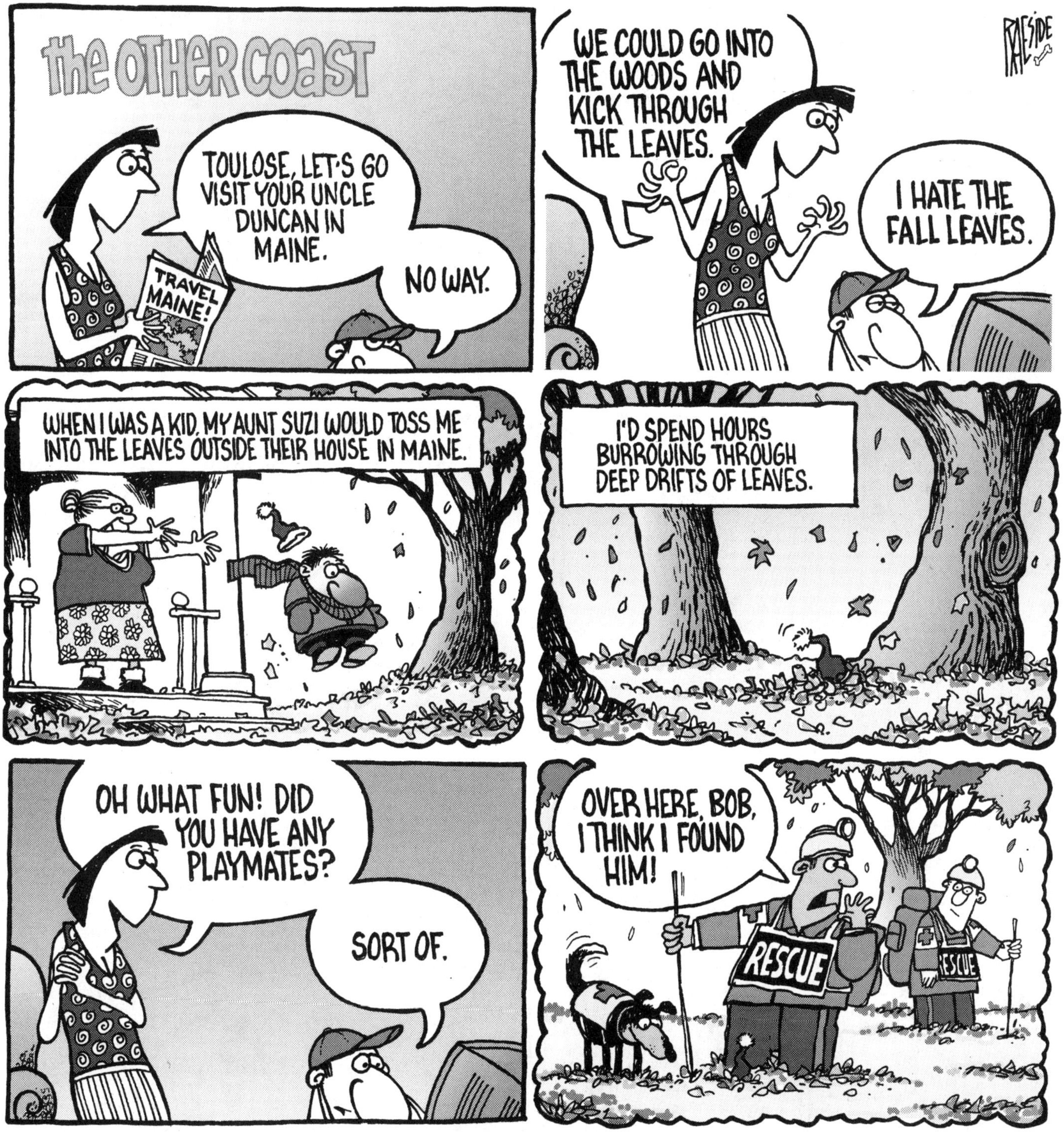
the OTHER COAST
RAESIDE
TOULOSE, LET'S GO VISIT YOUR UNCLE DUNCAN IN MAINE.
TRAVEL MAINE!
NO WAY.
WE COULD GO INTO THE WOODS AND KICK THROUGH THE LEAVES.
I HATE THE FALL LEAVES.
WHEN I WAS A KID, MY AUNT SUZI WOULD TOSS ME INTO THE LEAVES OUTSIDE THEIR HOUSE IN MAINE.
I'D SPEND HOURS BURROWING THROUGH DEEP DRIFTS OF LEAVES.
OH WHAT FUN! DID YOU HAVE ANY PLAYMATES?
SORT OF.
OVER HERE, BOB, I THINK I FOUND HIM!
RESCUE
RESCUE

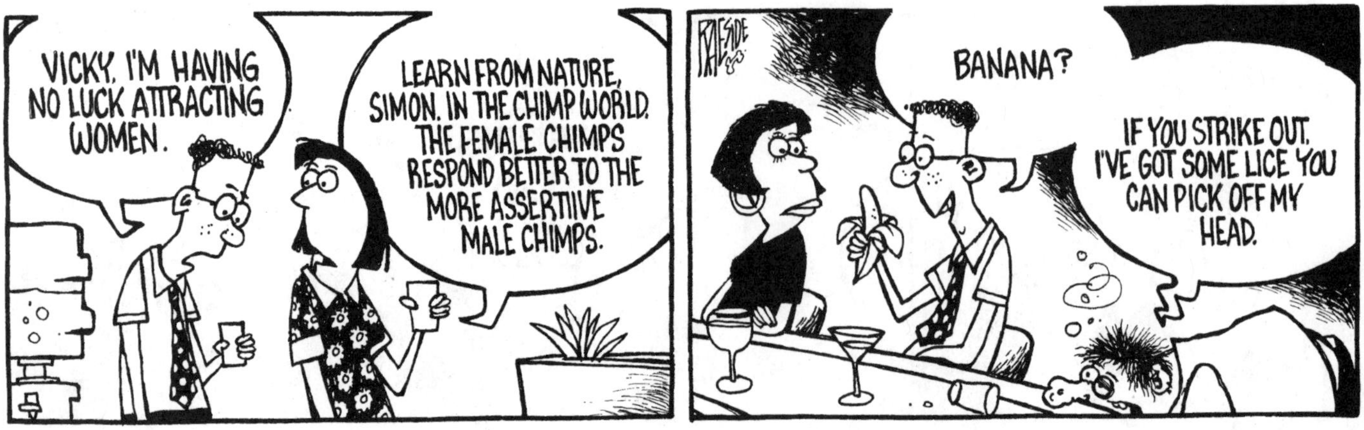
VICKY, I'M HAVING NO LUCK ATTRACTING WOMEN.
LEARN FROM NATURE, SIMON. IN THE CHIMP WORLD, THE FEMALE CHIMPS RESPOND BETTER TO THE MORE ASSERTIIVE MALE CHIMPS.
BANANA?
IF YOU STRIKE OUT, I'VE GOT SOME LICE YOU CAN PICK OFF MY HEAD.

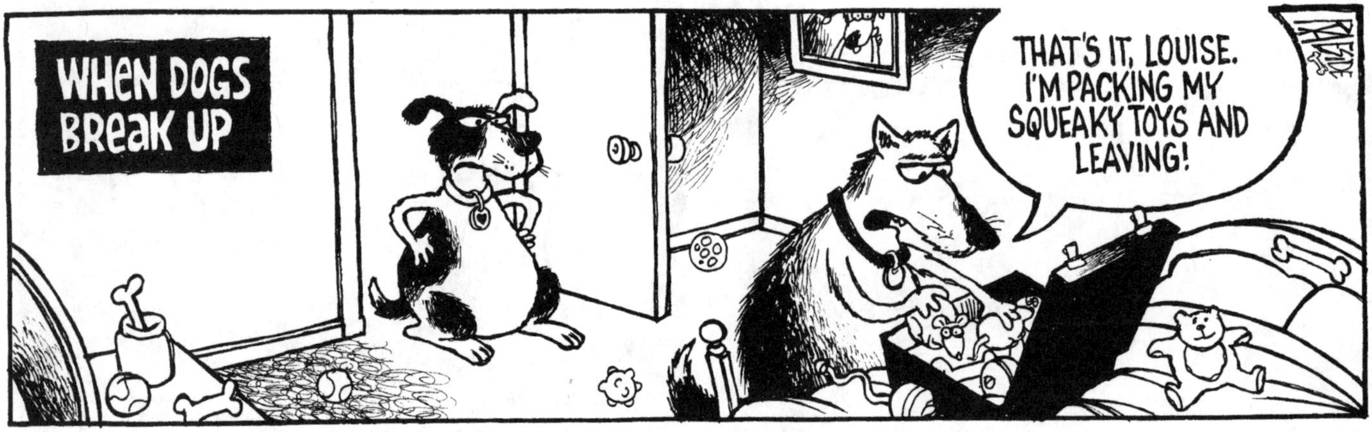
WHEN DOGS BREAK UP
THAT'S IT, LOUISE. I'M PACKING MY SQUEAKY TOYS AND LEAVING!

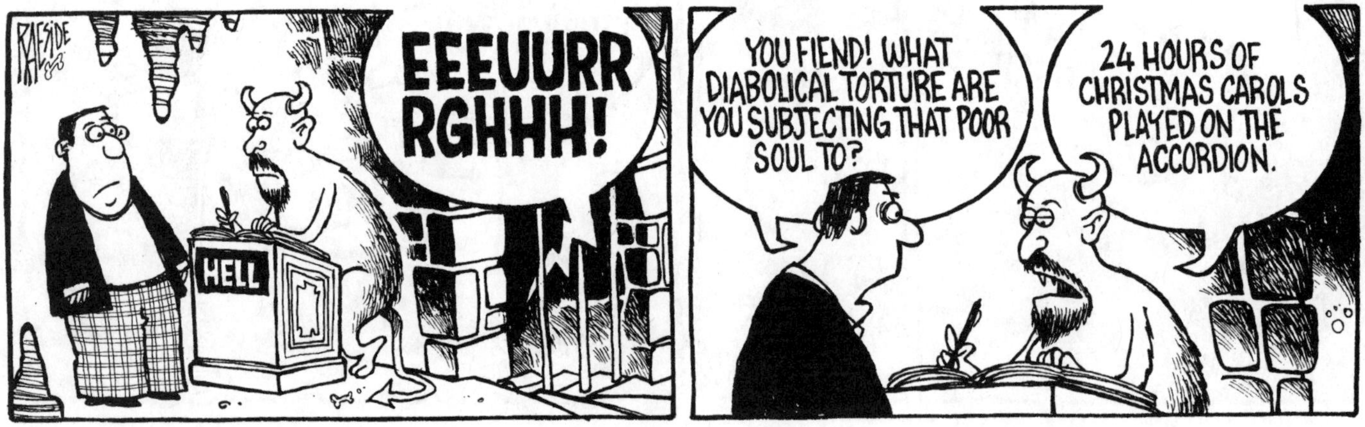
EEEUURR RGHHH!
HELL
YOU FIEND! WHAT DIABOLICAL TORTURE ARE YOU SUBJECTING THAT POOR SOUL TO?
24 HOURS OF CHRISTMAS CAROLS PLAYED ON THE ACCORDION.

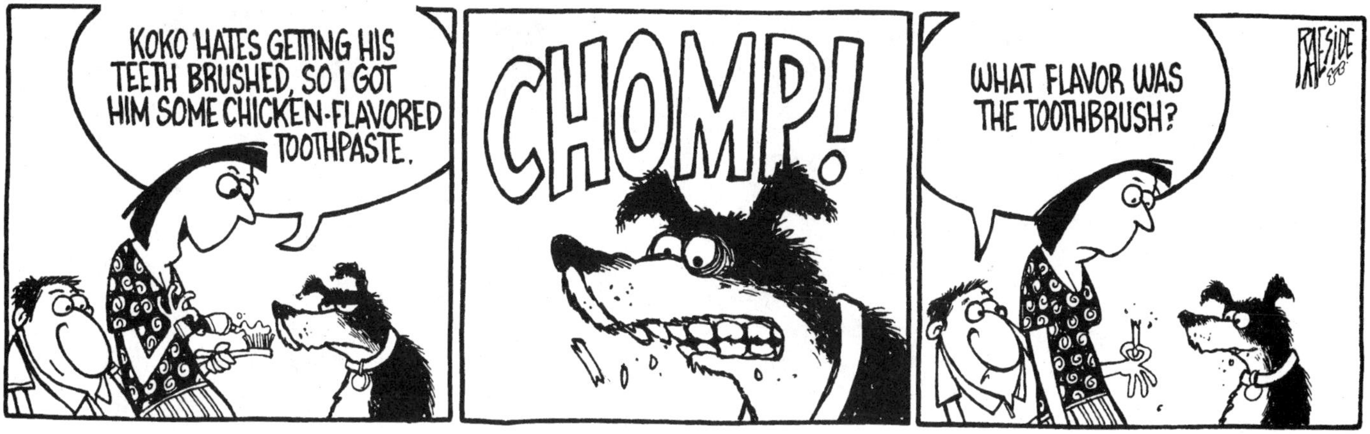
KOKO HATES GETTING HIS TEETH BRUSHED, SO I GOT HIM SOME CHICKEN-FLAVORED TOOTHPASTE.
CHOMP!
WHAT FLAVOR WAS THE TOOTHBRUSH?
RAESIDE

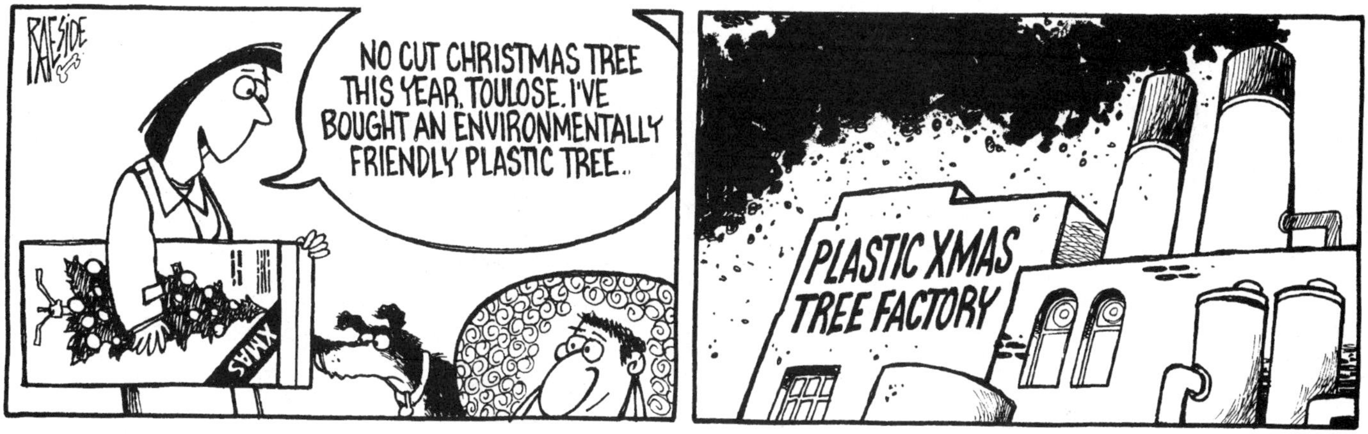
RAESIDE
NO CUT CHRISTMAS TREE THIS YEAR, TOULOSE. I'VE BOUGHT AN ENVIRONMENTALLY FRIENDLY PLASTIC TREE..
XMAS
PLASTIC XMAS TREE FACTORY

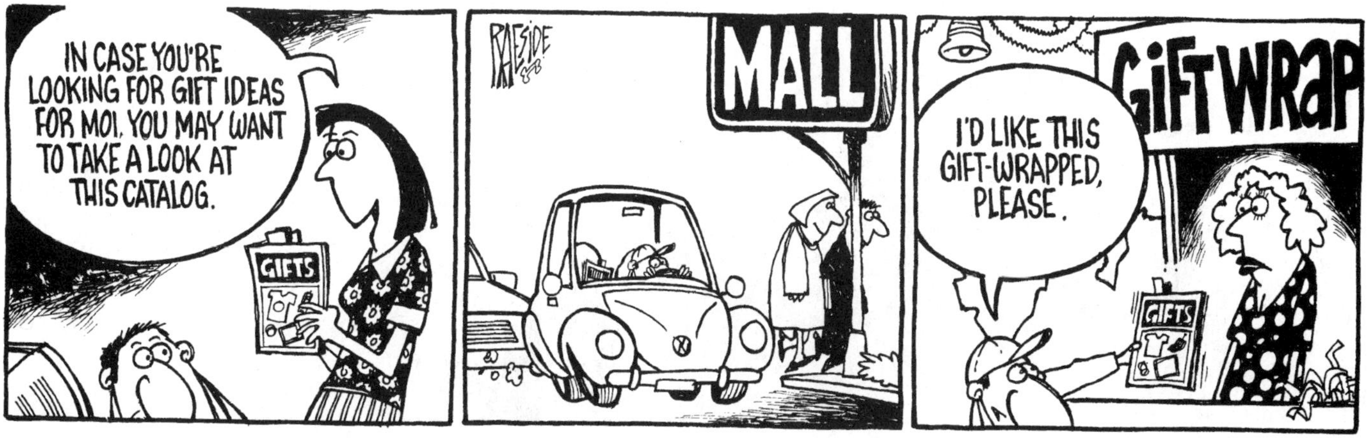
IN CASE YOU'RE LOOKING FOR GIFT IDEAS FOR MOI, YOU MAY WANT TO TAKE A LOOK AT THIS CATALOG.
GIFTS
RAESIDE
MALL
GIFT WRAP
I'D LIKE THIS GIFT-WRAPPED, PLEASE.
GIFTS

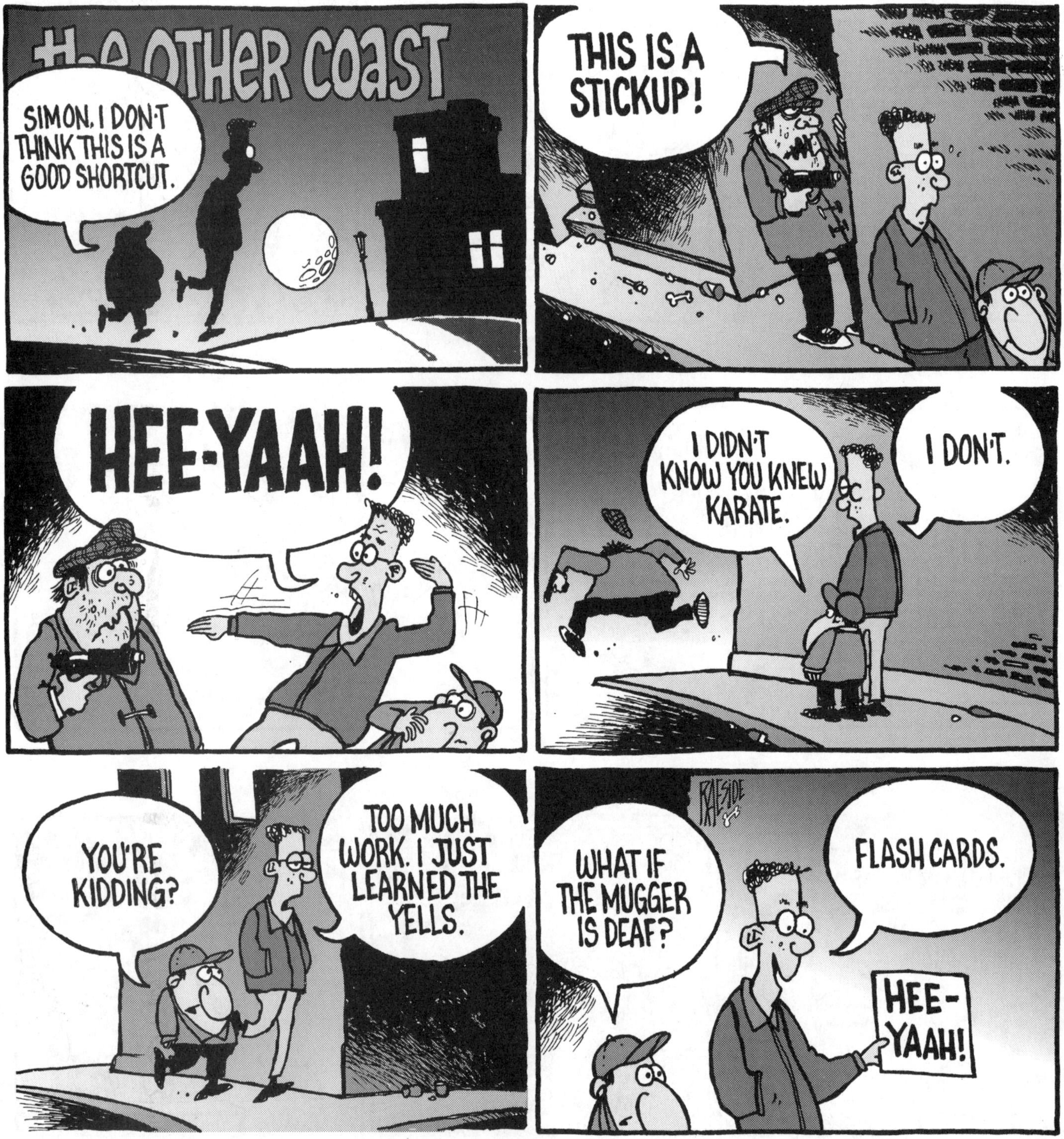
the OTHER COAST
SIMON, I DON'T THINK THIS IS A GOOD SHORTCUT.
THIS IS A STICKUP!
HEE-YAAH!
I DIDN'T KNOW YOU KNEW KARATE.
I DON'T.
YOU'RE KIDDING?
TOO MUCH WORK. I JUST LEARNED THE YELLS.
WHAT IF THE MUGGER IS DEAF?
FLASH CARDS.
HEE-YAAH!

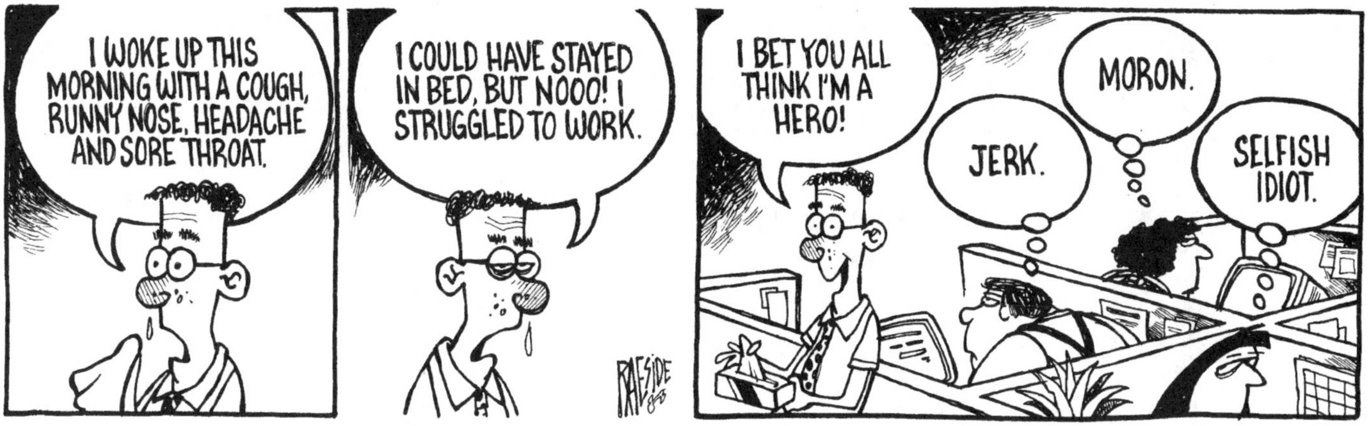
I WOKE UP THIS MORNING WITH A COUGH, RUNNY NOSE, HEADACHE AND SORE THROAT.
I COULD HAVE STAYED IN BED, BUT NOOO! I STRUGGLED TO WORK.
RAESIDE
I BET YOU ALL THINK I'M A HERO!
JERK.
MORON.
SELFISH IDIOT.

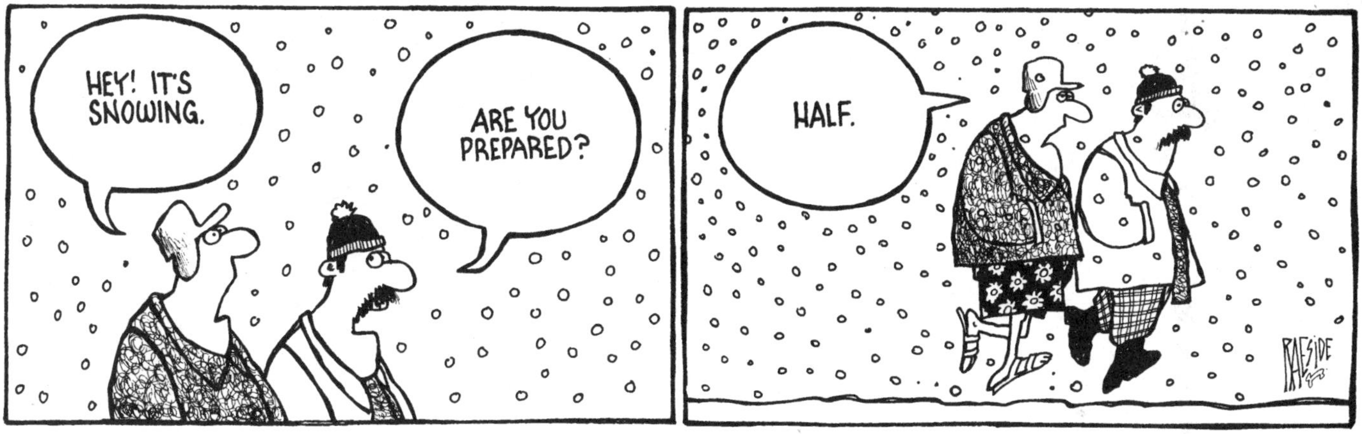
HEY! IT'S SNOWING.
ARE YOU PREPARED?
HALF.
RAESIDE

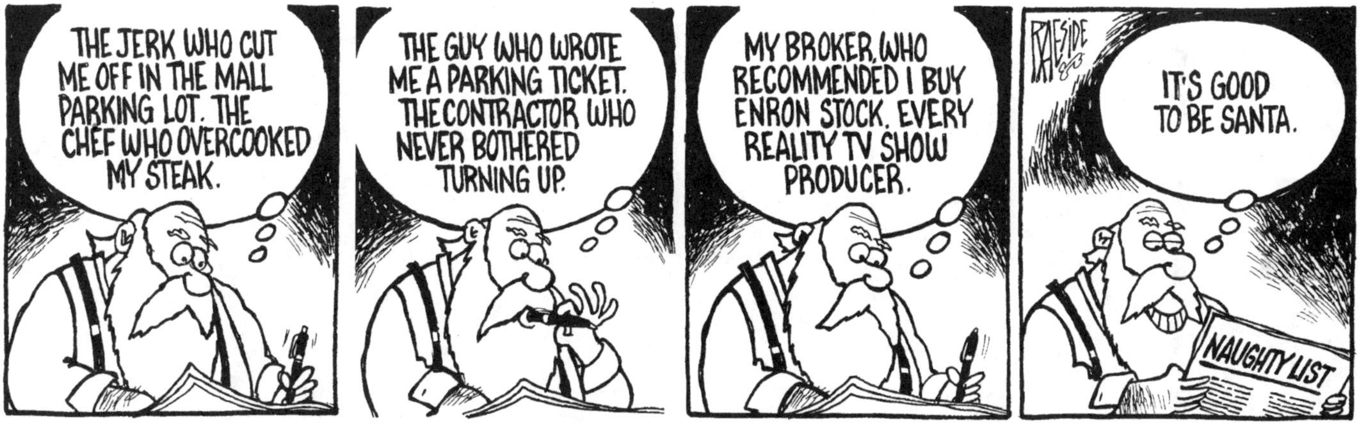
THE JERK WHO CUT ME OFF IN THE MALL PARKING LOT. THE CHEF WHO OVERCOOKED MY STEAK.
THE GUY WHO WROTE ME A PARKING TICKET. THE CONTRACTOR WHO NEVER BOTHERED TURNING UP.
MY BROKER, WHO RECOMMENDED I BUY ENRON STOCK. EVERY REALITY TV SHOW PRODUCER.
RAESIDE
IT'S GOOD TO BE SANTA.
NAUGHTY LIST

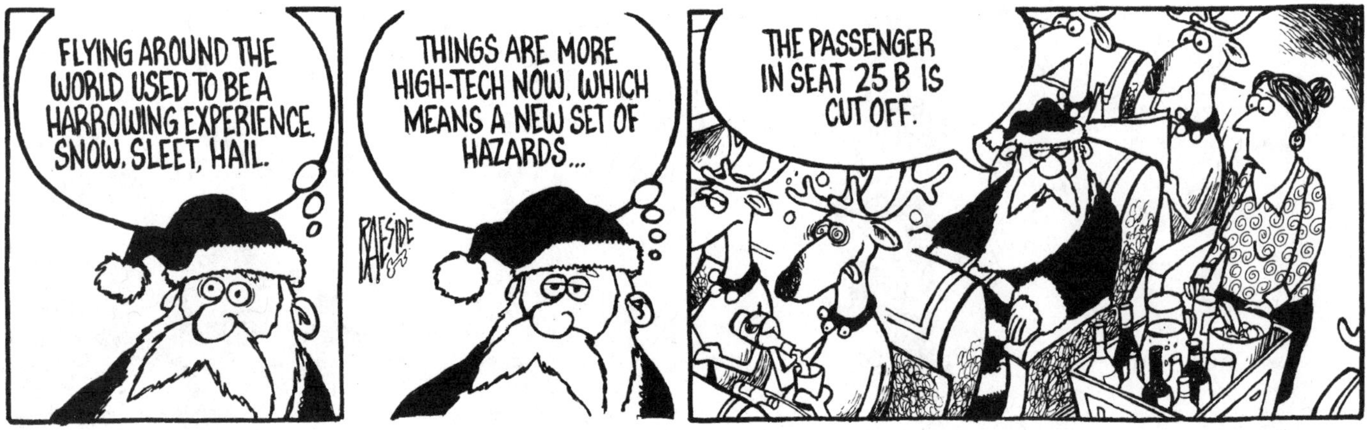
FLYING AROUND THE WORLD USED TO BE A HARROWING EXPERIENCE. SNOW, SLEET, HAIL.
THINGS ARE MORE HIGH-TECH NOW, WHICH MEANS A NEW SET OF HAZARDS...
RAESIDE
THE PASSENGER IN SEAT 25 B IS CUT OFF.

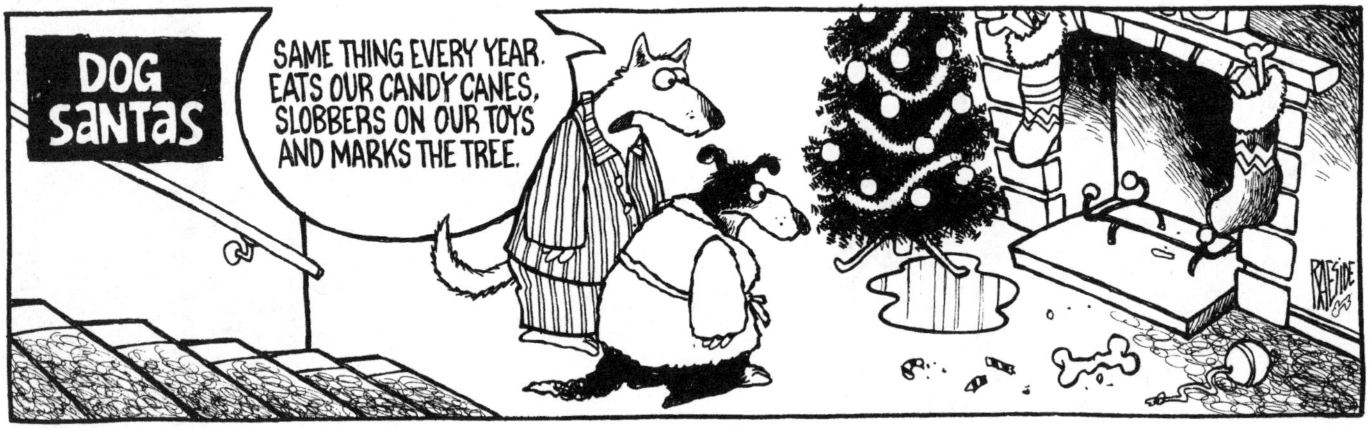
DOG SANTAS
SAME THING EVERY YEAR. EATS OUR CANDY CANES, SLOBBERS ON OUR TOYS AND MARKS THE TREE.
RAESIDE

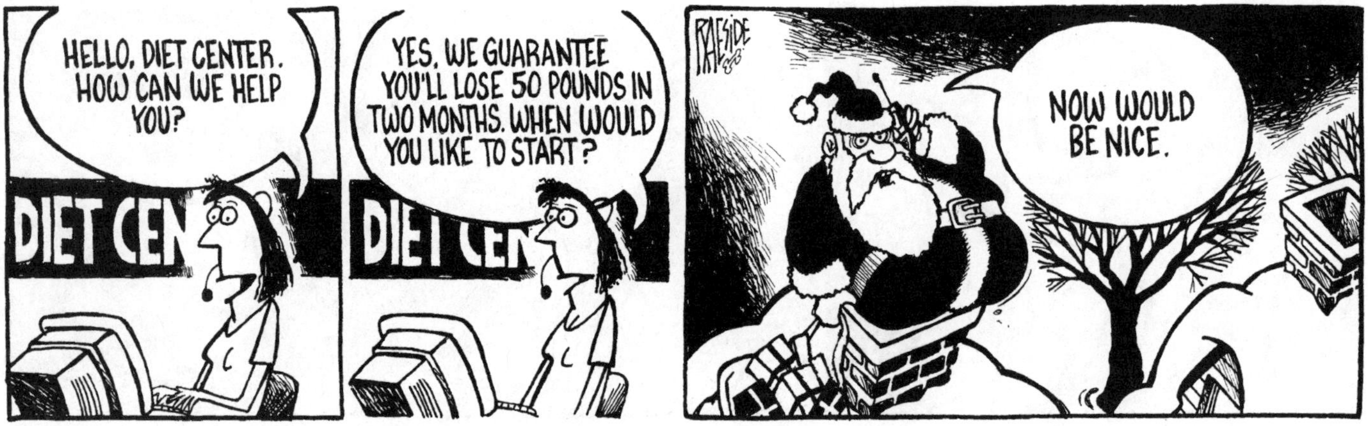
HELLO, DIET CENTER. HOW CAN WE HELP YOU?
DIET CEN
YES, WE GUARANTEE YOU'LL LOSE 50 POUNDS IN TWO MONTHS. WHEN WOULD YOU LIKE TO START?
DIET CEN
RAESIDE
NOW WOULD BE NICE.

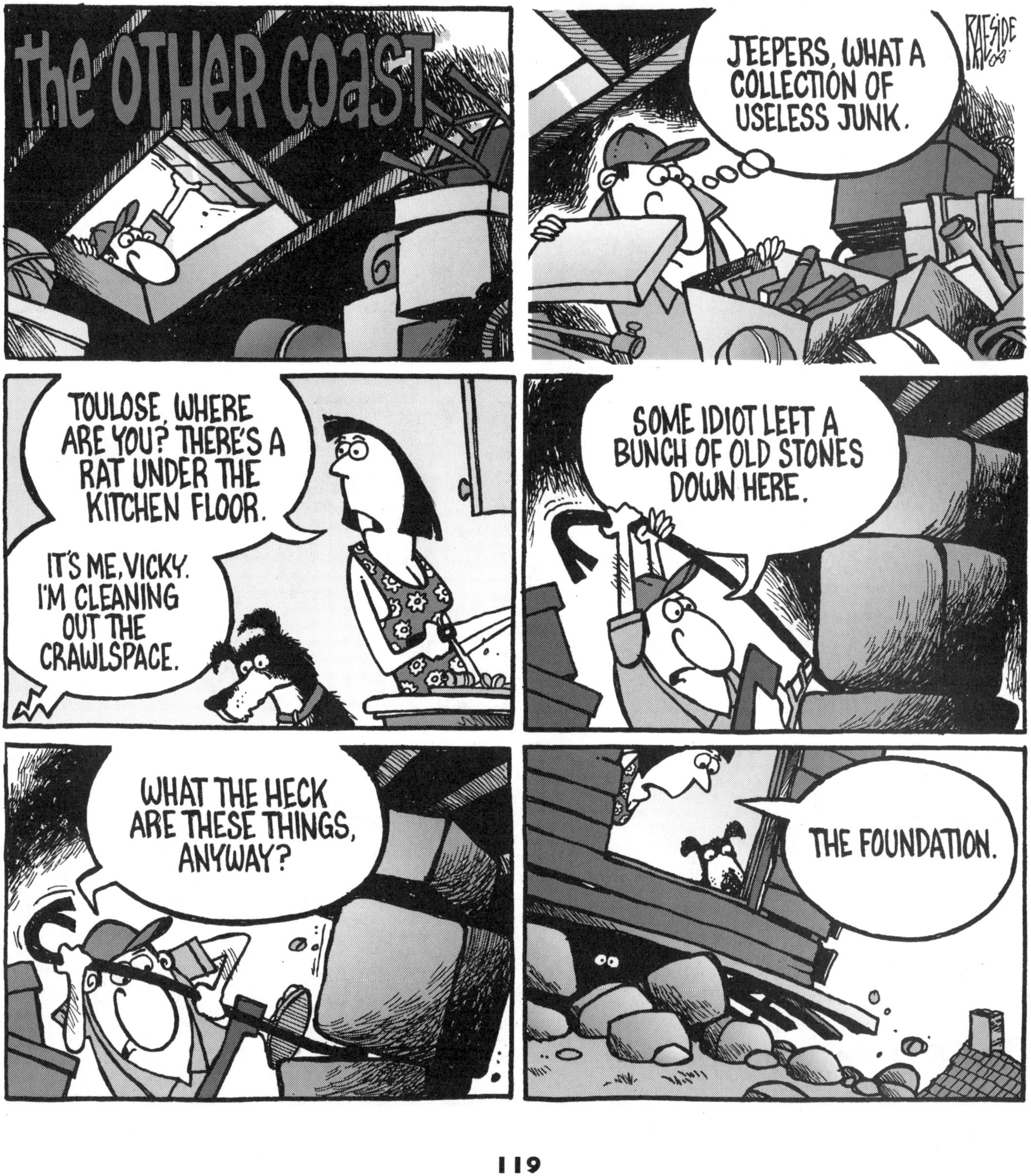
the OTHER COAST
RAFSIDE '03
JEEPERS, WHAT A COLLECTION OF USELESS JUNK.
TOULOSE, WHERE ARE YOU? THERE'S A RAT UNDER THE KITCHEN FLOOR.
IT'S ME, VICKY. I'M CLEANING OUT THE CRAWLSPACE.
SOME IDIOT LEFT A BUNCH OF OLD STONES DOWN HERE.
WHAT THE HECK ARE THESE THINGS, ANYWAY?
THE FOUNDATION.

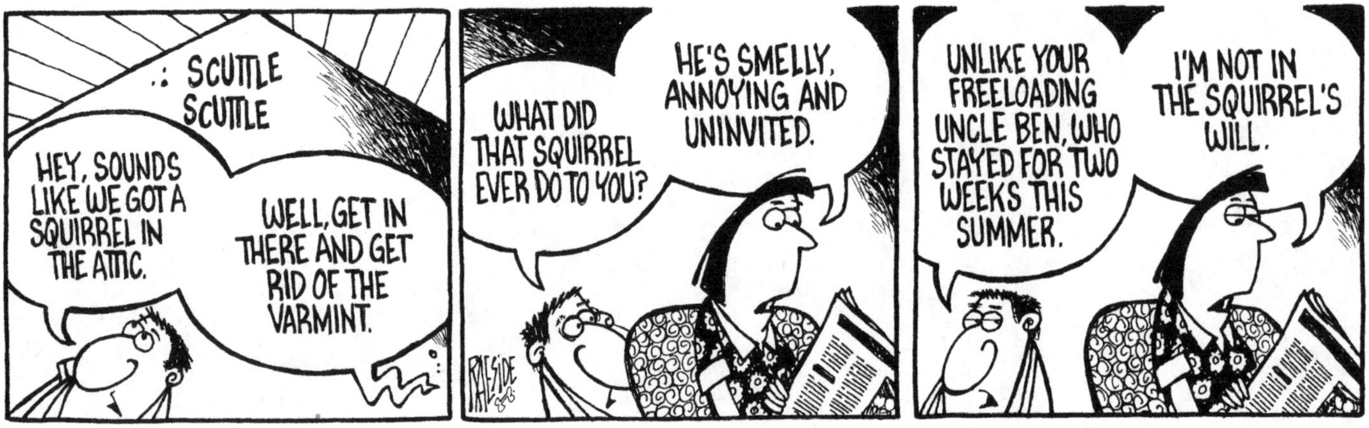
SCUTTLE SCUTTLE
HEY, SOUNDS LIKE WE GOT A SQUIRREL IN THE ATTIC.
WELL, GET IN THERE AND GET RID OF THE VARMINT.
WHAT DID THAT SQUIRREL EVER DO TO YOU?
HE'S SMELLY, ANNOYING AND UNINVITED.
UNLIKE YOUR FREELOADING UNCLE BEN, WHO STAYED FOR TWO WEEKS THIS SUMMER.
I'M NOT IN THE SQUIRREL'S WILL.

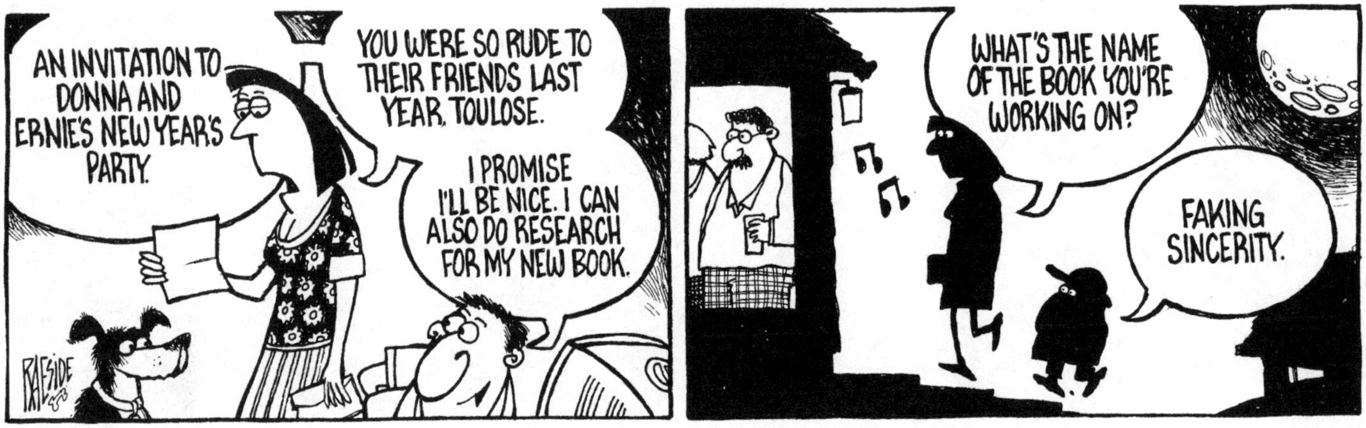
AN INVITATION TO DONNA AND ERNIE'S NEW YEAR'S PARTY.
YOU WERE SO RUDE TO THEIR FRIENDS LAST YEAR, TOULOSE.
I PROMISE I'LL BE NICE. I CAN ALSO DO RESEARCH FOR MY NEW BOOK.
WHAT'S THE NAME OF THE BOOK YOU'RE WORKING ON?
FAKING SINCERITY.

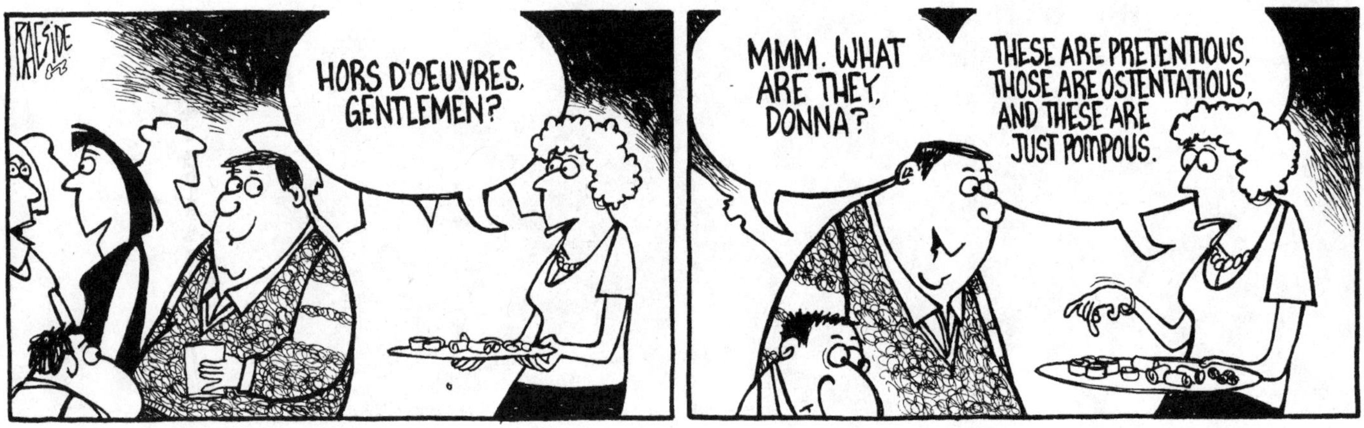
HORS D'OEUVRES, GENTLEMEN?
MMM. WHAT ARE THEY, DONNA?
THESE ARE PRETENTIOUS, THOSE ARE OSTENTATIOUS, AND THESE ARE JUST POMPOUS.

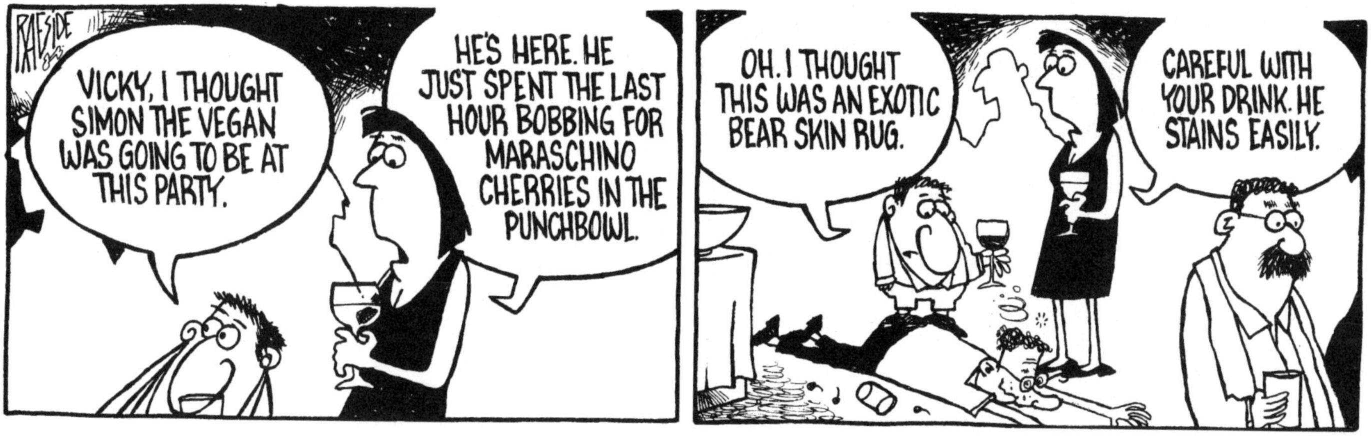
VICKY, I THOUGHT SIMON THE VEGAN WAS GOING TO BE AT THIS PARTY.
HE'S HERE. HE JUST SPENT THE LAST HOUR BOBBING FOR MARASCHINO CHERRIES IN THE PUNCHBOWL.
OH. I THOUGHT THIS WAS AN EXOTIC BEAR SKIN RUG.
CAREFUL WITH YOUR DRINK. HE STAINS EASILY.

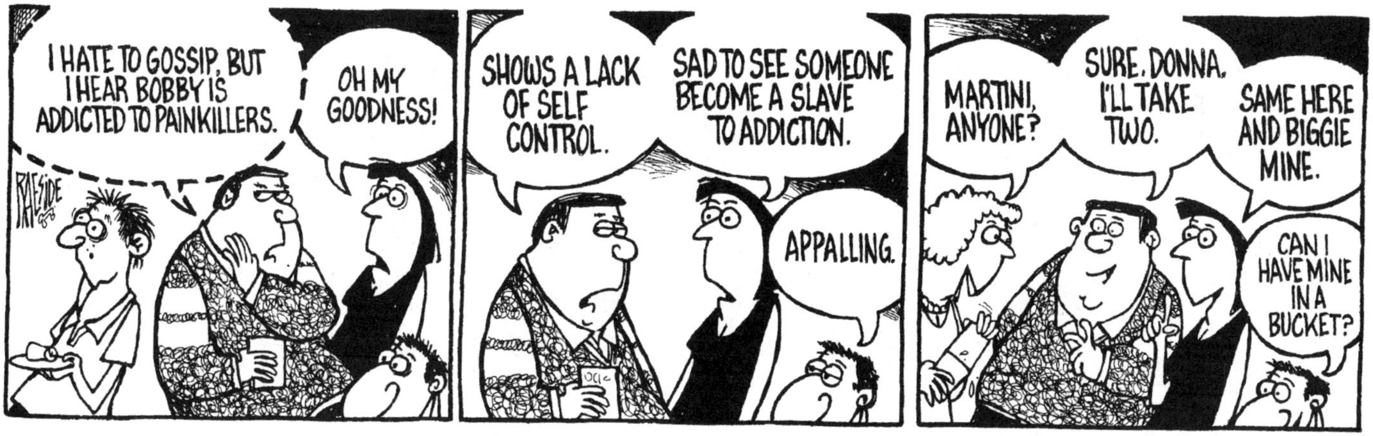
I HATE TO GOSSIP, BUT I HEAR BOBBY IS ADDICTED TO PAINKILLERS.
OH MY GOODNESS!
SHOWS A LACK OF SELF CONTROL.
SAD TO SEE SOMEONE BECOME A SLAVE TO ADDICTION.
APPALLING.
MARTINI, ANYONE?
SURE, DONNA. I'LL TAKE TWO.
SAME HERE AND BIGGIE MINE.
CAN I HAVE MINE IN A BUCKET?

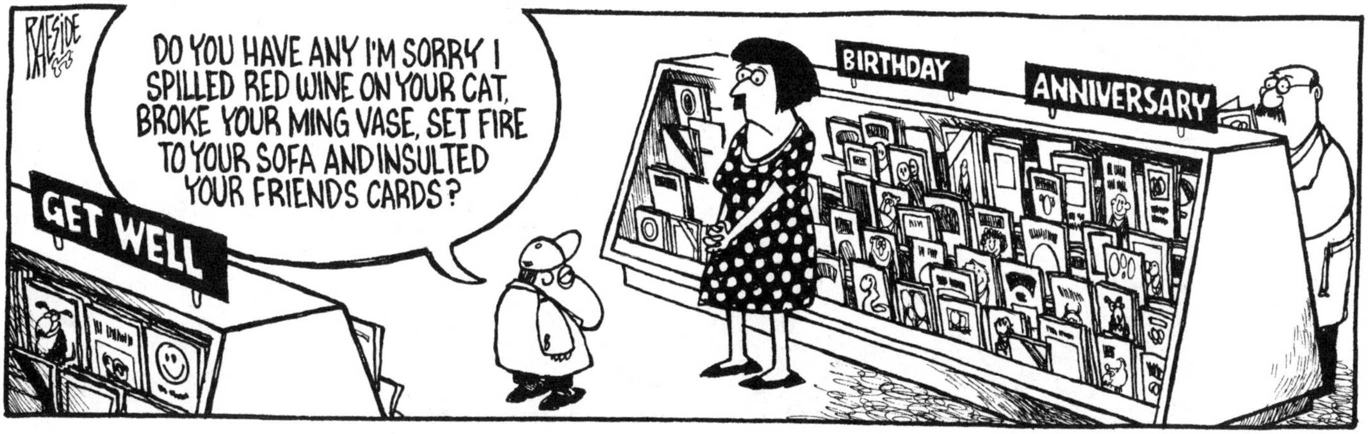
DO YOU HAVE ANY I'M SORRY I SPILLED RED WINE ON YOUR CAT, BROKE YOUR MING VASE, SET FIRE TO YOUR SOFA AND INSULTED YOUR FRIENDS CARDS?
GET WELL
BIRTHDAY
ANNIVERSARY

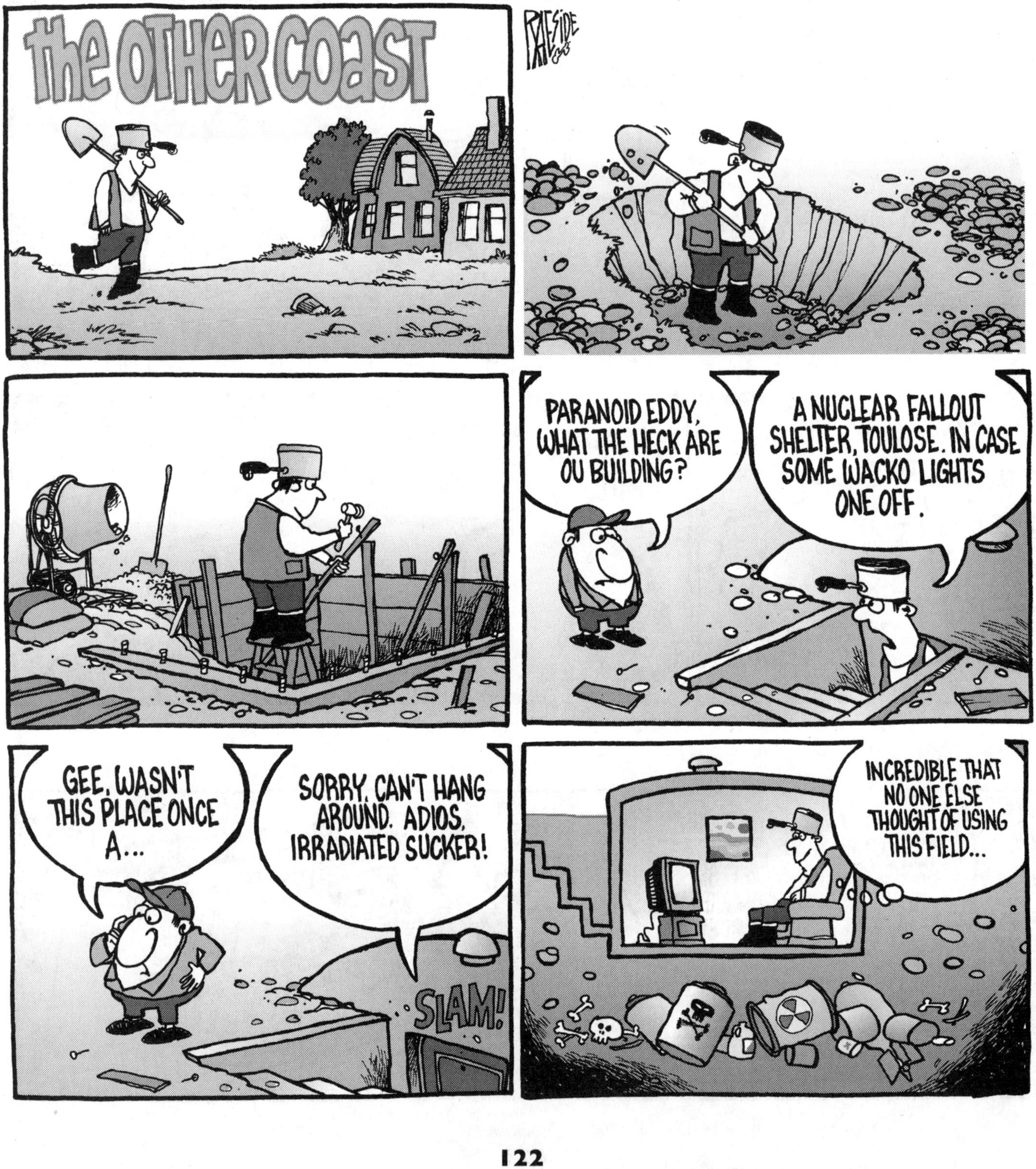
the OTHER COAST
RAESIDE
PARANOID EDDY, WHAT THE HECK ARE OU BUILDING?
A NUCLEAR FALLOUT SHELTER, TOULOSE. IN CASE SOME WACKO LIGHTS ONE OFF.
GEE, WASN'T THIS PLACE ONCE A...
SORRY, CAN'T HANG AROUND. ADIOS, IRRADIATED SUCKER!
SLAM!
INCREDIBLE THAT NO ONE ELSE THOUGHT OF USING THIS FIELD...

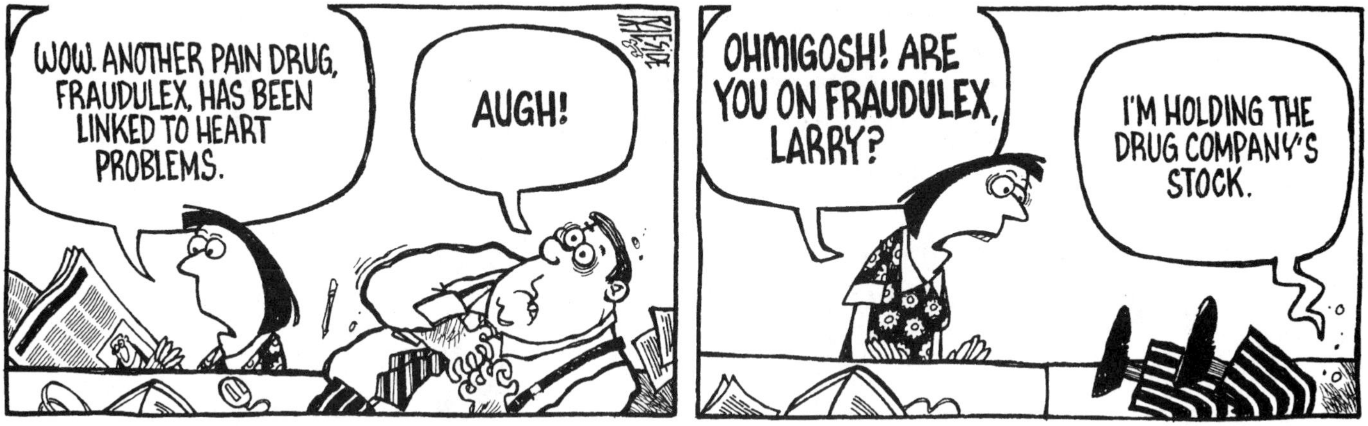
WOW. ANOTHER PAIN DRUG, FRAUDULEX, HAS BEEN LINKED TO HEART PROBLEMS.
AUGH!
OHMIGOSH! ARE YOU ON FRAUDULEX, LARRY?
I'M HOLDING THE DRUG COMPANY'S STOCK.

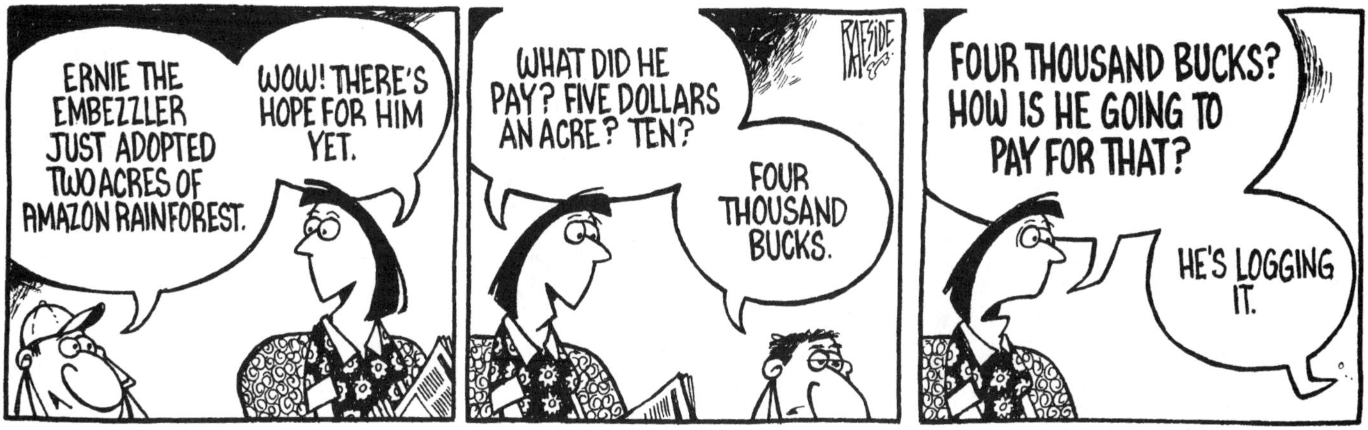
ERNIE THE EMBEZZLER JUST ADOPTED TWO ACRES OF AMAZON RAINFOREST.
WOW! THERE'S HOPE FOR HIM YET.
WHAT DID HE PAY? FIVE DOLLARS AN ACRE? TEN?
FOUR THOUSAND BUCKS.
FOUR THOUSAND BUCKS? HOW IS HE GOING TO PAY FOR THAT?
HE'S LOGGING IT.

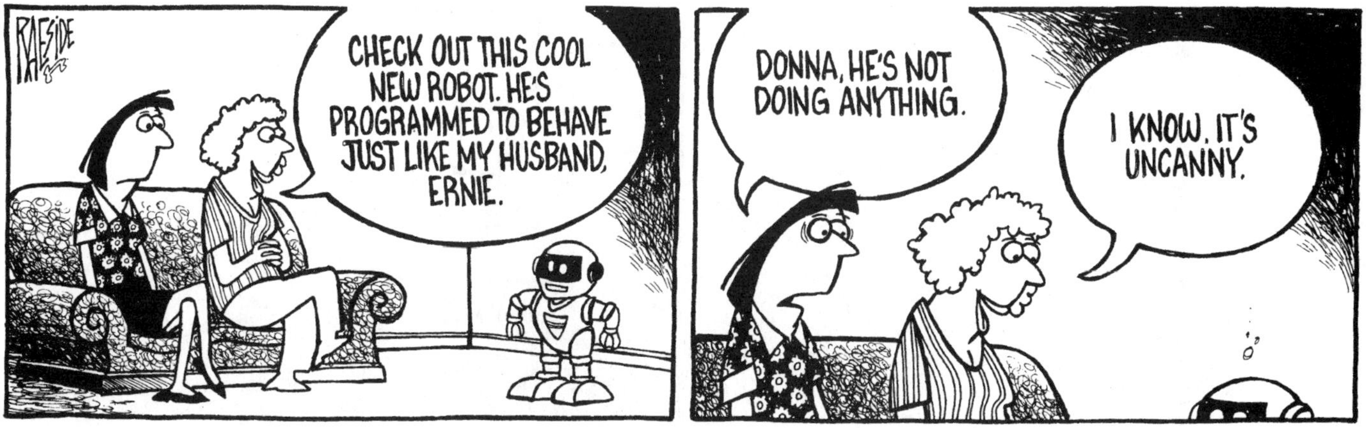
CHECK OUT THIS COOL NEW ROBOT. HE'S PROGRAMMED TO BEHAVE JUST LIKE MY HUSBAND, ERNIE.
DONNA, HE'S NOT DOING ANYTHING.
I KNOW. IT'S UNCANNY.

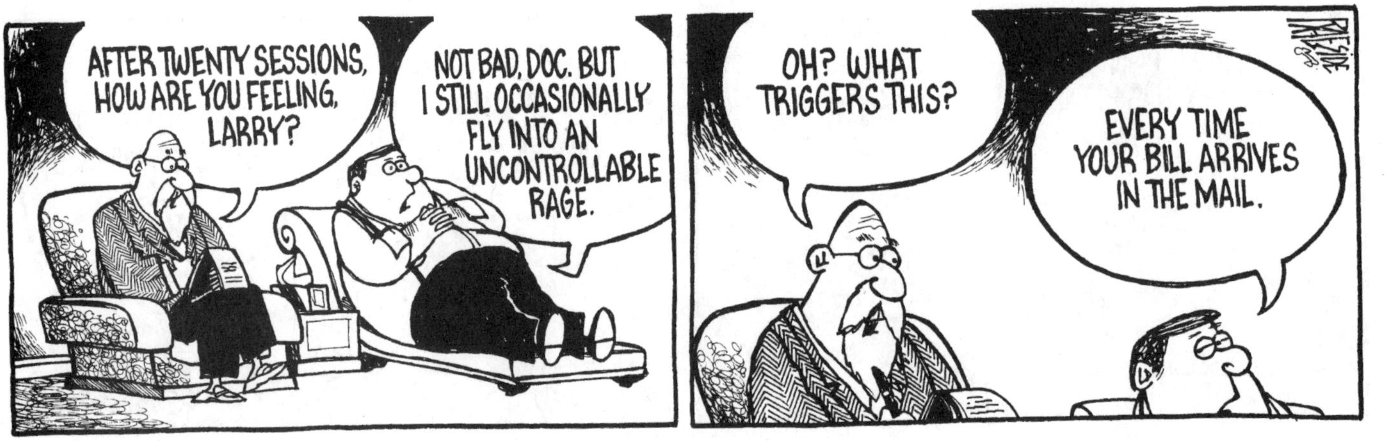
AFTER TWENTY SESSIONS, HOW ARE YOU FEELING, LARRY?
NOT BAD, DOC. BUT I STILL OCCASIONALLY FLY INTO AN UNCONTROLLABLE RAGE.
OH? WHAT TRIGGERS THIS?
EVERY TIME YOUR BILL ARRIVES IN THE MAIL.
RAESIDE

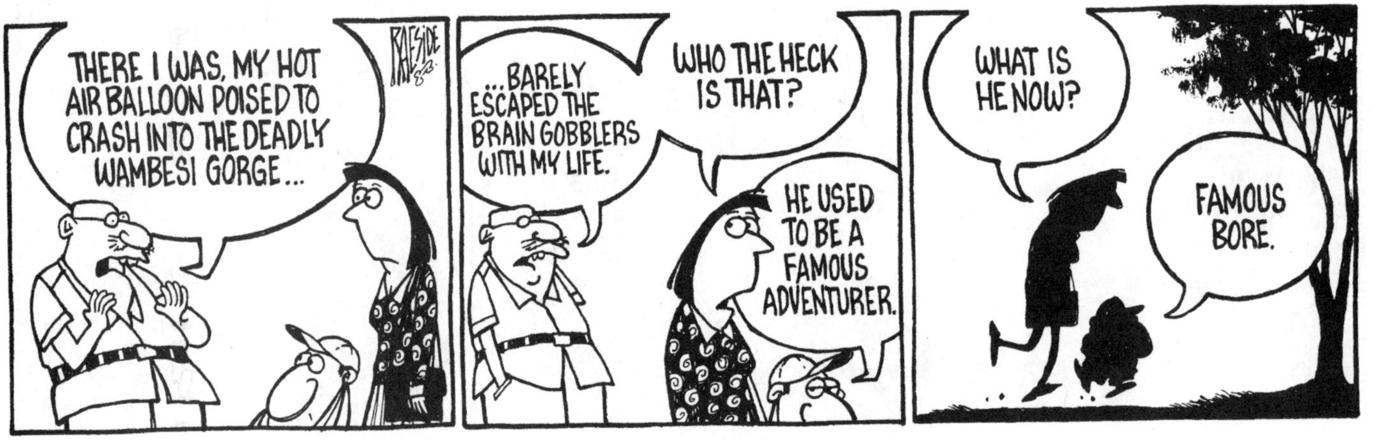
THERE I WAS, MY HOT AIR BALLOON POISED TO CRASH INTO THE DEADLY WAMBESI GORGE...
RAESIDE
...BARELY ESCAPED THE BRAIN GOBBLERS WITH MY LIFE.
WHO THE HECK IS THAT?
HE USED TO BE A FAMOUS ADVENTURER.
WHAT IS HE NOW?
FAMOUS BORE.

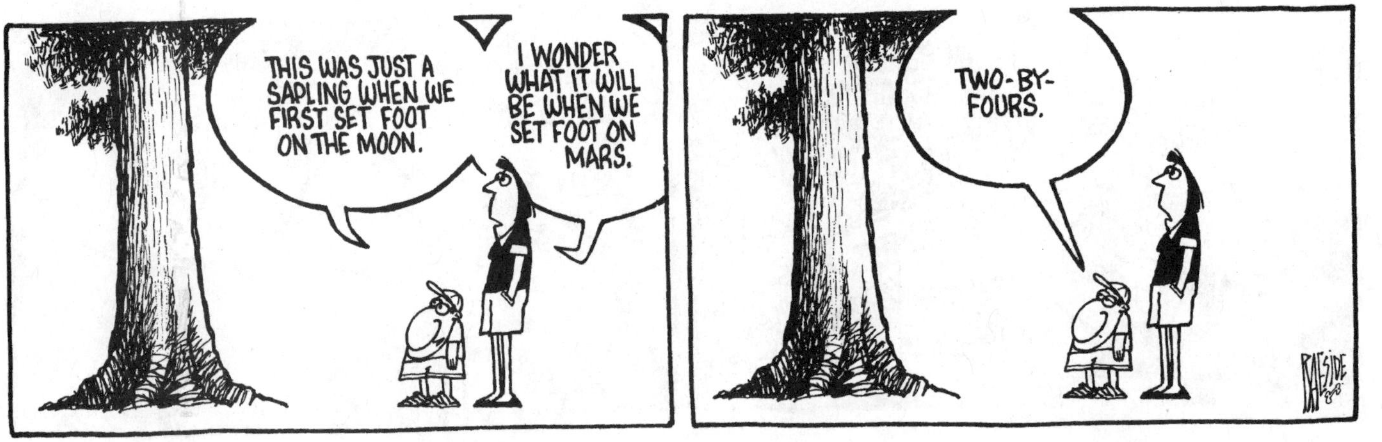
THIS WAS JUST A SAPLING WHEN WE FIRST SET FOOT ON THE MOON.
I WONDER WHAT IT WILL BE WHEN WE SET FOOT ON MARS.
TWO-BY-FOURS.
RAESIDE

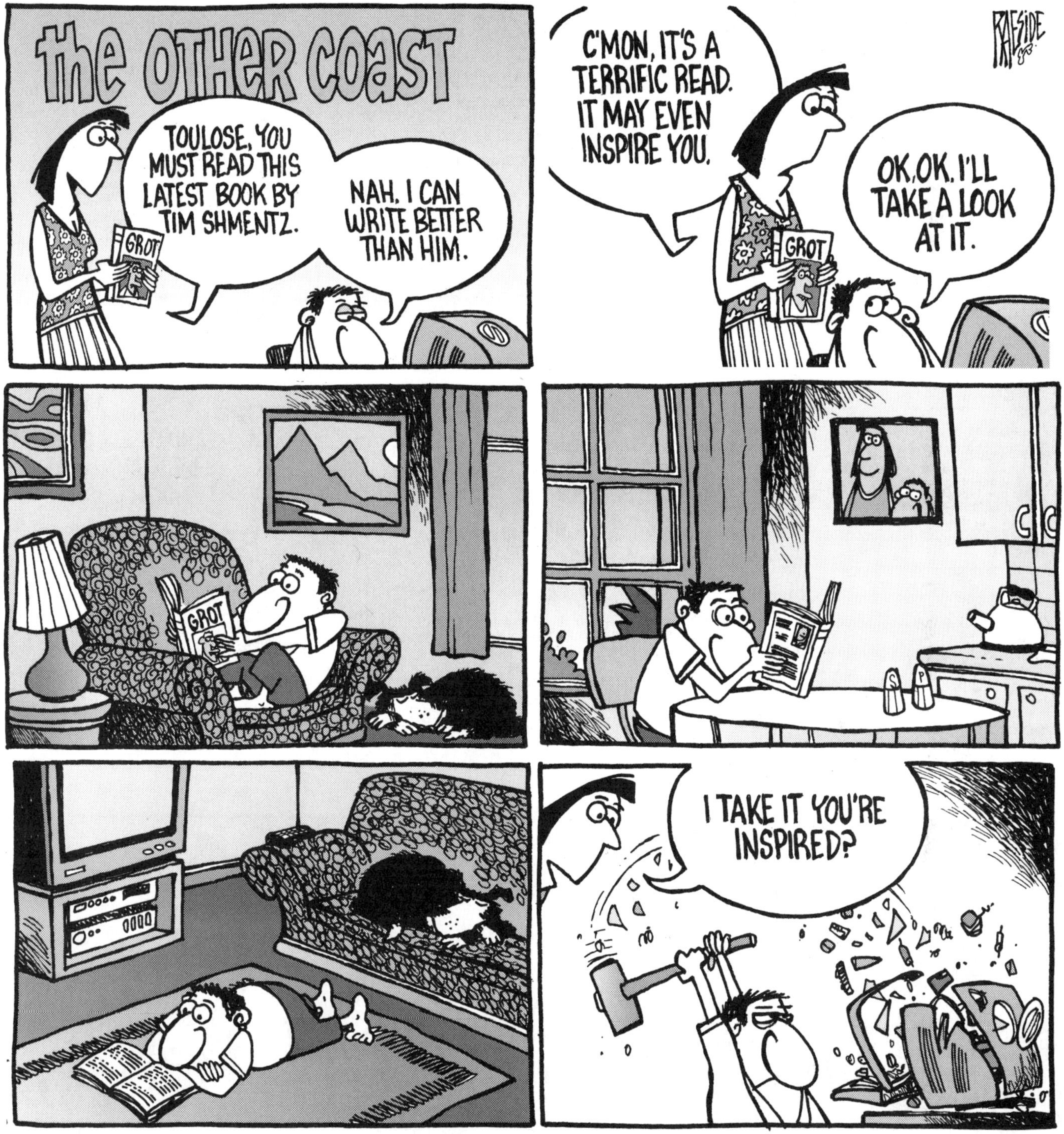
the OTHER COAST
RAESIDE
TOULOSE, YOU MUST READ THIS LATEST BOOK BY TIM SHMENTZ.
GROT
NAH. I CAN WRITE BETTER THAN HIM.
C'MON, IT'S A TERRIFIC READ. IT MAY EVEN INSPIRE YOU.
OK, OK. I'LL TAKE A LOOK AT IT.
GROT
I TAKE IT YOU'RE INSPIRED?

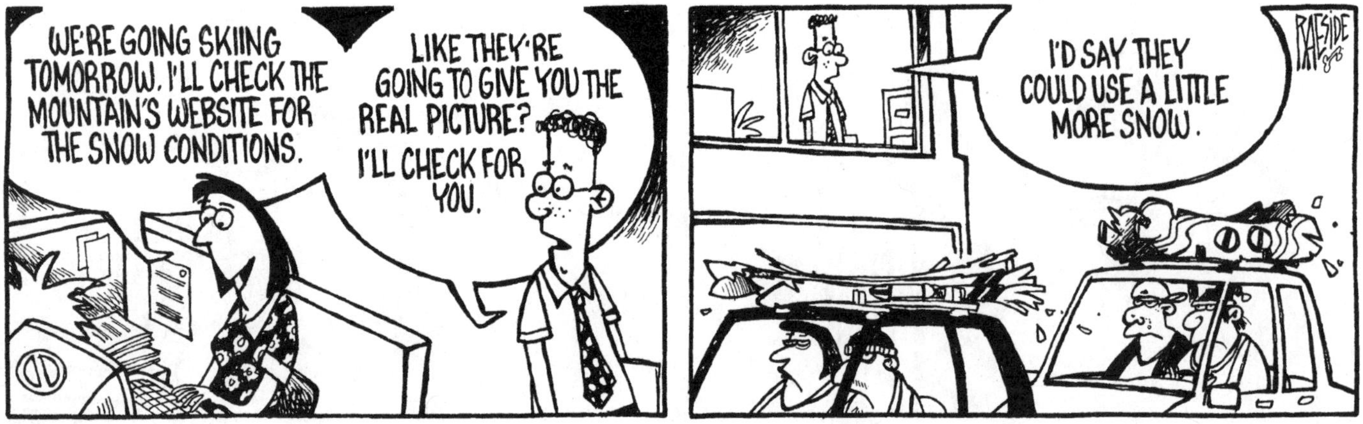
WE'RE GOING SKIING TOMORROW. I'LL CHECK THE MOUNTAIN'S WEBSITE FOR THE SNOW CONDITIONS.
LIKE THEY'RE GOING TO GIVE YOU THE REAL PICTURE?
I'LL CHECK FOR YOU.
I'D SAY THEY COULD USE A LITTLE MORE SNOW.
RAESIDE

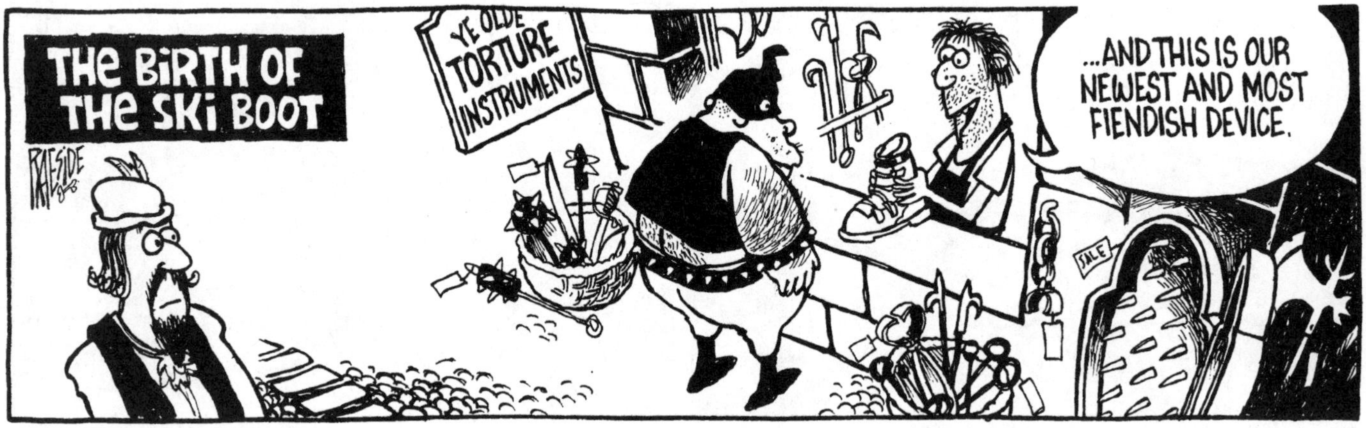
THE BIRTH OF THE SKI BOOT
RAESIDE
YE OLDE TORTURE INSTRUMENTS
...AND THIS IS OUR NEWEST AND MOST FIENDISH DEVICE.
SALE

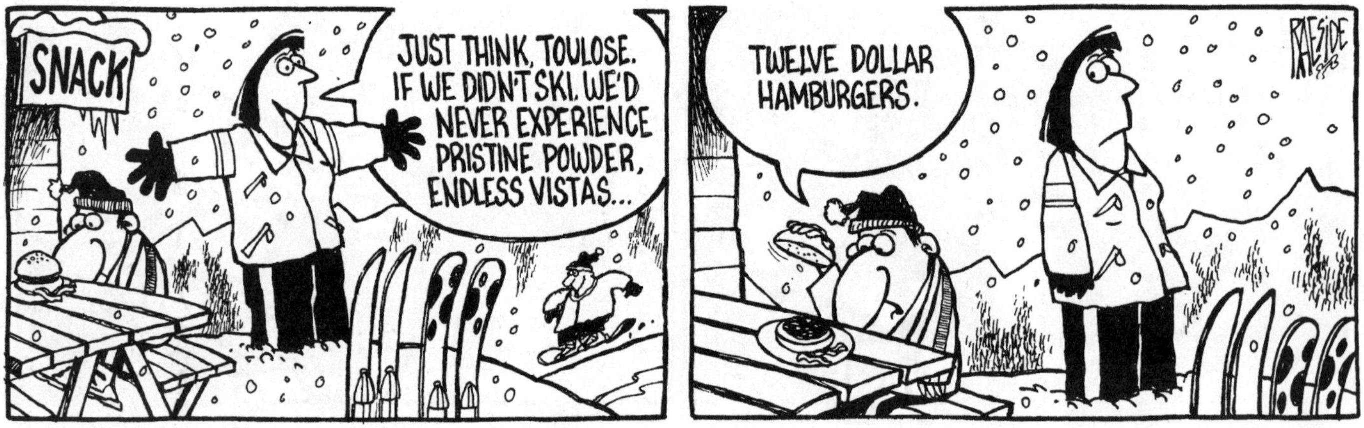
SNACK
JUST THINK, TOULOSE. IF WE DIDN'T SKI, WE'D NEVER EXPERIENCE PRISTINE POWDER, ENDLESS VISTAS...
TWELVE DOLLAR HAMBURGERS.
RAESIDE

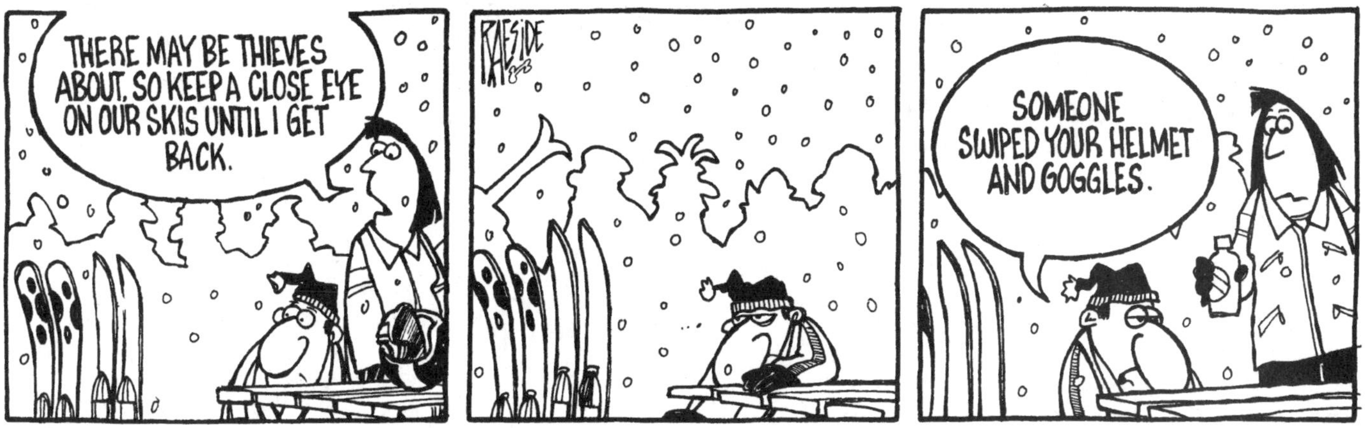
THERE MAY BE THIEVES ABOUT. SO KEEP A CLOSE EYE ON OUR SKIS UNTIL I GET BACK.
RAESIDE
SOMEONE SWIPED YOUR HELMET AND GOGGLES.

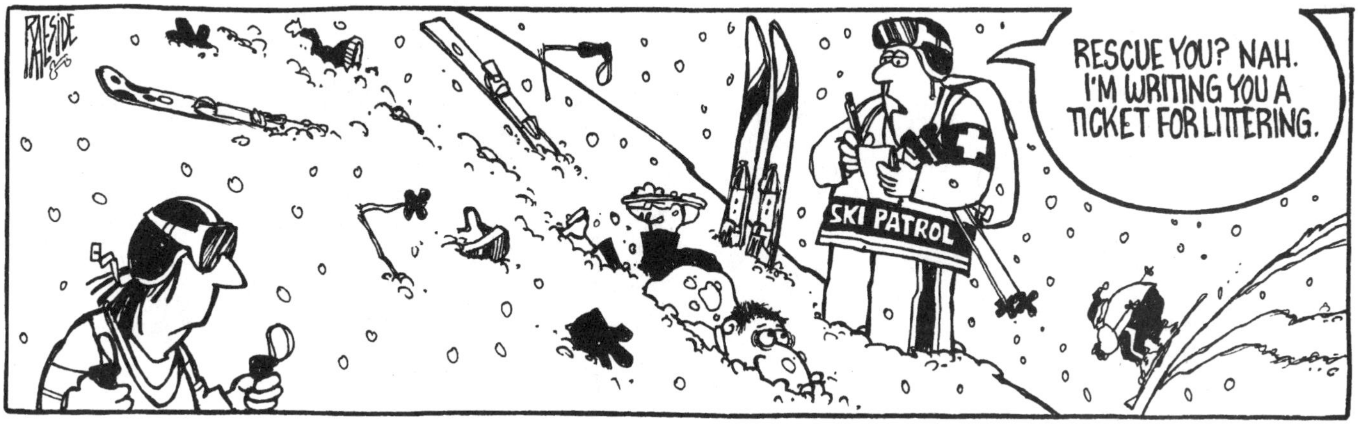
RAESIDE
RESCUE YOU? NAH. I'M WRITING YOU A TICKET FOR LITTERING.
SKI PATROL

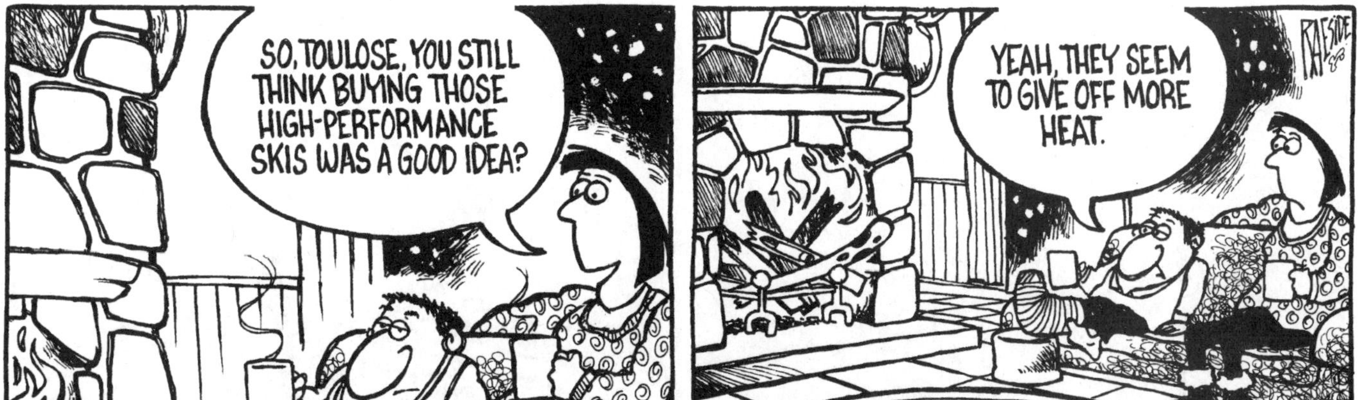
SO, TOULOSE, YOU STILL THINK BUYING THOSE HIGH-PERFORMANCE SKIS WAS A GOOD IDEA?
RAESIDE
YEAH, THEY SEEM TO GIVE OFF MORE HEAT.

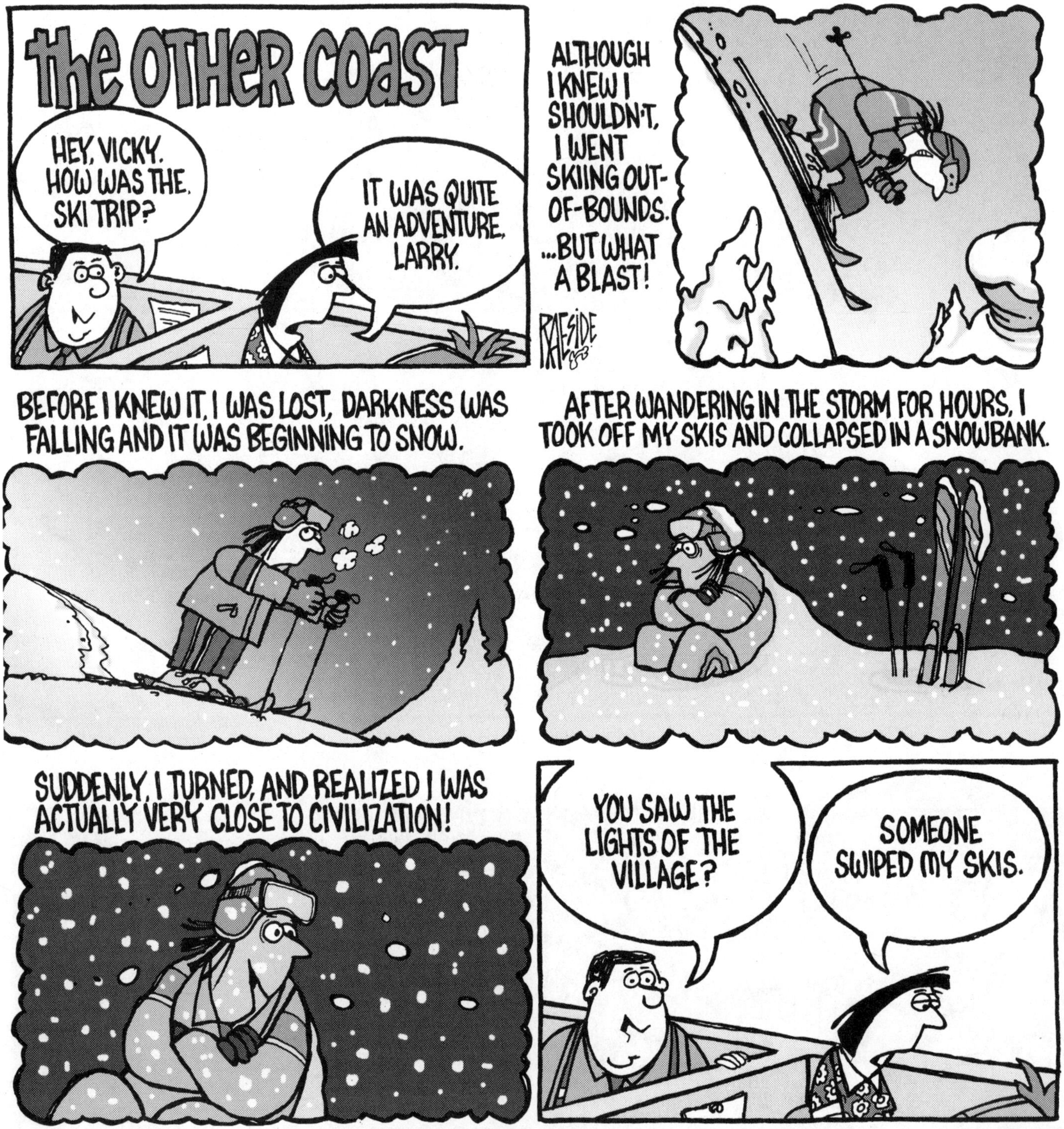
the OTHER COAST
HEY, VICKY. HOW WAS THE SKI TRIP?
IT WAS QUITE AN ADVENTURE, LARRY.
ALTHOUGH I KNEW I SHOULDN'T, I WENT SKIING OUT-OF-BOUNDS. ...BUT WHAT A BLAST!
RAESIDE
BEFORE I KNEW IT, I WAS LOST, DARKNESS WAS FALLING AND IT WAS BEGINNING TO SNOW.
AFTER WANDERING IN THE STORM FOR HOURS, I TOOK OFF MY SKIS AND COLLAPSED IN A SNOWBANK.
SUDDENLY, I TURNED, AND REALIZED I WAS ACTUALLY VERY CLOSE TO CIVILIZATION!
YOU SAW THE LIGHTS OF THE VILLAGE?
SOMEONE SWIPED MY SKIS.